Fries's Rebellion

Fries's Rebellion

The Enduring Struggle for the American Revolution

Paul Douglas Newman

PENN

University of Pennsylvania Press
Philadelphia

10   9   8   7   6   5   4   3   2   1

First paperback edition 2005

Published by
University of Pennsylvania Press
Philadelphia, Pennsylvania 19104-4011

Library of Congress Cataloging-in-Publication Data

Newman, Paul Douglas.
   Fries's Rebellion : the enduring struggle for the American Revolution /
Paul Douglas Newman.
      p.   cm.
   ISBN 0-8122-3815-X (cloth: acid-free paper); ISBN 0-8122-1920-1 (pbk.: acid-free paper)
   Includes bibliographical references (p.) and index.
   1. Fries, John, ca. 1750–1. 2. Fries Rebellion, 1798–1799. I. Title
E326 .N49   2004
973.4′4—dc22   *2004049462*

For Forrest and Leo . . .

and Bethany, Joe, and all the rest

Contents

Preface

On March 7, 1799, nearly four hundred men marched into Bethlehem, Pennsylvania, behind John Fries, to demand the release of seventeen prisoners jailed for resisting a federal tax. Fries (pronounced "Freeze") captained a company of militia from Bucks County, the same unit with which he had served as a Patriot in the Revolution. Two decades later he led a combined force of armed light horse, riflemen, and infantry into the peaceful Moravian village, marching in step to the cadence of fife and drum in defiance of the federal authority he had once fought to establish. Federal Circuit Court Judge Richard Peters had warranted the arrests of the seventeen prisoners in question for obstructing the fledgling national government's very first attempt to lay a direct tax on property. In 1791 the federal government had levied an indirect tax, an excise on spirituous liquors, and western Pennsylvanians had risen up in rebellion in 1794, impeding the officials and mustering an army. The Direct Tax Act of 1798 was a levy on lands, dwelling houses, and slaves. It used a progressive rate that taxed wealthy homes at higher percentages than modest ones but taxed improved farmlands more than the uncultivated holdings of speculators. In 1798–99, it was eastern Pennsylvanians, especially German Lutherans and the German Reformed, who rebelled. This standoff, which has come to be known as "Fries's Rebellion," was the culmination of seven months of tax resistance and political opposition to other odious federal legislation, such as the Alien and Sedition Acts, exorbitant military expenditures, and the creation of a peacetime standing army, all of which the Federalist Party implemented to provide national security from the threat of war and invasion by France during the Quasi War.

This is thus the story of a rebellion, but not of an insurrection. It was a rebellion in a figurative sense, as a popular, localized resistance movement against perceived injustices by aggrieved citizens who employed logical but illegal methods and Revolutionary ideals, but not in a literal way as an attempt to make war against the government. Inhabitants of western Massachusetts and western Pennsylvania were insurgents in 1786 and 1794, engaging in military actions against state and federal authorities. In the former case, thousands of Yankee farmers assaulted the federal armory at Springfield attempting to force the Massachusetts government into a convention to rewrite the state's constitution. In the latter, about 5,000 armed men gathered on Braddock's Field and threatened to sack the federal arsenal at Pittsburgh, perhaps intending to secede from the union when they stood behind the flag of "Westsylvania"—the symbol of three earlier attempts from 1774 to 1783 to secede from Pennsylvania to form an independent province or state. And later in 1799, even though the Federalist Party and its newspapers quickly sought to label the tax resistance and the jail break in eastern Pennsylvania the "Northampton Insurrection," these "rebels" never intended to make war against the governments of the state or the nation. They were trying instead to expand the role of the people within the political system, as they understood it, rather than attacking it from outside.

The rebels sought to manifest the national principle of popular sovereignty to participate in state and national politics in order to dominate and decide local affairs. Early in the decade they followed the party of their Revolutionary commander, George Washington. Later, the Republicans in state and national politics offered them greater opportunities for local control. As this transition progressed, the nation drifted toward war with its Revolutionary ally France, and the Fifth Congress passed the Direct Tax Act in the summer of 1798 to pay for armament and fortification, while it also passed the Sedition Act to silence partisan dissent. In the autumn, Federalists in the Adams administration appointed a wealthy Moravian as commissioner for the Direct Tax in Northampton County, and patriotic German Lutherans and Reformed then began opposing the Direct Tax, the Sedition Act, and the military build-up. In Bucks County the opposition developed later, after the New Year when their Direct Tax commissioner, an English-speaking Quaker, finally secured assessors to take the rates in the northwestern-most and predominantly German townships. But the Bucks County people had been watching their neighbors in Northampton County, and had been in communication with them. When a federal marshal arrested several Northampton County men for sedition and obstruction of process and prepared to transport them to Philadelphia for trial, John Fries led the Bucks County militia to Bethlehem on March 7 to assist his Northampton County neighbors in releasing the prisoners and securing local trials. In 1799, the Pennsylvania protesters added direct action to their political strategy, accompanying their constitutional arguments engaging the First, Second, and Sixth Amendments. The would-be rebels proved to be sophisticated and discriminating citizens in the "first party system," and even after the rebellion they did not commit themselves blindly to one party or the other.

Yet the Federalists labeled the event the "Northampton Insurrection" and branded the participants "miserable Germans," "insurgents," and "traitors" in 1799, just as they had marginalized western Pennsylvanians as "Whiskey

Rebels" five years earlier, and just as the eastern-dominated Massachusetts government renamed the Regulators as "Shaysite Rebels" seven years before that. Moreover, the Federalist Adams administration and the Federalist federal circuit court aggressively pursued treason convictions and executions for Fries and a few others. In the months that followed the Bethlehem rescue, the Federalists' district attorney brought charges against one-quarter of the rebels, but secured indictments for only one-third of them for lesser crimes, including sedition. Federal prosecutors sought to prove that Fries had led a concerted attack upon a federal force and that his actions constituted "levying war against the United States." By painting the tax resistance as an insurrection they denied the legitimacy of the resisters' real ideological, political, and economic grievances and encouraged the nation to form a patriotic bipartisan consensus between Federalist leaders and their Republican adversaries to quell the domestic threat of "civil war" while facing the threat of war with France. From the Federalist viewpoint, that consensus would perhaps distract other Americans from their opposition to the Federalist program of militarization, taxation, immigration restriction, and its attack on civil liberties. Maybe it would be enough to persuade the states to ignore the Republicans' Virginia and Kentucky Resolutions to repeal and nullify repressive Federalist legislation. Focusing on a handful of leaders and only a fraction of their followers allowed the Federalist Party to sacrifice a few scapegoats to the cause of national security without further antagonizing thousands of people who had engaged in tax resistance or public political protest. At least that was the plan. The Federalists secured a number of convictions in May 1799, including that of John Fries, but one of the presiding judges threw out Fries's conviction on a technicality. A year later another jury convicted Fries of treason for a second time, and another judge sentenced him to hang. Only President Adams's eleventh-hour pardon saved John Fries and his two neighbors, John Gettman and Frederick Heaney, from their date with the hangman.

While "Northampton Insurrection" is a misnomer, so too is "Fries's Rebellion" in some ways. While this was indeed a rebellion in the figurative sense, it did not belong to John Fries. He joined the resistance movement rather late and is known primarily for his role in the March 7 rescue at Bethlehem. Fries played a significant role, but the rebellion belonged to the thousands of German-American men, women, and adolescent children of eastern Pennsylvania, centering in Northampton and northern Bucks Counties, but spreading locally through Montgomery, Berks, Dauphin, York, and Lancaster Counties, as well as some western counties, who engaged in the varied acts of resistance. They rebelled against perceived "unconstitutional" legislation of an "aristocratic" Federalist Party, against Quakers and Moravians who received

Federalist patronage and assessed the tax, and they rebelled for the right of the people to govern themselves locally and nationally, with or without political parties, and to secure their property and future pursuit of happiness. The rebellion, to them, became another ethnicizing and Americanizing experience that, when added to their history, constructed the social and political contexts they used to guide their future decisions.

While one recent historian located Shays's Rebellion as "The American Revolution's Final Battle" and another described the Whiskey Rebellion as the "Frontier Epilogue to the American Revolution," the Fries Rebels would have disagreed with both implications. Rather than a story consigned to paper and concluded, the Revolution to them was a perpetual narrative for successive generations to retell, an experience to be relived, and an enduring struggle to be reengaged. Their rebellion testified to the democratizing forces in politics and society unleashed by the American Revolution. To them, the Revolution was more than a War for Independence, the founding of a national republic, or the parchment documents that defined each. It was a political, economic, and social process of expanding popular sovereignty. The Revolution was a spirit to be constantly revived and a set of political principles to be frequently redefined—always in a democratic direction—to provide more local and personal control of daily life as well as increased power over broader collective policies. The Fries Rebels believed they were upholding the Revolution's promise and founding ideals, even when they engaged in their own discriminatory, majoritarian behavior against some of their neighbors. Perhaps other Americans equally estimated that the people could directly expand their own role in local, state, and federal government, making it more democratic and less republican in the fluid days of the post-Revolutionary political settlement when parties were only beginning to form and authority seemed so weak. Even if this was not the case, the Fries Rebels appear to have thought that way, and if we listen closely enough, we can hear them tell us so.

Prologue: "The Constitution Sacred, No Gagg Laws, Liberty or Death"

Just days before Christmas 1798, Henry and Peggy Lynn Hembolt hosted a gathering of their neighbors near their Montgomery County paper mill. It was a private party among friends, nine of them in all. As they ate their meal, drank their toasts, and gave thanks for the closing year, their holiday mood turned, however, to political concerns. While they counted republican liberty among their blessings, they feared its erosion at the hands of the Federalist-dominated U.S. Congress and administration just a few miles south in Philadelphia. The Alien and Sedition Acts, recruitment for a professional standing army, a looming war with France, and the newly passed federal Direct Tax on lands and dwelling houses all seemed particularly onerous.[1] The Hembolts and their party questioned the constitutionality of this newly energized and centralized federal government. In 1798 they and their neighbors in northern Bucks County and Northampton County publicly opposed the Federalist legislation by drawing on both the republican ideals that fueled the Revolution and the democratic consequences radiating from it. Through the process of that opposition they reengaged the American Revolution.

Late that December day Henry Hembolt decided that they would raise a liberty pole, as the previous generation had done to proclaim their resistance to "unconstitutional" British taxation.[2] He instructed Morris Schwelein, George Britson, and Isaac Young to cut and hew a tall tree. He gave James Jackson some pasteboard, and Peggy Lynn gave him a needle and thread and some red, white, and blue ribbon to make a liberty cap with flowing streamers. Jackson fashioned the cap, added a tricolored cockade, and nailed it to the top of the pole. They mimicked the Republican Party in Philadelphia which had borrowed the French cockade to exhibit its dissent from Federalist foreign policy after the "XYZ Affair." The others prepared a sign that read, "The Constitution Sacred, No Gagg Laws, Liberty or Death," and fastened it about the middle of the pole. With the decoration complete, they dug a posthole and erected their liberty tree. Raising their glasses and toasting their accomplishment, they shouted "Huzzah for Liberty!"[3]

For more than a month, the Hembolts and their guests watched as federal tax officials assessed their property and their homes for taxes that in their opinion supported unrepublican, undemocratic, and unconstitutional Federalist policies. That Federalists appointed as assessors their Quaker and German sectarian neighbors, pacifists who had abstained from combat during the Revolutionary War, confirmed Republican Party charges of Federalist "monarchism" and counterrevolutionary intentions. The oldest among the Hembolt party, George Savage, had himself fought for liberty as a Patriot in the Revolution.[4] He and his German Lutheran and German Reformed neighbors in eastern Pennsylvania called themselves "Kirchenleute" (Church People) to distinguish themselves from their sectarian neighbors, principally the Moravians, but also from Mennonites, Anabaptists, and Schwenkfelders—the "Sektenleute."[5]

Using the term "Kirchenleute" also separated them from the English-speaking Quakers, who were still politically and economically powerful. Sectarians, Anglo-Quakers, and other English speakers dominated the towns of the Lehigh Valley. Easton, for example, was a busy commercial town and the Northampton County seat at the forks of the Lehigh and Delaware Rivers. It was dominated by Anglo Americans, while Bethlehem upriver to the west was a Moravian center of industry, commerce, and pietism. Allentown, an industrial and commercial hub inhabited mostly by Kirchenleute and Anglos, lay upriver and to the west near the confluence of the Little Lehigh Creek, Jordan Creek, and the Lehigh River. It was the first market town on the Lehigh in the center of Kirchenleute farms that drained their produce to the Delaware and beyond. In the towns they smelted iron and forged it into tools and hardware in smitheries, operated glassworks, tanneries and haberdasheries, and manufactured paper products and wagons. Newtown and Norristown to the south and east of the Great Swamp and Perkiomen Creeks were the county seats for Bucks and Montgomery Counties respectively. Quakers and other Anglos dominated the courthouses and businesses in both. Most Kirchenleute, who were the children and grandchildren of the great Rhine Valley and Palatinate migration from early to midcentury, farmed the rolling hills and valleys in the rural townships to the north and south of the Lehigh River, between the Blue Mountain and the Lehigh Hills. Some stoked forges and kilns and, like the Hembolts, operated grist, saw, and paper mills along the many creeks and streams that fed the Lehigh River.[6] Others kept taverns or owned small stores, but few engaged in skilled crafts, manufacturing, regional merchandizing, or the legal profession. Those were found in the larger towns dominated by English speakers and sectarian Germans. In terms of geography, economics, ethnicity, religion, and politics, the Kirchenleute of the Lehigh region were hemmed in on all sides.

Just south of the Lehigh Hills in the northwest corner of Bucks County lay Lower Milford, home to the rebellion's namesake, John Fries. Drained by the Great Swamp Creek (today called the Unami) that swept south into the Perkiomen Creek and eventually into the Schuylkill River, Lower Milford bordered both the Northampton and Montgomery County lines to the northeast and southeast and was typical of Kirchenleute townships in the region and the townships with fiercest tax resistance. Comprising 15,000 acres, it was home in 1800 to 1,109 people living in 192 households representing 93 nuclear families with three or four children on average. Fourteen years earlier when the state conducted its second "Septennial Census," the township had listed 190 taxable men; by 1800 that number had only increased by 5, but those 195 men had become fathers to 553 children under the age of sixteen, 269 of them boys

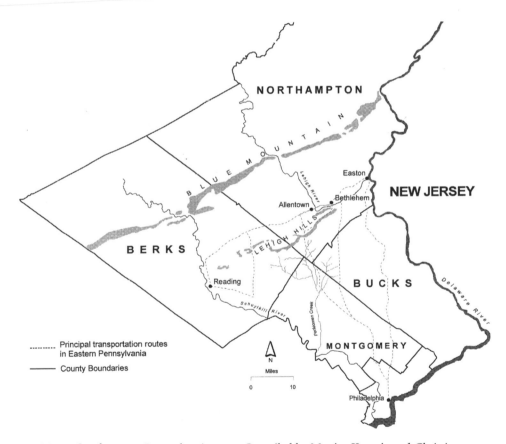

Map 1. Southeastern Pennsylvania, 1798. Compiled by Monica Kovacic and Christine Herchelroath, University of Pittsburgh at Johnstown Cartography Laboratory.

expecting land. Another 169 children were between sixteen and twenty-six years of age, 78 of them were young men who would soon head households of their own. Young men and women who would soon require land or dowries comprised 65 percent of the township's population in 1800. Germans made up 85 percent of the population, and most attended the German Reformed or Union (Reformed and Lutheran) churches. Of adult German men, 89 percent owned their own land and houses, 85 percent of the total taxable men were property holders. Two-thirds of them lived in small one-story log houses with barns twice as large that were valued together between $100 and $300, and they farmed between 26 and 150 acres of good land, averaging in value more than $12 per acre. Another 5 percent rented from family members. Only one in ten were renters in the true sense of the term. Of those tenants, half were Germans renting from German neighbors. Only six Kirchenleute paid rent to English-speaking landlords, while five Anglo-Americans leased property from those speaking Pennsylvania Dutch.[7]

Theirs was a tight-knit, homogeneous, rural farming community of nuclear families, and while the region was not yet overcrowded, they certainly could foresee the narrowing of local prospects for their children. Compared to the broader Pennsylvania German belt of settlement that extended west and south through the counties of Northumberland, Berks, Dauphin, York, and Lancaster, where on average only 70 percent of taxable men owned land, the Kirchenleute in the Lehigh area were doing a bit better. Still, threats to their economic liberty and that of their heirs were palpable. Following the Revolution, they and other Pennsylvanians had become accustomed to defending their property against taxmen and the sheriffs who followed them with summonses to appear in English-speaking courts in distant county seats and later presented them with foreclosure orders. Bucks County commissioners reported in 1783 that their taxmen were unable to collect the state taxes due to the scarcity of hard money, especially in the predominantly German northern townships, and when the sheriffs and justices of the peace commenced foreclosure sales, whole communities crowded the auctions and engaged in no-bid covenants to save their neighbors and buy them time. Agrarian communities throughout the state used their militias to intervene and to stop tax collection. By 1785 state tax collectors were more than $1 million in arrears. Through obstruction, militias and bands of farmers were able to prevent the state from collecting its excise in the 1780s; the legislature abandoned the tax in 1790.[8]

During the course of that resistance, in 1784 and 1785 the citizens of Lower Milford refused the Supreme Executive Council's call for their militia to go to Northampton County's Wyoming Valley to evict the "Connecticut Claimants" who had settled on lands ostensibly owned by Pennsylvania land speculators.

In a petition to the Council, the Lower Milford citizens wrote that they were filled with "abhorrence of the Idea of Staining [their] hands with the blood of their Countrymen & fellow Subjects" over "a dispute about private property." They deemed the effort "inconsistent with the Very Spirit of Our Laws and Constitution."[9] Northampton men also refused to fight "the quarrel of a set of landjobbers . . . to extirpate the whole race of Connecticut Claimants."[10] In the early 1790s, Bucks County farmers protected themselves and their neighbors from foreclosures by obstructing roads with fences and ditches on several occasions, and Northampton farmers did the same seven times between 1791 and 1795.[11] Through this post-Revolutionary struggle, the Kirchenleute of Lower Milford had succeeded not only in fending off taxes and policies they deemed unfair and unconstitutional but had protected their economic liberties as well since nine of ten men could still count themselves as yeomen farmers. Moreover, they had learned that strongly espoused political principles, coupled with community participation and political action, were fundamental to defending and maintaining all their liberties: individual, economic, local, and national.

Such defiance reveals that although they may have referred to themselves as "Subjects," the people of Lower Milford were good Pennsylvania Constitutionalists who took pride in the democratic state constitution of 1776 and the egalitarian ideals it represented. The drafters of the constitution of 1776 refused to concentrate power in the hands of a single executive and so created a limited Supreme Executive Council that paled in authority to the unicameral Assembly. Only a Council of Censors could recommend constitutional amendments to regulate the Assembly. All free taxpaying men of the commonwealth, white and black, elected the Assembly annually, and the legislation it passed was not enacted until after the following elections to allow popular approval of the legislators and their laws. The constitution of 1776 afforded the "people" with the "sole exclusive, and inherent right of governing" the entire commonwealth and in Lockean fashion told them to "take such measures as to them may appear necessary" if the government trod on their sovereignty. The decidedly undemocratic feature of the 1776 frame of government, however, was its provision of a "Test Oath" for citizenship that required freemen to swear their loyalty to the new government. Quakers, some sectarian Germans, loyalists, and neutrals were disenfranchised by this government and would not be reenfranchised until the drafting of a new state constitution in 1790. During the war, the patriotic Kirchenleute equated neutrality with loyalism, even neutrality inspired by faith, and thus overlooked the hypocrisy of waging a democratic revolution through exclusive and discriminatory means.

Through the Revolution and into the 1790s, the Kirchenleute regarded themselves as citizens and freemen, not subjects, and as citizens they were at liberty to oppose governmental authority when they found it unfair or threatening and, conversely, to support the parties or authorities when they thought it proper. In 1794, in spite of their refusal to march against agrarian insurgents a decade before, the Lower Milford militia, including John Fries, answered President Washington's call and marched west to suppress the Whiskey Rebellion. And this was during a period when Bucks County roads had twice been closed by resisters. The Kirchenleute either accepted the administration's argument that the western insurgents posed a real threat to the nation or, less likely, simply succumbed to federal authority, whereas nine years earlier the Council could not convince them that the Connecticut Yankees as close as the next county endangered them or the state. Either they were so local in their perspective that they could not see common ground with agrarian excise resisters in the west, who were also closing roads, or they perceived themselves as nationalists and patriots, bound by the call of their Revolutionary hero and president. It is possible that they held both perspectives at once.[12] In both 1784 and 1794, the community, through its militia, acted as one. Within the township, there was little to divide them. It was outside the township, in the larger towns and on the larger stages of the county and state, where divisions appeared.

Although Lutherans and Reformed often disagreed throughout the eighteenth century, by the mid-1790s they began to build union churches, and beginning in 1796 in the Lehigh region most voted for German-speaking Republican candidates over sectarian, Quaker, and Anglo-American Federalists in national and state elections. During the contest in state politics over the constitution of 1790, which broadened the franchise to include Quakers and sectarians but rolled back many democratic conventions of the constitution of 1776, Lutherans generally sided with the old Quaker Party while members of Reformed congregations bristled at sacrificing hard-won reforms.[13] Generally they cooperated in their jealous defense of individual liberties guaranteed by the federal Constitution and the Bill of Rights. Moreover, their common adherence to the Republican Party in the late 1790s and their shared democratic and republican political ideals allowed them to transcend their suspicions of one another and to struggle together as Kirchenleute in opposition to the Direct Tax and the broader Federalist national program. But the Kirchenleute were not simply opposed to national policies; they supported the Republican Party in state politics to work for militia, judicial and local government reforms that would give them greater control of local politics in their own tongue. In doing so, they invoked the Revolution's promise of self-government to gain greater control of their own lives.[14]

In the decade after the Revolution, depreciating paper money and the

scarcity of specie led to foreclosures and evictions throughout rural Pennsylvania.[15] During the 1790s, citizens of Bucks County besieged the governor's
office with petitions for appointments, reappointments, or removal of justices
of the peace, in many instances to obtain a magistrate within their own language, religion, or ethnicity. The justice of the peace settled minor legal disputes
and criminal cases but, more important, was responsible for the collection of
debts. Controlling the offices of county commissioner, tax collector, sheriff, and
justice of the peace could mean the difference between immediate eviction and
a continuance, between shelter and homelessness, between taxable citizenship
and landless subjection.[16] All these local issues and more, tied to state matters
by national political parties, would be resurrected by the Direct Tax in 1798 and
would provide the context for the Kirchenleute opposition.

In neighboring Berks County, the Kirchenleute were a solid majority
and thus had won control of local government as Republicans, and they had a
German language newspaper to voice Kirchenleute Republican dissent, Jacob
Schneider's *Readinger Adler*. In the region where Bucks, Northampton, and
Montgomery Counties met, three jurisdictions divided the Kirchenleute, and
they had no popular press of their own until the very end of the decade, though
Schneider's *Adler* came in from Reading, and Henry Kammerer's Republican
Philadelphische Correspondenz occasionally made its way up the Allentown
road as well.[17] Bucks and Montgomery Counties were dominated by Anglo and
Quaker majorities who controlled the county seats of Newtown and Norristown. Northampton County's Germans were divided between the rural Kirchenleute bordering the Lehigh Valley in the county's southwestern corner,
the town-dwelling Moravians of Bethlehem, Nazareth, and Emmaus, and the
Anglos and Scots-Irish to the east in Easton and north of the Blue Mountain. With the Moravians, they dominated county politics. Yet Northampton
County Kirchenleute had begun the process of winning control of local offices
as Republicans by the mid-1790s. In state politics, the Federalist Party courted
the sectarian pacifist vote by proposing to lower or eliminate fines for exemption from militia service and used patronage to appoint powerful and profitable local offices like justice of the peace and prothonotary. Republicans,
fearing the Federalists' national scheme of replacing militias with a standing
professional army, extolled the republican virtue of the militia and called for
stiff fines for those refusing to serve. They campaigned to end the gubernatorial appointments of militia captains and Justices of the Peace initiated by Pennsylvania's conservative constitution of 1790 and to return those powers to the
people through company and local elections. Following the adoption of the
federal Constitution, Pennsylvania conservatives had succeeded in devising a
new state constitution that not only centralized local authority but checked the

powerful Assembly with a popularly elected upper house and a single, veto-wielding governor. The 1790 constitution also ended the delay for enactment of legislation until ensuing elections and provided for appointment of a judiciary for tenure of good behavior instead of mandating regular elections for judges. Moreover, the vote was still limited to taxable men, which in Pennsylvania meant property holders. While many Pennsylvanians, especially the Kirchenleute of the Lehigh region, considered all of this counter-revolutionary, the constitution of 1790 did broaden the franchise by readmitting Quakers and German sectarian pacifists into the body politic and enfranchising Roman Catholics and Jews for the first time.[18] But when the Quakers and Sektenleute used Philadelphia connections to reclaim political control in the Lehigh region, the Kirchenleute saw little that was democratic about this new frame of state government that seemed to undermine the principle of majority rule.

Following this setback, Kirchenleute in Pennsylvania, especially in Northampton and Bucks Counties, petitioned their governor to translate state political and legal documents into German and to extend more authority to the local justices of the peace, particularly concerning the settlement of debts, rent collection, and actions of trespass. Simon Snyder of Northumberland, a German state representative and Republican partisan, took these petitions, as well as ones from his own county and the German counties of Berks and Dauphin, and turned them into Republican platform planks in the late 1790s. The proposed legislation, along with calls for elected justices of the peace, would provide local power and security to German speakers, who faced distinct disadvantages when appearing before Anglo judges in English-speaking courts in bustling county seats like Easton or Newtown.[19] It would also end the indignity of these Kirchenleute submitting themselves before magistrates whom they still considered "Tories."

Kirchenleute liberty, earned in the Revolution and threatened thereafter by economic uncertainty and political counterrevolution, depended upon the security of Kirchenleute property. It not only fed them and nourished their families but provided political freedom and privilege as well. The security of their property rested on their ability to use that political freedom to affect state legislation allowing them more local control of offices and their affairs. Liberty was a local concern.

Yet the Hembolts' liberty pole reminds us that while they were in the midst of a struggle for state and local control, they also prized their liberty in national and international contexts as well. The Federalists' Sedition Act, occasioned by the prospect of a war with France, America's former Revolutionary War ally, threatened the Republican opposition. Pennsylvania Republicans were working for more democratic state politics and local control and the Federalists used the Sedition Act to turn political dissent into sedition.[20] The Kirchenleute understood full well the implications that the nation's foreign and domestic policies held for their daily lives. In addition to the Sedition Act and the Direct Tax, they frequently railed against the creation of the "New Army" (a professionalized standing army) and other military preparations, the congressional scheme to borrow millions of dollars to pay for them, and the Alien Acts that empowered the president to deport immigrants and extended residency requirements for naturalization. To oppose this legislation and policy, they developed and used their own understanding of Revolutionary patriotism, nationalism and popular constitutionalism. In the century between the Seven Years War and the U.S. Civil War, members of German Lutheran and Reformed congregations underwent a process of ethnicization, like many later immigrant groups and their children. By the end of that period, their definition of liberty and democracy had evolved into an American attitude, splicing parochialism, cultural distinctiveness, and nationalism voiced through patriotic rhetoric. This was their answer to Pennsylvania's nineteenth-century common school movement that threatened their language, culture, and local control of education. Being American meant exercising the right to remain German Church People and to retain local majoritarian control.[21] The Kirchenleute opposition movement of 1798–99 took place within this broader ethnic ideological development and helped push it along.

Today the Hembolts' dinner party would seem to be an acceptable part of a proud American tradition of popular and partisan dissent. On any given day one can read letters to the editor or tune in to talk radio or television to read, hear, and see American citizens questioning the constitutionality of various matters. Public displays of opposition to federal laws, policies, and authority are commonplace now and are generally accepted as the norm in a democratic society, though individual exceptions abound especially during wartime when jingoism, xenophobia, and superpatriotic conformity ride high. When in 1798, only a decade after ratification of the federal Constitution, the nation faced what seemed to be an imminent war with France, Federalists regarded such expressions as seditious. Indeed, the Federalist press referred to symbols like the Hembolts' as "Sedition Poles." But the Hembolts considered public political dissent their First Amendment individual right of self-defense against government infringement and their constitutional and patriotic duty to protect their fellow citizens.

The Kirchenleute had come to understand liberty in both negative and positive forms and in very broad and interconnected terms, much more than had the Federalists and even more broadly than the national leadership of the Republican Party. They believed that as Americans they should be free from repressive government—"No Gagg Laws"; they also believed they should be free to express their political beliefs and overturn unconstitutional legislation and policy. They considered the Sedition Law unconstitutional not merely because it violated the First Amendment and their liberties as citizens of the nation but also because it threatened their regional and local political and economic liberties while they strove for judicial reform at the state level. As Republican leaders James Madison and Thomas Jefferson were theorizing about ways the states could interpret and challenge the constitutionality of federal legislation in 1798, the Hembolts and their neighbors decided that they, the people, held that right and responsibility. It is this pronounced popular constitutionalism that makes the study of this opposition movement so intriguing.[22]

Jefferson had of course used a strict construction of the Constitution in his attempt to block Treasury Secretary Alexander Hamilton's plan for a national bank, and Madison had likewise fought against Hamilton's funding scheme for a national debt at the beginning of the decade. From 1793 to 1796, the short-lived Democratic Societies, a loose collection of ninety-three clubs across the country that opposed many Washington administration policies, used the language of constitutional opposition in their printed declarations, resolutions, and addresses.[23] But these were formal organizations, with elected officers, committees of correspondence, dues-paying members, and newspaper editors like Henry Kammerer and Benjamin Franklin Bache. Many were leaders in society, commerce, and state and national politics like Benjamin Rush, Michael Leib, Alexander James Dallas, Blair McClenachan, George Logan, and David Rittenhouse. In the autumn of 1798, neither the Hembolts nor their neighbors were as prestigious as the leaders of the Democratic Societies had been, and as yet they were unknown and unorganized. But that changed when elections for state and national leaders brought in the Republican Party and as Federalist sectarian tax assessors made their way into the region. Pennsylvania had long been the scene of factional politics, and the Kirchenleute were seasoned veterans at selecting and changing their party affiliations based on religious, ethnic, and regional interests. The Republicans offered them an alternative to Federalism locally and beyond in what historians call the "first party system." While the partisans, especially Republicans, tried to play the game of ethnic association perfected by later parties, the Lehigh area Kirchenleute pragmatically chose the Republicans to fight for immediate and idealistic goals in the late 1790s, but they did not uniformly adhere to Jefferson's party after the turn of the century.

Through the party, their militia, newly created township associations, and other organizations, the Kirchenleute voiced constitutional opposition to Federalist legislation and policies that would deprive them of their liberty. They asserted that as the people, they had the right to obstruct unconstitutional laws while they were petitioning their legislators to overturn them. In this way, the Kirchenleute opposition movement of 1798–99 was not only more democratic than the Republican Party that sought its votes, but its conception of popular sovereignty was radical even when compared to subsequent opposition movements. Later movements such as the labor, agrarian, antiwar, and civil rights movements learned that disobedience or obstruction of laws considered unconstitutional would certainly lead to arrest and imprisonment; indeed they counted on it as a strategy of civil disobedience. In 1798 the Kirchenleute opposition in eastern Pennsylvania had not learned this lesson, as it would not be articulated and perfected for decades to come. Even though many of them, principally their leaders, had marched west under President Washington against the Whiskey Rebels four years earlier, the Kirchenleute resisters of 1798–99 believed that they could construct a legitimate constitutional opposition that would bring no criminal charges or military reprisal, by holding the authorities accountable to the Constitution and by using its provisions, especially the Bill of Rights, to frame their obstruction while demanding legislative repeal. They had successfully obstructed a hated state tax in the 1780s while they waited for their Assembly to repeal it, why wouldn't the same tactic work against federal legislation in 1798? The Pennsylvania constitution of 1776 had afforded the people the democratic right to nullify unpopular legislation before its enactment through the ballot, and in 1798 the Northampton, Bucks, Montgomery, and Berks County Kirchenleute and others had sent new Republican representatives to Philadelphia who would not take their seats in the Sixth Congress until March. Why not resurrect a democratic right afforded by the state during the Revolution (and only lost eight years since) to obstruct the Direct Tax until the new Congress could consider their petitions? Moreover, the western insurgents in 1794 had used militias, extralegal associations, and constitutional language, and had also engaged in extraconstitutional violence against taxmen to express their grievances and had threatened to sack Pittsburgh and seize the federal arsenal there. The Massachusetts' Regulators of 1786 had used militias and county associations to shut down courts but had also resorted to interpersonal violence and had actually attacked the federal arsenal at Springfield.[24] Perhaps violence had been their error?

The lesson the Kirchenleute took from the events of 1786 and 1794 was that violent obstructionism and threatening federal arsenals allowed the Massachusetts and U.S. administrations to slap the "rebellion" label on the opposition and launch armies of more than 4,000 and 10,000 respectively, to suppress them. The Kirchenleute opposition would try not to make those mistakes, yet all the while forcefully asserting that it was the people's right to interpret the constitutionality of federal law and to interpose themselves between Congress and the administration to settle their grievances. The Hembolts and others used the United States Constitution and its Bill of Rights not only as a shield to protect individual rights against government transgressions but also as a sword of popular sovereignty to fight for all the liberties they believed they had won during the war, including some that many "Revolutionaries" had never intended them to have. In many ways, they were demonstrating that the Revolution for them had not ended and that through popular participation and opposition in national and international affairs they might reignite and feed the democratic fires it had lit two decades earlier in order to secure the blessings of liberty at home. Such was the breadth and depth of the liberty that the Hembolts believed they had earned in the Revolution, and to maintain it, they knew they had to keep "the Constitution Sacred."

Chapter 1
Liberty

Scenes similar to the raising of the Hembolts' liberty pole unfolded throughout the upper Schuylkill, upper Perkiomen, and Lehigh valleys during the fall and winter of 1798–99. In Northampton, northwestern Bucks, northern Montgomery, Berks, and Dauphin Counties, Kirchenleute communities hoisted liberty poles and signed "associations" vowing to resist assessment of their homes, and they threatened and warned off assessors. Occasionally, housewives drove off assessors by dousing them with hot water, a novel technique (afforded by the requirement that assessors count and measure windows) that earned the event ridicule as the "Hot Water War."[1] Yet some of those women, like "Grandy Miller" (Figure 1) became local heroines, revered for decades after the event, revealing that this truly was a shared community struggle.[2] Meanwhile, the resisters petitioned Congress for repeal of the offending legislation.

Several townships successfully resisted assessment for a wide variety of interconnected reasons. Many considered any taxes excessively burdensome whether they were indirect excises placed on commodities or direct taxes on property, no matter how devised, by whatever body, or whatever their purpose. New taxes, especially those on land, drained cash-poor small farmers of income, and the inability to pay brought the specter of foreclosure. In addition to this common fear, ethnic, religious, class, democratic, patriotic, local, state, national, international, and constitutional concerns were expressed by the participants in words and deeds. Their language of opposition survives mainly in the form of depositions and as trial testimony, and in those contexts it makes sense that some would have tried to color their dissent as loyal constitutional opposition to avoid imprisonment. Perhaps some wrapped themselves in such patriotic dress after the fact, while many others truly held democratic, republican, and constitutional convictions, as evidenced by the Hembolts' liberty pole, the descriptions of events by frustrated tax assessors, and the various patriotic "Revolutionary" methods of protest employed by the resisters, whose actions reinforced and confirmed their words. Whatever their individual reasons or methods, the Lehigh area Kirchenleute collectively and openly opposed the Federalist legislative program in 1798 through local institutions, and their

Figure 1. "Grandy Miller" was the wife of David Shaeffer, a tax resister from Macungie Township, Northampton County. Shaeffer died of yellow fever while in jail awaiting his trial. "Grandy Miller" later married Jacob Miller. Hers is the only extant image of any resister. Date unknown, photograph courtesy of the Macungie and Lehigh County Historical Societies.

opposition language demonstrates their intricate and complex political ideology, their estimation of the people's broad and extensive role in local, state, and national politics, and the breadth and depth of their post-Revolutionary conception of liberty.[3]

When the question of popular participation in or dissent from federal government policy emerged with the Democratic-Republican Societies earlier in the decade, Federalists scorned such populism, and Republican leaders thought it something to be tightly controlled and contained at the polls. While the leadership of the two emerging parties differed on foreign, commercial, and military policies, they all believed that republican liberty was most secure in elite hands. But what did the people themselves think?[4] At least for the eastern Pennsylvania Kirchenleute, the Lehigh resistance can begin to answer this question. If they emerged from the Revolution with such an acute sense of republican, democratic, and economic rights, maybe other ordinary Americans did as well. Perhaps they took their Revolutionary leaders at their word: there really was such a thing as "the people" and they really were sovereign.[5] The Lehigh Kirchenleute's language and actions of opposition graphically demonstrate this belief.

"All those people who were Tories in the Last War mean to be the leaders, they mean to get us quite under, they mean to make us Slaves!" Captain John Fries made this warning to the Lower Milford Militia under his command on the seventh of March, 1799. "And if we let them go on," he continued, "things would be as they are in France," where the people were "as poor as Snakes." Fries was preparing to enter Bethlehem's Sun Inn to negotiate bail with a federal marshal for some prisoners, Northampton County men who had combined to resist the execution of the federal Direct Tax.[6] With the state and national midterm elections in swing, Jonas Hartzell, a German Reformed vestryman, brigadier general of the Northampton Militia, and first-term Kirchenleute state representative from Northampton County, campaigned for the Republican Party that fall. He denigrated the Federalists, their president's foreign policy, their domestic and military measures in the Fifth Congress, and their local Quaker and Moravian adherents when he warned, "if a War should break out, we would then show them who *The People* are, we're *The People*."[7] Then he told a crowd that if the Federalists won the elections for the Sixth Congress, they "are going to pass a great many damned acts, just as they used to do in the old country—Germany!"[8] U.S. Representative Blair McClenachan cautioned another Northampton County audience that the Federalists "wished to oppress the people" with the "Tax Law . . . 'til they got all their lands and then they would lease it out again to the people for their life," and he encouraged them to send petitions to Congress. But "if the people were to oppose it," he advised, "it might yet be altered."[9] Days later one township drafted a petition calling for the repeal of the Direct Tax because it "is now well known, that the owners of Houses in Pennsylvania will pay much more in proportion to the value of their property than the holders of uncultivated lands."[10] About the same time, the Reverend Jacob Eyermann, a German Reformed minister warned his congregation that they "would be as bad off as they were in Europe" if they did not actively oppose the Federalist legislation.[11]

Not long after, seventeen residents of Lehigh Township in Northampton County bound themselves in an "Association" to resist the tax, and ordered assessor "Friend Henry Strauss": "you shall cease to measure the Houses until further orders; and if it must be done, we will ourselves elect a sober and fit man to do the business in our Township."[12] In Bucks County, tavernkeeper George Mitchell informed assessor Samuel Clark that "the people were dissatisfied that their assessor was appointed without their having a choice; for they wished to choose themselves"[13] Elsewhere, some Upper Milford and Macungie militia gathered at Captain Henry Jarret's Millerstown home on Christmas Day, where Henry Shankweiler declared that "he would not suffer his house to be appraised by anybody that had been a Tory in the Last War," and many others present agreed but added that "they were willing to pay a land tax if it was laid as they had petitioned Congress."[14] Henry Shiffert remembered that Jarret sent his men outside to fashion a liberty pole, commanding that "they should never take up with the Stamp Act, if they did they would be sold for slaves."[15] Phillip Wescoe reported that Jarret then "ordered them to take off their hats, ride around the pole, and huzzah for liberty." The men fell in, "and they cursed and swore that they would rather die than submit to the Stamp Act and House Tax Law which was Slavery and Taking the Liberty Away!"[16]

"Slavery and Taking the Liberty Away," "as bad off as they were in Europe," "Tories," "'til they got all their lands," "Liberty Poles," "associations," "petitions," "we will ourselves elect": these words and actions comprised the Fries Rebels language of opposition to the Federalist legislative program of 1798. Within it, we can hear many dialects, including radical republicanism and patriotic Revolutionary nationalism, ethnoreligious conflict and bigotry, ethnic definitions of liberty, Jeffersonian-Republican partisanship, agrarian economic insecurity and class tensions, conservative, corporate, provincial and parochial localism, and the post-Revolutionary democratic impulse that inspired their radical popular constitutionalism. Sometimes their terminology was straightforward and voiced a single audible tongue, but many times they spoke in a kind of pidgin language, slurring several dialects together. Other times they were multilingual, shifting their syntax, drawing on one expression and then another to comprehend the political and economic situation surrounding them and to vocalize their dissent. Distinguishing all these subtle accents from the garbled din heard emanating from the depositions and trial testimony can lead us away from the mono-causal interpretations that have dominated the scholarship on Fries's Rebellion. Early observers and later antiquarians treated it as an aberrant event, the result of misguided and ignorant Germans who, in John Adams's opinion, were "as ignorant of our language as they were of our laws."[17] More recent scholars have found causes in explanations such as localism, agrarian radicalism, ethnoreligious tensions, Republican electioneering, Federalist miscalculation, and even transatlantic radical democracy. Yet few attribute more than a single cause.[18] Most hear one or two dialects that best suit their interpretation and seem to miss to the variety of idioms that voice alternate or confusing conclusions.[19]

The ideology and motivation of the Lehigh resistance movement are not simple matters. In 1798 the Kirchenleute faced a complex set of political and economic choices within multiple, layered contexts. Factoring individual, family, and communal interests, and combining them with ethnic, racial, class, cultural, gendered, historical, national, and spiritual understandings, they made these choices through social, religious, and political institutions on many levels, from the home, to the church, to the workplace, to the local, state, and national governments and beyond. In such a situation, people create ideologies or worldviews, sets of ideas that make sense of the various worlds around them and can integrate and interconnect those multiple worlds to sustain, protect, and nurture them. And of course, many times unanticipated change or outside intrusion forces people to adapt, stretch their preconceived notions, add new ideas or eliminate old ones.[20] In the process people create new contexts that simultaneously restrict and broaden their range of choices and the actions they take, creating new meaning and still new contexts.[21]

The Lehigh area resisters were not motivated by a single factor, or even just two or three, but they weighed multiple variables and reasoned their reaction from a number of perspectives, not just from their past and their present, but from a democratic future they dared to imagine. They drew upon several traditional assumptions and formed novel beliefs in the construction of their ideology of resistance that was at once pragmatic and idealistic, and when they articulated it, they did so in an opposition language that was never quite as clear or comprehensible as historians would like it to be. Instead, it varied in jargon and accent from place to place and from person to person. Yet listening to it all very carefully, we can discern the broad outlines of a single idiomatic pidgin language that the Lehigh Kirchenleute spoke in their opposition to the federal laws in 1798 and 1799.[22]

One of the first clearly audible dialects of the Kirchenleute opposition language was revolutionary republicanism, complete with warnings of slavery, standing armies, corrupt government, and conspiracy against liberty, while the creation of voluntary "associations" recalled Pennsylvania's "Committees of Safety" and Committees of Associators" in the American Revolution. Anglo-American Patriots culled their revolutionary ideology from England's seventeenth-century Commonwealth tradition and the "country" or "Whig opposition" to Crown and Tory Party that developed in the century that followed. Whigs espoused the contract theory of government, prized individual property holders, and extolled them as the virtuous and "disinterested" governing class who should rule themselves and their neighbors in a representative democracy for the common good and liberty of all. Whether Patriot leaders were firmly committed to these ideals or just employed the rhetoric of liberty for their own ends, classical republican discourse filled the air during the imperial crisis and war that followed.

Pennsylvania's revolution was more than just a republican revolt against aristocratic and imperialist rule from abroad. Similar to the conflict that historian Carl Becker describes in neighboring New York, the struggle in Pennsylvania was as much about "who would rule at home" as it was about simple "home rule."[23] Radicals, who were disenchanted with the neutral and loyalist leadership of both the Quaker and Proprietary Parties, supported the colonial resistance to the "Intolerable Acts" of 1774 by joining the extralegal Committees of Safety or Observation and the Associators. Through these bodies they relayed information from the happenings outside of Boston and inside the Continental Congress in Philadelphia and enforced the boycotts and nonexportation ordered by the latter. Companies of Associators from the heavily German-populated counties of York, Lancaster, and Berks made their way to Boston in 1775 following the Battles of Lexington and Concord. In June 1776, the Radicals seized control of the colony and drafted a constitution that created the "Commonwealth." While the Radical leadership certainly stood to benefit politically and economically from their takeover, their democratic constitution enfranchised many people previously denied power and created a democratic form of representative government. Classical republican ideology, which historians such as Bernard Bailyn and Gordon Wood have claimed was the principal Revolutionary motivation, was but one of many motivating factors in the Radicals' fight for independence and provincial control. They professed that Parliament conspired to rob them of their liberty; their mobs had attacked Benjamin Franklin's home in 1765 when he was appointed a distributor of stamped paper; they orchestrated their own Philadelphia "Tea Party" in 1774 to oppose parliamentary corruption; and they opposed Britain's standing army with their own militia in 1775.

Many of the Radicals were underrepresented westerners who had long resented eastern domination of the colony's Assembly and economy, and they courted other less powerful backcountry Pennsylvanians such as the Scots-Irish and the Germans. Seeking a republican and democratic correction, they overrepresented themselves with the constitution of 1776 by providing equal apportionment in the unicameral legislature, the Supreme Executive Council, and the Council of Sensors. Less populous western and northern counties empowered themselves at the expense of the dense southeast. They also eliminated specific property requirements for voting, admitting all free men with any taxable property who swore an oath to the new government, and they provided for an annually elected unicameral assembly directly elected and controlled by the people with no oversight by veto-wielding executives or placemen. The Radicals' behavior was decidedly not democratic from the standpoint of neutrals, Loyalists, and those whose conscience prevented them from swearing oaths, but compared to other state Revolutionary governments, their brand of republicanism was by far the most democratic in the role they assigned to popular participation. The Lehigh Kirchenleute shared this Revolutionary experience and remembered in it 1798.[24]

Of 211 people individually identified with any phase of the resistance in 1798–199 through the depositions and trial testimony, 83 (nearly 40 percent) had fought in the Revolution two decades before, and another 70 (one-third) were related to veterans; many were sons of veterans, like sixteen-year-old Daniel Fries. More than three-quarters were connected to the war.[25] According to historian Eugene Slaski, the Lehigh Valley Kirchenleute, particularly those between the river and the Lehigh Hills, "were among the more active revolutionaries." They helped to organize, and then served as members of, the Northampton County Committees of Observation and Correspondence in response to the Intolerable Acts in 1774, and with their Scots-Irish neighbors they formed an Associator militia (numbering 2250 a year later). During the conflict they tasted victory at the battles of Trenton and Princeton and defeat at the first engagement on Long Island. For the remainder of the war, they guarded the Delaware River, suffered the presence of refugees during the occupation of Philadelphia, and reluctantly parted with their flour and other provisions in return for depreciating "Continental" bills from Washington's army.[26] In spite of the hardships, their participation in that war—and their adherence to the principles that in part inspired it—helped form their identity as Pennsylvanians and American citizens while they remained Germans. Historian Stephen Nolt that contends Pennsylvania Germans spent the ensuing fifty years employing "revolutionary ideology" to defend "ethnic particularism with the rhetoric of liberty, equality, and natural rights."[27]

Thus in 1798 they revived the "Associator" tradition from Pennsylvania's revolution and signed township associations. John Fries wrote the document for Lower Milford, in Bucks County and emblazoned the motto "LIBERTY" across the top.[28] Another six hundred men from the three townships of Upper Milford and Upper and Lower Saucon "bound themselves under Jacob Lerch, to oppose all those laws respecting the Stamp Act and Tax Law."[29] The Federalist "Stamp Act" that Henry Jarret damned was a 1797 federal tax on legal documents to fund fortification and military measures, but its name served to connect the Federalist administration with the opprobrium of British imperialism. Many Kirchenleute referred to the Direct Tax assessors as "stampers" or "damned stamblers," and thus they connected their revolutionary republican memories of the imperial struggle to their opposition in 1798. Assessor Michael Bobst of Northampton County reported the revived Revolutionary tactic of boycotting through the Weisenburg Association, where "they have bound themselves together not to come to my store, or to my son's Tavern under a penalty of ten dollars."[30] Associations policed neighbors; one man claimed that when he refused to sign a paper, the group condemned him as a "stamp act man" and threatened him with the loss of his commission as a captain in the militia.[31] The Associations also drafted petitions to Congress that either questioned the validity or reality of the House Tax or called for its repeal along with the Alien and Sedition Acts and military measures. And like their Revolutionary forbearers who had opposed unfair taxation and infringements on civil liberties, the Kirchenluete too claimed that such actions were unconstitutional.[32] While prizing their recent Patriot experience, members of the Kirchenleute resistance still held onto their German past, convinced that they would be "as bad off as they were in Europe" were the Direct Tax to go unchecked.

Members of Congress "are going to pass a great many damned acts," Jonas Hartzell railed, "just like they used to do in the old country," as he reminded his people of their European past. The Kirchenleute opposition language, of course, voiced Revolutionary republicanism with a distinctly German accent. Of the 211 known resisters, a simple surname check reveals that at least 187 were German-American.[33] Seventy thousand Germans from the Rhine Valley and the Palatinate made their way to Pennsylvania in the six decades preceding the Revolution, using familial and communal chain migration, fleeing a region racked by war and poverty for more than a century. They had endured all sorts of taxation to fund one war, then another, and the most hated were direct taxes on houses, called "hearth taxes." In this climate, argues historian A. G. Roeber, "Palatines" (mostly Lutherans but some Reformed as well) understood liberty primarily in negative terms. *Freheit* meant freedom from outside transgressions on individual or community autonomy. To secure *freheit*, Palatines jealously guarded their *freheiten*, or privileges, and the most important of them was the ownership and transferal of property. For Palatines, the ownership of property afforded economic freedom and the limited rights of citizenship they could use to communally protect it. Acting collectively as the *Burgerecht*, they filed signed *Gravamina* (grievances) seeking redress when overbearing taxes threatened their property. Ownership preserved the domestic hearth for future generations in houses and villages and harbored the family and communities from danger in an age of turmoil.[34] When Henry Jarret's men "cursed and swore" against the "House Tax Law" as they rode around their liberty pole, many must have recalled stories about German "hearth taxes" in "the old country" from their parents' generation, and some in their sixties and seventies were old enough to remember these taxes themselves.

According to historian Aaron Fogleman, the German obsession with securing titles to land continued in the New World and was paramount among Germans' goals, and so they quickly naturalized as citizens and engaged in colonial politics "to make secure what they had acquired in the *Neuland*" and "played a crucial role in all the contentious elections" in Pennsylvania after 1740, shifting from Quaker Party to Proprietary Party candidates when it served their interests in property rights. German immigrants demanded four things: abundant land, a fair land office to balance settlers' needs and speculators' profits, a generous general loan office, and security in their property, for which naturalization and a fortified militia were absolutely necessary.[35]

These were still critical issues in 1798. When Jarret's men "cursed and swore" against the "Stamp Act," they did so in part because it taxed legal documents such as wills, deeds, probate receipts, and certificates of naturalization, all keys to Kirchenleute property ownership, transferal, and economic security, as well as political citizenship for themselves and their heirs.[36] Echoing were the many memories of their political battles in the 1740s-1760s to become naturalized and to acquire and protect their land. They had first attached themselves to the Quaker Party, which controlled the Assembly and afforded a liberal naturalization, and against the proprietor, Thomas Penn, who sought to deny unnaturalized Germans the ability to bequeath their land and to secure his own right of escheat. During the French and Indian War, Church Germans in the northern and western backcountry gradually joined the Proprietary Party, which sought military protection from, and forced eviction of, Native Americans. In 1755 nearly 600 Berks County men, largely Germans, marched into Philadelphia carrying the corpses of neighbors killed by Delaware Indians. The Quaker Assembly passed, and Governor Robert Morris (the proprietor's agent) signed a bill providing £60,000 to militarily defend their homesteads. After the war, when Franklin and the Quaker Party threatened Proprietary control by petitioning the royal crown to reclaim title and control of the colony, Penn enacted a populist land policy in 1765 that cut the price of a 100-acre lot by nearly two-thirds. Many Church Germans naturalized, secured title for their lands, and voted Proprietary that year, beginning to swell their conception of *freiheit* to include suffrage.[37] In 1798 many remembered participating in this struggle for property rights, and others had watched their parents struggle or learned of the fight as grandchildren. The Federalist "Stamp Tax" that targeted naturalization and inheritances rekindled memories real and shared and offended the Church Germans. It must have also reminded them of the Revolution, a national, state, and local experience that had expanded their notions of *freiheit*.

When the Radicals in Pennsylvania began pushing for greater western representation after 1774, Germans demonstrated that they had amplified their definition of *freiheit* to include not only the ballot but also the right to protect their *freiheiten* themselves by pushing for greater representation and their own positions of authority. In 1776 most Church Germans abandoned the two traditional parties and joined the Radicals in framing a new government. After the elections that year, Germans comprised 38 percent of the Assembly.[38] Lehigh area Kirchenleute expanded their notions of liberty as well and combined them with religious prejudice. During the war, many Scots-Irish began to leave the Lehigh Valley and the German sectarians declined in number. During the decade of the 1790s, the Moravian towns of Bethlehem and Nazareth shrunk by one-half and two-thirds respectively.[39] One historian notes that "the valley became more Pennsylvania-German," and while they exhibited "the inclination . . . to remain wedded to the soil" like Germans in other counties, they began to assume public offices.[40] Moreover, just as Revolutionary participation would provide Lehigh Germans with an American identity, it would also serve to bridge the gap between Lutherans and Reformed. Together as Kirchenleute they served on the Committee of Observation, and as Associators they harassed "non-Associators," their Sektenleute neighbors.

When John Fries warned that "Tories . . . mean to be the leaders" and "mean to make us slaves," he meant the pacifist Quakers and Moravians, who until the 1790s still held onto some local political appointments in Northampton County and most in Bucks County, despite their declining numbers, and who as Federalists had just been appointed to collect the Direct Tax by the Adams administration in Philadelphia.[41] Here his jargon is loaded with multiple meanings. The reference to "Tories" and "slaves" immediately recalls the Revolutionary republican rhetoric. Yet "Tories" also referred to the current situation, identifying the sectarian assessors. Henry Shankweiler was very clear about this when he refused to submit to an appraisal by "anybody that had

Figure 2. Christ Reformed United Church of Christ, Trumbaursville (formerly Charles Town). This is the third church, built in 1868 on the site of the original. This Union congregation dates to 1778. John Fries's remains lie buried in an unmarked grave. The headstone is Daniel Klein's, who as an adolescent boy in 1799 obstructed the Direct Tax with his family. Photograph by Paul Douglas Newman.

been a Tory in the Last War." Patriot Kirchenleute scorned the sectarian pacifists as Tories during the Revolution for their refusal to take up arms, despite the
Moravian contributions to Patriot military supplies and the medical services
their communities rendered as military hospitals. During the war, the Church
People assumed an "us versus them" mentality and divided the region into
"Whig" and "Tory" townships along religious lines. The Lutheran and Reformed Associators particularly harassed the Moravian community at Emmaus,
which lay within the Kirchenleute Northampton County township of Upper
Milford. The Milford Associators repeatedly jailed, fined, and verbally abused
Emmaus non-Associators for their refusal to take the oath of allegiance to the
state and to take up arms in the militia. The Kirchenleute demanded oaths,
which they knew the Moravians' religion would not allow them to profess,
even when the Pennsylvania law allowed for affirmations. Patriot Church People forced many of the Moravians to abandon their principles and swear oaths
of allegiance to avoid financial ruin from fines and detention.[42] A decade and a
half after the war's end, the wounds of religious bigotry still stung in 1798, as
the Lehigh Valley Kirchenleute still "patriotically" derided Friends and sectarians as Tories, and the Sektenleute remembered their mistreatment.

Because of the irregularity of church records, it is impossible to know
exactly how many of the participants in the opposition were Kirchenleute, but
fortunately very good records are extant for four of the townships of heaviest
resistance: Lower Milford in Bucks County and Upper Milford, Macungie, and
Heidelberg in Northampton County. Of the 123 identified participants in the
four townships, 83 were Lutheran, Reformed, or attended a Union church.[43] It
is not known exactly how many of the total number of resisters were Kirchenleute, but given their overwhelming predominance in the rural areas and
among the resisters from townships of heaviest resistance, they were unques-
tionably the bulk of the total. In fact, one of the most vocal leaders in
Northampton County at the high water mark of the resistance was a Reformed
clergyman, Jacob Eyermann. Another Reformed minister, Thomas Pomp,
launched an invective against Moravian Direct Tax commissioner Jacob Eyerle
in an Easton newspaper.[44] Nor do we know the exact ratio of Reformed to
Lutheran among the resisters, but there were 28 Reformed and 24 Lutheran
churches in Northampton County, and Heidelberg, Lehigh, Weisenberg, Whitehall, and Chestnuthill all formed Union churches by 1798, as did Lower Milford
in Bucks County.[45] John Fries attended the Christ Reformed United Church of
Christ in Charlestown, about halfway between his home and Milford Square
(see Figure 2). After several decades of religious rivalry and political competition, the Lutheran and Reformed found commonality in their German Protes-
tantism during and after the Revolutionary War. Those experiences "ethnicized"

their political consciousness as Kirchenleute by the 1790s.[46] In 1798 this ethnicization resounded loud and clear when they complained that their taxmen,
"Tories in the Last War," came from the peace sects and the Federalist Party. [47]

And therein resides another meaning to Fries's warning about the
"Tories." The appointment of "Tory rascals" to lay and collect the Direct Tax
confirmed the Republican Party's charges of a Federalist monarchical conspiracy to destroy republican liberty in America and return the nation to monarchy,
aristocracy, and political and economic slavery. Jeffersonian-Republicanism,
inspired by national and state politics as well, also rolled from Kirchenleute
tongues. Earlier in the decade, a congressional opposition to Washington administration policy had developed in Philadelphia, principally around Speaker
of the House James Madison. Madison had authored the Virginia Plan that the
Constitutional Convention revised into the national, federal frame of government at the Pennsylvania State House (now Independence Hall) in 1787. He
and other Federalists, Alexander Hamilton and John Jay, authored and distributed dozens of essays (the "Federalist Papers") to garner popular support for
ratification. Then, as a U.S. Representative, Madison drafted the Bill of Rights
and guided it through Congress and the ratification process. In 1790 he opposed Treasury Secretary Alexander Hamilton's plan for national economic
solvency through federal assumption of the individual state debts and the
funding of wartime securities at face value. In the years of depreciation and
skyrocketing inflation that attended and followed the war, wealthy individuals
and groups had opportunistically purchased the "Continental" notes for pennies on the dollar from the farmers and craftsmen who had patriotically
bought them or had accepted them as payment from the Revolutionary army.
Madison favored a system of "discrimination" that would provide some reim-
bursement to the original holders to reward their virtue. He also opposed
Hamilton's Bank of the United States, and so did Thomas Jefferson.

Jefferson, the author of the Declaration of Independence, the wartime
governor of Virginia, and American minister to France, returned home in 1789
to serve in President Washington's cabinet as secretary of state. He enthusias-
tically kept track of the democratic revolution evolving back in France that
summer. When Washington submitted Hamilton's bank plan to his cabinet for
advice, Jefferson balked, using the Constitution to argue that the central government did not have the right to charter a private corporation, a selection of
wealthy men, to be the sole repository of all the funds of the United States government. Such a creation threatened to tie the interests of Congress (and therefore the people) to the interests of the bank and its investments; that was
exactly what Hamilton meant it do. To Jefferson and Madison, the Bank of the
United States reminded them of the Bank of England, and Hamilton resembled

another Sir Robert Walpole, the mid-eighteenth-century English prime minister who financed a funded national debt with increased taxes housed in a national bank and raised a standing army and navy to fight wars of conquest. These armies and navies had intruded on American liberty not only in Boston after 1767 but had for years plied the coastal harbors impressing colonists for labor in the British war machine. In England, Walpole's policies and those of his successors led to a near permanent state of warfare fed by corrupt mercantilist industrialism, where cities, factories, the poor, monopolies, and customs duties grew and grew. By 1790 the English government was using poor houses as workhouses, and Hamilton's plans outlined in his reports on Public Credit and Manufactures seemed to portend such developments in America. As for Parliament's "country Whigs" that rose to resist Walpole early in the eighteenth century, an opposition developed around the two Virginians both within Congress and beyond as the century drew to a close.

In spite of Jefferson's and Madison's fears and opposition, Alexander Hamilton's plans passed through Congress one after another, occasionally with help from the former two. In 1790, Madison dropped his opposition to Hamilton's "Assumption" plan in exchange for the provision that the nation's permanent capital be situated in the South on the Potomac River across from Virginia, an event labeled the "Compromise of 1790" and brokered between the two men by their dinner host, Thomas Jefferson. Then Madison supported Hamilton's Excise Tax on Spiritous Liquors in 1791, a bill the Virginian had suggested a year earlier. Only after a series of Washington administration domestic and international policy actions between 1793 and 1796 (Washington's Proclamation of Neutrality, his censure of the Democratic Societies, the suppression of the Whiskey Rebellion, attempts to create a standing army, and the Jay Treaty) did Jefferson, Madison, and others begin to construct the framework of an opposition party. The term "first party system" is not an accurate descriptor in the days before the massive fundraising, conventions, lobbyists, wide-scale electioneering, national partisan adherence, and shared capitalist consensus that later characterized politics, especially after the Civil War. One historian has labeled these early organizations as "proto-parties," especially since the people were as likely to guide policy as their leaders.[48] During this period, all over the country citizens began forming popular Democratic-Republican Societies to communicate and inform the people of the actions of their government in Philadelphia. They memorialized and petitioned on a range of democratic issues, most in opposition to President Washington's domestic and foreign policies and in support of the French and their revolution.[49] In 1796, Jefferson contested for the presidency as a Republican against Washington's vice-president

John Adams, who with other supporters of the administration styled themselves Federalists.[50]

But more than just national politics were at stake in Philadelphia in 1796. A Republican political machine was taking shape there to wrest control of city and state politics from Pennsylvania's conservative counterrevolutionaries of 1790. Jeffersonian-Republican politicians from the west enjoined Germans and Scots-Irish working-class voters on the city's outskirts to oppose the conservative Philadelphia Federalist merchants who favored the president's foreign policy and its benefits for their trade. Both Philadelphia Federalists and Republicans had organized themselves in the elections of 1794 and 1795, and in 1796 they campaigned and organized ward-level committees to elect state assemblymen, a congressional delegation, and presidential electors. In all three races, the campaign issue was the Jay Treaty of 1795, the Washington administration's concession of America's neutral right to trade with belligerents (England was at war with France) in exchange for the opening of British West Indies ports to American ships and products. Republicans, of course, damned the administration's foreign policy as monarchical because it bound the United States to England in preference to the French revolutionaries. Federalists scorned the anarchy and licentiousness they saw in France's bloody frenzy, and blamed it on rampant democracy. But democracy remained popular among working people in Philadelphia, and the politics of association worked, as ethnics and new immigrants overwhelmingly voted Republican and succeeded in the city and county of Philadelphia in electing an assembly slate, a state senator, two U.S. Representatives, including Blair McClenachan, and electors for Thomas Jefferson. They performed well in the west too, but their results were mixed in the Kirchenleute counties in between.[51]

In heavily Republican Berks County, German candidate Joseph Heister, a wealthy land speculator, lost a congressional race to another German, Federalist ironmaster George Ege. When Ege resigned to take a judicial appointment, Heister defeated the Federalist lawyer from Reading, Anglo-American Daniel Clymer. It seems that in the latter race, in which another German choice did not exist, ethnicity trumped republican virtue. Kirchenleute townships only polled 16 and 17 percent in York and Lancaster County for Jefferson, but in Northampton County, Lehigh township gave the Virginian 93 percent. Northampton Republicans ran a slate of four Kirchenluetc candidates for State Assembly and succeeded in electing one, but the Federalists held the other three. Easton Federalist Samuel Sitgreaves retained his seat in an October election that drew only 27 percent of voters. The presidential election on November 4 drew even less, only 17 percent. National and international politics had yet to stir Lehigh

Valley residents, with the exception of the Moravian Federalists at Nazareth, who celebrated in 1796 when the Jay Treaty took effect.[52] Republicans spent the next two years building a party organization and installing newspapers around the countryside. Only days after the elections of 1796, Jacob Schneider began publishing his Republican *Readinger Adler,* which carried the party's opposition message in German to the Kirchenleute of Berks County and the Lehigh area.[53] When the next state and national elections came in 1798, Philadelphia Republicans moved out of the city and began to extend the politics of ethnic association into the Kirchenleute counties.

Schneider's *Adler,* along with other Republican newspapers like the *Philadelphische Correspondenz* and the *Philadelphia Aurora,* denounced the Federalist-dominated Fifth Congress, President Adams, and the Federalists' reaction to the crisis with France, describing them as the makings of a monarchical plot. Meanwhile, in 1798 state Republicans encouraged their Kirchenleute constituents to push for laws that would require the state government to print its documents in German as well as English, and to give them electoral control over justices of the peace and militia captains. Then Federalists in the Fifth Congress painted Republican dissent as treason with the Sedition Act, abridging the First Amendment and thereby threatening the ability of the Republican Party to enact its broader agenda of localizing state authority that appealed to the Kirchenleute. The Federalists passed Alien Acts that in Pennsylvania would rob Republicans of thousands of Irish votes in Philadelphia. They appropriated millions of dollars for defense and augmented a "standing army" at a time when state Republicans were attempting to stiffen the Pennsylvania militia law to further penalize conscientious objectors. And to fund it all, they authorized Congress to borrow millions of dollars, which they, the people, would eventually pay with a "Stamp Tax" and the "Direct Tax." Charges of Federalist "monarchism" made sense to the Kirchenleute who struggled against "Tory" assessors, as they combined local, ethnic, religious, state, and national concerns in the autumn of 1798 and commenced their opposition to laws that seemed to undermine both the letter and the republican spirit of the Constitution. Republican politicians like Jonas Hartzell and Blair McClenachan politicked for weeks around the Lehigh Valley in the fall of 1798 to make sure that the Kirchenluete made the connection. Not coincidentally, then, Jeffersonian "country opposition" became a powerful element in the Kirchenleute's language of opposition, as they read Republican newspapers, listened to Republican campaign speeches, and voted for Republican candidates who warned them that Federalists meant to enslave them by dispossessing them of their farms.[54] When McClenachan pronounced that Federalists "wished to oppress the people" by taking "all their lands" and leasing them back out "to the people for their life," this seemed a real possibility, and soon the Kirchenleute themselves appropriated this language.

When John Fries said, "they mean to make us slaves," the Kirchenleute drew upon a wealth of memories and cultural traditions to interpret this warning. Many were ideological, as "slavery" permeated the rhetoric of Jeffersonian-Republicanism and the radical Whig talk of the Revolution. But here also can be heard real issues of economic insecurity and personal liberty. Some remembered the Rhine lands. Historian Marianne Wokeck contends that most southwestern German immigrants fled a life of "bondage" in an "outmoded feudal system" characterized by inflation and burdensome taxes."[55] Perhaps others recalled bound labor in America, as one historian has estimated that as many as half of Pennsylvania's 70,000 eighteenth-century immigrants arrived as indentured servants or redemptioners.[56] The Quaker Party and its German press certainly kept alive Rhinelanders' fears of enslavement in the 1740s and 1750s by attacking the proprietor's quasi-feudal land policy. After the Revolution, many still remembered when Thomas Penn had vigorously prosecuted German squatters and titleholders who fell behind on their quitrents and had foreclosed and evicted them regularly. Then from the 1780s to the early 1790s, sheriffs delivered nearly 9,500 writs of foreclosure in the heavily German counties of Lancaster, Northumberland, and Berks. One historian estimates that more than two-thirds of the inhabitants of those counties faced foreclosure and eviction after the Revolution.[57] And postwar Pennsylvanians were not alone. From the 1720s through the 1780s, American agrarians built a tradition of rural "regulation." From the tenant riots of New York, the land rioting in New Jersey, to the regulation movements in North Carolina and Massachusetts, to the rebellions and resistance in Vermont and Maine, dispossessed farmers, squatters, and tenants rebelled against the consolidation of landed wealth, unfair taxation, imprisonment, and foreclosure. They claimed a right to ownership based on the virtue of their labor that improved the land, as opposed to speculators whose ready cash and access to courts stripped it away from them. They violently attacked taxmen and surveyors, forcibly shut down courts, broke their neighbors out of jails, and occasionally challenged the political systems that served speculators, bankers, and lawyers.[58] The militias of Lower Milford and Northampton either drew upon or entered into this tradition when they refused the call to evict the Connecticut Claimants in the Wyoming Valley.

Those too young to recall Germany or early colonization experiences likely learned about them from their elders, and the economic insecurity of their own time in the post-Revolution depression reinforced these lessons and memories. When Fries said, "they mean to get us quite under," he was referring to the specter of debt and the Quaker merchants and bankers who held the notes. As a vendue crier (public auctioneer), John Fries and his clients understood firsthand in the cash-poor days that followed the Revolution the issue of debt in a contracting economy. Historian Terry Bouton has shown that tax officials in Bucks and Northampton Counties complained throughout the 1780s that they could not collect the state and county taxes because of the "absolute scarcity of Money." Although the democratic Constitutionalist Party controlled the Assembly and issued paper money in 1785, most of it was paid to the holders of wartime securities, 96 percent of which were held by fewer than 500 speculators in 1790. Tax assessors, who were fined for noncollection, also complained that sheriffs, justices of the peace, and constables stubbornly refused to do their duty of prosecuting and foreclosing on offenders. Bouton contends that while Massachusetts farmers "regulated" their credit, tax, and legal system, rural Pennsylvania farmers constructed "concentric rings of protection around their communities" that began with a sympathetic constabulary, extended to juries that refused to convict delinquent taxpayers, and ended with direct regulation by the farmers themselves. Jacob Arndt, a Moravian Northampton County tax collector complained to the state comptroller general in 1787 that local justices of the peace and constables "seek in the first place to indulge their neighbors." Arndt continued that "dissatisfaction among the people is great, they complain of the weight of Taxes weighed upon their shoulders."[59]

Agrarians across the state pledged to no-bid covenants at auctions, violently abused threatening officials, or closed the roads that led from county courthouses to rural farms. In eastern Pennsylvania, there is direct evidence of one covenant in Berks County in 1780 and another in Bucks in 1783, and Northampton officials complained they "could get no purchasers" for sales once in 1783, again in 1786, and twice in 1788. Violence was less frequently employed in the Lehigh area. Only Robert Levers, a tax collector for Northampton County, reported an attack. In 1785 a group of men he described as "yeomen" and "gentlemen" attacked his home, knocked in his door, threatened and assaulted him, although the extent of his injuries and the ritual employed are not clear. Road closings were more popular, as officials reported four in Bucks and seven in Northampton over the period, the last as late as 1795. Yet all of this was mild compared to the violent treatment that officials received farther west in the state, where crowds administered beatings and tar and feather jackets liberally, and in 1798–99 eastern Pennsylvanians would become milder still. Westerners in the 1780s and early 1790s suffered both from the postwar depression and extreme distance from eastern markets, which made the excise on distilled grain particularly threatening to their economic survival. By 1798, eastern Pennsylvanians were relieved to see a slowly improving economy, and the Direct Tax fell more lightly on the poor than the rich.[60]

While the progressive House Tax was relatively innocuous to those whose homes were valued at less than $500, many feared that the house measurements, especially the measuring and counting of windows, signaled the duty would become an annual rate or that the federal government would use it as a precedent for even more taxes, direct or indirect. Five townships of heaviest resistance—Lower Milford (Bucks County), Upper Milford, Macungie, Heidelberg, and Lehigh (all Northampton County)—have excellent records remaining and can serve as a representative sample for the resistance as a whole. These modest communities yielded 134 of the 211 resisters identified. The Pennsylvania Septennial Census of 1800 recorded 1,009 taxable men from the five townships, and the U.S. Census counted 1,151 households.[61] Most of the 783 homeowners lived in log homes valued between $100 and $400, with an average

Figure 3. A two-story hewed log home in Lower Milford Township on Foulkes Mill Road, just south of Milford Square. Of thirty-one homeowning resisters in Lower Milford, only one lived in a two-story log home. Another owned a two-story frame house, twelve lived in one- or two-story stone houses, and the rest resided in one-story round or hewed log houses like John Fries's home, pictured in Figure 4. Photograph by Paul Douglas Newman.

value of $306, and most of the 868 landowners owned less than 300 acres (half less than 100 acres), with an average value of $8.81 per acre. Modest though they were, in recent years they had fared much better than other Pennsylvanians, such as those to the south in Chester County where only 54 percent still owned their own land in 1799.[62] In the five townships, 70 percent of adult men owned their own houses and ten of eleven owned at least some taxable property. Through naturalization, land purchases, political action, and extralegal communal defense strategies, more than three of four Kirchenleute in these townships had managed to acquire and maintain enough property to sustain themselves and their families and to create a stable rural community life. Even still, this was not enough land to continue carving it up among their sons, and in a 1795 petition to the governor for a German justice of the peace, the men of Lower Milford humbly referred to themselves as "the Lower sort of the People."[63] The Kirchenleute in 1798 had survived the postwar depression but remained vulnerable.

The average taxable man paid less than $1 on his home and less than $5 on his lands for the Direct Tax of 1798. Of the 211 identified resisters, 99 owned taxable homes and 98 owned taxable land. This figure sounds low, but the 211 identified resisters represent only 172 households; therefore, 58 percent owed federal taxes. Even this number is deceptively low because in many cases more than two resisters came from a single household. Teenage sons and younger brothers often joined their fathers and uncles in resistance. Another factor pulling the numbers lower is that eight resisters' home townships and counties were not revealed by the depositions or testimony, so verification of their status as property-holders is unattainable. Furthermore, of the remaining 101 who did not appear on the Direct Tax enumeration, 52 appeared as taxable men in the Pennsylvania Septennial Census of 1800 or on the Bucks and Northampton County rates. Considerably more than 58 percent of the resisters probably owned taxable property in 1798, perhaps as high as 75 to 93 percent; given the accuracy of the numbers for the five townships of heaviest resistance, that range seems quite likely.

Furthermore, in the five townships of heaviest resistance where the records are precise, the overall figure of 75 percent land ownership reflects the projected 75 to 93 percent range for resisters. In Lower Milford, 36 of 43 resisters owned land or houses, and 4 of those who did not were younger sons still living at home. Across the county line to the north in Upper Milford, 19 of 29 identified resisters owned property, with 3 boys being still at home and a grandfather living with his son's family. Northward in Macungie, where at least 35 men protested the laws, 21 held property and 3 lived in their father's homes. Heading northeast to Heidelberg, 11 of 15 faced the Direct Tax, and across the Lehigh

River to the east in Lehigh Township only 5 of 16 did not. At least 79 percent of these resisters either owned their own property or lived with an adult relative who did. Moreover, tax-resister property owners are almost identical to the general home and landowners of the five townships (see Tables 1–3).[64]

These figures refute contemporary Federalist charges that the resisters were rabble who held no taxable property.[65] They also reveal that the resisters had weathered the troubled economy of the 1780s much better than some historians believe. When Fries warned his people that if they failed to act they would be "as poor as snakes," it is the conditional "would" to which we should pay particular attention. As of 1798, these Kirchenleute were not impoverished. Actually, about four in five were landholders, and they were rather average both in the value of their taxable property and in the size of their farms, houses, and outbuildings when compared to the rest of their local neighbors. Most resisters of the total sample (more than 60 percent) lived in a house valued between $100 and $300 and operated farms of around 115 acres whose average value was $949.41—about the size that James Lemon claims was owned by a typical middle-class, profitable eighteenth-century farmer who supplied

Table 1. Comparison of Home Value, Resisters and All Homeowners in Five Townships of Heaviest Resistance

Home value in dollars	99 resisting homeowners	783 homeowners
Less than 100	2—0.1%	2—0.2%
100–499	80—80.8%	675—86.2%
500–999	18—18.18%	99—12.65%
1000 and above	2—2%	9—1.15%

Table 2. Comparison of Acreage, Resisters and All Property Owners in Five Townships of Heaviest Resistance

Number of acres	98 resisting property owners	868 property owners
Less than 300	98—97%	838—97.1%
100–299	46—45%	390—44.93%
More than 300	3—2.9%	24—2.76%

Table 3. Comparison of Home and Property Values and Acreage, in Five Townships of Heaviest Resistance

	Home value	Acreage	Property value
Average resister	$319.38	115.5	$8.22 per acre
Average home and property owner	$306.81	105.7	$8.81 per acre

many of his own needs and produced a modest surplus for the market.[66] At the county level, Bucks County resisters lagged a bit behind the average landed wealth of $1095.02, while Northampton County resisters fared significantly better than the $647.26 average.[67] Eight of ten resisters owed less than a dollar in tax on their homes. Few owed more than two or three dollars for their houses and lands combined. Some—especially the tavern owners like Conrad Marks and George Mitchell—were actually quite well off, while a few others, such as John Fries, owned very little property. Fries and his wife raised their family of ten children in a one-story log cabin, sixteen feet wide and fourteen feet deep (see Figure 4). The barn that stood on his thirteen acres of land was twice that size. Fries owed a total of forty-five cents for the Direct Tax of 1798.

In spite of this relative prosperity, many may have worried that the Direct Tax Act would lead to future economic hardship perhaps even "slavery." Of the 6,646 people inhabiting the five townships, 648 were men between twenty-six and forty-five, and they were fathers to 4,494 sons and daughters twenty-five or younger, who would soon require land and dowries. Of the 1,151 households, 996 (83%) were homes to young men and boys under twenty-five. Moreover,

Figure 4. John Fries's house, Lower Milford Township. Today covered in a stone veneer, this one-story, 16′ x 14′ hewed log structure was only a bit smaller than the typical homes that sheltered seventeen of thirty-one Lower Milford resisters. The structure is still a home today. Photograph by Paul Douglas Newman.

Macungie Township experienced an increase of adult taxable males from 252 in 1786 to 359 in 1800, as Heidelberg grew from 158 to 220.[68] While few expressed fears that the levy collected in 1799 would break them immediately, their future (and their children's future) was growing more crowded and uncertain. So unlike desperate "Regulators" who used violence and threatened insurrection, these resisters focused on changing the laws and the assessors to prevent or forestall future economic turmoil rather than angrily responding to immediate hardships.

Another element of agrarian economic insecurity faced by the Kirchenleute, attendant to the fear of foreclosure, was an ideological and class-based contempt for land speculators and for Pennsylvania and U.S. land policies that favored them, exhibited by the Kirchenleute refusal to evict the Connecticut claimants in 1784–85.[69] Republican U.S. Representative Blair McClenachan (a speculator himself) played upon this prejudice in a Northampton County campaign speech in 1798 when he charged that the Federalists would employ their economic policy "'til they got all their lands" and then "lease it out again to the people for their life." In the climate of foreclosures that the Kirchenleute had regularly experienced since the days of Thomas Penn and in the wake of their parents' or grandparents' serfdom in Germany, the threat of permanent tenancy was more than a political bogeyman—it was a menacing and all too possible reality. Furthermore, the rhetoric of Revolutionary and Jeffersonian republicanism was also filled with scorn for dependency and equated civic virtue with "yeoman" farmers, independent artisans, and small shopkeepers. The Kirchenleute employed this rhetoric in their petitions that attacked the Direct Tax because it favored the "holders of uncultivated lands," speculators whom they, the "Lower sort of the People," considered "landjobbers." One farmer quoted in the *Aurora* lamented, "these are strange times, when the speculator goes free, and the industrious farmer is become the object of Taxation."[70] Here they objected to Pennsylvania land policies that allowed speculators to claim rights to millions of acres of land while only paying relatively small down payments. Every year from 1786 to 1791 and then again in 1793 the Assembly attempted to prosecute small farmers who fell into arrears on their taxes and granted extensions to delinquent speculators who held large unsettled tracts.[71]

These memories were still fresh in 1798, and thus many argued that taxing houses in addition to lands would unfairly target small farmers, who would pay both a house and a property tax. Moreover, taxes would be higher for improved land than for speculator holdings, as farmers would "pay much more in proportion to the value of their own property than the holders of uncultivated lands." The Kirchenleute's "virtuous" accomplishments therefore made them eligible to pay higher taxes that could ultimately lead to their dispossession.

While the House Tax was "progressive" in that its rates increased in proportion to the increase in home values, the tax on land applied a fixed rate to the land's assessed value. It is important again to recognize that the Kirchenleute feared that they might become tenants in the future, as their words have shown. They had thus far avoided bankruptcy, foreclosure, and tenancy, and they meant to continue to do so.

The above figures tell us several other things about the resisters' communities as well. First, although the counties at large may not have been ethnically or economically homogeneous, the townships were. In Northampton County, Bethlehem was a Lehigh River village of about five hundred, mostly Moravians involved in industry. Easton was a town of more than a thousand artisans and merchants, many Anglo-Americans and Scots-Irish, crowded at the forks of the Lehigh and Delaware Rivers. The resisting townships bordering these towns were rural farming communities with populations of as much as one thousand but spread out over ten to twenty thousand acres; they were inhabited almost exclusively by Church People.[72] And those most active in the resistance tended to be neighbors in the literal as well as figurative sense. The assessors for Lower Milford Township were fastidious enough in their data collection to record properties adjoining each taxable estate.[73] Of the forty-three identified resisters there, thirty-four lived adjacent to one another. Additionally, the figures above attest to their economic homogeneity.

The ethnic and religious county divisions combined with the demographic and economic ones made for a town and country contrast in sharp relief that would give otherwise intangible ideological differences clearly recognizable faces and, as mentioned above, ones that had been in conflict for years past. Moreover, the homogeneity of the resisting townships and the direct similarities of resisters to the whole population produced the feeling of broadly shared corporate ideals and values and likely lent an air of communal sponsorship and self-legitimization to the resistance. When John Fries explained Lower Milford's decision to march to Bethlehem to rescue the prisoners, he reflected that the "township seemed to be all of one mind" to do so, and the sheer numbers of men who signed associations also attest to such community consensus.[74] The language the resisters used indicates that extralocal ideas of republicanism, revolutionary patriotism, Jeffersonianism and class, confirmed local economic and ethnoreligious realities and infused multiple meanings into their oppositionist terminology.

When Fries charged that the "Tories mean to be the leaders," he was also, in effect, saying, "*We* mean to be the leaders!" vocalizing the increasing homogeneity the resisters experienced in the postwar Lehigh area in a dialect of localism. Sometimes they objected to particular leaders of dubious character, as did the Lehigh resisters who advised their friend Henry Strauss that they would rather have "a sober and fit man do the business." More important, they wished to exclude the diminishing sectarian minorities and English speakers from positions of local power, particularly the posts of sheriff, justice of the peace, prothonotary, constable, county commissioners, judges, and of course, tax collectors, in order to attain local control. They wanted government business printed in both English and German, German-speaking public officials, and Kirchenleute-controlled communities. Yet to achieve these ends, they had to join in state and national politics to change the way those posts were filled. By 1796 the Northampton Kirchenleute had begun to fill some offices, but many of the most crucial still resided in sectarian, Quaker, Anglo, and Scots-Irish hands. Moravian John Arndt was both registrar of wills and recorder of deeds, Quaker Peter Rhoads was a president judge, Anglo William Henry and Scots-Irish John Mulhollan were associate judges, Federalist Anglo Samuel Sitgreaves represented them in Congress and three out of their four assemblymen did not speak German. In some cases, judiciary appointments were the reason, but for state and national level elective offices the Kirchenleute had yet to push for representation. In addition, the county commissioners were Scots-Irish and Anglo, and the appointed prothonotaries historically had been so as well. On the latter note, Governor Mifflin that year appointed Quaker Daniel Stroud as notary in spite of German pleas for Henry Spering.[75]

Kirchenleute in upper Bucks County waged similar battles. Lower Milford petitioners sought to replace Quaker Justice of the Peace Everhard Foulke with George Weichart in 1795 because the latter "is well acquainted with the English and German Languages." Nearby Kirchenleute in Rockhill Township entreated the governor, saying "being German, and being Inclined not to be Intirely Excluded from the Executive Office . . . pray that you . . . grant a Comition of the Peace to a Descendent of a German."[76] In the 1798 and 1799 elections, the Kirchenleute would turn out in massive numbers to vote for Republican and Kirchenleute state representatives to work in the capitol with Simon Snyder for judicial reform and local control. In 1798, Northamptoners placed Kirchenleute Republicans in all four of their assembly seats, and Nicholas Kern became their state senator. Through participation in the state political arena, they would assert their local hegemony, but this would be a moot point if the Federalists threatened to dispossess them of their property through taxation and of their Republican political voice through the Sedition Act. Paradoxically, the struggle for local control took them all the way to the national government, where they demonstrated both the negative and positive definitions of their *freheit* and demanded redress of their *gravamina*. Although they drew some of their inspiration from parochialism and they fought to retain their language and culture, their words and actions reveal that the Kircheleute opposition clearly understood the importance of extralocal ideas, issues, and politics.

Directly tied to Kirchenleute localism is the dialect of Revolutionary democracy and self-government. Members of the Lehigh Association thought that they had the right to "elect" a federal collector for "themselves," and George Mitchell spoke for all of Lower Milford when he said that "they wished to choose themselves." On March 7, the day of the rescue, Judge John Mulhallon reported that he had met a company of Northampton militia as they marched toward Bethlehem. When he asked who was in command, they responded that "they were all commanders."[77] The Revolutionary experience had indeed unleashed democratic consequences for American politics, society, and the people's conception of their political power, and the 1790s bore witness to the emergence of democratic popular participation in the Lehigh Valley area.[78] In addition to local and state politics, by 1798 the Kirchenleute believed they not only had the right to representation on the national level, but that they should have the right to inject themselves between their representatives and the executive when they deemed laws or actions to be unconstitutional and to forestall those laws at least until their petitions for repeal could be heard. Here they were not merely resurrecting Revolutionary language; they were crafting new meaning for the term "unconstitutional" by using their state and national experience, combined with their own notions of natural rights.

The Kirchenleute's democratic "popular constitutionalism" was a hybrid of ideals and practices. Echoes of the Pennsylvania constitution of 1776 can be heard in Blair McClenachan's advice to Northamptoners that "if the people opposed" the Direct Tax, "it might yet be altered" as the state excise taxes had been defeated a decade before. There was a real U.S. Constitutional logic at work as well because federal "Gagg Laws" certainly seemed to violate the First Amendment. When federal marshal William Nichols arrested Northampton County resisters and prepared to transport them out of the region to Philadelphia for trial, Captain Henry Jarret damned Nichols for taking the prisoners "from place to place against the laws of the Constitution."[79] Jarret understood his neighbors' Sixth Amendment right to a trial in the district where their crimes were alleged to have been committed. This national constitutionalism also had a state and local meaning because local juries served as buffers protecting indebted neighbors from taxmen and merchants. In addition to the Sixth Amendment, the Kirchenleute had also used their First Amendment right of petition in the autumn and winter of 1798–99 and had determined to wait until the new Sixth Congress met to learn if the law stood. Congressman

Robert Brown brought before the House of Representatives in the winter of 1799 a petition signed by 1,100 Northampton County men that declared the Federalist legislation "contrary not only to the spirit but to the letter of the Constitution."[80] In March, Jarret and one hundred of his Upper Milford and Macungie men used the Second Amendment when as the militia they marched to Bethlehem to invoke the Sixth Amendment and bail their neighbors out of jail before the spring planting. Militias had also been a popular local tool in Pennsylvania for protecting indebted neighbors in the postwar period. The Kirchenleute's state and local experiences underwrote their attachment to the Bill of Rights.

Other actions and words from the opposition similarly evinced the Kirchenleute nationalism and popular constitutionalism. The Hembolts' liberty pole bore the message "The Constitution Sacred," another pole had "a flag with fourteen stars and the motto LIBERTY underneath," one more sported "the patriotic sign of the Federal Eagle," and still another pole decried the Federalist foreign policy that favored Great Britain and affirmed, "The United States of America, Free, Sovereign, and Independent."[81] Resisters' actions around the poles exuded the same constitutional and nationalistic tones, used democratic and republican terms, and of course mixed them with Republican partisanship as well. Captain Jarret's men circled a pole and "huzzahed for liberty," others toasted liberty with whiskey and huzzahed even louder, and another Northampton County group burned mock copies of the Alien and Sedition Laws around their pole.[82]

Via the resurrection of Revolutionary tactics and petitioning, the resisters spliced republican words with democratic action for a combination of parochial, state, partisan, and national concerns that included local control, economic liberty, and national independence. The nation was only beginning its "great transition" from a rural, semisubsistence-based agrarian economy to a more cosmopolitan capitalist society; Gordon Wood and a host of other scholars have argued that the Revolution had earlier touched off a shifting of political cultures in which republicanism served to bridge a monarchical world to a liberal and democratic one.[83] To be sure, there were cash economies, corporations, expanding banks, urban settings, manufacturing, class structures, interest group politics, and even political parties and electioneering in times and at certain places during the colonial era, especially in Pennsylvania, but in the nineteenth century these would become ubiquitous. And the culture did change from one of small communities with strict rules for social order to more urban conditions where impersonal forces increasingly controlled daily life, loosening the bonds of patriarchal political authority, and money, not birth, granted access to power. Yet the growth of these factors did not produce a steady march toward either liberalism or democracy. Democratic rhetoric abounded, interest-driven parties formed, and more people voted, but this did not necessarily increase the people's sovereignty. Instead, the centennial celebration of the American Revolution would coincide with the beginning of what historians label the "Gilded Age," a time when democracy was for sale and conservative politics, not liberalism, enriched "Robber Barrons" at the expense of the people. But in 1798–99, Thomas Jefferson's fears for the future implications of Alexander Hamilton's policies had yet to be realized. Perhaps aware of these implications, perhaps not, the Kirchenleute "rebels" of the Lehigh region stood in the middle of this national transition while also passing into the realm of local governance over their sectarian neighbors. In either case, they were demanding a type of democracy that the Farmers Alliances and the Populist Party craved a century later, a sort of direct action democracy heedless of parties and money and bureaucracy. And to do so, they abandoned Federalism and enjoined the cause of the Republican Party when it seemed appropriate, as their parents had expediently joined one party and then another during the colonial era.

Although they opposed the Federalist legislation and policy in 1798, the Kirchenleute did not regard their opposition as extralegal, and they had no designs on creating their own party. On the contrary, they asserted that they were acting within the bounds of acceptable political behavior, at least in their own interpretation of the Constitution, and the Republicans' state and national agendas seemed to make them the people's party in spite of the wealth and power of its leadership. So unlike later Populists who either disdained the two political parties or fused with the Democrats, the Kirchenleute oppositionists were both Republican partisans and independent popular constitutionalists at once. In the very first years of party politics, it seemed to them that they could be both; thus they were attempting to construct their own version of post-Revolutionary democratic political culture. In 1785 the citizens of Lower Milford spoke of "the Idea we have of Justice & the Spirit of Our Laws and Constitution" when they refused to evict the Connecticut Claimants, fellow citizens whom they did not know, but who were struck similarly by hard times and squeezed by speculators. In 1798 and 1799 the people of Lower Milford and Northampton County reiterated their beliefs in both "the Spirit" and "the letter of the Constitution" (or constitutions), revealing that they considered these constitutions as much a set of unwritten Revolutionary principles as they were frames of government.[84] The unwritten "Spirit" they invoked was a combination of democratic popular sovereignty and republican civic virtue. They demanded the right to govern themselves locally, to legislate for the state and the nation, and to be represented by the state executive branch. This much is not extraordinary, given the political history of the Revolution. What is unique is that they also used their popular constitutionalism to demand the right of direct action, the right to block legislation that violated either the spirit or the letter of the Constitution. In 1799 they used *their* "Constitution" as yet another ring of defense against the advancing threats to their property and their liberty.

A quick glance at the Reverend Jacob Eyermann, a Northampton Kirchen-leute clergyman, can illuminate the mixture of ethnic, religious, historic, economic, political, local, and national dialects that formed the popular con-stitutionalism of the Lehigh area Kirchenleute. In a direct confrontation with an assessor before his congregation, Eyermann "drew from his pocket a book . . . which he pretended contained the Constitution . . . telling the people that they (Congress) had not the right to pass such laws."[85] This was as democratic an action as the writing of petitions. With both events, the resisters insisted that they, the people, had the right, the ability, and the duty to interpret the consti-tutionality of federal laws and directly influence pending or passed legislation. Like Thomas Jefferson, Eyermann was demonstrating a belief in strict con-struction. Yet his argument reveals a more radical philosophy than the Repub-lican Party's contemporary Kentucky and Virginia Resolutions, which argued for state nullification or at least state power to repeal unconstitutional laws. Eyermann stated that "there was no such law" as the Direct Tax but concluded that the Moravian Commissioner "Jacob Eyerle had made the House Tax Law." The minister then carefully set forth a plan of action for his flock, "the people should only oppose the [Direct Tax] law, if they oppose the law then Eyerle would have to draw back and then the people would be free, otherwise they would be bound and tax after another would ensue, the people would have to pay tythes . . . and they would be slaves."[86]

Eyermann's argument serves as a compendium of Lehigh resistance lan-guage, blending republican fears with democratic pronouncements, urging constitutional opposition to one law, and harkening back to German hearth taxes, feudal serfdom, and American servitude. He warned of religious dis-crimination and focused his attack on Jacob Eyerle, the Moravian commis-sioner for the Direct Tax and Federalist candidate for Northampton County's House seat in 1798. The book he waved around was not the actual Constitution, but the gesture represented something much more important, the power that the people demanded to exert over their own lives and for their country as well. This was a creative power. The Kirchenleute did more than just derive their rights from the Constitution, they claimed the right to recreate it, to reimagine it, to nurture it, and to interpret the actions of their governments through the lens of "the principles of *Our* Constitution." *Their* Constitution was an amalgam of democratic rights not bound by written laws or won as a prize, but claimed as inherent, as inseparable from themselves, as unalienable. Natural rights and the right of popular sovereignty formed *their* Constitution, "the Idea" they had "of Justice," and that was more powerful than any scrap of parchment.

All this language led many townships in the region to actively resist the assessment of their homes while they waited for word from the upcoming Sixth Congress. Moreover, it shaped the character of that resistance. Throughout the entire affair, not a single assessor or any federal official came to harm. There was absolutely no interpersonal violence, outside of threats, and there was no ritualistic violence. This presents a curious dilemma for scholars of premodern crowd action, particularly those who study mobs and riots in Pennsylvania, because the Kirchenleute resisters seem to measure up to historiographical standards for premodern crowds. They asserted their own "moral economy," to borrow E. P. Thompson's phrase, by exercising their own political philosophy and locally preventing the assessment of the Direct Tax. And to borrow from George Rude, that political philosophy resulted from the merger of their own local "inherent political ideology," German *freheit*, and a broader "diverged ideology" learned from American experience, producing a "radical popular ideology" that informed their resistance.[87] Yet in terms of popular political protest in eighteenth-century colonial America, the Kirchenleute resistance also comports to Pauline Maier's and Gordon Wood's models of organized, mainly peaceful extralegal activity.[88] Riots regarding land, food, impressment, vigilante justice, or other issues in which lives and livelihoods were immediately at stake tended to be more radical and more likely to employ interpersonal violence. Almost all outdoor eighteenth-century politics, no matter what the issue, exhibited ritualistic violence such as burning effigies or forced public humiliation, a characteristic conspicuously absent from Fries's Rebellion. The Lehigh area resistance movement's simultaneous conformity to and divergence from the colonial American trends of the eighteenth-century political opposition make it a problem also in light of Pennsylvania's history of popular protest and the national trend at the turn of the nineteenth century.

Pennsylvania was a colony and state defined by demographic pluralism—ethnic, class, national, racial, religious, occupational, regional, and economic pluralism—in which many groups continually competed for various resources and violent conflict often erupted because of the striking differences between the competitors.[89] Pennsylvania's political and social protests were renowned for their radicalism and violence during the eighteenth century. For instance, one account of the history of rioting in America notes that a single Pennsylvania riot, the infamous "March of the Paxton Boys" in 1763, provided half of all rioting fatalities for America from 1700 to the imperial crisis of the 1760s.[90]

The Paxton Boys, mostly Scots-Irish, Presbyterian frontiersmen, massacred 20 unarmed Moravian Indians and threatened to sack Philadelphia, the colonial capital, if they were not given military protection for their farms and families in the wake of Pontiac's War. They also demanded that the Quaker colony hand over Indians protected by Moravians and Friends. In Pennsylvania's popular protests from the mid-eighteenth century and into the nineteenth, violence was an inherent trait.[91] The nonviolence of Fries's Rebellion obviously does not fit the Pennsylvania mold, even though its sources seem to be rooted in the typical Pennsylvania ethnoreligious conflict. During the postwar economic crisis, another historian identified 86 cases of interpersonal violence against state and federal officials collecting taxes and enforcing foreclosures and evictions in Pennsylvania from 1781 to 1794. Even Pennsylvania Germans were not strangers to forming violent mobs when governments or other ethnic groups offended them. As late as 1793, one hundred German farmers from the nearby Lebanon Valley attacked an Irish construction crew digging the Schuylkill and Susquehanna Canal near Myerstown because they believed the state had allowed the company to pay them unjustly low prices for the right of way.[92] Moreover, the dockets of the Northampton County Quarter Sessions papers in the 1780s and 1790s are replete with cases of riot, assault and battery, and other violent crimes.[93]

Furthermore, the absence of violence, even the symbolic violence of a burnt effigy, makes Pennsylvania's Fries's Rebellion stand apart from the national trend at the turn of the nineteenth century. The typical riot of pre-Revolutionary eighteenth-century America entailed little interpersonal violence and instead crowds usually channeled their aggression against effigies and property. Most American communities were homogenous agricultural villages that developed, shared, and expressed corporate ideals through a combination of voting and nonvoting citizens. The Revolutionary era unleashed democratic participation and the competition between equal interests. In America's early national and Jacksonian periods, as the nation became more individualistic, industrial, capitalistic, urban, populous, and stratified by racial, ethnic, and class divisions, rioting became more interpersonally violent.[94]

Yet Fries's Rebellion is conspicuous for its nonviolence, both interpersonal and ritualistic, in spite of its post-Revolutionary timing during the "Great Transition," its Pennsylvania setting, and its ethnoreligious and rural versus cosmopolitan accelerants. In an age when symbolic and interpersonal violence were the norm in outdoor popular politics, the Kirchenleute intentionally chose to refrain from it. This choice is key to understanding their political maturation as Germans locally and as Americans nationally and to understanding their resistance. They chose not only nonviolent tactics, but they borrowed forms and devices from the Revolutionary generation in order to robe their dissent from federal policies in the patriotism of the War for Independence. Thus they donned constitutional and nationalistic conservatism while democratically waging political dissent. The Revolution, its aftermath, and the creation of the federal Constitution all challenged the meaning and role of popular political dissent out of doors. Revolutionary leaders who encouraged crowd action in the struggle toward independence disdained it in the decades that followed, and the governing elites used the people themselves to squelch popular uprisings. Twenty-eight Kirchenleute resisters (more than 10 percent of the sample), including their most influential leaders; John Fries, Frederick Heaney, Henry Jarret, George Shaeffer, Adam Stahlnaker, Henry Ohl, and Henry Huber, had marched west under President Washington and Generals Henry Lee and Alexander Hamilton to subdue the Whiskey Rebels. Yet in 1798–99, they too reformulated the role of the crowd and public political dissent.

The Lehigh area resistance movement exhibited remarkable restraint when compared to the Shays and Whiskey Rebellion, or even the agrarian rebellions of the colonial era, for a number of reasons. The resisters focused their opposition on the laws and the Federalist Party, not the authority of the federal government. They attempted to use the political system both as Republicans and popular constitutionalists. They drew on their Revolutionary heritage to legitimize their opposition as citizens and Jeffersonian-Republicans. Many of their leaders had participated in the armed suppression of the Whiskey Rebels. Their communities were homogeneously united in opposition under careful leadership, and their targets were their pacifist neighbors who either laid down their commissions or refused to put up a struggle.[95] Indeed, there were many *threats* of physical violence. Andrew Lentzinger, for example, threatened Heidelberg assessor Nicholas Miller, saying that he "would shoot the assessor if he would come to take the assessment," and he said that if Jacob Eyerle should come around, he would "cut him to pieces and make sausages of him."[96] Northamptoner Herman Hartman, on hearing of an approaching assessor, exclaimed that "he had his gun ready" and that he and others were prepared, and if "forced . . . would go from house to house and cut off the heads of those Stampers."[97] But in spite of threats like these, no shots were fired, no one was decapitated, and not a single assessor was ground for sausage. In fact, several times the threats were accompanied by offers of assistance made to assessors, such as the overture made by the people of Plainfield to Northamptoner James Williamson. Williamson reported that an association warned him to discontinue his assessments, but some of its members told him that if "I should incur any penalty for not bearing the execution of my duty they would reimburse me."[98] The absence of interpersonal and symbolic violence, or rather the intentional exercise of nonviolent resistance in the events comprising Fries's Rebellion is perhaps the most intriguing and most significant aspect of the Kirchenleute language of opposition. [99] In comparison to other crowd or mob behavior in the eighteenth century—where mobs coated officials' bodies with hot tar and feathers or gave them "Hillsborough Paintings" with human excrement, rode them out of town on rails, whipped them, destroyed their homes, and in some instances murdered them—the few threats made by the Kirchenleute seem rather mild.[100]

Probably the most important factor for understanding why the various "mobs" that comprised the Kirchenleute resistance did not administer "rough music" to ensure that the government upheld a local moral economy is that they did not envision themselves as a mob or as an extralegal crowd of civil vigilantes. They construed their opposition as thoroughly within the law, the republican system of government, and "the Ideas" they had "of Justice." The leaders of the Kirchenleute opposition—militia captains, tavernkeepers, clergymen, local constabulary, storekeepers, millers, and one vendue crier—exerted remarkable control over the hundreds of farmers who at one point or another resisted the assessment of their property. There were a number of occasions when crowds threatened to get out of hand, but every time there was a Kirchenleute community leader on hand to assure the safety of the tax officials, the local judiciary, and even the U.S. marshal who came to make arrests. This restraint was intentional. They opposed "unconstitutional" laws by framing their resistance with patriotic, Revolutionary practices in accordance with the Bill of Rights and their own popular conception of the Constitution and its principles. They did so not only in hopes of avoiding a government reprisal, but in the sincere belief that the people were entitled to interpret the laws, that popular action—legitimized by the Revolution and the Constitution—could persuade Congress to repeal unconstitutional legislation that they considered "Slavery and Taking the Liberty Away!"[101]

Kirchenleute political language and the ideology it reveals represent the milieu of political experiences that shaped the lives of men like John Fries and Henry Jarret. These leaders and many of the resisters were teenagers during the imperial struggle, soldiers in the War for Independence, witnesses to two constitutional conventions in Pennsylvania and founding of the nation and the subsequent partisan division, survivors of a postwar depression, soldiers again in the "Watermelon Army" that quelled the Whiskey Rebellion, crusaders for local Lutheran and Reformed control through parochial and state action, and, by 1798, dedicated Republican partisans. They were not republicans *or* democrats, localists *or* nationalists, Germans *or* Americans. They were all these things at once. With such a broad and democratic understanding of republican liberty, they claimed the right of direct participation in their own governance and thus challenged those who would deny it, specifically, conservative Federalists in Philadelphia who had passed the hated laws and appointed their "Tory" assessors.

Since the Revolution, many of its leaders had retained a narrower definition of liberty in a republican society, and by the 1790s they sought to prevent the erosion of "public liberty" in America in what they envisioned as a torrent of rampant democracy. Federalists in 1787 managed to rein in the power of democratic state governments with the creation of the federal Constitution, and in Pennsylvania, conservatives in 1790 managed to curb the people's power with a new and counterrevolutionary frame of government. Yet even still the 1790s witnessed a swelling tide of democratic aspirations by Pennsylvanians and Americans elsewhere. Democratic Societies publicly challenged Washington administration domestic policy and praised the French Revolution in spite of its increasing violence. Western farmers rose up in rebellion against the federal excise, and crowds in New York and Philadelphia protested the Jay Treaty in the streets. Concern mounted among Federalist leaders and the Adams administration in Philadelphia, particularly within a group of conservative "High Federalists" who followed the lead of Alexander Hamilton.

By the end of the 1790s, Hamilton's influence had coalesced around a small group of powerful and connected Federalists, specifically George Washington, President Adams's Secretary of State Timothy Pickering, Secretary of War James McHenry, Secretary of Treasury Oliver Wolcott, U.S. Senator Theodore Sedgewick, former senator and leader of the New England Federalists George Cabot, and U.S. representatives such as Fisher Ames, William Loughton Smith, and Uriah Tracy. Although none of them were by any means simple mouthpieces of the nation's first treasurer, they corresponded with Hamilton regularly and often used his advice when advocating policy or directing legislation. Together with the disturbing examples of democratic outbursts seen throughout the decade, the obstructionism in the Lehigh area seemed a proof to these "Hamiltonians" that popular opposition to the federal government and the Federalist administrations were indeed real threats to the Republic.

To Hamiltonian minds, these threats demanded the accelerated imposition of public order in the face of expanding democracy. The contemporaneous explosion of the French Revolution early in the decade, its democratic principles and violent tactics, the intrigues of "Citizen Genet" in America's east and other French officials in the west, the nefarious XYZ Affair, the eruption of Wolf Tone's democratic rebellion in Ireland, the late immigration of thousands of Irish to Philadelphia, and the looming war with France in 1798 all lent credence to Hamiltonian conservatism and popularized it among many other

Federalists in Congress.[102] The party's reactionary posturing during the Fifth Congress (which gave rise to the Kirchenleute's dissent) evidenced opportunistic anti-Republican partisan subterfuge as well as the Hamiltonians' real fears for the future of the Republic in the face of perceived foreign and domestic threats. Through these laws they sought to implement a system of national security and public order. The Hamiltonians' distortion of the tax resistance as an "insurrection" and their overzealous pursuit of executions were a direct result of the fears of 1798 and their desire to uphold order and public liberty in the Republic. The politics of fear precipitated attacks upon constitutional rights and the sacrifice of American civil liberties by the Fifth Congress. Fear of the "Jacobin Phrenzy" emboldened even moderates in Congress to pass the Alien and Sedition Acts: it also led the Federalist Party to consider any opposition to its program of national defense as evidence of treason, even if it consisted merely of liberty poles, threats, and pails of hot water.

The "Northampton Insurrection" would be both more and less than the rebellion Hamiltonians and other Federalists claimed it to be. It was indeed a large and concerted effort to prevent a federal tax, though thanks to the politicking of disingenuous Republican politicians many believed the Direct Tax was still under debate and not yet law. As a result, it was mostly peaceful and devoid of interpersonal or even symbolic violence. Perhaps the resisters believed that by public demonstration and obstruction they could stave off the tax without violence. Yet it was a "rebellion" in a sense, as an assertion by a small body of people who in the infancy of the Republic, in the face of federal armies and the Alien and Sedition Acts, claimed the rights to govern themselves locally and nationally and to participate directly in the perpetual evolution of constitutional democracy. That is what Jonas Hartzell meant when he exclaimed, "we're *The People!*"

Chapter 2
Order

As is clear in the language used by the Lehigh Kirchenleute, liberty was the most significant component of the American conception of republican politics. But it is one of the great historical ironies of the period that, despite the unifying power of the desire for liberty, American Revolutionaries never actually agreed on its meaning.[1] For some, it originated from a desire to free government from English corruption and to establish the rule of popular sovereignty; for others it meant the expansion of popular participation in government and the protection of citizens against their leaders while pursuing individual happiness. Out of this confusion, many Americans, including the Kirchenleute, emerged from the war with a broadened concept of liberty that gave rise to heightened expectations of participation in their government and, therefore, a greater determination to protect the conditions, especially private property, that afforded such privilege.

At the same time, others worried that too much liberty could lead to democracy and anarchy, and they believed that true liberty was found in a republican commonwealth that required submission of individual freedoms for the good of the whole.[2] Some began to sense that the expansion of liberty's definition was leading the Confederation toward a democratic politics of self-interest, the decline of deference, and the decay of republican virtue. In drafting the federal Constitution, they stressed the need for an energetic national government led by a natural aristocracy that could ensure an ordered republican liberty for the American community.[3] Federalists like George Washington and Alexander Hamilton typified this stance. When Hamilton rose to speak at the Constitutional Convention in 1787, he advocated a vigorous, centralized government: "we must establish a general and national government, completely sovereign," Hamilton demanded, "and annihilate the state distinctions and state operations." In reality, it was not the state governments themselves that Hamilton feared; it was their localist orientation and tendency to bend to the sway of the people, who "seldom judge or determine right," that influenced him to advocate an aristocratic, sovereign national government based on the British model.[4]

As much as the specters of localism and popular democracy, the omni-presence of well-fortified European forces surrounding the infant nation haunted Alexander Hamilton. Foremost among the defects of the democratic Confederation of independent states, Hamilton feared, were security matters: the states "can raise no troops nor equip vessels before war is actually declared. They cannot heretofore take any preparatory measure before an enemy is at your door." In order to attain an internal security, or "individual security" as he deemed it, Hamilton called for a limited electorate of elites, lifetime tenures for presidents and senators, and a national government veto of state laws. This powerful national state, invigorated with "public strength," could then provide a military defense to meet external security threats. Security could also be achieved by consolidating and funding a national debt to foreign and domes-tic creditors, tying their economic interests to the survival of the republic and justifying national schemes of taxation to pay the interest and fortify the mili-tary. Hamilton's liberty was a national independence that relied on the wealthy and the powerful and intentionally sought to overrepresent their interests. While most supporters of a federal government in 1787 were unwilling to go to the lengths advocated by Hamilton, events in the ensuing years, including Fries's Rebellion, pushed many in that direction.[5]

Resisting the Hamiltonian push for a stronger national government in 1787 were Antifederalists, who were more willing to put legislative, military, and taxing powers at local and state levels, closer to the people. They were quicker to court popular political participation, and they were more jealous of protecting individual civil liberties.[6] Despite such ideological differences, most delegates to the Philadelphia convention and the state ratifying conventions did agree on one thing: liberty, however defined, depended upon the security of private property, and republican governments at the state and national lev-els provided that protection.[7] Private property and the contracts that secured it served the interests of landed and mercantile wealth, while simultaneously affording basic economic and political liberty for small farmers, artisans, and shopkeepers, attaching their interests to those of their more prosperous neigh-bors and fastening their loyalty to governments.

The Federalist Party that emerged during the 1790s—especially the Hamiltonian Federalists—clung to the notion of liberty with order.[8] Although the Federalists had a sincere commitment to republican government and agreed with their Republican Party adversaries on the necessity of individual virtue among citizens to sustain republican government, Hamiltonian Federal-ists' pessimistic view of human nature prevented them from believing that the mass of citizens possessed the innate virtue for self-governance. Democratic participation and self-interested, factionalized politics would in their opinion paralyze government and lead to anarchy and then to submission to a European power. To cap this democratization of republican liberty and thus to protect the people from themselves, Federalists demanded order—both political and social. They would hold the line on voting requirements, allowing only free men of property to elect wealthier, elite men of leisure to govern. The latter would do the governing in a republic with the consent of a deferential public. Thus, to most conservative Federalists of the 1790s, American society hinged on a paternalistic social elite that extended patronage and demanded deference from common people like the Kirchenleute. While the Kirchenleute position in the Constitutional debate is unclear and many joined the party of Washington in the 1790s in deference to their Revolutionary military leader, by 1798 they were increasingly advocating an Antifederalist commitment to localist democracy as they grew impatient for their expanded definition of liberty.

But public criticism or opposition, especially by the common stock of people, was out of the question to Hamiltonians, as democracy was akin to anarchy in their minds. Ordinary people were to voice their opposition only at the polls, where Hamilton believed that "the general sense of the people will regulate the conduct of their representatives."[9] This was the extent to which Hamilton and his allies were willing to understand popular sovereignty. The liberty they sought to secure, then, was less concerned with individual rights and liberties than with collective pursuits of happiness: an ordered public liberty. The purpose of government was to create order in society, the economy, domestic politics, and foreign relations to ensure the survival of independent republican government and to concurrently erect an economic and political world in which American citizens such as the Kirchenleute could pursue their economic happiness.[10]

While the Federalists were in control of the nation for twelve years, their policies often evinced an obsession with order.[11] As secretary of the treasury, Alexander Hamilton sought to stabilize and energize the national government in the early 1790s so that the government could do the same for the national economy. According to Hamilton, the two qualities "which are essential to public strength & private security" are "*stability* and *order* in Government."[12] Toward this end, Hamilton initiated his controversial policies with the assumption and funding of the Revolutionary War debt, his creation of the Bank of the United States, the excise tax on whiskey, and his "Report on Manufactures." He intended these programs to create an environment of economic expansion and diversification that would be naturally beneficial to the merchant class, bankers, and speculators in land and government securities, who would of course take advantage of their opportunities and thus increase the national wealth. Ideally, their success would increase the opportunities of others and undercut domestic economic discontent so evident during the postwar depression.[13] Hamilton and those in Congress who enacted his plan thus tied the American future to the immediate needs of merchants, financiers, and holders of public securities and signaled to the American people that the Revolution was over, democratic change would cease, and stability would take its place. Clearly, citizens such as the Kirchenleute did not share this outlook.

Hamilton's vision for extending the American republic into the nineteenth century required fashioning the young nation on the British industrial and commercial model. He and other Federalists advocated a trading relationship with Britain over opening newer avenues with the French or other nations, and they confirmed it with the Jay Treaty. Great Britain occupied the powerful position of either being America's most dangerous enemy or its greatest ally—especially as Britain and France resumed warfare in the middle of the decade.[14] Siding with France would have drawn the ire of the world's most powerful nation. On the other hand, utilizing the "neutral right" to trade with Britain offered America the opportunity to take advantage of the British trade network and market for American agricultural exports while satisfying a domestic demand for manufactured goods from the British Empire and beyond. President Washington and the Federalists believed such a course would benefit the governing class of plantation owners, merchants, and incipient industrialists as well as agrarian and working Americans—farmers, shopkeepers, and artisans—by providing security and lifting the national economy out of depression.[15] Moreover, Hamilton and other Federalists feared that the Jacobin excesses of the French Revolution would wash up on American shores, and they argued that the French Revolution and regicide had cut the ties of the 1778 Franco-American Treaty of Alliance. Therefore, adhering to a plan that mimicked the British model and favored Britain over France would concurrently sustain order and ensure the growth of the Hamiltonian brand of limited, ordered republican liberty for all.[16] With the memory of the Revolutionary alliance and their sacrifices during the war with Britain still fresh, many Americans, including the Kirchenleute resisters, disagreed.

When an opposition party formed to counter the Hamiltonian formula for an ordered republic, conservative Federalists recoiled in draconian fashion, fearing that the Republicans, should they ever gain power, would destroy all that Federalism had planned for the Republic. Hamiltonians particularly feared the Republican attachment to the French and their revolution, which had toppled the aristocratic order in a bloody fashion and seemed to threaten the moral order of America as well. Republicans opposed funding the debt, assumption, the Bank of the United States, the Proclamation of Neutrality, and the Jay Treaty. By 1798 they opposed the impending war with France, the Alien and Sedition Acts, and the military expansion. Hamiltonians simply could not tolerate dissent, however, when the prospect of war with a foreign enemy seemed to threaten national security, especially when that outcry came from those like the Pennsylvania Church People whom they heretofore had considered among their own party.

The Republican leadership, men like Jefferson and Madison, were not the Hamiltonians' greatest fear. What frightened them most was the popular following the two Virginians attracted and the fact that citizens had begun to publicly criticize and directly oppose Federalist policies. This was unthinkable, but it was a product of the Federalists own doing. By forging a revolution to create an independent nation of independent citizens, and by securing it with a constitution based on the theory of popular sovereignty, the Federalists unintentionally had helped to create what historian Gordon Wood identifies as "the first society in the modern world to bring ordinary people into the affairs of government—not just as voters but as actual rulers."[17] Many Americans seemed immediately to realize this radical transformation and challenged the authority of their governors in the Shays and Whiskey rebellions; they formed grassroots political organizations like the Democratic-Republican Societies, and even contested the Republic itself with failed western secession schemes like "Franklin" and "Westsylvania" and successful ones like Vermont.[18] While Thomas Jefferson mused that "the tree of liberty must be refreshed from time to time with the blood of patriots and tyrants" and Madison affirmed that the "eyes" of the "people . . . must be ever ready to mark, their voice to pronounce, and their arm to repel or repair aggressions on the authority of their constitutions," Republicans and Federalists alike feared democratic outbursts and insurrection and sought to channel them into the acceptable political outlets.[19] Federalists favored the poll, but Republicans added aggressive petitioning and even suggested state nullification as avenues of democratic participation. Through the 1790s, Federalist toleration for the Republicans and their partisans dwindled and then vanished with the outbreak of hostilities with France and the passage of the Sedition Act in 1798. Hamiltonians connected the two crises and feared that the French would use internal dissent to pave the way for military invasion. Should that happen, they worried, liberty of every description would be in jeopardy.

Like the Lehigh Kirchenleute resisters, Hamilton and his High Federalist allies made choices within the context of multiple structures. Hamiltonians chose to craft their program of economic stimulation, international relations, internal domestic order, national defense, and taxation while weighing a complex set of historic, economic, security, political, diplomatic, racial, ethnic, religious, class, and cultural factors. Those same issues would in turn color the

Hamiltonians' view of Fries's Rebellion and guide their reckless reaction to it. Their experiences in the 1790s reinforced the High Federalists' narrow conception of liberty and popular sovereignty and led to their increasing distrust of its use by the American people. They feared popular democratic and insurrectionary tendencies and the terror of the French Revolution, held serious apprehensions over the emergence of a pro-French opposition party in America, and exhibited anxieties over French interference in American politics and society. As the decade wore on, Hamiltonian Federalists had increasing difficulty separating these issues, and by 1798 they appeared to be parts of a concerted whole: democratic ingredients in a recipe for the destruction of Federalism, republican government, and national independence. The Hamiltonians' perceptions of the domestic political events and international crises in the decade after the Philadelphia convention convinced them to exert and expand their governmental authority, to demand order over individual liberty as necessary to secure republican liberty for all. To meet the challenges to stability and order both from within and from without, they constructed the first federal program of national security that included sacrifices of individual civil liberties, the quieting of dissent, exaggerations of the danger of treason and sedition, appeals to patriotism and Christianity, extraordinary defense spending, and of course, taxation. During international hostility, they painted partisan dissent as sedition and labeled the obstruction of federal law as treason. Federalists, especially Hamiltonians, implemented these policies to maintain and fortify an independent republic defined by ordered liberty and to retain and amplify their authority to govern it. The Lehigh Kirchenleute resisted Federalist policies and authority and would be among the first objects of this American mode of domestic control during an international crisis. These High Federalist overreactions contributed in varying degrees to the party's defeat in 1800, and to the collapse of Federalism in the decades that followed.

On March 7, 1799, while the crisis with France remained unresolved, the armed, uniformed, and French-cockaded force of Kirchenleute who marched into Bethlehem bore the appearance of an insurgency. Federalists were quick to treat it accordingly, as they had been preparing to meet rebellions for years. Alexander Hamilton first began calling for a professional army to guard against domestic insurrection during the ratification process for the federal Constitution. In *The Federalist*, No. 6, he recalled the 1784 attempt by western Carolinians to forcibly secede and form the independent nation of Franklin, and he cited similar plans by Pennsylvanians and New Yorkers. Of course, Shays's Rebellion in Massachusetts and related violence in other states were more frightening still. Referring to Shays in *Federalist*, No. 25, Hamilton insisted that "cases are likely to occur under our government . . . which will sometimes render a military force in time of peace essential to the security of society." And in stark contrast to Jefferson's metaphor that rebellions manured the tree of liberty, Hamilton noted in *Federalist*, No. 28 that insurrections are "maladies as inseparable from the body politic as tumours and eruptions from the natural body" and "whatever may be its immediate cause, eventually [endanger] all government." At the Constitutional Convention, his pleas for a strong, centralized state focused on the need for military preparedness. When violent resistance to his excise tax on whiskey erupted throughout the backcountry only a few years later, Hamilton and President Washington marched at the head of a volunteer army to make an example of frontier Pennsylvanians.[20] In the few years after national unification under a republican constitution intended to secure both national independence and personal liberty, Americans proved to Hamilton their capability for violent insurrection and signaled the necessity for a peacetime army. Hamilton's controversial arguments so shortly following the Revolution—itself precipitated partly by a fear of standing armies—revealed the gravity of the threat to order that he perceived.[21] They reveal the risk he and Washington were willing to take, so soon, of magnifying what anti-insurrectionary public sentiment existed to justify the strengthening of the state.

The threat to order also had roots outside the United States. In the summer of 1789, the French Revolution commenced with the meeting of the Estates-General, the formation of the National Assembly, the storming of the Bastille, and the adoption of the Declaration of the Rights of Man and Citizen which was intended to be prefixed to a written constitution. By 1793 the revolution in France had failed to stabilize, much as Hamilton had feared, and violence was increasing. After the Girondins executed their king, they fell to the Jacobins and "The Terror" as Robespierre and his allies settled political and social scores with a torrent of bloodshed. In a series of published essays under the titles "Americanus" and "Pacificus," Hamilton began to ask "Whether the cause of France be truly the cause of liberty?" In a 1794 essay, he answered that theirs was "the cause of Vice Atheism and Anarchy." Hamilton's anxiety over the French Revolution stemmed not from his concern for the French people, however, but rather from its threat to order and government in America.[22]

As early as 1792, Hamilton had identified Thomas Jefferson and James Madison as "the head of a faction . . . subversive of the principles of good government and dangerous to the Union." To Hamiltonians, the danger emanated from their "*womanish attachment to France and their womanish resentment against Great Britain,*" emotions that would inevitably lead to war with England if the Republicans should control the government.[23] Hamilton worried that "the Spirit of faction and anarchy" it had spawned "in this country . . . [is] the only enemy which Republicanism has to fear." Oliver Wolcott, a Hamilton ally and secretary of the treasury under President Adams, also worried that "the French count upon the support of a party in this Country," fearing it was "a systematical measure of France to destroy the publick confidence in the Friends of Govt." The Republicans, or the "French Party" as Federalists referred to them, challenged the authority of the "Friends of Govt." John Adams's secretary of state, Timothy Pickering, furthered the Hamiltonian rhetoric by referring to the Republicans as "our internal enemies."[24] Federalists like U.S. Representative Fisher Ames of New England dreaded that the Republicans could not—or worse yet would not—control their constituents and the people would overtake their leaders with democratic zeal and then overturn republican government and replace it with a "mobocracy."[25] During the decade of the 1790s, neither party willingly admitted the legitimacy of the other. Leaders of both denigrated their opponents as "factions" that in unrepublican fashion served a narrow collection of interests instead of the common good. Republicans generally clustered in the plantation south and agrarian west, while Federalists appealed to more diverse commercial economies in the east, although there were many exceptions. Both believed themselves to be the true heirs of the Revolution. The thin band of consensus that connected them and their mutual belief in republican government tethered a Republican participatory republicanism on one side and the Federalists' ordered republic on the other. International and domestic events throughout the decade strained that consensus, however, nearly to the breaking point by the turn of the century.[26]

In the spring of 1793, many Americans cheered the French regicide and their new experiment in republican government. Soon after the execution of the king, the French Republic declared war on Great Britain. When Citizen Genet arrived in Philadelphia that May to represent the Republic, the people feted him with banquets and balls. One particular group that expressed support for Genet, the French Republic, and the cause of republicanism everywhere asked its honored guest to suggest a name for its club. He replied with the title "Democratic Society." Within the following two years, ninety-three Democratic Societies (also known as "Democratic-Republican Societies") would form, with at least one in every state except Rhode Island and Georgia. Pennsylvania led the nation with nine, including one composed of Germans in Philadelphia whose memorials circulated through the state's German-language press and reached the Lehigh area Kirchenleute nearby. The societies styled themselves after the Jacobin Clubs in France and proposed to eradicate popular ignorance, that "irreconcilable enemy of liberty." Furthermore, out of "love for their country," they vowed to "examine into the conduct of its officers."[27] From 1793 to 1796, they continually and openly criticized the policies and the

politicians of the Washington administration. Federalists were shocked at the
nerve of these unelected people, interposing themselves between the voters and
the administration, breaching the principle of popular deference central to the
order-oriented Federalist political culture. Federalists deemed these groups
illegitimate and dangerous to republican society. When three Democratic-
Republican Societies in western Pennsylvania agitated resistance to Hamilton's
federal excise tax, they convinced Federalists of the danger.[28]

For more than two years following the implementation of Hamilton's
"whiskey tax," trans-Appalachian farmers individually and collectively condemned the excise tax and harassed its collectors. Hamilton worried that if
the government did not enforce the law—either through proclamation or by
force—"the authority of government would be prostrate."[29] In 1793 the three
Democratic Societies that formed in southwestern Pennsylvania at Washington, Yough, and Mingo Creek immediately drafted petitions and planned
resistance.[30] Their rhetoric too had a Revolutionary tone, declaring central government taxes upon an under-represented and remote people, levied on the
basis of their livelihood, to be unconstitutional. Some threatened secession and
the construction of a western republic. After the shooting of one of the "rebels"
and the August 1794 militia rally of more than 5,000 resisters at Braddock's
Field who threatened to sack the federal arsenal at Pittsburgh, Washington and
Hamilton led an army of more than 10,000 federalized militiamen to eradicate
the resistance. Among them were John Fries and many of his Kirchenleute
neighbors. Even young Republican men saw an opportunity to "support the
Glorious cause of Liberty" by joining the expedition, such as Meriwether
Lewis.[31] In his annual address to Congress the following November, President
Washington declared that "a prejudice festered and bittered by the artifice of
men" or "certain self-created societies," as he called them, had "produced
symptoms of riot and violence."[32] The Democratic Societies interjected themselves between the people and the government, were not accountable to the
people or controllable at the polls, and criticized the policies of the federal government at will. Federalists could conceive of no greater threat to republican
order and government.

The connection between the societies and the insurrection afforded the
Federalists the opportunity to increase the power of government by raising
an army, making an example out of western Pennsylvanians, censuring the
Democratic Societies, and quieting the Republican Party. As Republican leader
James Madison correctly perceived, the Federalists' "game was to connect the
democratic societies with the odium of the insurrection—to connect the Republicans in Congress with those societies—to put the President ostensibly
at the head of the other party in opposition to both."[33] While Washington's

condemnation tarnished the societies and they soon faded from existence, the Federalists could not silence Republican opposition and in less than a year Republicans presented their most vocal resistance to Federalist policy in the ratification debates over the Jay Treaty with Great Britain.

Once again, more disturbing to Federalists than the Republican congressional opposition were the popular outbursts opposing the treaty. Some opposed the solidification of economic ties between the United States and its former parent, some resented policies that favored merchants over producers, while others resented that the agreement still did not satisfy American demands supposedly won by the 1783 Treaty of Peace signed at Paris. Popular protests sprang up all around the country. Protesters burned John Jay in effigy and pelted Alexander Hamilton with stones when he attempted to defend the treaty on a street in Manhattan.[34] Oliver Wolcott described a protest in Philadelphia as being composed of a "generally ignorant mob, of that class which is most dissatisfied and violent."[35] While there is no record of Kirchenleute protest, they likely viewed the Northampton Sektenleute public celebration of the treaty at Nazareth in 1796 with contempt.[36]

During the Revolutionary era, many of the the men who later became Federalists accepted and even approved of crowd action. But in the 1790s, when such action was directed against their authority, they viewed all crowds as mobs and saw any protest as illegitimate. Hamiltonians believed that the people were capable of launching a violent, bloody, democratic insurrection in the United States on the model of the French Revolution.[37] They resisted assertions by average people that they had a right to participate in the governing of the republic by attempting to shape public policy. The formation of the Democratic Societies, the insurrection in western Pennsylvania, and the Jay Treaty riots also provided Hamiltonians and other Federalists with more reasons and opportunities to increase governmental power and to exert their authority for the cause of order and public liberty. And the activities of French officials in America in the 1790s would provide them with more reasons still.

In the winter of 1799, Hamiltonians projected their fears of French subversion onto the Kirchenleute resistance in order to raise an army to crush it. During the trials that followed, they learned that there was no French connection, but French activity earlier in the decade had conditioned Federalists to imagine one. Between 1793 and 1797, France had sent three ministers to the United States: Edmond Genet, Jean Fauchet, and Pierre Adet. Federalists accurately believed that each of the three ministers had tried to mold American public opinion and influence its politics in order to pull the United States into the war against Great Britain.[38] When Genet arrived in America in April 1793, he was greeted in Charleston, South Carolina, by wild celebrations in favor of the establishment of a French republic. Within a month he received a similar welcome in Philadelphia, but by June his actions had cast him into disrepute with President Washington and his entire cabinet. In his "No Jacobin" essays, Hamilton publicly denounced Genet and charged that his involvement in the Democratic Societies amounted to "direct violations of our sovereignty," tended "to divide a free country," and led to "dissention, commotion, and in the end, loss of liberty."[39] Hamilton and other Federalists (and indeed even Jefferson) were outraged by Genet's attempts to outfit American vessels as privateers against British shipping, even after Washington had issued his Proclamation of Neutrality on April 22 forbidding American citizens from taking part in any hostilities on the seas with or against any belligerent and denying France the use of American ports for attacking British shipping.[40]

Early in July, while President Washington was at Mount Vernon, Genet arranged for the captured British vessel, the *Little Sarah*, to be outfitted in Philadelphia as the privateer *Little Democrat*. Pennsylvania Governor Thomas Mifflin sent his secretary of state, Alexander James Dallas, to advise Genet not to put the *Little Democrat* to sea against the president's proclamation. Genet angrily refused and declared that he would go over the president's head and appeal his cause, and the cause of France, directly to the American people. An irate Washington exclaimed, "Is the Minister of the French Republic to set the Acts of this Government at defiance, *with impunity?* and then threaten the Executive with an appeal to the People. . . . What must the World think of such conduct, and of the Governmt. of the U. States in submitting to it?"[41] The next day the president met with his cabinet and decided to request the French government to recall Genet. Neither the president nor Genet knew yet that only a month earlier the Girondins had fallen to the Jacobins, the guillotines were chopping away, and one was waiting for Genet should he ever return home. He never did.[42]

When the Jacobin Fauchet succeeded Genet in 1794, Hamilton declared, "Twas a *Meteor* following a *Comet*" because Fauchet attended meetings of Democratic societies like his Girondin predecessor, "swallowing toasts full of sedition and hostility to the Government" in open defiance of President Washington's condemnation of those clubs after the Whiskey Rebellion. A year later, Pierre Adet replaced Fauchet, and he too mingled at Republican Party meetings. But Adet's political machinations far surpassed those of Genet and Fauchet. He arrived in Philadelphia while the Senate was considering ratification of Jay's Treaty, and he publicly supported congressional Republican opposition to the treaty with Britain. Adet again overstepped the bounds of diplomatic protocol just days before the presidential election of 1796. He published two open letters to Washington's secretary of state, Timothy Pickering, in the Republican newspaper, the *Philadelphia Aurora.* On October 27, he charged that the Washington administration had failed to respond to French inquiries about Jay's Treaty. Then on November 15 he criticized the Federalist policy of disallowing American trade with French privateers.[43] Such subversion was insufferable to Federalists.

An outraged Hamilton fired back his "Answer" in New York's *Evening Advertiser.* Adet's "apparent intention," Hamilton charged, "is to influence timid minds to vote agreeable to their wishes in election of the President" by "the apprehension of War with France." The "agreeable" candidate to French wishes was Thomas Jefferson, of whom Hamilton lamented, we "have everything to fear if this man comes in."[44] While the minister's attempts to secure a Jeffersonian victory and to block Jay's Treaty failed, his political activity and sway in the Republican Party motivated the Federalists to take action to stamp out French influence.

Time and again Hamilton's fears of domestic insurrection and his anxieties over French intervention in American politics intertwined after 1793. He condemned Genet's recruitment of American privateers "in open defiance to the government," but he found even more alarming Genet's "covert" acts to ensnare the United States in the French war against Britain and Spain. "He sets on foot intrigues with our Southern and Western extremes," Hamilton warned, "and attempts to organize . . . and to carry on . . . military expeditions against the territories of Spain in our neighborhood." Indeed, Genet attempted to outfit a military expedition among Kentuckians to mount an attack on Spanish posts along the Mississippi River; the expedition was to have been led by George Rogers Clark. Pickering wondered "whether some secret French agent was not employed before Genet's arrival, to tamper with the Western people relative to the conquest of Louisiana?" Even more shocking was Fauchet's behavior during the Whiskey Rebellion. He publicly applauded the insurrection. According to Hamilton, "he knew and approved of a conspiracy which was destined to overthrow the administration of our government." Hamilton noted, however, "Mr. Adet has been more circumspect than either of his predecessors."[45] Adet conspired to regain North American territory for France through covert operations involving American citizens. In December 1796, Timothy Pickering received a distressing letter informing him that "Mr. Adet is in some kind of improper negotiation with one or more of the citizens of Kentucky." By spring, Pickering, Hamilton, and Secretary of War James McHenry all suspected that Adet intended to foment rebellion among Kentuckians and use the independent state as a base to invade Spanish Louisiana and create a republic west of the Mississippi.[46]

Soon after the Kentucky affair, Pickering learned of Adet's attempt to stir a French-Canadian rebellion against the British. More alarming, Adet had recruited Americans from New England to assist in the liberation. Before Adet left for France in April, Pickering learned that he had commissioned David McLean of Rhode Island and Thomas Butterfield of Vermont to raise American troops and march on Quebec. The British successfully thwarted the insurrection and subsequently hanged its leaders, including McLean and Butterfield, but to Hamiltonians the Canadian rebellion and the Kentucky affair posed dangerous precedents. McHenry worried that it "would seem as if nothing, short of a dismemberment of the Union, and having part of it under French protection, would satisfy the directory." And after "gaining this point," he warned General Washington, "France will then play for the whole." Pickering had more precise ideas of how the French plotted to overrun the United States. The "designs of France to repossess Canada" and its "means to regain Louisiana" proved to him that the French schemed "to renew the ancient plan of her monarchs of *circumscribing* and encircling what now constitutes the [United] States" and ultimately controlling the continent. In May 1797, Hamilton noted the possibility of a French naval invasion of America but emphasized that "an internal invasion" seemed more likely. Even before the Quasi War began, Hamiltonian Federalists were convinced that the French intended to subvert American independence and republican government from within.[47] By 1799 armed and organized opposition from a non-English-speaking force of Republican voters sporting tricolored cockades seemed proof of that suspicion. In the meantime, hostilities with France were escalating and the Federalists were planning for internal and external security.

Hamiltonians had good reason to doubt the protection of the Atlantic Ocean in the 1790s. Indeed, by the 1790s the British, French, and Spanish had been warring with one another on and around the American continent for nearly two centuries. For most of the decade, Spain and Great Britain maintained armed forces on the American continent. Moreover, since 1793, France and Britain had waged war against one another on the seas—with the help of the Dutch and the Spanish—not only on the Atlantic, but particularly in the Caribbean, where the United States enjoyed substantial trading advantages during wartime. Meanwhile, American diplomatic relations with France steadily deteriorated after the 1793 Proclamation of Neutrality and the 1795 Jay Treaty. French minister Jean Fauchet was so outraged that he demanded that Americans be made to hear "the voice of France thundering against the treaty and demanding justice." In 1796, French privateers in the Caribbean took advantage of the souring relations and began attacking American commercial shipping in the West Indies. The French Directory then sanctioned the piracy with a decree of July 2 authorizing the condemnation of neutral ships trading with belligerents. In the summer and fall of 1796, American newspapers reported the loss of scores of commercial vessels to French privateers.[48]

In November the United States dispatched Charles Cotesworth Pinckney as minister plenipotentiary to France, but the Directory refused to receive him formally and Franco-American relations appeared to be at an impasse.[49] Hamilton knew the U.S. military was unprepared, and he desperately wanted to avoid a war with France. When John Adams came into office in March, Hamilton fervently pressed cabinet members Pickering, McHenry, and Secretary of the Treasury Oliver Wolcott to impress upon the president the importance of an "Extraordinary Mission" to negotiate with France.[50] On March 22, 1797, Hamilton wrote to the secretary of state and presented him with a list of actions the government should take in response to the Pinckney rejection. Along with the dispatch of an extraordinary mission, Hamilton wanted the president to declare a national day of humiliation and prayer, to call the Fifth Congress into session, and to urge Congress to prepare defensive measures. Among those measures, Hamilton suggested the creation of a navy and a Provisional Army of 25,000 in case of war, commissions for merchants to arm themselves, and a means for collecting the revenue to fund the military buildup. "The governing passion of the Rulers of France has been revenge . . . to force us into a greater dependence may be the plan," Hamilton warned Pickering, and in "this time of general convulsion, in a state of things which threaten all civilization, 'tis a great folly to wrap ourselves up in a cloak of security." Three days later President Adams issued a proclamation calling for the convention of a special session of Congress on May 15, as "an extraordinary occasion exists . . . in order to consult and determine on such measures as in their wisdom shall be deemed meet for their safety and welfare of the said United States."[51] To the Kirchenleute, preparedness meant bolstering the militia, but to Hamilton it meant something else entirely.

Within weeks, Hamilton got to work impressing his ideas on the coming Congress. He chose to operate through South Carolinian William Loughton Smith, who chaired the Ways and Means Committee in the House of Representatives. On April 5, he wrote to Smith expressing concern over the situation with France, and on the 10th, he wrote again, this time with a detailed plan of action for the Fifth Congress. Hamilton first insisted that a commission should be sent "to avoid . . . a rupture with France." He worried that if war erupted and "a sudden peace in Europe takes place," France could concentrate all her energies on America and then "what is to hinder an invasion?" Internally, Hamilton dreaded "the very large party infatuated by a blind devotion to France." He asked Smith, "In a contest so dangerous" who will guarantee that "these [Republicans] on considerations of ambition, fear, interest, and predilection would not absolutely join France?" Further distressing to Hamilton was "the vast body of blacks" in the South. Referring to the French alliance with Toussaint Louverture of Haiti against Britain, Hamilton reasoned, "We know how successful the French have been in inoculating this description of men and we ought to consider them the probable auxiliaries of France." Therefore Hamilton urged "a further attempt to negotiate," and in case that should fail, "vigorous preparation for war."[52]

After quickly outlining his ideas for a commission, Hamilton turned to defensive measures. He presented Smith with a detailed list of eight proposals for national security that Congress should pursue. He called for a new tax and for authorization for the executive to borrow $5 million on the basis of that revenue and also advocated the completion of the U.S. frigates *United States*, *Constitution*, and *Constellation*, obtaining more ships from Great Britain, commissions for merchant ships to arm and protect themselves, an embargo on trade with France, an order to force merchant vessels to sail armed or under convoy, and the fortification of principal ports. In addition, he demanded the establishment of a provisional army of twenty thousand infantry which would be better able to defend the country than the militia in case of invasion. Hamilton expected stiff opposition to the creation of an army from the Republicans, who would deny the probability of a French invasion. He instructed Smith to answer that those "who may think an Invasion improbable ought to remember that it is not long since there was the general Opinion the U[nited] States was in no danger of War . . . the present opinion that there is no danger of invasion may be as chimerical as that other which experience proves to be false." Besides, Hamilton reasoned in another letter, their arguments should be moot because he was offering a *provisional* army in substitute for a *standing* one, "the men to be regularly *inlisted* upon condition not to be called into actual service *except in case of Invasion*." Yet he further suggested raising additional regular artillery and augmenting the cavalry by two thousand, which "will be useful guards against the Insurrection of the Southern Negroes—and they will be a most precious arm in case of Invasion."[53] Here Hamilton played upon the fears of the Republican Party's southern base and hoped this tactic would buy support or at least the grudging acceptance of a modest professional standing army in peacetime.

In winding up his letter to Smith, Hamilton made one final suggestion for mobilizing public opinion against France and in favor of the military measures. He was quite worried that should war break out the people might view it as a failing of the Federalist Party and not as a result of French outrages and that they would then throw their support behind the Republicans (hence his desire to send the extraordinary commission). To counter the Republican influence, he recommended that "a day of humiliation and prayer besides being very proper would be extremely useful" as a "philosopher may regard the present course of things in Europe as some great providential dispensation. A Christian can hardly view it in any other light. Both these descriptions of persons must approve a national appeal to Heaven for protection. The politician will consider this an important means of influencing Opinion, and will think it a valuable resource in a contest with France to set the Religious Ideas of his Countrymen in active Competition with the Atheistical tenets of their enemies."[54] God could be the ultimate secret weapon in the national security arsenal, rallying the people to the cause of Federalism and convincing them that their party was synonymous with independence, nationalism, safety, and Providence.

Some argue that America's isolation from Europe afforded the nation an "age of free security" in the eighteenth and nineteenth centuries.[55] But Hamilton certainly doubted the security of oceanic barriers to the invasion of America by a foreign power whose core values he deemed antithetical to America's, a foreign power that held significant sway over a certain population of American citizens—some of whom held prominent positions in government (indeed, one was the vice-president). Therefore, he also called for the mobilization of public opinion, by appealing to the people's religious sensibilities, to create a popular attitude of anti-Jacobinism that would allow the creation of a military establishment and the collection and expenditure by Congress of sums then unheard of by the American people. Hamilton wanted Federalist politicians to play upon Christians' fears of atheistic anarchy, but many German Church People of the Lehigh region would not be cowed.

In April, President Adams issued a list of fourteen questions to his cabinet about the French situation. Secretary of War McHenry transmitted these to Hamilton, and Hamilton quickly fired back a set of responses that mirrored his letter to Smith. McHenry thanked Hamilton for the plans and promised to use them to help the president draft the speech he would deliver to the new Congress.[56] When Congress convened on May 16, President Adams delivered a speech that reflected Hamilton's opinions in his letters to McHenry and Smith. Adams warned Congress that France

evinces a disposition to separate the people of the U.S. from the Government; to persuade them that they have different affections, principles, and intents from those of their fellow citizens: and thus to produce divisions fatal to our peace. . . . While we are endeavoring to adjust all of our differences with France by amicable negotiation, the progress of war in Europe, the depredations on our commerce, the personal injuries to our citizens, and general complexion of affairs, render it my indispensable duty to recommend to your consideration effectual measures of defense . . . to guard against sudden and predatory incursions.[57]

Three weeks later William Loughton Smith presented ten resolutions to the House that followed Hamilton's plan nearly verbatim, with an additional call for a prohibition of the export of arms, ammunition, and military and naval stores.[58] For the remaining four weeks of the first session, Congress debated Smith's national defense resolutions and enacted some into law. Congress prohibited the exportation of arms, provided for the defense of ports and harbors, commissioned the completion of the three frigates along with appropriations to arm and man them, raised revenue by levying a "stamp duty" on legal papers and licenses, and authorized the president to borrow $800,000 on the credit of that tax.[59] While Congress could not agree on a provisional army during the short first session, it did pass "An Act authorizing a detachment of the Militia of the United States," which ordered the states to place 80,000 men in readiness to be called by the president to defend the nation in case of invasion or war.[60] Also during the special session, Adams, with the help of his cabinet, formed an "Extraordinary Commission" to be sent to Paris. Massachusetts Republican Elbridge Gerry would serve along with Federalists Charles Cotesworth Pinckney of South Carolina and John Marshall of Virginia. The three men sailed for Paris later that summer, while the president, Congress, and American people waited nervously.[61]

The commission arrived in Paris to discuss settlement for American commercial losses and to pursue an agreement that would secure American trading rights as a neutral nation and preclude further French attacks. After a considerable time Talleyrand, the French minister of foreign affairs, sent three lesser anonymous officials to receive the ministers; these officials refused to receive the American delegation without payment of tribute to the French Directory. This generated the XYZ Affair in April 1798, when the Republican Party demanded proof of French corruption and John Adams subsequently released the "XYZ Dispatches."[62] Timothy Pickering complained bitterly about the "apologies our internal enemies [the Republican Party—Jefferson in particular] make for the French Government."[63]

The dispatches shocked the nation, and letters, memorials, petitions, declarations, and toasts of support poured into Adams's office from all corners of the nation, vowing "Millions for defense, but not one cent for tribute!" Citizens pledged to stand behind the president, even in the case of war, to protect the honor, integrity, and security of the republic. Many wore black ribbons or cockades on their hats to show their support for the president and their disapproval of France and French Jacobinism. Republicans, however, took to wearing red, white, and blue cockades, opposing war with the Revolutionary ally. The ribbons became badges of party loyalty in the streets of Philadelphia.[64]

Under normal circumstances, the Hamiltonian Federalists found criticism and opposition to their authority hard to swallow, but during times of crisis it was unthinkable.

The insult of April's XYZ Affair was compounded by the injury of more serious French depredations on American commercial shipping. French privateers had captured more than three hundred American vessels in the previous eighteen months, and by the spring of 1798 they no longer confined their piracy to the Caribbean. They began patrolling America's coastal waters, waiting outside its harbors and bays to pounce upon unarmed ships. The three U.S. frigates were still under construction, and war between the former allies appeared imminent. The Federalist Party in Congress was now ready to implement Hamilton's long awaited military schemes. So, as the dominant majority in the Fifth Congress, Federalists manipulated the popular attitude of anti-Jacobinism—the "Black Cockade Fever"—to draft anti-Jacobin (read also anti-Republican) legislation, to fortify existing defenses, and to create new defense institutions to provide for national security.

Hamilton detected a sinister conspiracy. By May he was convinced that the United States would most likely fall into a war, not only with France, but with a body of its own people as well. He wrote a distressing letter to George Washington:

There is certainly a great possibility that we may have to enter into a very serious struggle with France; and it is more and more evident that the powerful faction which has for years opposed the Government is determined to go every length with France. I am sincere in declaring my full conviction . . . that they are ready to *new model* our constitution under the *influence or coercion* of France—to form with her a perpetual alliance *offensive and defensive*—and to give her a monopoly of our Trade by *peculiar and exclusive* privileges. This would be in substance, whatever it might be in name, to make this Country a province of France.[65]

He then called on Washington to abandon his retirement and to tour through Virginia to fan the flames of the "black cockade fever" by speaking out against the French and their American sympathizers. Finally, he regretfully informed the general that his services might again be necessary at the head of the army.

Other Federalists worried that the French were ready to invade the United States. On March 21, Timothy Pickering wrote to Robert Goodloe Harper, a Federalist representative from South Carolina, and warned him that the French intended to foment a slave rebellion in the South and then launch an invasion from Haiti. In April, Harper declared to the House that 5,000 French troops were prepared "to make a blow on the Southern country whenever the word of command shall be given." Former Secretary of War Henry Knox concurred with Pickering and Harper when he warned the president that the French would raise an army of "ten thousand blacks" and "land on the defenseless parts of South Carolina or Virginia." On May 8, Speaker of the House Jonathan Dayton publicly announced that the troops France had been amassing in its ports were not bound for England, but for the United States.[66]

The following day President Adams proclaimed a national day of fasting and prayer. He agreed with Hamilton that an appeal to the people's religious sensibilities would foster national unity. Moreover, Adams knew that much of the American clergy would directly assist the Federalists in the mobilization of popular opinion against the secular French revolutionary government. That morning the well-known Reverend Jedediah Morse delivered a sermon in Boston's North Church that sent shockwaves through New England and the Federalist Party. Morse held forth a book written by John Robison, a Scottish professor of science at the University of Edinburgh, *Proofs of a Conspiracy against All the Religions and Governments of Europe*, which had recently been reprinted in New York. In this book, Robison contended that in 1775 a Bavarian professor of Canon Law had founded a secret society, the Order of the Illuminati, which was dedicated to masterminding a world democratic revolution by undermining Christianity, fomenting class warfare, and overturning all the governments of Europe, replacing them with anarchy and licentiousness. The Illuminati, Robison claimed, plotted the French Revolution and designed England's social unrest during the Pitt administration of the 1790s. In his sermon, Morse gravely reported to his congregation and to America that the subversives of the Illuminati, under the influence and direction of France, had crossed the Atlantic and were busy with their work of fostering a godless, democratic world revolution in the United States, although at the time he had no conclusive evidence to prove it.[67] A few weeks later Harvard divinity professor (and Morse associate) David Tappan delivered a sinister warning to Harvard's graduating class. Like Robison, Tappan worried that the Illuminati's radical, democratic ideas were deliberately engineered to contaminate the minds of the young. Tappan charged that "under the mask of universal philanthropy," the Illuminati "has been aiming at complete dominion over the minds and bodies of mankind" by infiltrating the media and spreading their ideas "among young people with the help of young writers."[68]

A year after his sermon at the North Church, Jedediah Morse returned to the subject of the Illuminati in Charlestown, Massachusetts, this time with "complete and indubitable proof" of its operation in America. He began by reminding his congregation and readers that the Illuminati first targeted Christianity and that its destruction would topple government:

In proportion as the genuine effects of Christianity are diminished in any nation . . . in the same proportion will the people of that nation recede from the blessings of genuine freedom, and approximate the miseries of completed despotism. . . . If so, it follows that all efforts made to destroy the foundations of our holy religion, ultimately tend to the subversion also of our political freedom and happiness. Whenever the pillars of Christianity shall be over thrown, our present republican forms of government, and all the blessings which flow from them, must fall with them.

Then Morse dramatically drew from his pocket "an official, authenticated list of names, ages, places of nativity, professions, etc. of the officers and members of a Society of *Illuminati* . . . consisting of *one hundred* members, instituted in Virginia [the center of Republicanism], by the *Grand Orient* of FRANCE." Most were emigrants from France and Haiti, with only a few Americans. Nonetheless, Morse proclaimed that they were "enemies whose professed design is to subvert and overturn our holy religion and our free and excellent government" and whose actions had already born fruit with the Whiskey Rebellion, the creation of Democratic Societies, the formation of an opposition party, and infiltration of the media by Republican newspaper editors. Although Morse had an audience with Federalists such as Adams, Washington, Wolcott, and Pickering, it is unknown how much of his Illuminati theory they accepted. There has never appeared sufficient evidence to prove that the society was ever any more than a limited, short-lived philanthropical association. But many Federalists certainly believed that there was a French conspiracy to undermine America's republican government, Illuminati or no Illuminati.[69]

In his 1799 essay "Laocoon," Massachusetts Federalist Fisher Ames heeded Hamilton's call to mobilize public opinion for Federalist national security designs, seeing the hysteria over the Illuminati conspiracy as the perfect vehicle to that effect. Federalists were only just learning how to play the game of popular politics, and they did well by stealing the Republican tactic of using the issue of popular sovereignty to justify their actions. Ames professed that "public opinion is the great auxiliary of good government," and he asked, "Where can its weight fall so properly as on the conspirators who disturb its tranquility." Taking aim at the Republicans and their charges of Federalist monarchism, Ames continued, "Our government has not armies, nor a hierarchy, nor an extensive patronage. Instead of these auxiliaries of other governments, let it have the sword of public opinion drawn in its defense, and not only drawn but whetted by satire to an edge to hew its adversaries down."[70]

Many Federalists in 1798—especially those from New England—began calling for a declaration of war against France, as the public opinion they created seemed to support it. Theodore Sedgwick, George Cabot, Fisher Ames, and Timothy Pickering all clamored for war during the second session of the

Fifth Congress to assuage the national honor, attack the Republican Party, and unify Americans under the Federalist Party. But many other Federalists, including Adams, Hamilton, Harper, Jay, and Marshall, still opposed it. Hamilton certainly expected war, but in the spring of 1798 he did not believe it was America's best course. If war was to come, Hamilton and the moderates believed that France must initiate it to obviate any political capital the Republicans might try to gain from a Federalist declaration. French attacks on "neutral" American commercial vessels would not suffice. Enough moderate Federalists in Congress agreed with Hamilton to prevent a vote on war.[71] In that spring and summer of the second session, domestic party conflict, divisions among the Federalists, and military unpreparedness prevented the Adams administration from declaring an offensive war against France.[72] The Federalists instead adopted a defensive strategy to guard against an overt French invasion or, more likely, covert stimulation of domestic insurrections. The French policy, as Fisher Ames described in a letter to Pickering, would be to "Wage war and call it self-defense."[73]

Initially, the Fifth Congress began implementing that policy much in the way President Adams had hoped by taking measures to protect American commercial shipping. In the second session, Congress appropriated over $2 million to complete construction of the three warships, to refurbish and build new fortifications for America's ports and harbors, and to outfit the newly created Department of the Navy and Marine Corps with two dozen armed ships, a number of supporting vessels, and the arms, ammunition, and crews to man them. On May 28, the Federalists launched their unofficial "Quasi War" against the French by passing an act "to protect the commerce and coasts of the United States," which authorized the president to instruct American ships to seize any French vessel suspected of committing depredations on U.S. commerce or merely suspected of *intending* to commit such offenses by "hovering on the coasts of the U.S." In June, Congress authorized merchant vessels to defend themselves against French depredations, and in July, Congress expanded these laws further by ordering the commanders of armed ships to capture *any* armed French vessels and by authorizing the president to commission privateers to do the same. In the meantime, President Adams signed laws declaring an embargo on all trade with France and nullifying all previous treaties between the two quarreling nations.[74] Adams was satisfied with the congressional plan of naval armament that followed his suggestions, and he thought it would sufficiently meet national security needs without the need for an expanded army. Alexander Hamilton and the Fifth Congress were not so sure.

Along with naval provisions, Federalists and Republicans joined in Congress to augment the military establishment on land as well. Southern Republicans worked with Federalists on these measures to answer their constituents' fears of a French invasion from the West Indies, and it was their involvement that drastically cut the numbers of troops and the president's discretion for using them desired by Hamilton and William Loughton Smith. Republicans, much more so than Federalists, held to the fear of professional "standing" armies inherited from seventeenth- and eighteenth-century country oppositionist thought, particularly because of their self-imposed role as the opposition party in America. They feared what they saw in the standing armies of Europe, which were mustered from the impoverished and the imprisoned, marshaled by the aristocratic kin of elite leaders, and used arbitrarily by tyrannical governments to impose their authority by squelching opposition while wreaking havoc on the civilian communities that hosted them.[75] When Congress authorized the president to raise a Provisional Army of 10,000 volunteers—instead of Hamilton's 20,000—Republicans and moderate "Adams Federalists" in the House would not grant the executive the power to do so "whenever he shall judge the public safety requires the measure," as the original Federalist Senate bill stipulated. Instead, the House bill that Adams signed on May 28 allowed the president to raise the force only "in the event of a declaration of war against the United States, or of an actual invasion of their territory by a foreign power, or of imminent danger of such invasion discovered in his opinion to exist, before the next session of Congress."[76] Not only was the law substantially weaker than High Federalists had wished, it was scheduled to expire within seven months. Nevertheless, this was still a victory for the Federalists, who had sought to create an auxiliary reserve force during the 1794 crisis with Britain and also in 1797 when hostilities had erupted with France—on both occasions to no avail. Their Provisional Army was more than just a protection against French invasion, however. Hamiltonians hoped to use it as a precedent for strengthening the military during peacetime.

Some weeks later, as the nation prepared to celebrate the twenty-second anniversary of its Declaration of Independence, Robert Goodloe Harper presented a bill to the House that would vastly expand both the Provisional and the regular United States Armies. After years of military troubles on the frontiers of the Northwest Territory in the early 1790s, Congress had established a regular peacetime army of 3,000 professional soldiers in 1796. By eighteenth-century European standards, this was a very small army, and it was primarily concerned with defensive operations (although certainly not from a Native American perspective) and was relegated to frontier areas away from the centers of population.[77] Harper's bill would change all that. Out of the 50,000 men he proposed, over 12,000 would be immediately activated for service as regulars. But once again Republicans and moderate Federalists substantially modified Hamiltonian designs. The bill that resulted let the Provisional Army Act stand and augmented the regular army by the addition of 12,000 troops, but not indefinitely; the auxiliaries would only serve for the duration of the current emergency.[78] Nevertheless, as with the Provisional Army Act, this was still a High Federalist victory. An elated Alexander Hamilton viewed the "New Army" as an opportunity to extend the principle of a peacetime standing army into the republic's future—a plan he had deemed necessary for national power since he had chaired the Continental Congress's military committee in 1783.[79]

With the convention of the third session in the winter of 1799, as protests erupted, petitions poured into Congress, and the Virginia and Kentucky Resolutions made their way from state to state, the Provisional Army Act expired. With the Quasi War continuing, and regardless of the popular opposition, Congress still felt the need to give the president the authority during the coming recess to raise an army in defense of a foreign invasion. The bipartisan "Eventual Army Act," signed into law on March 2, 1799, gave the president the authority to augment the regular army with a requisition of state militias, not only to meet an invasion, but to "suppress insurrections" as well.[80] Five days later John Fries led 400 armed men into Bethlehem to secure the release of federal prisoners who had publicly opposed and obstructed the legislation of the Fifth Congress. Only a few weeks after its creation, the Eventual Army would crush this insubordinate and subversive "insurrection." With their militia the resisters opposed the standing army, with their French cockades they opposed the prospects of a war with France, with their liberty poles they opposed the Sedition Act, and by releasing the prisoners jailed for obstruction they opposed the Direct Tax and the Stamp Tax that funded the national security program, all defying Federalist governance even in spite of the appeals to Heaven. As the Kirchenleute resistance movement reveals, they correctly perceived the Sedition Act and the new system of taxation as additional pieces of a national security framework that threatened their liberties while claiming to protect them.

The military, religious, and propagandistic elements of the Hamiltonian system of national security seemed to be working in the second session of the Fifth Congress. The president's May 9, 1798, proclamation of a day of humiliation and prayer, combined with the popular outpouring of support for the president and the Federalist Party after the XYZ Affair, seemed to evince a popular attitude of anti-Jacobinism. Congress managed to establish institutions—the Department of the Navy, the Marine Corps, the Provisional Army, the Eventual Army and the "New Army"—to meet the national security demands of that policy. But many Federalists in Congress were not prepared to stop there. Six days earlier Pennsylvania congressional representative and Federalist Samuel

Sitgreaves from Easton, who represented the Northampton Kirchenleute, had risen on the House floor and addressed what he believed to be at the heart of the matter:

the business of defense would be very imperfectly done, if [Congress] confined their operations of defense to land and naval forces, and neglected to destroy the canker-worm which is corroding in the heart of the country . . . there are a great number of aliens in this country from that nation [France] with whom we have at present alarming differences . . . there are emissaries amongst us, who have not only fomented our differences with that country, but who have endeavored to create divisions amongst our own citizens. They are . . . assiduously employed at this moment, and it is much to be lamented that there exists no authority to restrain this evil.[81]

That restraining authority would come in a series of laws called the "Alien and Sedition Acts."

The infamous Alien and Sedition Acts were a compilation of four laws: the 1798 Naturalization Act, which extended the residency requirement for U.S. citizenship from five to fourteen years; the Alien Act, which gave the president authority to deport "all such aliens as he shall judge dangerous . . . to the United States"; the Alien Enemies Act which provided the president with the power to deport alien men from nations with whom the United States was at war; and the Sedition Act, which outlawed "false, scandalous, or malicious writing or writings against the Government of the United States . . . either House of Congress . . . or the President" in addition to combinations and conspiracies to defeat the laws of the United States. While this defensive legislation was born in an age of fear, Federalists used the measures in an offensive manner to suppress their political opposition.

In the spring and summer of 1798, Hamiltonians anticipated a French invasion of the United States. They knew that for years French officials had meddled in American politics and had attempted to enlist more than just American support for French military causes. Moreover, they had witnessed the immigration of thousands of Irish and French refugees into America over the decade. While the Republicans enjoyed the political support of French and Irish immigrants, Federalists recognized that the French émigrés could have obvious connections with an invading force and that the Irish had long supported the French as enemies of Great Britain. Furthermore, many of the arriving Irish had witnessed Wolf Tone's failed democratic rebellion in 1798. Considered in this context, the various alien laws were indeed real national security measures in their intention, designed to remove potential instigators of domestic unrest, but they proved to be more useful as elements of a repressive Federalist program to quash Republican dissent.[82] Similarly, the Sedition

Act appeared to some to be a reasonable defensive measure. It did improve upon the common law interpretation of seditious libel because truth was allowed as a defense, juries became judges of the fact of libel, and prosecutors had to prove malicious intent. But the temptation for partisan mischief by the Federalist administration was too great. Hamilton, for his part, was none too happy about the Alien laws or the Sedition Act, but not because he disagreed with them in principle. The Alien Act and Alien Enemies Act placed a great deal of power in the president's hand during peacetime, and Hamilton worried they would provide grist for the Republican opposition mill. Hamilton particularly worried about the political backlash of the Sedition Act. Federalist representatives and senators were also eager to augment the power of the state, just a bit too hastily in Hamilton's mind. Such rash measures could jeopardize the pro-Federalist, anti-Jacobin popular attitude that he and his party had worked so hard to attain and thereby dash this opportunity, which if handled carefully, would significantly increase the power and authority of the national government, particularly the military.[83] Moreover, he worried that the partisanship of the Alien and Sedition Acts would destroy the consensus that Federalists needed should they have to go to war.[84] His worries were justified indeed as the sedition trials (the most prominent against Republican newspaper editors and one Republican representative) and their backlash attested. Indeed, the Kirchenleute resistance began with the Hembolts' liberty pole denouncing the Sedition Act, and most of the Direct Tax opposition included displays and language targeting the "gag law."

Perhaps even more radical than standing armies, alien acts, or sedition bills in 1798 were the tax bills to fund all the national security creations, including the Direct Tax and Stamp Tax that drew Kirchenleute contempt. Congress apparently swallowed whole the "Millions for defense" slogan in 1798. The total defense appropriation by the Fifth Congress was a staggering $10,519,367.84, almost $4 million more than the normal expenditure on the entire federal budget would have been for 1798. For most of the decade, the federal government was able to fund its domestic and foreign debt and pay for its operating expenses with the impost and tonnage duties and internal excise taxes on items such as liquor and salt. In fact, many years ended with a balanced budget or with a surplus, but not 1798, as the House Ways and Means Committee was learning in the second session. In its first session, the Fifth Congress allocated $454,000 for defense—a heavier defense allocation than usual for a single session, but not extraordinary. Then in the days that followed the XYZ Affair, the second session passed thirty-three pieces of national defense legislation with a price tag of $3,887,971.81—more than the entire First Congress had appropriated for all government expenditures. The third session would add over $6,000,000.[85]

On May 17, 1798, Philadelphia's *Universal Gazette* reported on the Ways and Means Committee's calculations for the annual budget. The income of $8 million would more than satisfy the normal expenditure of $6.9 million, but the government owed the Bank of the United States a payment of $400,000 on December 31, and Congress had to allocate an additional $1.4 million to meet the foreign debt. To this $700,000 shortfall, the committee added the "Extraordinary costs" of the military preparations, which as of May 17 totaled nearly $2.5 million. The government was operating in a hole $3.2 million deep and growing deeper every day, and Congress realized that these "Extraordinary costs" would require some extraordinary measures to meet them in the form of two federal taxes and loans from the Bank of the United States.[86] The first tax was extraordinary in name; the "Stamp Tax" eerily resembled the British Stamp Act of 1765. The other was extraordinary in nature; the "Direct Tax" was the federal government's first attempt to lay a direct levy on the people, a method previously the sole domain of state and local governments. Prior to 1798, the federal government used only indirect taxes, such as excises on consumer goods. One could avoid the tax, or at least control the amount paid, through one's purchasing habits. But the Direct Tax would levy a rate on every property-owning individual. It was an unavoidable tax that many Lehigh area Kirchenleute sought to evade and repeal.

Even in the days before the federal Constitution, the men who later became Hamiltonian Federalists began to favor direct modes of taxation.[87] In January 1787, Alexander Hamilton introduced a bill in the New York legislature for a direct tax on houses that would guide his thinking toward a federal direct tax a decade later.[88] Then, after the Constitution was ratified, the question of taxation rose again with the task of managing the lingering Revolutionary War debt. Hamilton's funding scheme included only indirect taxes and imposts to pay the interest on the debt, but he knew that preparing a professional army— a goal he had not yet given up—would require that the government use its constitutional power to lay a direct tax. In a letter to President Washington, Hamilton's assistant secretary of treasury, Oliver Wolcott, stressed that if "a direct taxation . . . is not introduced upon the first establishment of government, and with the influence of all the public creditors, it is not likely that it can be hereafter adopted, but with the greatest public disturbance."[89] Later events in eastern Pennsylvania would prove Wolcott right, but most legislators were not ready to grant the central government such authority in 1790. In eighteenth-century America, taxation often provoked immense controversy. In 1765 a debate over taxation began the road to revolution, and after the war many attempts by states to meet requisitions of the Confederation Congress met stiff opposition in Massachusetts and elsewhere. In the 1790s, the Federalists knew that while they desperately needed cash, they had to be extremely cautious in procuring it, and thus Congress approved only indirect taxes. They levied external taxes such as customs duties on foreign imports, and internal taxes assessed throughout the country such as excises on consumable commodities. One of those indirect, internal taxes was the 1791 excise on spirituous liquors. Western Pennsylvanians violently opposed the excise on whiskey, and the federal and state governments spent thousands to suppress the insurgency. In all these cases, constitutional questions about representation formed part of the resisters' political grievances, but conservatives such as Hamilton dismissed the Shays and Whiskey Rebellions as illegitimate violent insurrections that threatened liberty and security. The western Pennsylvanians' behavior earlier in the decade was not lost on Hamiltonians, and they would see and project the eastern dissent of 1798–99 in much the same light.

In 1796 the question of direct versus indirect taxation surfaced yet again. With the progress of the French Revolution and the first signs of French hostility toward American vessels on the high seas, Hamilton and Wolcott began to fear for the security of the young republic. "Our external affairs are so situated," Hamilton wrote, "that it seems to me indispensable to open new springs of revenue and press forward our little naval operation & be ready for augmenting it."[90] The Hamiltonians believed that it was their responsibility to preserve the Republic, and so they began planning both indirect and direct taxes. On April 1, the chairman of the House Committee of Ways and Means, William Loughton Smith, reported the need to secure additional revenue to support appropriations for that year, pay the expenses of suppressing the Whiskey Rebellion (more than $1.2 million), and continue funding the foreign and domestic debt in the years to come. He explained that indirect taxes would not suffice, because the depredations on American commerce by French and British forces made the collection of duties irregular at best. Therefore the committee suggested a direct tax to complement indirect duties, but the committee only made this suggestion to the House instead of drafting a resolution because the subject of direct taxation was "untrodden ground." Even Republican Albert Gallatin, a western Pennsylvanian critic of the whiskey excise, favored the suggestion, as he thought it would provide a fairer distribution of taxes. Three days later, on April 4, 1796, the House resolved to direct Secretary of the Treasury Oliver Wolcott—Hamilton had resigned the year before—to draft a plan to lay and collect a direct tax and to present a report to the next session of Congress.[91] Wolcott made his report on December 14, 1796, calling for Congress to declare lands, houses, and slaves taxable and levy and to collect the tax in a uniform manner.[92] On January 12, 1797, Smith unveiled Wolcott's specific proposal to raise $1.2 million in a Ways and Means Committee report, and later the House passed a resolution ordering the Ways and Means Committee to bring forth a bill.[93]

While Hamilton and Wolcott agreed that the most expedient method for raising the necessary revenue was through a federal direct tax, they split over the means of valuation. Wolcott's plan favored land over houses because houses, he argued, were indices of expense, not wealth. Upon reading his protégé's report, Hamilton immediately put his ideas to paper. For months he besieged Wolcott in the administration, Smith in the House, and Theodore Sedgwick in the Senate with his ideas for the "House Tax."[94] He emphasized to Sedgwick that since the "Leaders of the opposite party favour it now . . . it will be well to take them while in the humour and make them share the responsibility."[95] Hamilton explained that he agreed with the secretary's "general principles and objects" but he preferred a tax on dwellings, believing that houses were a more accurate index for assessing individual wealth, especially in cities and towns, and thus would provide a fairer distribution of the tax burden across class lines and reduce the risk of resistance, riot, or rebellion. Indeed, his plan for taxing houses was fair in comparison to indirect excise or sales taxes because the House Tax was a graduated tax that applied a sliding scale to the tax rates from poor to wealthy by counting the number of rooms in a house and taxing extravagances such as tiled chimneys and papered walls (See Table 4 for schedule).[96]

By summer 1797, the French had been attacking American shipping in earnest for a year, and still there was no direct tax bill. In June an impatient Hamilton chastised William Loughton Smith, whose committee was slowly

Table 4. The House Tax

Lower class limit of value ($)	Rate assessed	Taxes due ($)
100	.002	0.20
500	.003	1.50
1000	.004	4.00
3000	.005	15.00
6000	.006	36.00
10,000	.007	70.00
15,000	.008	120.00
20,000	.009	180.00
30,000	.010	300.00

Source: Reprinted from Lee Soltow, "America's First Progressive Tax," *National Tax Journal* 30 (March 1977): 540.

drafting the bill, saying "Our country will first be ruined and then we shall begin to think of defending ourselves."[97] In the same month, he fired off a pair of letters to Wolcott, urging him to work more quickly with Congress to produce a tax, but he still preferred a tax on dwellings over land. He also suggested that the president should be authorized to open a loan of $5 million dollars to defray coming military expenses while Congress formulated and collected the taxes.[98] In the meantime, Smith presented another tax proposal to Congress on June 17, this time for an indirect duty. He proposed that certain legal transactions be required to appear on government-issued, stamped paper, a proposal not unlike the British Stamp Act of 1765. Besides targeting documents used by the business classes, such as various licenses, bills of exchange, certificates of shares in banks and insurance companies, and insurance policies for the shipping industry, the stamp duty also affected immigrants and ordinary citizens. It placed a $5 duty on naturalization certificates, and it specifically taxed documents essential for the transfer of property: grants, deeds, wills, and receipts for probated legacies. The Kirchenleute relied on these documents to secure property, citizenship, and the pursuit of happiness for themselves and their children. Passed on July 3, the law would take effect on January 1, 1798 and amass at least $200,000. In December, however, the second session postponed the commencement of the Stamp Act until July 1, 1798. Meanwhile the direct tax bill was still incomplete.[99]

In March, Adams learned of the French Directory's treatment of the American officials. When Hamilton found out, he could no longer tolerate further delays on the direct tax. He warned Theodore Sedgwick that "eventual dangers of the most serious kind hang over us and that we ought to consider ourselves bound to provide with the utmost energy for the immediate security of our invaded rights & for the ultimate defence of our liberty and Independence."[100] The explosion of the XYZ Affair in April 1798 brought a new sense of urgency to the Ways and Means Committee for finishing the direct tax. By this point, Hamilton had persuaded Smith of his plan, and the Ways and Means bill, introduced to the House on May 1, strongly reflected Hamilton's designs. Over 65 percent of the $2 million prescribed would come from a graduated tax on dwellings, the rest from slaves and land.[101] When Congress passed "An Act to provide for the valuation of lands and dwelling-houses, and the enumeration of slaves, within the United States" (known as the "House Tax") on July 9 and passed the "Direct Tax Act" authorizing collection five days later, Hamilton thought he had corrected the error of his previous federal tax through careful attention to fairness in his graduated House Tax.[102] Surely the people would appreciate his efforts and show more respect for this internal tax than they had for the excise of 1791. The duty attempted to be fair in distributing the burden.

Westerners and rural people could not complain that city folks in their fancy townhouses went free. Moreover, houses valued at less than $500 owed only $.20 per $100 of value, or one-fifth of 1 percent, while those worth over $30,000 paid $1.00 per $100 of value on a graduated scale, or 1 percent (See Table 4).[103]

Slaves were taxed at the rate of $0.50 each, regardless of age or gender. The remainder of the $2 million not raised by the house and slave taxes was to be collected by a tax on lands. The land tax, like the slave tax, was not progressive, but a fixed rate attached to the assessed value of land, set at $0.19 per $100 of value. Hamilton understood that such a rate would behave regressively when applied to improved small farms of modest taxable men as compared to the unimproved lands of wealthy speculators. But he also knew that very little and perhaps none of the $2 million would have to come from taxes on land because the slave tax would more than likely make up the difference left from the House Tax. Nevertheless, the assessors were responsible for completing a schedule that included house measurements and value, land measurements and value, and the number of slaves. In addition, on the house schedule, the 1798 law required the assessor to record the number and measurements of a dwelling's windows. There was to be no tax on windows for the meantime, but Hamilton and Wolcott saw the scheduling as an opportunity to collect information that might be useful should future direct taxes on luxuries be considered. This provision led many Americans to refer to the House Tax as the "Window Tax," because assessors counted and measured the number of windows, and it indeed stirred suspicions about future and further federal government direct taxation, as the Kirchenleute rhetoric revealed.

Since it required the assessment of every dwelling, piece of real estate, and slave in the nation, the Federalists' tax called for the formation of a bureaucracy. The law divided each state into several districts, each with its own commissioner. Each commissioner had several assessors, and, of course, each assessor had to have several assistants. Pennsylvania's share of the amount to be raised would be $237,000. Pennsylvania's Gradual Abolition Act of 1780 had, however, dramatically reduced the number of slaves in the state to 1,700 from a high of over 6,000 a few decades before.[104] Therefore only $850 would come from slaves; still most officials in the national and state government believed the number and value of impressive homes in and around the capital city would make land tax negligible. With Philadelphia as the nation's political and economic capital, officials in the Keystone State believed that the House Tax would account for so much of this amount that, even though the slave tax returns would be low, combined with the House Tax they would eliminate the need to collect taxes on Pennsylvania land. Yet the Direct Tax law called for an accounting of lands and improvements anyway. Not until October did the assessment teams make their way out into the country.[105] To procure capital in the meantime, Congress authorized the president to borrow $2 million against the prospective income of the Direct Tax and another $5 million to cover the massive costs incurred by the construction of national security institutions.[106]

Wolcott used the Direct Tax as an opportunity to spread patronage to Federalist supporters. He appointed Seth Chapman, a Quaker, and Jacob Eyerle, a Moravian, as assessors for Pennsylvania's third and fifth districts, covering Northampton, Bucks, and Montgomery Counties. Most of the assistants they appointed were also Friends and Moravians.[107] Meanwhile, the Lehigh Kirchenleute were growing ever more outraged over the national security measures of the Fifth Congress. They became convinced that Congress and the administration were fomenting a monarchical conspiracy, and in congressional elections that fall they turned out the peace sect Federalists in favor of Republicans—one a Kirchenleute and the other an Anglo-American Presbyterian.

With perhaps the worst possible timing, the assessors would not reach the area until just after the elections, the most heated contests the region had seen all decade. The unpopular Federalist administration had sent sectarian tax collectors into a political, ideological, and ethnoreligious minefield.

Chapter 3

Resistance

Competing definitions of republican liberty—the broadening idea of liberty and extensive participation versus the narrowing conception of the need for a deferential ordered liberty—produced the national partisan conflict between Federalists and Republicans and colored local events in the Lehigh Valley in 1798. This competition informed the Lehigh Kirchenleute resistance to the Direct Tax and the rest of the Federalist program, their pronouncement of their right to govern, and their association with the Republican Party. By the fall of 1798, the controversial legislation of the Fifth Congress had raised their suspicions of Federalist monarchism. In ethnically homogeneous Berks County, the Kirchenleute had for several years openly championed the Republican Party. In heterogeneous Northampton and northern Bucks Counties, the Republicans had only begun to make headway with the rural Church People. At the elections for state assembly in 1797, the *Philadelphia Aurora* reported a "great change" in Northampton County's delegation, as three of their four new members were Republican. In 1798, contemporary opinion still considered the region to be pro-Federalist in national concerns, but the national security measures passed by the Fifth Congress that spring slackened the bond between the Kirchenleute and the Federalists even further. And by October, three full months after the second session had adjourned, coordinated opposition had yet to develop. It took the congressional elections that month, fueled by partisan and Revolutionary rhetoric, to provide the impetus for action. Republican politicians and their press would do all they could to help the Lehigh Kirchenleute to tie their local enmity for Friends and sectarians to the national constitutional crisis created by the Federalists. [1]

In Berks County, the rural farmers sought to send Joseph Heister, a Kirchenleute Revolutionary War hero, back to the United States House of Representatives for the Sixth Congress, while the Scots-Irish, Quakers, and German Moravian Federalists in Reading looked to replace him with Anglo-American Daniel Clymer. Playing the ethnic card should have been simple for Heister in Berks County, where Germans outnumbered Anglo-Americans by almost 4 to 1, but Heister had one serious flaw—he was a speculator. After the war, Heister had bought Continental certificates and land grants from cash-poor veterans at pennies on the dollar. When Alexander Hamilton's redemption plan for reimbursing domestic creditors at face value passed early in the decade, Heister made a fortune. This did not set well with the patriotic Republican Kirchenleute of Berks County, many of whom had contributed to Heister's prosperity. Local Federalist newspaper editor, Gottlieb Jungmann, joined in too and exploited Heister's unrepublican behavior in his *Weekly Advertiser*. Jungmann and Reading's Federalist leaders forced the debate away from ethnicity to the broader plane of republican principles. The election then focused on the candidates' republican character and their attachment to the Republican and Federalist Parties. Unfortunately for Clymer, these issues would prove even more detrimental to his chances than his ethnicity.

Jacob Schneider's *Readinger Adler* provided commentary on a wide variety of issues drawn from presses around the country. Its German language in the familiar fraktur print commanded broad appeal throughout the region, and the paper was clearly superior to Jungmann's *Weekly Advertiser*. By 1798 the *Adler* was popular throughout Berks County and even in neighboring Northampton County and northern Bucks and Montgomery Counties. When Jungmann and the Federalists pushed republican and partisan arguments into the debate, Schneider jumped in with both feet. In July he helped establish a Republican political club called the "German Society" in Reading and published all their addresses, reminding the Kirchenleute of their duty to preserve the republic against "aristocratic" and "monarchical" schemes. Schneider and the society presented an impassioned plea for the people to honor their German immigrant fathers and grandfathers who had shed their blood and sacrificed their lives in the Revolution for the liberty and independence of all Americans, reminding them that Heister had voted against the Alien and Sedition Acts and the Direct Tax in the Fifth Congress.[2] All the while, the Federalists organized militia companies in Reading in support of the Adams administration and published addresses and memorials pledging their allegiance to the administration during the "Black Cockade Fever."[3] In September they organized a rival club, the "Reading Association," to aid "the civil magistrates to preserve the borough's peace" during the election.[4] The county sheriff, whose duty it was to manage the polls, was the German-American John Christ, president of the Republican "German Society." The Federalists were more than a little nervous.

As the farmers harvested their crops in late summer and election day neared, political concerns and debates began filling Berks County's taverns and meeting places, aided of course by Schneider's partisan editorials. Like the Republican editors in Philadelphia, Schneider contended that the Federalist Party was selling America to British interests and that its aristocratic tendencies were proof of a monarchical conspiracy to subvert American republicanism and constitutional law. The House Tax, he claimed, was only the beginning of a plan to slowly dispossess Americans of their property rights. He argued that the Federalists' monarchical conspiracy aimed at nothing less than enslaving the American people, a charge reminiscent of the revolutionary Whigs' conspiracy theories that had led to the American Revolution. They would be as landless and powerless, Schneider warned, as their parents and grandparents had been as redemptioners in America and under the serfdom of Germany.[5] Some may have remembered the dreaded "hearth taxes" from the old country, others likely had heard of them from their parents or grandparents. Schneider's Republican rhetoric convinced much of Berks' Kirchenleute, just as Republican charges of a Federalist monarchical conspiracy activated Anglo Americans in Virginia and Kentucky that same fall. The Kirchenleute even began to question the veracity of the "XYZ Dispatches" from the previous spring that had demonstrated France's contempt for the United States by revealing the attempt to extort tribute from American emissaries. The event had signaled the continuation of French attacks on American commercial shipping. But if war with France really was not imminent, then perhaps the Republicans were right— what else could then be made of the Fifth Congress's military buildup?[6] In the October election, a record turnout of seventy percent of eligible Berks County voters came to the polls to protect liberty, property, the Constitution, and republican government, returning Heister to Congress in a landslide.[7]

In the neighboring congressional district that encompassed all of Northampton County and the northern reaches of Bucks and Montgomery Counties, October brought not one but two congressional elections. The first was held to fill a vacated seat in the House of Representatives for the upcoming final session of the Fifth Congress. Over the summer, Samuel Sitgreaves had accepted a presidential appointment as commissioner to Great Britain under the auspices of the Jay Treaty; he resigned his congressional seat in August and left for London in September. Sitgreaves's appointment must have only heightened the Kirchenleute's suspicions of his monarchism, especially after his sponsorship of the Sedition Act and support for the Alien Acts earlier that summer. The second election was to fill the House seat for the Sixth Congress that would convene in the spring of 1799. November brought still another election, this one to decide upon a state senator.

This region had long been divided politically—not between Federalists and Republicans, but along ethnic, religious, and class lines. Anglo-Americans held most local, state, and national political offices in Bucks County and were frequently members of old, wealthy Quaker families. This was true both in the Anglo south and the Kirchenleute north and had led to considerable tensions during the 1790s in the predominantly German townships where "the Lower Sort of the people" farmed the piedmont of the Lehigh hills. In 1794 one justice of the peace, Theophilus Foulke, served Lower Milford and Richland townships. The Foulkes were an influential Quaker family in northern Bucks County, and they held a variety of local offices. When Theophilus Foulke resigned his commission in December that year, Quakers and other Anglos petitioned the governor to appoint his kinsman, Everhard Foulke, already a county commissioner, in his place. No less than seven other Foulkes signed the petition.[8]

Four years later Everhard Foulke would be Lower Milford's assessor for the Direct Tax, and not a single person who would later resist that rate signed the 1794 petition on his behalf. Instead, twenty-one later resisters from Lower Milford signed competing petitions requesting George Weikert in place of Foulke because Weikert "living in Milford, about half a mile from Richland Township line" was more centrally located than Foulke who lived "at the outermost corner of Richland, and being upwards of ten miles distance from a great number of the inhabitants of Lower Milford." Moreover, they argued, Weikert "is well acquainted with the English and German languages, and three-fourths of the inhabitants of the district are Germans." One hundred and fifty-four citizens signed the petitions for Weikert, about three-quarters of them Germans, and the rest Quakers and Anglos from nearby Quakertown, which sat on the Richland-Lower Milford line. On the list were the men who would lead the resistance against Foulke and the Direct Tax just four years later: John Fries, Reverend Thomas Pomp, Henry Huber, Henry Mumbower, John Klein, and others. Despite their efforts, Governor Thomas Mifflin appointed Foulke.[9] About three weeks later, the people of Richland met at Quakertown to petition the governor again, this time to remove Foulke because of his plural office holding and "his family connections in this District . . . which we conceive may have a disagreeable influence in deciding suits in which they may be concerned." They further charged that as a justice of the peace, he would be expected to administer "oaths" that he himself would not swear and that he lived too great a distance from the majority of the population around Quakertown. No matter, when the Federalist Party ran Quaker John Chapman for U.S. representative in 1798, Everhard Foulke still carried the title "Esquire" with him.[10]

In Northampton County, the German Americans themselves divided between the town-dwelling, pacifistic peace sects of Bethlehem and Nazareth (and Anglo/Scots-Irish Americans of Easton, the county seat) and the rural Kirchenleute who surrounded them. Yet they were faring better than their neighbors in Bucks County. By the middle of the 1790s, Northampton Kirchenleute had assumed control of most local constabulary, and by 1797 they had taken a majority of the county's state Assembly seats. But the Kirchenleute of the district had yet to crack national offices. Indeed, their congressional representative was Samuel Sitgreaves, the Easton Anglo-American Federalist whom they perceived as being part of the aristocratic monarchical conspiracy. The elections in the tumultuous year of 1798 brought their first opportunity to compete for federal governance.[11]

To fill Sitgreaves's seat for the third session of the Fifth Congress, the Easton Federalists proposed to run Jacob Eyerle, a Moravian from Nazareth, and for the Sixth Congress they backed Eyerle for Northampton's district and Quaker John Chapman for Bucks and Montgomery Counties. The Republican Party saw an opening. They had been battling the Federalists in Pennsylvania, especially the Northampton-northern Bucks County region for two years, but although Pennsylvanians and Northamptoners had favored Jefferson over Adams in 1796, Federalists still held federal offices in the district. In this election, the Republicans would use the religious division for political capital. Against Eyerle they ran Revolutionary War veteran Robert Brown, a Scots-Irish Presbyterian from Northampton.[12] For the Sixth Congress, they again nominated Brown, along with another Revolutionary War hero, German Lutheran Peter Muhlenberg from Montgomery County, for the southeastern district.

Republicans in the Lehigh region did not have a newspaper editor with the skills of Jacob Schneider, though the *Adler* did make its way into the area via the Allentown-Reading Road. They also relied on Benjamin Franklin Bache's *Philadelphia Aurora*, while Federalists subscribed to John Fenno's Philadelphia *Gazette of the United States*.[13] When in the summer of 1798, Philadelphia fell into the grips of a yellow fever epidemic, Bache and Fenno—who had competed with one another for most of the decade—contracted the disease in September and died within three days of one another. Temporarily without the *Aurora*, Northamptoners relied even more heavily on the *Adler*. Schneider realized this, and repeating his advice for Berks County voters, he urged the Kirchenleute from Northampton and Bucks Counties to honor the achievements of their Revolutionary fathers who had sacrificed their lives for liberty and to preserve their legacy and the Republic by voting Republican, or more specifically, by voting for Kirchenleute and Patriots over Sektenleute Tories. All along he continued to rail against the "aristocratic" Federalist Party, whose actions in the Fifth Congress seemed proof positive of a monarchical conspiracy against liberty.[14] In spite of Schneider's efforts, his paper simply did not have Bache's circulation. To compensate for the loss of Bache, Republican politicians from Philadelphia who sought refuge from the fever stumped for Republican candidates through the Lehigh region that fall. The Federalists would have been well advised to have done the same, but they remained confident that the Germans would continue to defer to the party of Washington for national offices despite their recent losses in state and local positions, and they sent no one from Philadelphia to campaign.

First to arrive was the U.S. representative from Philadelphia, Blair McClenachan, who had been a bitter a bitter opponent of the Alien and Sedition Acts and the Direct Tax in the Fifth Congress.[15] He rented a room in a Heidelberg Township tavern and traversed Northampton County for eight weeks campaigning for Brown and Muhlenberg. Like Heister, though a self-proclaimed democrat, McClenachan had speculated in securities after the war and had earned a fortune after he supported a paper money bill in 1785 (as a Constitutionalist in the Pennsylvania Assembly) that directed most of the funds to speculators. By the 1790s, he had joined the nascent Republican Party in Philadelphia to counter the conservatives who had become Federalists, and like Joseph Heister, he played the ethnic politics of assimilation to distract voters from his less than virtuous past. He was shortly followed by former Republican state assemblyman Jonas Hartzell. Hartzell was a war veteran, a former sheriff in Northampton County, a brigadier general in the Northampton militia, a tavern owner, and a vestryman of the German Reformed Church in Nazareth Township west of Easton. Like Schneider, McClenachan and Hartzell played on the ethnoreligious division and the popular fears of a Federalist monarchical counterrevolution. In Millers Town, a small village in Macungie township, Hartzell "was very industrious . . . in telling the people that they should endeavor to put other people into the Legislature that the laws of congress lately made were very dangerous to the liberties of the people, particularly the Stamp Act and other late laws as the Direct Tax." Hartzell explained that the Federalists were threatening constitutional government by "taking much of the liberty of the people and that the people should not be so still about it and that everybody ought speak badly of them and stick together."[16]

Echoing Schneider's attacks in Reading, Hartzell accused the Federalists and President Adams of fabricating the XYZ Affair to "deceive" the people into forfeiting their liberties. "The dispatches lately published were all . . . untrue," he argued. Hartzell asserted that Philadelphia Republican "George Logan was sent to France" by Thomas McKean, Republican State Supreme Court Judge, and Vice-President Thomas Jefferson and Logan "would let us know who the X, Y, and Z were." In the summer of 1798, Dr. Logan, a wealthy Philadelphia physician and influential Republican state politician, met with Thomas Jefferson and Edmond Genet, and the three of them schemed to win an audience with the French Directory to defuse the "XYZ Affair" and the "Black Cockade Fever" that threatened war, and during the fall elections Logan was still abroad.[17] Hartzell further complained that the House Tax law "was too *suspicious*" and seemed to be a Federalist attempt to first deprive the people of their

property and then rob them of their liberty. He then charged that "the Mennonites, the Quakers, and Moravians had hitherto had everything in their own
hands, and directed the Government, but if a War should break out . . . we
would then show them who *The People are*, we're *The People*."[18] And Hartzell
meant "we." He was one of them. He led them in war, he led their militia, he
led them in prayer, he led them in law, he led them in community affairs, he
led them in state politics, he led them into the Republican Party, and he led
them to see the interconnection of all these things. Ultimately, the local Kirchenleute themselves determined from their own experiences that Hartzell's
charges made sense, and they decided that they indeed were "The People."

U.S. Representative McClenachan similarly warned the voters that the
Federalists "wished to oppress the people . . . 'til they got all their lands and
then they would lease it out again to the people for their life . . . and that if
[they] . . . and other people did not oppose the laws they would certainly lose
their lands." "And," he continued, "if things were to go on the way they had
begun we should have a number of great Lords and the people would be
slaves," as "the President would make himself to be a king of the Country."[19]
McClenachan's message was clear; Federalists in Philadelphia planned to subvert constitutional republican government with monarchy and tyranny unless
the people stood firm. Not so coincidentally, German-American Republicans
then began to satirize the Federalist administration, concocting a parody of
the Alien Acts. The "Alliance" bill, as the story went, betrothed the president's
son, John Quincy Adams, "to marry a daughter of the King of Great Britain
. . . to hold the United States in trust for the King! And it is for these purposes that an army is to be raised and *window* taxes levied."[20] McClenachan
then concluded by purposefully misleading his constituents, as one deponent
claimed that he advised the people that "the Tax Law was not fixed and finally
determined upon but if the people were to oppose it, it yet might be altered."[21]

It is possible that these were the words that ignited and fueled the opposition to the Direct Tax in eastern Pennsylvania, as the depositions and later
trial testimonies reveal that many believed that the tax was only a bill under
consideration and not yet law. McClenachan knew full well that the tax had
been passed into law in July, but he played upon his constituents' Pennsylvania
persuasion that popular action could subvert unpopular laws. McClenachan,
like Hartzell, dealt in half-truths not only to stir up opposition but to rally
support for the maturing state Republican Party and its infant national cousin.
Votes meant more to these men than popular sovereignty or truthful democracy, and in this way they were at best only marginally more democratic than
the Federalists they opposed. That margin in Pennsylvania included direct
election of justices of the peace and militia captains, and in 1798 that was good

enough for the Kirchenleute, who believed that Republican U.S. representatives could perhaps roll back the Alien Acts, the Sedition Act, and the growing regular army that stifled their chances in state politics, blocking local control.

Local Republican associates of Hartzell and McClenachan assisted in the campaign. In a 1799 deposition, one resister testified that Hartzell and State Assemblyman Abraham Horn together lied outright to the people of Plainfield Township, telling them that "all houses between the value of 100 and 500 dollars were to be taxed, and those above 500 were not to be taxed . . . and if we don't take particular care of our elections . . . the ruin will be irretrievable."[22] Nicholas Kern, another Hartzell aide, and candidate for state senator, went one step further. After Kern had denounced the Fifth Congress and encouraged the people to resist the Stamp Act and the Direct Tax, an eye-witness charged that he instructed area militia captains to "collect their companies and advise them to provide themselves with plenty of powder and balls." The "great many pidgeons" who "would be up from Philadelphia next spring . . . would find out whether they were the Rogues or the Stamp Act Folks were the Rogues."[23] Joseph Horsefield, a Northampton County justice of the peace from Bethlehem, testified to the organization of the Republican Party in the county, and of its use of the militia in electioneering that fall. The officers from many companies held meetings "to prepare a ticket for the election." They also passed "several resolutions," drafted "petitions for the repeal of the Alien and Sedition Acts and the house tax law," and sent the captains back to their companies to collect signatures.[24] In November, at the election for state senator, Henry Jarret, a captain of a Macungie troop of Light Horse and a justice of the peace, followed Kern's advice, declaring that his company "would petition against the tax law . . . and if that would not do they would take up arms and oppose the laws."[25]

With their republican and democratic sensibilities stirred not only by Schneider and the Philadelphia politicians, but by their own interpretation of the Fifth Congress's actions, the people of Northampton and northern Bucks Counties prepared themselves to fight the Revolution all over again in the fall of 1798. The press described the region as being divided between "Whig and Tory" townships—Kirchenleute and peace sect/Anglo-American, respectively, of course.[26] And on election day, Robert Brown easily defeated Eyerle to fill Sitgreaves's seat, while Brown and Muhlenberg defeated Eyerle and Chapman by nearly 2-to-1 margins for the Sixth Congress which was to convene in March 1799. Pennsylvania sent eight Republicans and only five Federalists to the House of Representatives that fall. The Republicans also made substantial gains in the state assembly. Although in that body the Federalists still maintained a slim majority, Northamptoners swept all their district seats in the lower house, removing French Huguenot Stephen Balliet and sending the Church-German

Nicholas Kern to the Senate.[27] Balliet, like Eyerle, would serve as an assessor for the Direct Tax in Northampton County just weeks later. Charged by the republican hysteria of antimonarchism, the Kirchenleute "Whigs" won the election for the Republicans and stunned the Federalists, who had steadily controlled the region throughout the decade. Such defeats would become routine for Federalists in the months and years to come in much of the country, as the blowback from their counterrevolutionary legislation and policies mounted. But in 1798 they rode the "Black Cockade Fever" to victory in most congressional districts throughout the country, reclaiming the majority for the first time since the Second Congress. So in November 1798 the Kirchenleute must have seemed to Federalists as nothing more than a few dark clouds on an otherwise promising horizon.

Aside from the partisan battle, the campaign of 1798 found the Kirchenleute fighting for their republican conception of liberty: political participation not only as the voting governed but as office-holding governors as well. More ominously, the election left the region emotionally charged as the people repeatedly assured themselves that it was their duty to keep fighting the American Revolution. Less than a month later Federalist assessors—Moravians and Quakers—including the defeated Eyerle and Balliet, made their way through the region to take the rates for the House Tax. Their timing could not have been worse.

In an effort to stave off ethnic tensions, President Adams and Treasury Secretary Oliver Wolcott appointed a fairly equal mixture of Anglo and German-American Federalist assessors for the region. Jacob Eyerle, the defeated Federalist German Moravian candidate for Congress, received the post of commissioner for Pennsylvania's fifth district (Northampton, Wayne, and Luzerne Counties), while Seth Chapman, a Quaker and a relation of the Federalists' other defeated congressional candidate, John Chapman, was commissioner for the third district (Bucks and Montgomery Counties). They subsequently appointed fellow Federalist Quakers and Moravians as assessors and assistants to levy the House Tax. Seth Chapman appointed his brother James to assess the northern district of Bucks and Montgomery Counties, and James appointed several Quakers—John Roderock, Everhard Foulke, and Cephas Childs—as assistants along with Samuel Clark.[28] Finally, Eyerle appointed a mixture of Moravians and Anglo-American townspeople from Easton, Nazareth, and Bethlehem as his assistants in Northampton. Jacob Eyerle received his post as commissioner for the valuation and collection of the Direct Tax in Pennsylvania's fifth district in August 1798. In Wayne and Luzerne counties, he had no trouble filling his roster with assessors and assistants, but in Northampton

County, he admitted, "I was not so successful." There he placed advertisements for nominations at local public houses, but two months later he had received only two names. He then began to make a list of his own nominees to fill the posts.[29]

Had Adams appointed nonsectarian Federalists to do the business, there likely still would have been liberty poles and petitions, but active resistance to the actual assessment would have been less likely. As mentioned above, the language of the tax resisters culled from the depositions and trial testimony contains various dialects: republican and democratic, localist and nationalist, idealistic and pragmatic, but the one constant refrain throughout was the disgust for the "Tory" assessors. Neighboring Berks County was predominately Kirchenleute, and, as mentioned above, it too experienced a tumultuous partisan battle in the 1798 elections. In 1799 they sent petitions to Congress and erected liberty poles in opposition to the Direct Tax, yet there were few instances of tax

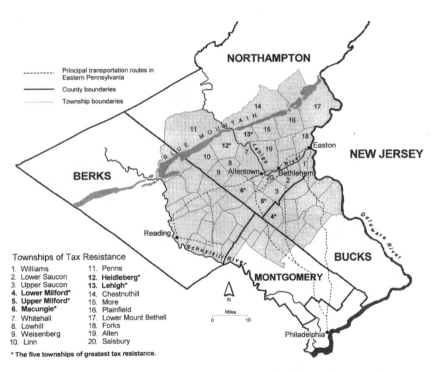

Map 2. Townships of Tax Resistance, 1798–99. Compiled by Monica Kovacic and Christine Herchelroath, University of Pittsburgh at Johnstown Cartography Laboratory.

obstruction in that county. Their tax commissioner was the Irish lawyer from Reading, Collinson Read, and Reading's collector was Federalist Daniel St. Clair. What separated Berks County political opposition from Bucks and Northampton County's resistance was that the antitax sentiment was so universal among the overwhelming Kirchenleute majority that Read and St. Clair did not push the assessments in the rural townships. Conversely, President Adams and Treasury Secretary Pickering appointed sectarian and Anglo assessors for the Lehigh Valley Kirchenleute who insisted upon taking the rates.[30] While resistance to the Federalists' Direct Tax, the Stamp Act, the Alien and Sedition Acts, and the military measures spread broadly across the state—in Berks, Dauphin, Northumberland, Westmoreland, York, Chester, and Philadelphia Counties— the most concerted opposition and the only organized obstruction arose in the Lehigh region, where a sectarian minority persistently attempted to assess a Kirchenleute majority.

The resistance movement had two distinct centers of operation: the townships surrounding the Lehigh River in Northampton County, and Lower Milford and some neighborhoods in its surrounding townships in Bucks and Montgomery Counties. At first, there was little correspondence between these two areas, but as the resistance mounted in December, townships within Northampton County began coordinating their resistance, and by February it was clear that they and the people of Lower Milford in Bucks County were sharing information. Geographic proximity, the lay of the roads and the public houses along them, the use of militia companies, and the continued encouragement they received from national and state Republican politicians in Philadelphia all assisted them in coordinating their efforts. In addition, both shared the experience of the October congressional elections and the same affliction: "Tory" assessors. The combination of these factors exaggerated their fears of Federalist monarchism. In Bucks County, John Fries, a militia captain, vendue crier, and veteran of the Revolution and the "Watermelon Army," led the opposition along with Conrad Marks, a fellow Revolutionary War veteran and tavernkeeper in Lower Milford Township. Fries's job took him to Richland, Rockhill, and Bedminster Townships, where more Kirchenleute lived, and Marks's tavern lay on the Summany Town Road in Milford, connecting the village to Quakertown and then north into Northampton's Saucon Valley, down the southern slopes of the Lehigh Hills.

Northampton County on the other hand, had no center per se; the resistance spread out in the townships that surrounded the Moravian and Anglo-American towns along the Lehigh River—Allentown, Bethlehem, Easton—forming almost a C shape. They stretched in a line beginning at the Delaware River from Williams Township, southwest through Lower Saucon, Upper Saucon,

Upper Milford (bordering the Bucks County center of resistance in Lower Milford), and then northwest through Macungie, Weisenberg, Lowhill, and Linn, over into Berks County's Albany Township, back across the county line and over the Blue Mountain to Penn, back northeast through Heidelberg, Whitehall, Lehigh, Moore, and Plainfield, and over the Blue Mountain once again to Chestnut Hill (see Map 2). The heaviest opposition took place in two sets of neighboring townships where citizens and militia attended one another's meetings and assisted each other in their obstruction: Heidelberg and Lehigh, Macungie and Upper Milford. The Bucks County township of Lower Milford lay adjacent to the south, and the roads and economic ties loosely bound the "Milfords" between the Upper Perkiomen and the Great Swamp Creek. The resistance was first and heaviest in Northampton County by far and spilled from there into Bucks County later.

Resistance began in Northampton County as early as August, when Michael Krumrein and his two sons, Henry and Adam, erected a liberty pole on their Williams Township farm along the road to Easton. It apparently attracted considerable attention from Easton's Federalists, and on September 8, a Moravian justice of the peace, Philip Arndt, rode out to the Krumrein farm to destroy the symbol of opposition. Just four years earlier Federalists had witnessed liberty poles in the western part of the state connected to the excise resistance, and they had called them "sedition poles." In 1798, Federalist reporters in depositions revived that term for the Kirchenleute poles. As Arndt rode up to the Krumrein farm, he saw Michael Krumrein and his two sons. Michael was armed with a stake, and Adam carried a large stone; someone had alerted them to Arndt's mission beforehand. As Arndt stepped down from his horse, Adam drew forward, raised his stone, and threatened to "knock [Arndt] down if he attempted to cut down the . . . liberty pole." His father then added "that he had fought once against the Stamp Act" in his youth "and would fight against it again." Outnumbered, Arndt conceded and rode off, leaving the Krumreins and their liberty pole standing.[31]

Raising celebratory liberty poles, like the Krumreins' exercise, was the most common form of Kirchenleute resistance to the Federalist legislation of 1798–99. They drew the practice, as the elder Krumrein related, directly from their Revolutionary experience. In August 1765, Boston's Sons of Liberty deemed a tree on Newbury Street their meeting place and used it to hang ritualistic effigies of Andrew Oliver, George Grenville, and others they blamed for the "unconstitutional" Stamp Act. They called it the "Liberty Tree." The following summer New York City residents erected two flagpoles on the common, ostensibly to celebrate the king's birthday. The public ceremony that surrounded the poles, however, was more celebratory of Parliament's repeal of the

Stamp Act, and it offended British soldiers, on whose parade grounds the poles stood. The British troops cut one of the poles down and with bayonets drawn prevented a crowd from reerecting it. As Paul Gilje writes, "suddenly a flagpole became a 'Liberty Tree,' and throughout the imperial crisis, liberty poles grew in popularity with patriotic Whigs in other colonies." Revolutionaries used the poles to fly flags and display patriotic slogans, usually positive affirmations of British rights and liberties. Occasionally, as in Boston, the positive ritual of "Liberty Trees" was used in combination with the negative ritual of effigies, in which a crowd pinpointed an enemy of liberty and figuratively hanged, burned, and dismembered the offender of the corporate ideal. Other rituals that negatively targeted enemies of liberty included the destruction of the offenders' property. More painful was the ritual humiliation of an offender with the "tar and feathers" of a "New England Jacket" or forcing him to "ride the stang," an eighteenth-century version of being ridden out of town on a rail while the crowd hurled insults or objects. The intention of such personal rituals was not to kill the victim but to humiliate. Nevertheless, the application of searing hot tar to bare flesh was a violent experience for the unfortunate recipient; so too was a "Hillsborough Painting" with human excrement or public whippings and beatings. All these methods were common to tax revolts and agrarian uprisings throughout the eighteenth century, but they were not as common in Pennsylvania during the early years of colonial opposition as they were in Massachusetts and Virginia. After 1774, when the presence of the Continental Congress in Philadelphia emboldened the push for an anti-Proprietary revolution within Pennsylvania, Revolutionary rituals increased in frequency and intensity. Although, the Krumreins may or may not have erected a liberty pole or designated a liberty tree in 1765, they and their neighbors had certainly been exposed to such rituals, both positive and negative, during the course of the opposition and the war that followed.[32]

In 1798–99, the Krumreins and their Lehigh Valley neighbors revived the positive, affirming ritual of the liberty pole but there never appeared an effigy of Jacob Eyerle or Seth Chapman. Neither did they pull down assessors' homes or subject any of them to tar and feathers or beatings. The absence of effigies and ritualistic violence in the Kirchenleute tax resistance is particularly conspicuous because both practices were still alive in the 1790s. The Whiskey Rebels employed ritualistic violence quite liberally from 1791 to 1794, and in 1795 during the Jay Treaty debates in the Senate, John Jay mused that he could traverse the American countryside at night by the light of his burning effigies.[33] When the Direct Tax resisters engaged in Revolutionary rituals, they did not do so randomly. Rather, it seems, they carefully chose their rituals, preferring affirmative declarations of liberty such as the poles, or the signing of township

"Associations" and petitions, over the negating symbol of the effigy, property destruction, or interpersonal violence.

Moreover, the Lehigh region's liberty poles should be considered actual acts of opposition rather than merely symbols. When militia companies, families, or neighborhoods joined together to construct and erect a liberty pole, they engaged in a political and social ritual that did more than simply mirror their political opinions. The celebrations that attended their construction and the actual poles themselves, which stood in town squares and along highways for months, served as agents and sentinels of political action. The connection the poles made between the Revolution and the collective and individual action needed to rescue liberty in 1776 and the contemporary need to keep up that spirit in 1798–99 served to legitimize and even sanctify their democratic opposition and likely convinced otherwise passive and indifferent spectators to resurrect the democratic spirit of '76 and join in opposing the monarchical Federalist conspiracy to silence, disenfranchise, and dispossess them.[34]

The Krumreins are also instructive of the familial connections that defined Kirchenleute resistance and how the Revolutionary experience educated even those who were too young to remember the war. Michael Krumrein had lived through the War for Independence. When he passed the Revolutionary practice of the liberty pole on to his two sons, he did more than simply revive a cultural symbol of opposition from his youth; he taught his sons an ideological lesson about liberty and their republican duty to defend it. One son had already learned this lesson because he had marched west in 1794 with General Hamilton to rescue liberty from disorder. The testimony of William Nichols, the U.S. marshal who had the unfortunate duty of arresting tax resisters, further demonstrates how the adult children of war veterans became versed in Revolutionary rhetoric. Nichols reported that one leader of the tax resistance, Henry Shankweiler, "spoke a good deal about the stamp act, and the house tax." When Shankweiler "said he had fought against it, and would not submit to it now," Nichols "told him he appeared to be too young to have fought on either side during the war." To that, Shankweiler responded "his father had; he then added that there were none in favour of those laws but Tories." Revolutionary parents passed on their struggle to the first post-Revolutionary generation. Children listened and learned basic lessons about politics and republican government and their right to participate in them democratically as American citizens, a right earned by their parents' wartime sacrifices.[35]

Liberty poles like the Krumreins' were not confined to the hotbed of resistance in the Lehigh Valley. They appeared all over the state in the winter of 1798–99, and they all delivered the same message. They used the language of republicanism to explain to the local community and the Federalist authorities in Philadelphia that the laws of the Fifth Congress were a direct violation of the Constitution and a repudiation of the republican and democratic principles upon which it stood. The Hembolts in nearby Montgomery County adorned their pole with the slogan "The Constitution Sacred, No Gagg Laws, Liberty or Death," directly challenging the Sedition Act with an affirmation of the Constitution's protection of free speech in the First Amendment.[36] Poles also went up that month in neighboring Berks County and its neighbor to the west, Dauphin County. The people of Berks County erected a pole in Millers Town on the road into Dauphin County, which in turn inspired the people there to raise liberty trees in nearby Myerstown and further off in Jones Town and Lebanon. In Jones Town, they erected such a magnificent pole that one reporter exclaimed that it looked "at least a hundred feet high." Two poles went up in Lebanon, one bearing the "Patriotic sign of the Federal Eagle." The Myerstown tree flew a large flag with the affirming motto "THE UNITED STATES OF AMERICA, FREE SOVEREIGN, AND INDEPENDENT," decrying Federalist Anglophilia on the one hand and hailing the Constitution that guaranteed the slogan on the other. Back in Berks County, the people of Vassalboro celebrated liberty during the holidays by raising a town pole, and at the conclusion of the festivities they burned mock copies of the Alien and Sedition Acts and the legislation of the Fifth Congress.[37] They chose the laws, not the officials, as the subjects for their effigies.

Far off in Westmoreland County, in the western Pennsylvania region of the earlier excise resistance, a pole appeared in Greensburg that was decorated with a rather cryptic slogan: "The Father is gone to the Grandfather, and will come again and bring with him 70,000 men. In the year 1799. Tom the Tinker." Others reported that the signature read "Tone" rather than Tom, referring to Wolf Tone, the leader of Ireland's failed republican revolution of 1798. One citizen from Westmoreland suspected that the message caricatured the Tinker as the common man, the people, and that "The Father" referred to Albert Gallatin, leader of western Pennsylvania's Republican opposition in Congress, who would go to "The Grandfather" (revolutionary France, which had attempted to assist Wolf Tone's rebellion) and secure the promise of a French invasion of America to overthrow monarchical Federalists and reestablish true republican government should they refuse to repeal the hated laws of 1798.[38] Anonymous messages from "Tom the Tinker" (or "Tinkerer"), a typical tactic of popular opposition movements in the Old World as well as the new, had appeared in western Pennsylvania earlier in the decade warning neighbors not to register their stills with the excise officials lest the "tinker" would destroy the contraptions. Most liberty poles in 1798 were not so ominous or mysterious. Resisters throughout Pennsylvania, especially in the Lehigh Valley, joined the Krumreins of Williams Township in voicing their opposition with the postive language of Revolutionary republicanism, patriotic nationalism, and democracy.

Later in September, following Philip Arndt's trouble at the Krumreins' farm, the people of Penn Township held meetings to select candidates to run for local offices in the upcoming general elections. In addition to selecting candidates who opposed the Federalists' national security program, they drafted the county's first petitions for the repeal of the House Tax while using the militia to conduct meetings and drum up signatures. During the imperial struggle, institutions such as the Sons of Liberty and Committees of Public Safety had served as organizing tools for local leaders to direct the crowd. The Associator militia had similarly mobilized the Patriots during the Revolution just two decades before, and during the Whiskey Rebellion, Democratic Societies had served that function. By 1798–99 those political clubs had all but disappeared, but the militia had not.[39]

The Direct Tax resisters chose the militia as their organizing body for several reasons. First, it was an organization revered by republicans for its virtue and remembered by Revolutionaries as the source of their patriotism and nationalism. As historian John Shy contends, the militia may not have been successful on the battlefield, but it made up for that in its ability to win or coerce the "hearts and minds" of Americans to the Patriot cause. And in eastern Pennsylvania, the Associator militia was particularly effective in ethnicizing Reformed and Lutherans into Kirchenleute "freedom fighters." Second, much of their and their father's Revolutionary military service had been with those same militia units, which therefore lent an air of republican legitimacy to their actions. Militias conformed to republican notions of popular participation in the protection of republican governance, a notion reinforced by the Second Amendment to the Constitution. Another reason, of course, was that their Republican political leaders were advising them to use the militia to choose candidates, draw petitions, and gather signatures. Finally, the militia was at the heart of the Kirchenleute's state and local battles for political control. While it was an organization with "elected" officers that the Kirchenleute dominated (as sectarians shunned military service), the constitution of 1790 provided that the governor had to approve of their "recommendations," the same as for justices of the peace. As state and local Republican partisans, they pushed for the right to directly elect their officers, while at the same time pushing for increased fines for militia exemption, once more turning the screws on their Sektenleute competitors.[40]

In October, as the elections stirred the opposition further, the tax became the object of conversation in taverns throughout Northampton County. Just days after the Northampton Kirchenleute defeated Eyerle and John Chapman at the polls, Eyerle and Pennsylvania's eight other Direct Tax commissioners held a board meeting at Reading to plan the assessment of the state. Seth Chapman, commissioner for Bucks and Montgomery Counties, warned Eyerle that he had heard a report from a man who had recently traveled through southern Northampton County that "in every tavern where he stopped, the tax law was the general topic of conversation" and that the people there endeavored "to find out who the persons were that were friends of the government so much as to be assessors, in order to persuade them not to accept the appointment." Such warnings seemed to the commissioners reminiscent of those given to stamp distributors, customs officials, and tea merchants during the imperial struggle and to excise officers during the Whiskey Rebellion. Undaunted nevertheless, Eyerle divided Northampton County into three districts (the first north of the Blue Mountain—the second south of the Lehigh River—the third between the Lehigh River and the mountain) and appointed one assessor for each township. But as Chapman had warned, this proved to be a difficult chore.[41]

Eyerle started meeting with his appointees for orientation on Thursday, November 15, beginning with his third district at Nazareth. At the Moravian town, two failed to show and several others "begged to be excused from serving . . . because the people . . . were very much opposed to the law," adding that "they thought it was dangerous for them to accept" their positions. On Friday, moving south, he met with his nominees for the second district at Allentown, where one failed to attend and the others similarly pleaded to be excused and only accepted their commissions with a great deal of persuasion from Eyerle. Over the weekend things got worse as word of the appointments reached the Kirchenleute. On Sunday, Mr. Kearne, an assessor from the second district, came to Eyerle and refused his commission, recommending instead Jacob Snyder. On Monday, when Eyerle met with his appointees from the first district across the Blue Mountain at Chestnut Hill, two appointees failed to appear and a third, Nicholas Michael from Hamilton Township, refused his position outright. Eyerle managed to persuade him to accept, although it was clear that Michael still had serious reservations when the meeting adjourned. As they were leaving, Jacob Snyder arrived after traveling all day from the second district, traversing the river and the mountain, he just caught Eyerle. Kearne had recommended Snyder without even consulting him. Snyder flatly refused to do the job because "the people were very much opposed to the law."[42]

Later that week, as Eyerle headed to Luzerne County for similar meetings, he experienced another setback. Nicholas Michael from Hamilton caught up with him and told Eyerle that he had been forced to flee from his house in the middle of the night and would not do the assessing. When Eyerle arrived the next morning to take Michael to swear a deposition against the people who threatened him, Michael refused to do even this; he begged, "Mr. Eyerle, for God's sake, put me to jail so that I may be secure of my life, for if I inform against these people, I and my family will be ruined." Eyerle thought he was exaggerating, refused to accept his resignation or to put him in jail, and instead offered to go with him to Hamilton and explain the law to the people.[43]

More threats like these would come from the resisters, but there remained a great distance between threatening harm and actually engaging in physical abuse. In that distance lay a conscious decision, in this case a collective conscious decision made by hundreds of people. At this point two explanations are readily apparent. First are the communities themselves. The commissioners for the Direct Tax, Jacob Eyerle and Seth Chapman, may have lived in distant urban settings, but their assessors and assistants resided in or near the rural townships they assessed. They were the neighbors and trading partners, customers or vendors, and sometimes friends of the agrarians they assessed. Therefore, in addition to threats there were offers of assistance such as the Plainfield Association's pledge to James Williamson that if "I should incur any penalty for not bearing the execution of my duty they would reimburse me."[44]

Figure 5. Jacob Ritter's tavern near Emmaus, Macungie Township, today known and operated as the Commix Hotel. John Fries and his Bucks County militia stopped here to water their horses on March 7, 1799, on their way to Bethlehem to release the Northampton County prisoners. Photograph by Paul Douglas Newman.

These people knew one another, and they knew that they would have to continue living side by side, Direct Tax or no. The occasions when violence nearly broke out occurred mainly when the assessed perceived their assessors to be outsiders, in addition to being "Tories." The same sense of community that inspired violent emotions and threats against assessors also ameliorated hard feelings among neighbors. Their objective was to protect collective values, not to inflict harm and violence.

A second factor that mitigated violent action was the identity and actions of the assessors themselves. Since they were neighbors but also Quakers and Moravians, and therefore pacifists, the assessors consistently sought to avoid violent confrontations if possible. Assessors John Butz and John Wetzel were met by a cursing, swearing, and threatening homeowner Daniel Heverly in Macungie. Moravian Christian Heckenwelder suffered a similar reception when he attempted to assess the Upper Milford home of Revolutionary War veteran John Adam Engleman. Heckenwelder, Butz, and Wetzel all judiciously decided to temporarily quit their attempts at assessment to let tempers cool. When they perceived resistance, pacifist assessors informed the property owner that they could measure and deliver their house measurements and acreage themselves within ten days for appraisal.[45] The assessors deserve much of the credit for the nonviolent nature of the Fries Rebellion. Had these men been more insistent on taking the rates, or had they returned threats with insults, perhaps resisters would have hanged and burned them in effigy, or worse, perhaps they might have beaten or "tarred and feathered" an assessor, or torn down his home, as in scenes from the Whiskey Rebellion.[46] Yet the Kirchenleute deserve credit as well. Twenty-eight of them had been to western Pennsylvania to quell that earlier disturbance and knew firsthand the effects of a marching army on a civilian population. Their own intentional restraint, combined with the assessors' good judgment, helped to forestall even cases of spontaneous interpersonal violence.

Instead of pushing on the day after Nicholas Michael reported being threatened, Eyerle, Michael, and Northampton County Judge William Henry went to Hamilton and met with 60–70 of the people at Heller's Tavern the next day to hear their grievances and to explain the law to them better. Many of the townspeople wore their militia uniforms.[47] Eyerle probably chose Heller's tavern for his meeting likely because it was the largest (nonsacralized) public venue in Hamilton Township. Not coincidentally, when the resisters of Hamilton and other Lehigh Valley villages met to coordinate their opposition, they too chose taverns and inns for their meetings. Taverns were more than simply local watering holes in the eighteenth century, they were community centers. Taverns served as places of business, politics, mail distribution, legal disputes, and repositories of local and extralocal newspapers; they served as "public houses." They were also, of course, a good place to "tie one on" in an age of such heavy drinking that one scholar has renamed the "Early Republic" the "Alcoholic Republic."[48] Finally, taverns served as centers of militia activity. When companies gathered for muster day, they rendezvoused at public houses, drilled for a bit, fired their pieces, and then returned to the bar to dine and drink the rest of the day. Being the confluence of news, politics, and the militia, it is no wonder that taverns played such a pivotal role in the obstruction of the Direct Tax. Even more significant is the fact that tavernkeepers were at the center of Pennsylvania's tax resistance in the 1780s, when they refused to pay tavern licenses and the state excise on liquor.[49] By 1798 they were seasoned veterans of tax obstruction and occupied the perfect position for organizing resistance.

The use of taverns for meeting places of resistance many times produced drunken resisters which peaked the possibility for violence, as Commissioner Eyerle was soon to discover. When Eyerle read the law to the assemblage at Heller's Tavern, the "obstinate" crowd refused to listen and loudly "complained against the assessors." When Eyerle offered to let them elect their own assessor as they had requested, they responded that "they would do no such thing, for . . . if we do this, we at once acknowledge that we will submit to the laws, and that is what we won't do!" This was a telling remark. Even this early in the resistance, when offered the opportunity to elect their own man in place of the peace-sect adherent Michael, they still refused. The assessors were a key part of the problem to the Kirchenleute, but they were not the only issue. New assessors would not suddenly make the tax law or the other legislation of the Fifth Congress constitutional, stop future taxes, or impede any other Federalist monarchical designs.[50] These Lehigh Valley Kirchenleute had constructed their own popular brand of democracy, republicanism, and constitutionalism that combined their local concerns with national and international issues. This ideology and the people's commitment to solve their problems politically also helps to explain the movement's nonviolence and the absence of ritualistic violence toward assessors beyond threats and warnings.

As the assessors and their assistants accepted their posts and began work in the townships, nonviolent resistance was swift. In Plainfield Township at the end of November, assessors James Williamson and Abraham Shortz reported that the citizens "expressed a dislike of the law and complained of it as unconstitutional." Williamson attributed the opposition to ignorance and determined to hold a meeting at Mechler's tavern to read the law as Eyerle had done in Hamilton. Over one hundred people crowded into and around the tavern. After Williamson finished, the people remained recalcitrant, and he soon learned that they were not as ignorant as he supposed. "They connected with this law the Stamp tax, and Alien and Sedition Acts," Williamson reported, "and said they had fought against such laws once already," referring to the Revolution, "and were ready to do it again."[51] Two weeks later at Hachler's Tavern in Albany Township, Berks County, the people similarly warned assessor Valentine Bobst not to make the assessments until a petition could be drawn, but promised that if he ran into trouble, they would not let him suffer. As Williamson reported in Plainfield, the people in Albany promised to reimburse Bobst for any fines he might incur.[52]

In Heidelberg Township, the mood became considerably more heated, especially around the tavern of militia captain Henry Ohl, a veteran of the "Watermelon Army" that had put down the Whiskey Rebellion in 1794. Ohl was a bombastic local character who enjoyed being the center of attention. He freely used his position as a tavernkeeper and a militia captain to air his opinions and boast of how he would handle the assessor, George Lintz, if he should come to measure his house and lands. In late November, the local county tax collector and Revolutionary War veteran Michael Best asked his comrade-in-arms Henry Hunsecker to call a town meeting to prevent the assessment of the House Tax. Best said the people thought Hunsecker should call this meeting because he was a captain of the militia. Hunsecker refused, but on December 1 another militia captain and war veteran, Nicholas Miller, called a meeting at Ohl's tavern for the people to meet with Lintz. They wanted to see Lintz's "commission and the Law under which he was to Act." At the meeting they threatened to take his papers but did not. They also repeatedly threatened to shoot him and Eyerle if Lintz insisted on making the assessments. Ohl demanded that Eyerle himself come make the valuations, and to raucous laughter and applause, he added that he would "cut him to pieces and make sausages of him." Ohl added that he would shoot even his own father were he to come to assess the rate. This concern with seeing the written law and inspecting the assessors' papers would become a common occurrence during the resistance, echoing the Republican lies that it was "not yet a law," and "might yet be altered." Historian Alan Tully has demonstrated that rural Pennsylvania German Americans displayed literacy rates above 70 percent, so it is likely that many demanded to see the law because they could read it and determine its validity for themselves. Confirming Tully's findings, the petitions sent to the governor from German townships in the 1790s almost exclusively bore signatures instead of marks.[53]

The following day 150 men from Heidelberg (a township of only 158 taxable men in 1798) met at Ohl's tavern again. First they signed an "Association" drafted by George Horn, the schoolmaster, binding themselves together in agreement to resist the assessment of their property. These associations were extralegal institutions that may seem redundant in light of the resisters' use of the militia, but they proved to be quite integral to the resistance for several reasons. First, like liberty poles, they were a Revolutionary tradition that heaped further republican legitimacy on their undertaking. Similarly, they offered more men the opportunity of joining in these corporate expressions of political culture, particularly those whose age and physical stature prevented them from serving in the militia. Indeed, as Heidelberg shows, they produced near unanimous incorporations of township residents. Townships also used associations pragmatically to call forth neighbors to warn off assessors, and, as was the case with the Revolutionary Sons of Liberty, to police themselves to prevent any of their own from submitting to the assessors. And like their predecessors from their Revolutionary past, the associations proved useful for coordinating resistance between communities.

For example, as the Heidelberg people were meeting at Ohl's tavern, Conrad Spering, a militia captain and local liberty pole raiser, was drafting a paper in neighboring Weisenburg Township in which the people pledged to defend themselves against the government in case of reprisal for the tax resistance. When George Lintz arrived at Ohl's tavern to read the law, this time with Justice of the Peace Michael Bobst, the people informed the officials that "they were willing to pay a Tax but not in the manner required by the tax laws of Congress." Their mood had tempered, but they still resisted assessment of their houses in addition to their lands. The idea of taxing one's home seemed onerous and reminded many of the hated German hearth taxes.[54] It just could not be "constitutional." Two months later Henry Hunsecker met Jonas Hartzell in Philadelphia, and the Republican politician told the militia captain to tell his company and the association to "stand fast" against the House Tax.[55] Those organizations, of course, spread the word.

The Kirchenleute resistance stiffened as winter blew into the Lehigh Valley in December. The resisters began to use the Constitution itself, in addition to Revolutionary tactics, to frame their active resistance to the Federalist legislation. It seemed the logical thing to do. After all, the founders had added a Bill of Rights for the express purpose of providing the people protections against their centralized, federal government. But the Kirchenleute took this idea one step further. In their view, not only did the Constitution (as a compact among the governed to license the authority of their governors) defend their liberties from the encroaching power of government, but its Bill of Rights was an offensive tool as well. The people could use the Bill of Rights to prod the government back into line whenever it transgressed on their republican or economic liberties and to claim still further democratic political rights. In the days before *Marbury v. Madison* and judicial review, the Lehigh area Kirchenleute asserted by their actions and words that in a government based upon popular

sovereignty the people ought to have a role in determining the constitutionality of the laws. By this assertion they participated in the expansion of popular
democracy which they believed—as confirmed by their words and deeds—
defined the American Revolution.

To prevent unnecessary violence and to assure the repeal of the odious
legislation, they decided to oppose an "unconstitutional tax" by acting in
accordance with, rather than in defiance of, the Constitution. They used their
First Amendment right of assembly to organize public meetings to coordinate
the resistance. They drew on the First Amendment again when, during those
meetings, they drafted and signed petitions asking assessors not to collect the
tax or petitioned Congress to repeal the law.[56] One petition addressed to Congress reveals not only the petitioners' attachment to the Constitution, but
the yeoman character of their resistance as well. "That while we are warmly
attached to the Union," they affirmed, "we cannot but express our concern at
several acts passed in the last two sessions of Congress: 1. The law for erecting
a standing army." Here they objected to the "Provisional Army Act" and the
augmentation of the regular "New Army" by thousands of professional soldiers, while assuring and reminding Congress that "we are ready at any call,
to defend our country against any foreign enemy or domestic insurrection"
by way of the militia—the citizen army. They opposed, second, the Alien and
Sedition Acts, which produced "more disunion than union" and contradicted
the First Amendment. They further disputed "the inconvenience of procuring
and using stamped paper" and suggested that "the name of a Stamp Act [was]
odious to most Americans." And last, they objected to the Direct Tax because
"It is now well known, that the owners of Houses in Pennsylvania will pay
much more in proportion to the value of their property than the holders of
uncultivated lands." The tax seemed to punish those who settled on their land
and improved their property—those who virtuously pursued liberty—while
allowing speculators to continue their self-interested, aggrandizing pursuits
unabated and without subjection to the public interest.[57] This last grievance
was less concerned with the written Constitution than with the "Spirit" of their
Constitution that they voiced in other petitions after the Revolution.

Republican newspapers printed these petitions before they were sent to
Congress in order to attract more signers, and they further fanned the flames
of discontent. A reporter from the *Aurora*, which was by this time edited by
Irish immigrant and staunch Republican William Duane, recorded a supposed
conversation with a husband and wife concerning the Direct Tax. The wife told
him that it "was a hard case for her husband to pay a Tax on his hard earned
property, while her neighbour paid no tax on 10,000 dollars which he bought
of a number of Soldiers, who were obliged to sell their notes at 2–6 on the

pound." When she finished, her husband nodded and replied, "Ah Wife . . . these are strange times, when the speculator goes free, and the industrious farmer is become the object of Taxation."[58] An editorial in another paper complained of the law that allowed the president to borrow $2 million on the credit of the tax, claiming that "Congress have empowered the President to borrow as much money as he pleases, and to mortgage any or all of the states" and "that he will mortgage Pennsylvania first, because it is the richest!" "And," he continued sarcastically, "when he has got all of the money, he will run off to England, buy himself a lordship, and marry one of his daughters into the royal family."[59] Such editorial satire was not unlike the "Alliance Bill" yarn told at Kirchenleute Republican gatherings at the fall elections. Another claimed that the Federalists were drumming up a war with France to justify their unjust taxation and the creation of a military establishment.[60] Of course, these echoed the words of Schneider's *Adler* and Republican campaigner Jonas Hartzell during the fall elections.

Federalist newspapers tried to counteract the petition movement, which by January encompassed Pennsylvania, Kentucky, and Virginia, and was quickly spreading to other states. In Pennsylvania, Federalist editor John Wyethe used his *Oracle of Dauphin and Harrisburg Daily Advertiser* from the middle of the state to answer complaints from the east and mounting concerns in the west. "Those who grumble at our Land Tax, etc. should turn their eyes abroad," he demanded, "and see how the Republicans under the French yoke are obliged to contribute to the necessities of the state." He then ran a series of articles over three months trying to convince the resisters that the tax was a fair one and that their burden would be light.[61] But he, like other Federalists, had misjudged the character of the resistance. First, the Kirchenleute exhibited little or no affinity for the French or their Revolution, other than the wearing of red, white, and blue cockades. Federalist circuit court judge Richard Peters commented in 1799 that the resisters "were generally disposed against the French" and from all that he had heard and seen while taking depositions "he found none in favour of them."[62] Moreover, it was not the immediate burden of the levy that they protested but its future economic implications, its constitutionality, its antirepublican character, and its "Tory" assessors.

During the holiday season, signs of opposition to the laws of the Fifth Congress increased and resistance to the tax stiffened. Yet the people's commitment to constitutional principles and nonviolent action remained steady. At a mid-December meeting in Chestnut Hill called for the election of a state senator, Lutheran minister Jacob Eyermann asked assessor John Serfass to refuse his appointment because "the Congress nor the President had no right to make those laws; that they were cursed damned Villains and Robbers and that the people were under no obligation to obey." At that point he pulled from his cloak a book he pretended was "the Constitution," charged that Eyerle had made-up the law, argued that it was unconstitutional, and told the people that if they obstructed the tax law only and no other, then the government would draw back and future taxation would be thwarted. Then Eyermann toned down his rhetoric for the assessor's sake and said "I did not think any the worse of you for being an assessor, because you were sworn to support the government, and had a right to speak for it." Two weeks later, however, on the Second Day of Christmas, Eyermann prayed for the president and Congress during a sermon, but when he left the pulpit he told the people, "if we let that [the Direct Tax] go forward, it would go on as in the old country." He "would rather lay his black coat on a nail and fight the whole week, and preach for them on Sundays." Then, on Little Christmas while at Conrad Kroesy's house, Eyermann told a holiday crowd that "if he met Eyerle he would pull off his black coat and would beat" him and then once more produced his "Constitution" as justification.[63]

Eyermann had only emigrated from Weisenbach, Palzgrave, three years before when the French had destroyed his home and his town, yet he quickly became a popular minister in parson-starved eastern Pennsylvania. He arrived in Philadelphia in June 1796 and stayed there but two weeks, preaching once or twice at the Calvinist Church on Race Street and then set out to preach in Springfield Township, Bucks County, which borders Richland on the east and Northampton's Saucon Valley to the north, due south of Bethlehem. He stayed there through the end of 1797 and in the New Year moved to Hamilton Township, where he preached to four congregations. Like the militia and the Associations, Eyermann is an excellent example of the interconnecting networks that facilitated a coordinated resistance. In his role as pastor to four churches, he whipped up opposition in and between the two townships of Hamilton and Chestnuthill, the only two townships north of the Blue Mountain to obstruct the tax. Moreover, his eighteen months in northern Bucks County had made him well known and remembered there. When John Fries led the men of Lower Milford to rescue the Northampton prisoners at Bethlehem in March 1799, the only one of the nineteen they knew personally was the Reverend Jacob Eyermann. Witnesses, including the marshal, testified at Fries's and Eyermann's rials that "Fries expressed a great solicitude for the safety of Eyermann." So too did Captain Henry Jarret of Macungie Township fret over the preacher, revealing that Eyerman's reputation and obstructionism rolled down the southern slope of the Blue Mountain into the northern basin of the Lehigh Valley and beyond.[64]

At another holiday gathering, a New Year's Day celebration in Whitehall

Township, Major Loeb of the militia went farther when he proclaimed that "the people should first petition against the laws . . . and if that would not do they had their swords and pistols." If he "had seven or eight men," he declared, "he would go to Colonel Balliet's . . . house and would make him give out the Stamps and burn them to hell." While avenues of peaceful resolution remained open, however, violent action was unnecessary. As Loeb's threat makes clear, only when all peaceful options failed were they ready to resort to violence to preserve republican government, democratic rights, and pocketbook interests, otherwise known as "life, liberty, and the pursuit of happiness."[65]

On Christmas Day, Henry Jarret mustered his Macungie troops for the election of officers and raised a liberty pole in Millers Town. After Jarret commanded his troops to huzzah for liberty, one of his men, tavernkeeper Henry Shankweiler, "declared he would not suffer his house to be appraised by anybody that had been a Tory in the last War." The people of the neighborhood who had come out to watch the pole raising and to celebrate agreed with Shankweiler, and much like the people of Heidelberg, they "declared that they were willing to pay a land tax" though not a house tax, but only "if it was laid as they had petitioned Congress," to which Jarret added that if they submitted now "they would be sold for slaves." There was also talk that day among the citizens concerning news they had heard about growing resistance in the state of Virginia. Indeed, Virginians had been busy petitioning Congress against the Alien and Sedition Acts, and Jacob Schneider's *Adler* had carried such news in a series of articles throughout December. Thus, they decided to collect a fund to send a representative south to Virginia to determine the nature of their resistance and, if it was comparable, to coordinate their efforts with the Virginians. Someone passed a hat, and the group raised $40 in no time with patriotic donations as high as $10.[66] The results of this mission (if indeed it even materialized) are unknown, but it attests to the local Kirchenleute's knowledge of other extralocal opposition movements outside of Pennsylvania, and their desire to fight Federalism alongside Jefferson's and Madison's neighbors, who were at that time framing the Virginia Resolution.

A week later, on January 2, assessors John Wetzel, Jr., and John Butz began measuring houses in Macungie Township around Millers Town. Like those in Heidelberg, most in the village opposed the tax law and the legislation of the Fifth Congress and had bound themselves together in an association to resist assessment of their homes. The people there even bullied the few villagers who remained passive or neutral in politics by refusing to join the association. When George Shaeffer, another Revolutionary War veteran, Whiskey Rebellion expeditioner, and Direct Tax resister, learned that his neighbor Daniel Reisch was indifferent to the House Tax, Shaeffer damned him and called him a "cursed Stamper." And when Reisch retorted that Shaeffer would be arrested for his resistance, Shaeffer scoffed that "if they put me in prison here before Saturday there would be fifty of [my] neighbors there that would rescue [me] by force." Another who refused to sign a petition was condemned as a "stamp act man" and threatened with the loss of his commission as a captain in the militia.

Not surprisingly, Butz and Wetzel ran into trouble from the start. Their frustration began with the assessment of Daniel Heverly's home. As they approached, Heverly came running from the front door of his large, two-story farmhouse cursing and swearing; he warned Butz and Wetzel, "I have seven swords under my bed . . . and gun ready." He thundered that "he would not be famished like the Irishmen or the New England men."[67] With this statement, Heverly acknowledged the new Republican coalition of Irish émigrés and Kirchenleute. Perhaps he understood that he and his neighbors might soon share in Irish poverty and that they should overcome their differences to work together for their common class interest. He implied the same when he invoked the cause of the "New England men," referring to the Connecticut claimants who rival speculators sought to control or remove from Northampton's Wyoming Valley. Butz and Wetzel got the point and they left Heverly's, deciding to try again later, and went to the home of Revolutionary War veteran, wheat farmer, and successful miller, Herman Hartman. Hartman gave the two a similar welcome, exclaiming that "he had his gun ready," that he and his Macungie neighbors were prepared, and that if "forced" they would "cut off the heads of those Stampers." Butz and Wetzel then jotted Hartman's name down under Heverly's and determined to try one more house down the road. They next arrived at the home of storekeeper-farmer Adam Stephan, brother-in-law of resistance leader Henry Shankweiler. Stephan had heard the commotion at Heverly's and Hartman's and met the assessors in the street before his house and store. He warned them that if they attempted "to make the house tax appraisement he would not suffer it to be done that he would load his rifle immediately and would fight against that law." Disgusted and frustrated, Butz and Wetzel gave up their attempts to assess Macungie until they could talk to Eyerle.[68]

The following day, Thursday, January 3, the Moravian assessors Christian Heckenwelder and Henry Kooken set out to assess neighboring Upper Milford Township. They had just begun when Kooken received word that his wife was ill and left to attend her. Since Heckenwelder lived in the Moravian village at Emmaus, in the township's extreme northern corner over the Lehigh Hill, he did not know Upper Milford as well as Kooken. Thus he decided to retire for the evening and find a guide for the next day. He slept that night at John

Mumbower's public house, and Mumbower agreed to assist him in the morning. When the people of Upper Milford learned of Heckenwelder's intended assessments and heard that Mumbower planned to assist him, they sprang to action. John Shymer, a tavernkeeper, and John Adam Engleman, a Revolutionary War veteran who milled grain and lumber on the Upper Perkiomen Creek in the center of the township, called a meeting that night at Shymer's tavern.

Like tavernkeepers, millers such as Engleman and Herman Hartman assisted in coordinating resistance, as did families, preachers, militia captains, and associations. Farmers came to millers regularly to process their wheat and rye, and Engleman and Hartman stored it for them and likely traded it at Allentown just a few miles away, where it began a journey down the Lehigh River past Easton, and down the Delaware to Philadelphia, and then on out to the national and international markets. Engleman and Hartman would have credited the farmers' deposits and then traded back to them flour for their bread, lumber for their homes and barns, and some cash to purchase manufactured farm implements, leather goods, glass, clothing, and the like from local producers and the international market. Millers were at the center of the farmers' world. Who better to help coordinate the opposition?

Over eighty people convened for the township meeting. They drafted and signed a petition to Congress for repeal of the tax law, and they determined not to allow Heckenwelder to make the assessments while they waited for Congress's reply. John Shymer took charge of the meeting and proposed "that the question should be put about whether the people would stand by one another to give warning to Mr. Heckenwelder." Shymer called for "all those who would stand by him and Liberty, should follow him into the Road." About sixty men then got up and filed out into the street. Then Shymer commanded, "Now all those that are for Liberty shall swing their hats and huzzah for Liberty." After the shouting, they went back into the tavern and Shymer concluded, "Now the Township are all agreed that Heckenwelder shall be forbid to measure the houses, and that three men shall be sent to forbid him." They elected a delegation of John Moritz, George Seider, and Shymer himself—all veterans of the Revolution—and the township instructed them "that Heckenwelder should be warned not to make the assessments for some time, until we could hear what was done in other townships." McClenachan's lie during the October campaign still lingered, and the people were unsure whether the Direct Tax was yet a law.

On Friday morning, January 4, Heckenwelder and Mumbower set out to take the rates. When they reached Peter Keefer's house, Mumbower was called away to attend to business, but he told Heckenwelder that he would meet up with him down the road. Heckenwelder then took Keefer's assessment without incident—Keefer even left halfway through the measuring—and then headed next door to assess John Adam Engleman's home. When the assessor arrived he found Engleman, his two adolescent sons, and Peter Keefer. They verbally abused him and prevented Heckenwelder from measuring the house. Just then Mumbower returned and informed the Moravian that he could no longer serve him. It seems the "business call" he had answered was a hoax; what he had found at his tavern was an angry group who threatened to kill him if he persisted in aiding the assessor. A frustrated Heckenwelder then quit for the day seeing that the job would now drag through the weekend and keep him from returning home. He decided to let things cool down and not to continue the next day—he was still waiting for Kooken to return, and until then he had no guide. Instead, he contacted Eyerle and asked him to call a township meeting on Saturday night to read and explain the law to Upper Milford.

Between sixty and seventy men showed up on Saturday night at Shymer's tavern, about one-third sporting French cockades (feathers colored red, white, and blue) according to Jacob Eyerle, who came at Heckenwelter's request to read the law. The crowd first damned Eyerle as a "Tory Rascal" and protested that the law was a scheme of his. As Eyerle attempted to explain the Direct Tax, George Shaeffer interrupted, "admitting it is a law, we will not submit to it!" Then he and his kin Jacob and John Shaeffer, the latter a war veteran, threatened to beat Heckenwelder right then and there, but did not. Instead, cooler heads prevailed and the assessors left; the Upper Milford Association had stopped the rates.[69]

By Sunday, January 6, "Little Christmas," Kooken's wife had improved, and he rejoined Heckenwelder. The two then decided to try again, setting out to make more assessments. Almost immediately, the township delegation of Shymer, Moritz, and Seider interceded, warning the assessors to stop the assessments because they thought "there was no such law in existence." Heckenwelder assured them that there was indeed a law and that Commissioner Jacob Eyerle would meet with them again in one week at Klemmer's tavern and read the law. The next Sunday, Eyerle read the law in English and in German to a crowd of about eighty, many of whom belonged to Captain Anton Stahler's volunteer rifle company, some in uniform and wearing "cockades of red, blue, and white." George Shaeffer once more jumped up and exclaimed, "Mr. Eyerle, it is no law." Others agreed and charged that Eyerle had concocted the tax himself to avenge his defeat at the polls in October. When Eyerle warned that their actions could land them in jail, they vowed, "by God, if [he] should only attempt to take one to jail, we would soon have him out again!"[70]

On Monday, January 14, Eyerle learned of other troubles in Northampton County. On January 4, the people of Weisenberg had prevented Michael Bobst from making assessments. Bobst warned the people that they could go to jail and told them how a man from Berks County had landed in jail for harassing an assessor. Jacob Greenwalt of Reading had threatened to tie assessor John Witman to a liberty pole and hold him there until he accounted for all the money he collected, as he believed Witman was a "dirty Ragamuffin" who "spent the money on Drink and Idle Women." Greenwalt was later arrested under the Sedition Act for slandering a federal official. When the Weisenbergers heard of this, one of them declared that they were not afraid because they knew that over 600 men south of the Lehigh River from Williams, Lower Saucon, Upper Saucon, and Upper Milford had bound themselves in an association under Jacob Lerch, an assessor who had resigned his commission, "And in case any one of them was put into confinement" Lerch's men "would rescue them." This massive association spanning four townships from the Forks of the Delaware all the way to Upper Milford was the work of a Williams Township Revolutionary War veteran, Nicholas Kline, who for three weeks carried "news from one part of the county to the other to raise the spirits and keep up the opposition." The Weisenberg citizens echoed the Upper Milford charge that the House Tax was not a law but merely a contrivance of Eyerle and Samuel Sitgreaves, indicating contact between the two. The people then agreed to boycott Bobst's store and his son's tavern, and they imposed a $10 fine on anyone doing business with the Bobst family. The role of Jacob Lerch is key too because Lerch knew Eyerle. Eyerle had nominated him for the assessor's post when he advertised and received no recommendations. And since he had actually accepted the commission and then resigned, it is almost certain that Lerch indeed knew the Direct Tax was law. Yet, Lerch, like Jonas Hartzell and Blair McClenachan, let the people persist in questioning it.

Eyerle also learned on January 14 that the assessor from Millers Town, John Romig, was too frightened to assume his duty, "not even for $500," and that Peter Zeiner had resigned his commission as assessor for Penn Township after the people there "raised a mob." Associations had been formed to resist assessment in Heidelberg, Linn, and Lowhill Townships as well. In all three districts of Northampton County, resistance prevented the assessments for the Direct Tax, and the people seemed to grow more obstinate with each passing day. Eyerle decided to nip the resistance before it turned violent and to complete the assessments and collection in time to turn over the funds to the federal treasury. He called on Northampton County common pleas judge William Henry to issue subpoenas and compile depositions to determine the cause of the resistance, the extent of its organization, and the names of its leaders. Henry dispatched the subpoenas on January 15, calling the deponents to meet him on Monday, January 28, at Trexler's tavern, at the crossing of the Weisenberg and Allentown Roads in Macungie.[71]

When the day came for the depositions, a crowd assembled outside of Trexler's Tavern in Trexlertown, and Captain Jarret's company of light horse rode into town dressed in uniform. They loudly protested against the tax law and harassed would-be deponents for cooperating with Eyerle. George Shaeffer and Henry Shankweiler stopped deponent Jacob Sterner before he went in and told him to warn Henry and Eyerle that "Millers Town would not be assessed, and they would make sure with pistols and swords." Judge Henry remembered that Jarret's men kept "looking in at the window, and seemed to make game at us, and mouths." In spite of all the excitement and the monkeyshines through the window, the depositions progressed smoothly throughout the week. At one point, Henry testified, Captain Jarret even "assured me he would do all that lay in his power" to control the angry townspeople. When Henry finished with the depositions weeks later, he sent them back to U.S. Circuit Court Judge Richard Peters to make out federal warrants for arrests. Peters originally wanted to make the warrants returnable to the local constabulary, but since most of the minor judiciary in Northampton was caught up in the opposition, on February 20 he made them returnable to himself in Philadelphia and handed them over to U.S. Marshal William Nichols to serve.[72]

Meanwhile, at the close of the depositions in Trexlertown, citizens of Macungie and Upper Milford met together at Lorash's Tavern in the middle of Upper Milford on Saturday, February 2. The legal action by Henry and Eyerle seemed to convince them that the House Tax was truly a law and tempered their opposition. Yet the assessments did not begin. They drew "a petition against the House Tax, the Stamp Act, and the Sedition Law" and bound themselves to an association "to support each other in opposing the tax law, until the meeting of the new Congress [in March] and until they had heard that other counties had accepted the laws and that they would petition Congress for the repeal of [the] laws and if that would not doo that they would submit." If, however, they must obey, "no Tories as those who had not served their Country during the last War should be employed"; rather, it should be done "by those who had done their duty for their country." Similarly, the people of Lynn Township informed Moravian Jacob Oswalt that he "should stop 'til the lower townships began to measure, as Philadelphia and Germantown."[73] And still there were those who looked to Virginia. During the winter, the people of Weisenburg and Upper Milford circulated rumors that Virginians were preventing the tax as well and that they might join the Northampton County men. Conrad Spering went about collecting "money to go Virginia to raise Troops to cut the Stamper's heads off," and Captain Henry Jarret advised his men that "if the Army should come up from Philadelphia against the people here, they must join the army from the backcountry which . . . would come to support them." And both Spering and Jarret seemed to think that General Washington might lead the Virginians in their mutual defense of constitutional rights and liberty against the Federalist Party. Many Kirchenleute still revered the general for his military service and leadership in the Revolution and never connected him with the Federalist Party, Hamilton, or the Adams administration. Of course they were wrong about Washington, who supported the law and the Federalist Party, but their hope was a testament to the "cult of George Washington" as the living embodiment of civic virtue and the Revolution as conceived by many Kirchenleute and other Americans too.[74]

And if all this was not enough, Eyerle faced not only the opposition of men and adolescent boys but of Northampton County women as well. John Romig complained at Macungie that "a woman came to me and said I should not go along with the business, before I was prepared with an iron cap"; this could have been "Grandy Miller," David Shaeffer's wife. Romig reported a rumor that folks in "some houses . . . kept hot water against the assessor come round to do his duty." After the March 7 rescue, the *Aurora* seized on this rumor and reported that women were dousing assessors with hot water and that the "Northampton Insurrection" was nothing more than a "Hot Water War."[75] This may have been a Republican deflection or ridicule of Federalists fears of civil war, or perhaps John Romig really needed an iron helmet. Other than the newspaper reports, there is no evidence that any assessor was ever scalded. But women did play an important role in the communities' obstruction of the laws. Peggy Lynn Hembolt was central to the liberty pole raising at her family's paper mill in December, and as assessor and Justice of the Peace Isaac Schmyer reported in Lower Saucon when "the men had gone from their homes . . . a quantity of women were gathered there, and compelled him to desist" from measuring the houses. Schmyer did not relate how they compelled him, a magistrate, to stop the business, but as a group they enforced the association signed by their husbands and fathers and demonstrated that they too could fight for democratic liberty even if the laws of the state and nation did not permit them to fully exercise it.[76]

By the end of February, Northamptoners remained determined in their resistance, but the confirmation that the House Tax was a law, not simply a bill or a contrivance of Eyerle's, calmed tempers and washed away the threats of violence, even though they still considered it unconstitutional. So they returned to petitioning and constitutional means of conflict resolution, that is, until Judge Peters sent U.S. Marshal William Nichols to the neighborhood to make arrests.[77] And Philadelphia Republicans continued to encourage their obstruction. Republican Representative Robert Brown instructed John Fogel, Jr., to go back to his district and instruct the people that "if the measuring of the Houses could only be stopped till the new session of Congress, he thought there could be no doubt but that the Law would be repealed." Assemblyman Jonas Hartzell similarly told Leonard Miller and Abraham Reedy to return to Northampton County "to tell the People not to submit to the laws, and they would carry the day."[78] The new Sixth Congress would convene in March and would consider the people's petitions then, not just from eastern Pennsylvania but from all over the country. Perhaps their newly elected Republican representatives would succeed in repealing the Alien and Sedition Acts, the Direct Tax, and the military measures. In the meantime, things cooled down in Northampton County, but just across the border in Bucks County, around Lower Milford, the resistance to the Direct Tax had only just begun.

Chapter 4

Rebellion

After the October county commissioners' meeting in Reading, Seth Chapman scheduled a meeting of his assessors for the upper twelve townships of Bucks County for late December. He had none of the troubles Eyerle had experienced trying to convince his appointees to accept the positions. He appointed his brother James as his principal assessor for the district, and James then appointed three Quaker assistants, Everhard Foulke, Cephas Childs, and Israel Roberts, and two nonsectarians, Samuel Clark and John Roderock. Each assessor was responsible for two townships.[1]

There was a distinct difference between tax collection in Bucks and Northampton Counties. Although the rebellion is named for Bucks County leader John Fries, the ideological and organizational epicenter of opposition lay in Northampton County. The movement there began several months before it crystallized in Bucks County, during the October elections for state and national offices. Shortly afterward, German sectarians under Jacob Eyerle assessed the Kirchenleutes' homes in December, and that action was egregious enough to produce wide-scale resistance and to warrant an inquest and then arrests. Bucks County resistance was much slower to materialize, only surfacing in the form of a liberty pole in Milford Square at about the time of the elections. Furthermore, Lower Milford's assessor, Samuel Clark, fell ill in December and delayed the assessments until after the first of the year. His efforts thereafter were half-hearted at best.[2] An Anglo-American, Clark lived near Milford Square, next door to resister and war veteran Daniel Weidner. During the war, the Lower Milford Associators had fined Clark for delinquency, and in the 1780s and 1790s, he attempted to reconcile with his neighbors by signing every Kirchenleute petition for German-speaking officials. But this was not enough to shield him from the threats of an outraged community majority in 1799. Clark lived on a one-hundred-acre tract with two fine houses and a number of barns, a spring house, and a carriage house, all valued at over $1,600. He was worth about twice as much as his neighbors.[3]

It was not until Everhard Foulke and Cephas Childs attempted to take the measurements in February 1799 that the opposition matured in Lower Milford.

The presence of Quaker assessors particularly energized the resistance and led to more drastic and potentially violent action there for several reasons. For one, throughout the 1790s, the Kirchenleute had struggled to wrest control of public offices away from Anglo Americans who did not speak the German language. In particular, they had targeted the Foulke family. Only four years before, nearly every adult man had signed a petition requesting the governor to remove County Commissioner Everhard Foulke from his seat as their local magistrate. Everhard had taken the justice of the peace position after Theophilus Foulke had resigned it to take another judicial position. Several years earlier in 1791 the people of Lower Milford had attempted to unseat Theophilus Foulke because he lived at a great distance, spoke little or no German, and most important, he did not represent "the inhabitants of Lower Milford, which is seemingly very Prejudicial especially to the Lower sort of the people." No less than eleven Foulkes owned land and houses in neighboring Richland Township, most in its southeastern corner along the Perkiomen Creek's Northeast Branch. Between them they owned thirteen houses, five of them stone, most with separate kitchens larger than the average Kirchenleute home. They owned more than 1,000 acres of the township's best land valued at more than $17,850, or more than $17 an acre. Not a single Bucks County Foulke answered the Associators' call to arms during the Revolution, opting to pay fines instead. Everhard Foulke owned two houses, each with separate and spacious kitchens, a cooperage, a "smoak house," and a large "shop" on 233 acres of land. Theophilus Foulke owned 47 acres and lived in a large, two-story home, with a generous detached kitchen and a "smith" shop all valued at nearly one thousand dollars. While the Foulkes' wealth and political power did not equal that of Quakers down-county, they were conspicuously successful when compared to their more modest up-county Kirchenleute neighbors. Neither of them seemed appropriate candidates to settle local disputes, keep the peace, or enforce debt procedures among the "Lower sort of the People" who had "done their duty for their country in the Last War."[4]

As they did later in 1795, the people of Lower Milford suggested George Weichert in place of Theophilus Foulke in 1791 because Weichart lived in the township, he was bilingual, and had "in the course of fourteen years served as Justice of said township to the entire satisfaction of the inhabitants."[5] Weichart had served as township magistrate since 1777. During the war, the job of enforcing the law of the Associators and collecting fines from non-Associators fell to him. After the war, Weichart represented one of the several protective shields that agrarian Pennsylvanians employed against state taxes and foreclosure. But in 1791, Pennsylvanians had a new government that had reenfranchised many non-Associators, like the wealthy Foulke family. To the Kirchenleute they were

"Tories" who sought to retake control of Bucks County politics, at least in its northern corner.[6]

In addition, as Pennsylvania conservatives the Foulkes fell into the Federalist Party, and by 1798 this lent further credence in Lower Milford to the theory of a Federalist aristocratic conspiracy tied to Great Britain. Together with the Kirchenleute's Whig-versus-Tory, republican-versus-monarchist, and Republican-versus-Federalist mindset in 1799, ethnic tensions and local politics further explain why the resistance in Lower Milford grew in little more than a month's time from simple meetings to a mission to rescue Northampton County men, most of whom they did not directly know.

Overt resistance in Lower Milford—the only center of opposition in Bucks County—developed slowly because of assessor Samuel Clark's illness. By February the measurements had yet to be taken. When it became clear that Clark would not take the rates, Chapman called on Everhard Foulke to assess Lower Milford, and that was more than the people could take.[7] The township was a powder keg because of its predominantly Kirchenleute character and the bad feelings between them and the Foulkes. Moreover, Lower Milford's proximity to Upper Milford, Northampton County's hotbed of resistance, was a prime vantage point from which to learn the language and technique of opposition. And most important, Lower Milford had a diligent and well-respected leader of the opposition in John Fries.[8]

According to his youngest son, Daniel, John Fries was the son of a Welsh immigrant, Simon Fries. Simon arrived in Maryland from Wales sometime before the middle of the eighteenth century and from there moved on to Montgomery County, where his son John was born in Hatfield Township in 1750. How a German came to be a Welsh immigrant is a mystery, but his surname and his subsequent American experience reveal his probable German ancestry. During his time in Wales, Simon must have acquired some English skills, and he passed them to his son. John Fries passed the first third of his life in Hatfield, a farming community in northeastern Montgomery County that bordered Bucks County and was populated by both Germans and Anglo Americans. John learned enough English as a child that by adulthood he was bilingual. In his adolescence, Simon apprenticed John to the coopering trade, and his master provided him with craft skills and saw to his academic instruction. According to one nineteenth-century chronicler who interviewed those who remembered the young man, John Fries was "some degree better educated than his neighbors." When he approached adulthood, he was "about six feet high, brawny formation, and adept in all athletic sports." He had brown hair with black eyes, "as keen as the eyes of a rabbit," one neighbor remembered.[9]

In his twenty-first year, John Fries married a German, Margaret Brunner,

perhaps another indication that Fries was himself German. The two immediately started a large family, and just as the Revolutionary War began in
1775 Fries moved his wife and children to Lower Milford where, according to
Daniel, the young family rented land from none other than Joseph Galloway.
Galloway was the famed Philadelphia lawyer and absentee Bucks County land-
owner who had served in the first Continental Congress in 1774 as a "Whig" but
had abandoned the American cause after it turned toward independence in
1776. Galloway permitted Fries to build a house on his Boggy Creek tract in the
Perkiomen watershed. As a Tory, Galloway lost control of his Bucks County
lands during the course of the war, but John Fries does not appear to have been
the beneficiary. One can imagine, however, that having the most infamous
Pennsylvania "Tory" for a landlord during the war helped Fries make the decision to cast his lot with the "Patriotic" cause.[10] Moreover, as residents of Lower
Milford, John and Margaret Fries surrounded themselves with other growing
Kirchenleute families who viewed the war opportunistically through ethnic
and religious lenses. After the Seven Years War, nonsectarian Germans in greater
Philadelphia had increasingly engaged in the political process and had begun
to disengage from the Quaker Party. In 1776, Lower Milford Church People and
their neighbors in the Lehigh Valley seized the Revolution. On the one hand,
they fought to secure home rule from a distant, unrepresentative, and corrupt
British Parliament and the mercantilist, aristocratic, and monarchical economic,
social, and political structures it served. On the other hand, they exploited the
war self-interestedly (and democratically) to assume local governance of their
own affairs in order to protect the modest farms they had built in the previous
half-century and to ensure economic opportunity and the personal and political liberties it would afford for themselves and their heirs in the years ahead.
Like so many other average Patriots, John Fries entered the war with mixed
motivations, combining a conservative backward-facing republican patriotism,
radical forward-looking democratic views, and aims of self-advancement.[11]

Fries made a name for himself locally and garnered the trust of Lower
Milford's citizenry during the Revolution. Although one of the township's
most recent arrivals, he immediately joined the local company of Bucks Associators under the command of Captain Henry Huber. At twenty-five, a married
father living independently of his own parents, Fries entered adulthood as an
Associator. In Bucks County that was a dubious distinction. Most of the
county, especially the Quaker-dominated lower townships near Philadelphia,
were opposed to the war, and even the Bucks Associators as a group were at
best ambivalent, drawing the scorn of General Washington on several occasions. But Lower Milford was about as far away from the prosperous down-
county Quakers as one could get in Bucks County. The area had been settled

by Germans around 1725, and a half-century later Church People dominated the population. They were much closer to the Lehigh Valley in distance and culture than to the larger Quaker towns of Bristol or Newtown forty miles away.[12]

In the fall of 1777, after the British had seized Philadelphia, George Washington called Huber's company into active duty to support the Continental Army at Whitemarsh until the winter encampment at Valley Forge. The Bucks Associators returned home for the winter and patrolled the area between the Schuykill and the Delaware Rivers under General John Armstrong. Just before dawn one morning, the clatter of hoofbeats and the lowing of cattle awakened Margaret Fries. When she peered out the window, she saw a company of British light horse herding the local farmers' livestock through Charles Town toward Philadelphia, and she immediately stirred her husband. John Fries dressed in a hurry, grabbed his musket, and flew out the door to alert the town. He roused Captain Huber and Justice of the Peace George Weichart, and they gathered a force of neighbor Associators to pursue the foragers. By the middle of the morning, Fries, Huber, Weichart, and their men overtook the enemy halfway to Philadelphia and compelled them to turn over the livestock, which they drove back north, returning the animals to their owners.[13]

Margaret's alarm earned John a promotion, and by that spring he was captaining a company of his own under General John Lacey when the upper Bucks County men again joined the Continentals down county. Over the winter the people of lower Bucks County traded freely with the British (and their gold) in Philadelphia, and when they sold to Washington's men, they extorted inflated prices for the depreciating Continental paper currency. In return, Washington threatened to seize their mills and take the war to the people. His frustration must have been felt by the upper Bucks County men who shared the Continentals' defeat at Crooked Billet on May 1, 1778, when British troops bayoneted the Patriot wounded and burned their bodies on the tops of haystacks.[14] This was the last of Fries's recorded military service, as the British abandoned Philadelphia the following year, turning the war southward. He and his neighbors, those in Lower Milford as well as Associators all over the county, turned their attention toward stripping non-Associators of their political power and economic resources and stepping into their places. Paradoxically, their "democratic" revolution within the county catapulted a decided minority into governance over a disenfranchised majority. The state's three Test Acts between 1777 and 1779 helped them in this endeavor. But what was true for Bucks County as a whole was the inverse for Lower Milford. There a German Reformed and Lutheran majority had been governed by the local Anglo-Quaker minorities with down-county connections. Therefore they were unique among the county Associators in that their fight for home rule was also a fight for majority rule at home, though they employed the same undemocratic exclusionary tactics to achieve this end.[15]

Sometime during the war John and Margaret Fries moved off the Galloway tract and rented twelve acres of land in Charles Town (today Trumbaursville) on the east side of the Great Swamp Creek, about four miles south of Milford Square on the road between Sumany Town and Allentown. They built a two-room, sixteen-by-fourteen-foot log cabin. Their landlord was William Edwards, who early in the Revolution had enlisted in the militia as a "fighting Quaker." He paid a fine for his absence, however, when he refused to answer the call in 1780. [16] Perhaps Fries remembered this in 1798, but even if not, Edwards's absence from all the township's petitions requesting German officials in the 1790s made him part of a conspicuous minority.[17] After Fries managed to purchase the tract outright, he continued to live on the property adjoining his former landlord. On that homestead, John and Margaret raised seven children to adulthood, having suffered the loss of one baby in infancy and two more in childhood. At the time of the Direct Tax, they still had two teenage daughters and one teenage son, Daniel, still in the house. There is no definitive record that the other surviving children were living in Bucks County at the time of the resistance, but a number of Frieses with first names matching

Figure 6. Another view of John Fries's house, where he and Margaret raised ten children. Photograph by Paul Douglas Newman.

those of John and Margaret's children appear in the tricounty region. It appears likely that they stayed relatively close to home because twenty years later two of John's sons executed his will and divided the estate among his remaining children. Daniel, the sixteen-year-old boy still at home, accompanied his father in several episodes surrounding the tax resistance and the rescue, but no other Fries children appear to have followed suit, so perhaps they had moved out of the neighborhood.

After the war, Fries's informal education combined with his popularity to elevate him from the coopering trade to assume a new and more profitable career as an auctioneer. He was bilingual and well trusted in the community, making him the perfect man for a job that took him all over Bucks County and occasionally into Northampton County and Philadelphia. Fries was a talker, a storyteller, and a man whose sense of humor easily won him friends. In addition, he was reported to have been an avid reader, consuming all the newspapers and pamphlets of the day, both English and German. In 1794 he had served his country once again by captaining a company of militia in the march west to put down the Whiskey Rebellion. And until 1798, he and his neighbors were known to have supported the Federalist Party, but the actions of the Fifth Congress, especially the Direct Tax, strained that relationship. The arrival of "Tory" assessors—in particular Everhard Foulke—to take the rates severed the patriotic bonds that had tied the local Kirchenleute to the party of George Washington. Like their Northampton County neighbors, however, the men of Lower Milford also erroneously believed that General Washington himself must have cut his ties to the Federalists as well. The idea that their Revolutionary leader could support such a monarchical scheme seemed inconceivable to them. Fries did not appear to have believed that Washington would ride to Pennsylvania in support of the resisters, but neither did he endeavor to dissuade his neighbors of that notion.[18]

In spite of John's successful career, the Fries family certainly seems to have been strained and stretched by 1798, as they lived in the shadow of William Edwards's 35'x20' two-story stone house. All Edwards's outbuildings also dwarfed the Fries cottage and out-valued it by a margin of five to one. So while not a farmer, Fries was nevertheless an excellent example of the typical tricounty Kirchenleute and the tax resisters who had survived the economic crisis of the postwar era, even improved their situation a bit, but sat precariously perched on the edge of economic vulnerability and worried about providing for the future of their maturing families.[19]

John Fries was forty-eight years old in 1798, and his age and experiences conferred an air of wisdom to his opinions; by December he began to share these opinions in private conversations with his Lower Milford neighbors. Like his contemporaries in Northampton County, Fries considered the Direct Tax and the laws of 1798 "unconstitutional" because, in his words, "the Acts for the assessment and collection of a direct Tax did not impose the Quota equally upon the Citizens; and therefore was wrong."[20] Here Fries specifically pointed to article 1, section 9 of the federal Constitution, which states, "No capitation, or other direct, tax shall be laid, unless in proportion to the census or other enumeration."[21] Yet it is probable that he used this simply as a rhetorical and legal device when federal Judge Richard Peters examined him in April, after the March rescue, because the Direct Tax did include an enumeration. Like others in the district, Fries believed that using houses as the main index instead of lands unfairly saddled the bill on industrious farmers and artisans who had improved their lands instead of on speculators and merchants. The resisters were, however, probably no more willing to shoulder a tax on their land than they were on their houses, as both portended threats to their economic liberty and their dreams for their children. This tax could not be constitutional, they assumed, and someone would have to act. By February the Kirchenleute of Lower Milford would get their chance.

By late January, assessor Samuel Clark's health had begun to improve, and he prepared to make his assessments to return to James Chapman at John Roderock's house on February 6. One day at the end of January while Fries was crying a vendue in Lower Milford, he spotted Clark. After the sale, he warned Clark not to go on with the assessments or he would "be confined in an old stable . . . and fed on rotten corn." Another man threatened to "tie him to the Liberty Pole" in Milford Square "and let him stay there." Clark suddenly felt ill again and made no attempt to assess the township by the required date. But Fries and his two coleaders, German-American Revolutionary War veterans and tavernkeepers George Mitchell and Conrad Marks, knew that the Chapmans would not give up as easily as Clark, so they called a township meeting for Friday, February 8, at John Klein's tavern to determine their next course of action.[22]

Meanwhile, James Chapman held his meeting to receive the assessments at Roderock's on February 6, and Samuel Clark came empty-handed. Clark explained the threatening situation, and Chapman asked for a volunteer to help him take the rates. An awkward silence befell the table, followed by a flurry of excuses why none of them had the time to help their friend. Chapman finally appointed Plumstead Township Quaker Cephas Childs to the detail and rescheduled the meeting for ten days later. In the meantime he made plans to read the law to the citizens of Lower Milford. Two days later, on Friday February 8, Fries and Mitchell drafted an association paper at Klein's tavern, and emblazoned it with the title "LIBERTY" in large print across the top. More than 50 citizens signed the pact and agreed that "the Valuation or measurement of the houses . . . should not be submitted until the people should have further time to consider of it, inasmuch as they considered it a Grievance and were doubtful whether it was really authorized by law." Then they resolved to send Valentine Kuyder, a militia captain and Revolutionary War veteran, to serve the message to Clark and Childs. Kuyder delivered the message to Clark on Sunday, and Clark went with him to Mitchell's tavern to talk to some of the people, who "expressed a wish to chuse an assessor for themselves." On Monday, February 11, James Chapman arrived at Mitchell's with Clark to hear the complaints, and when he offered to allow the people to choose their own assessor (an act not even the commissioner was allowed by law), the people refused. Again, as in Northampton County, the person taking the measurements was only a part of the larger problem. The tax, if indeed it was even a law, still seemed unconstitutional, and selecting assessors for themselves would only condone an unconstitutional act.[23]

Chapman met once more with his assistants on February 16, and this time Clark and Childs were nowhere to be found. Once again Chapman called for volunteers, but when he looked around the table, he saw no one willing. He decided to hold one more meeting in Lower Milford to read the law, and he scheduled it for the following week at George Mitchell's tavern. When Chapman arrived at Mitchell's on a cold and snowy Saturday afternoon, February 23, accompanied by Everhard Foulke and Isreal Roberts, they were followed closely in the door by twelve uniformed Kirchenleute resisters, marching with a large flag with the word "LIBERTY" sewn on it. Foulke's presence must have been especially galling; he realized this and took pains to keep as low a profile as possible that afternoon. He sat quietly in a corner of the tavern, speaking to no one. For three hours Chapman and his assessors attempted to explain the law, but each time they started they were shouted down, most often by Conrad Marks and his son, John, who whipped up the crowd by "huzzahing for liberty and democracy, damning the Tories" and declaring that "Congress had no right to make such a law." To this point, Marks's ranting was predictable, but his next comments were particularly revealing. He damned Jacob Eyerle and Stephen Balliet, assessors for Northampton County, charging that "they had cheated the public, and what villains they were" because they "never paid into the treasury." Through his own tavern, Marks had channeled the information and language of Northampton County's resistance into Lower Milford, and here he brought it to Mitchell's tavern, but that was not all that had made the voyage. While Israel Roberts was attempting to read the law, the crowd circulated a letter with information about tax resistance and petitioning in other parts of the country, particularly Virginia. It stated that 10,000 men were on their way to join them. With that information, the Lower Milford men became even more belligerent as Roberts tried in vain to read the law. Roberts remembered, "they would not suffer it" and "said they wanted to hear none of our damned laws" and one man who stamped "his musket on the floor said, 'we have made a law of our own, and we are determined to support it!'"[24]

Fries was away crying a vendue, and his restraining influence was sorely missed. Yet even without him, the crowd did not harm the assessors, although they had ample opportunity to do so. They had, however, demonstrated that they were in contact with Northampton County resisters and like them would not suffer the assessments. Chapman had been in touch with Eyerle and knew about his trouble in January and knew of the depositions that had been taken in Trexlertown by this point. The realization that the Northampton County obstruction had bled over into Bucks County gave him cause for alarm and convinced him that stiffer measures would be necessary to complete the business.[25] Disappointed, frustrated, and angry, Chapman finally gave up without reading the law, got in his sleigh, and rode off to Jacob Fries's tavern (John's cousin but not a tax resister) to confer with Foulke, Roberts, and Clark. Clark resigned immediately and ran out of the tavern; Chapman later that evening called for a meeting of all his assistants on Monday, March 4, at Quakertown. They would, all of them together, set out that day to assess Lower Milford. The business had to be finished.[26]

Thus by February 24, Lower Milford and most of the townships in Northampton County's second district had blocked assessment of their homes. In both regions, the resisters protested against specific laws, particularly the House Tax, and not governmental authority in general. They sought to protect their liberty in a manner they considered consistent with *their* Constitution and the ideals of the Revolution, while waiting for a response from the next Congress—the one that would include their two new Republican representatives, one a German American. In January and February 1799, petitions containing more than 18,000 Pennsylvanian signatures reached the House. Robert Brown, representing the district including Bucks and Northampton Counties, presented several petitions bearing the signatures of more than 3,000 of his constituents, decrying the legislation of the first two sessions "as contrary not only to the spirit but to the letter of the Constitution."[27] Many Kirchenleute from the counties of Berks, Montgomery, Dauphin, York, and Chester supplied petitions containing another 5,000 signatures.[28]

On February 25, the select committee presented its report on the petitions to the House Committee of the Whole during the last days of the Fifth Congress's third session, and the language they used to defend the national security system reflected the Federalists' anxiety concerning the subversion of American principles by French democrats and atheists. The committee declared that the Direct Tax, the Alien and Sedition Acts, and the military buildup were necessary

to guard not only against the usual consequences of war, but also against the effects of unprecedented combinations to establish new principles of social action, and the subversion of religion, morality, law, and government. France appears to have an organized system of conduct towards foreign nations; to bring them within the sphere, and under the dominion of her influence and control. . . . Her means are in wonderful coincidence with her ends; among them . . . is the direction and employment of the active and versatile talents of her citizens abroad as emissaries and spies.[29]

Since the national security laws were "parts of a general system of defence, adapted to a crisis of extraordinary difficulty and danger," Congress voted 61–39 to accept the committee's finding that the laws were wholly constitutional.[30] Only two weeks later this same rhetoric led Federalists, especially Hamiltonians and the press, to assume that the resistance in eastern Pennsylvania was French directed. Nevertheless, the resisters never heard the congressional response. Moreover, they had expected the new Sixth Congress, which would contain their new representatives, to consider their petitions, not the outgoing Fifth Congress. They would get their answer instead from federal Judge Richard Peters, who at this time issued warrants for the arrest of several Northamptoners for obstructing the assessment of the Direct Tax. U.S. Marshal William Nichols set out from Philadelphia on February 26 and served his warrants over the following week, while at the same time James Chapman and his assessors attempted to assess Lower Milford one last time. The coincidence of these two events transformed the tax resistance into Fries's Rebellion.[31]

As February drew to a close, it seemed logical to the Kirchenleute to consider the Direct Tax unconstitutional. It was a tax that resembled the British Stamp Act, a tax assessed and charged by those whom they considered treasonous Anglophiles, a tax shouldered by industrious farmers that passed over merchants and speculators, and a tax that funded a standing army conceived by a party that the local Republican press portrayed as pro-British and part of a monarchical scheme of counterrevolution. Most important, it was a tax laid on Kirchenleute property and their homes, the core of their ideological conception of republican, democratic, and economic liberty. If this rate truly was to be the first of many designed to tax them out of their property, as Republicans claimed, it not only threatened their future economic independence and the future of their families, but in Pennsylvania the prospect of debt and the loss of taxable wealth would have also meant disenfranchisement. And without the right to vote or their newfound ability to hold office, and therefore without actual representation, the Kirchenleute were sure to fall into what eighteenth-century republicans considered slavery under tyrannical rule. The Kirchenleute's constitutional logic may not have been legally precise, but it was certainly not the product of base ignorance as Federalists and Republicans alike later charged. They built their logic on their German inheritance and their American experiences, especially the Revolution and its talk of natural laws and social contracts. And it was their faith in republican government, the Constitution, democracy, and expanding popular sovereignty that convinced them that nonviolent popular avenues of redress remained available, even in the face of a monarchical conspiracy, the specters of taxation and dispossession, and the threat of political and economic slavery.

After riding for two-and-a-half days over snowy, slushy, and muddy roads, Marshal Nichols reached Eyerle's house in Nazareth, Northampton County, on March 1. The next morning he and Eyerle left for Lehigh Township to serve warrants for arrest to the men who had issued the February 9 warning to Henry Strauss. On March 2, they took twelve of them into custody; five of them surrendered to Nichols voluntarily. All twelve then provided assurances that they would deliver themselves to Nichols at Bethlehem before the end of the week. On March 3, Nichols and Eyerle met in Bethlehem with another assessor, Stephen Balliet of Northampton County's third district. Meanwhile, word had spread rapidly among the Kirchenleute about the arrests, but what concerned them most was that those arrested were to be transported to Philadelphia for their trials. Once more the Kirchenleute framed their opposition on constitutional grounds, beginning to protest the arrests as a violation of their Sixth Amendment rights and their local means of protecting themselves against prosecution. Although Philadelphia County borders Bucks and Montgomery Counties, Judge Peters's federal court lay fifty miles away and across a broad cultural boundary from the center of the resistance and the resisters' homes in Northampton County. The rural Kirchenleute feared that Philadelphia, an Anglo-American city, could not provide the Northamptoners with a jury of their peers. That night at Lorash's tavern in Upper Milford, someone told Captain Jarret that Nichols had a warrant for him, and Jarret replied that "if there was I would not give a damn for it." How could the "Spitzbuben" (rogue) arrest people, he demanded, and take "them from place to place against the laws of the Constitution!" Jarret went on to connect the arrests to the monarchical conspiracy, charging that "the President" only "pretended to send ambassadors to France, but the Rascals had got no further than England." During the winter, Adams had sent an "Extraordinary Mission" to

France under Oliver Ellsworth and William Vans Murray to seek a peaceful solution between the United States and that country. Jarret had no faith, however, in President Adams, a "damned Rascal" who told "nothing but lies."[32]

On the morning of March 4, Nichols, Eyerle, and Balliet made their way down the Allentown Road, crossed the Lehigh River, and continued west into Macungie to make more arrests. Both Eyerle and Balliet were defeated Federalist candidates in Northampton the previous fall, so when they came with a federal marshal to arrest Republican voting Church People the monarchical Federalist conspiracy must have seemed greater than just a theory. The officials first stopped at the house of George Seider to issue a subpoena for him to serve as a witness in the tax resisters' trials. Seider's wife emerged and cursed them vociferously with a torrent of foul and abusive language; then her husband came out with a club and swore that he would not submit himself to the "rascals." Nichols left the subpoena with a neighbor, and the three departed for Millers Town to make more arrests. In addition to the resisters' constitutional stance, credit for the nonviolence must also be attributed to Marshal Nichols's restraint. Nichols reached Millers Town by afternoon and attempted to serve George Shaeffer's warrant, but Shaeffer had heard that he was coming and had left home early that morning. Meanwhile, the presence of the marshal and Eyerle stirred a commotion at the center of town, where a crowd of about fifty began to form in Henry Shankweiler's tavern to prevent his arrest.[33]

As Nichols and the two assessors moved toward the crowd, Balliet spotted Shankweiler and pointed him out to the marshal, who quickly headed after him. When Shankweiler slipped into the crowd, Nichols pursued him into the crush, grabbed his arm, and placed him under arrest. But Shankweiler escaped again and ran into his barn. The crowd followed the command of David Shaeffer, George's son, and placed themselves between the barn and the marshal, chanting "Schlaget! Schlaget!" (Strike! Strike!). Shankweiler called out and swore that neither he nor his neighbors would hurt Nichols but that "Eyerle and Balliet were damned rascals," and he railed against the Stamp Act and the House Tax. With this speech the crowd roared, and Nichols grew quite anxious. He later recalled that "I had a pair of pistols, and finding the danger we were in, I pulled the buttons of my great coat," exposing the firearms to the crowd. This had no effect whatever, as one of the crowd ran up and stole the feather from Balliet's hat, to great applause and laughter. When Nichols demanded that Shankweiler go with him to Philadelphia, Shankweiler said he would not do it, even "if it was to the destruction of his property and children." The tavernkeeper eventually agreed to go to Bethlehem to meet Nichols later in the week, intending to post bail, but he never consented to submit himself for arrest. As Nichols, Eyerle, and Balliet left Millers Town to find a more hospitable place in

Macungie to spend the night, the crowd cheered and huzzahed for liberty, satisfied that they had preserved the guarantee of the Sixth Amendment. On March 5, Nichols and the assessors enlisted the help of a local constable to finish the business in Macungie. They arrested three more resisters that day, Daniel Heverly, Adam Stephan, and Herman Hartman, and headed back toward Bethlehem the next day. On the sixth, Nichols sent a deputy over the Blue Mountain to bring in the Reverend Jacob Eyermann, who was preaching a funeral at the moment of his arrest.[34]

On the same day that Nichols stirred up the people of Millers Town in Northampton County, James Chapman met with his assistants in Bucks County to begin the team assessment of Lower Milford, though only Foulke, Childs, and Roderock showed up as planned. Samuel Clark was conspicuously absent. He was helping his friend, tavernkeeper David Sellers, move into a new home in adjacent Rockhill Township. The others waited through the night for Clark and Roberts, but by morning neither had arrived, so Chapman ordered his three men to go on about the business. Chapman went to southern Milford

Figure 7. The Trum Tavern, Allentown Road, Trumbaursville. Some locals today believe that this was the tavern of Jacob Fries (John's cousin), but Davis's sources told him that Jacob Fries's tavern was well off the Sumany Town-Allentown Road. The Trum Tavern does match the description of Fries's tavern in the Direct Tax records. The Trum Tavern is currently a bar and grill. Photograph by Paul Douglas Newman.

and sent the others west across the Great Swamp Creek. They agreed to meet at Jacob Fries's tavern in Charles Town for dinner in the afternoon.[35]

The four assessors had little trouble at first. They did not take the time to measure or inspect the outbuildings. To expedite the process, they knocked on doors and asked the owners for the number of buildings on their property, their approximate sizes, and an approximation of their acreage. By dinner time they had completed almost one-third of the township. They targeted the Anglo minority first, only one of whom protested. Their luck changed when Cephas Childs reached Daniel Weidener's house and ran into Kirchenleute resistance. Weidener protested the measurement, saying that he was not sure that the House Tax was a law, but he soon gave way and left his house for George Mitchell's tavern, allowing Childs to make the valuation. When he finished, Childs also went to Mitchell's tavern to meet Roderock and Foulke to make the trip to Charles Town. At Mitchell's, Weidener again complained against the House Tax, but the three assessors ignored him and headed off to dinner.[36]

In the meantime, Chapman finished his morning assessments early and waited for his associates at Jacob Fries's tavern. While he waited, Samuel Clark pulled up with John Fries, the two having just finished moving the Sellers family. As Fries secured the team, Clark made his way inside, where he was surprised to find a disappointed and disagreeable James Chapman. Clark told Chapman that he simply would not make the assessments, that it was too dangerous for him, and that he would pay a fine instead. He then hurried out of the tavern, passing John Fries heading in. Fries was unaware that Chapman and his assistants were busy assessing the township so he greeted Chapman cordially and apologized for the way he and Foulke had been treated at the township meeting on February 23. Fries assured Chapman that the assessor would not have been so insulted had he been present, but he had been away on business. When the other assessors arrived, Fries greeted them as well, shook their hands, and bought them a round of drinks, and then he left them to their meal in their private room. After dinner, Fries rejoined the assessors and warned them that it would not be wise to make the assessments. He could not restrain the entire community, and he worried especially that Chapman and Foulke— both small men—could be hurt. Chapman then informed Fries that they were already making the assessments, and a surprised John Fries responded that "he did not believe it was an established law" and that he opposed both the tax and the Alien and Sedition Acts. Fries said "he was sorry to see" Foulke there, as "he was a man that [Fries] had great regard for." "I now warn you," Fries continued, "not to go to another house to take the rates, if you do you will be hurt." Because of their positions, Fries the vendue crier and Foulke the justice of the peace knew each other quite well. They worked together often, and they were both Federalists. Fries's warning to Foulke was not a threat but a caution. He understood how much his neighbors resented Foulke and the potential harm that could befall him. But when the assessors ignored his protests and headed back out to their business, Fries progressed from warning to threat, when he shouted that he would get "500–700 men under arms here tomorrow morning by sunrise."[37]

That afternoon Daniel Weidener and George Mitchell got to talking, and they worried that they might face recriminations from the townspeople for allowing Cephas Childs to assess their homes. After all, they had signed the association pledging to resist the law. Seeking advice, they went to Weidener's brother-in-law Jacob Huber, captain of a Bucks County company of light horse. Huber suggested that the three of them should convince the township to allow the assessment and preclude any trouble. But as the three conferred, John Fries and five others had already headed out to detain the assessors.[38]

Just before sunset, as Roderock and Foulke turned their mounts off the main road, heading toward Philip Singmaster's out-of-the way residence, they heard a command to stop. Spinning around, they saw Fries with five other men on foot. "I warned you not to proceed," that you might "get hurt," Fries called out to Foulke. "We are come to take you prisoner." At this, Fries grabbed for the reins of Roderock's horse but missed and instead caught his coattail. Roderock squirmed free and rode off. Meanwhile, Frederick Heaney and the others surrounded Foulke and took him into custody. When Fries returned from chasing Roderock, he ordered his men to release Foulke, and they let him go unharmed. As Foulke remembered, they "offered him no violence but said they would take him the next day" if he continued his work. Fries repeated his threat to gather hundreds of armed men the next day. That evening Fries, Heaney, Valentine Kuyder, and the others convened back at Jacob Fries's tavern, where Heaney and Abraham Samsel were "drumming and fifing." They decided to muster the militia the next morning at Kuyder's mill and march through the township to be sure the assessments had ceased.[39]

Fries and Kuyder assembled about thirty of their men in the middle of the morning on March 6 and marched them to Quakertown, a village just across the Richland Township border from Milford Square, to meet another group at Enoch Roberts's tavern. They sent Conrad Marks and George Gettman to find the assessors and bring them to Roberts's tavern. As they marched ahead of the fife and drum, people turned out at the roadside to watch and cheer them on. Their numbers swelled along the way, and when they combined with the Quakertown men, they were one hundred strong, many armed with muskets but most with clubs and staves. William Thomas remembered that when they entered Quakertown after the half-mile march, they "all stood in a rank and fired off, and hallowed Huzza!" Then some went into Enoch Roberts's house, and others went down the street to David Sellers's tavern. Daniel Weidener treated the troops to a quart of whiskey and two buckets of hard cider.[40]

About that time, Chapman met with his three assistants back in Milford, and in light of the previous day's resistance, they agreed to discontinue the measurements and head for home. Foulke and Roderock headed east out of Milford, and moving toward Richland Township they reached Quakertown about 3 o'clock in the afternoon. Childs followed that same route a few minutes later. While the militiamen waited for them, Conrad Marks made his way back and forth, in and out of Roberts's tavern, carrying whiskey out to the people. John Jameson remembered that the people who filled the street were "a great deal intoxicated." John Fries, by all reports, was known for his sobriety and was not drinking that day.[41] When Foulke and Roderock approached the town, they could see the drunken commotion in front of Roberts's tavern. Though nervous, they determined to try to pass through the crowd unnoticed. The assessors made it by Roberts's tavern and down the street to Sellers's tavern before the crowd recognized them and began shouting for them to stop. Hearing the roar, Fries emerged from Roberts's tavern and called for them to halt. Roderock claimed that some leveled their guns while another ordered "Shoot!" although he could not be certain who issued the command. At trial, Foulke refused to corroborate Roderock's testimony, and Roderock admitted that he spoke no German, so his implication that Fries gave a command to fire is a dubious one at best.[42] One resister, William Thomas, remembered that "John Miller snapped after Roderock, but his gun did not go off." Thomas's deposition was not corroborated by either Foulke's or Roderock's testimony. In any case, no one fired, and Roderock escaped into Richland.[43]

Foulke was not so lucky. The crowd surrounded him, and Valentine Kuyder (thoroughly inebriated) took hold of Foulke's reins and threatened to pull him from his mount. At that point, Captain Jacob Huber grabbed the bridle from Kuyder and scolded the drunk, telling him not to abuse little Foulke. Kuyder then grabbed Foulke's foot and tried to pull him down, but Foulke pulled free. Fries made his way down from Roberts's porch and asked the assessor to step down, saying "Foulke, you shall be taken, if you will get off there shall no man hurt you." As Fries spoke, a besotted George Mumbower knocked Huber with the butt of his musket and screamed for the men to pull Foulke down. Huber's brother John came to his defense, and the two then turned on Mumbower, rebuking him and others who called out for violence. Just then a musket was leveled at Foulke from the crowd, but the marksman was so drunk he fell over and passed out before he could pull the trigger. When Fries examined the gun, he found that the would-be assassin had rammed the ball in the muzzle before the powder. Apparently the same alcohol that contributed to the day's volatility prevented bloodshed as well. Foulke remembered that Fries advised the crowd that "no man should hurt him" and then led him and his horse to the stable. Fries knew that he had to get Foulke into the tavern and away from the drunken mob.[44]

At this point the crowd took out its frustrations on Captain Seaburn, "an old grey headed man" who was traveling through Quakertown on business, and had stopped to watch the excitement and got drunk in the process. When Peter Gable called for the crowd to huzza for liberty, Seaburn remained quiet, and when Gable asked whether he was for liberty or government, the old, inebriated man unfortunately replied "government." At this, Gable, a modest landholder and war veteran from Rockhill Township, ordered Peter Huntsberg, a landless laborer, to whip the hapless traveler in the name of liberty. Huntsberg eagerly laid two blows on Seaburn before William Thomas stepped in to stop the beating. Thomas was also a landless laborer, but a Revolutionary War veteran as well. Captain Seaburn's identity is a mystery, but as an outsider he

Figure 8. Enoch Roberts's Tavern, Quakertown. Today Roberts's public house still serves patrons as the Red Lion Inn. Photograph by Paul Douglas Newman.

provided a tempting target upon which the frustrated crowd could finally vent its pent-up aggression toward the Federalists and the Adams administration. Yet Thomas's defense of Seaburn reveals that even resisters caught up in throes of ritualistic violence could rise above such cultural forms and take a stand *against* their community's thirst for retribution through violence and *for* the maintenance of social justice. As a landless laborer, perhaps Thomas was the least likely person to defend Seaburn. The fact that he did shows that he had internalized the ideals of nonviolent constitutional resistance favored by the moderating leaders like John Fries. Not all had accepted these ideas, but some had, enough for Thomas to successfully end the attack on Seaburn, which was the only example of interpersonal violence in all the tax resistance and public protest.[45]

When Foulke got down from his horse and followed Fries into Roberts's tavern, he was met with insults and declarations by the people that "They would not submit to the law yet" but "if all the rest of the United States submitted they would." "We shall never submit to the law," Fries countered, "but it shall be repealed." Others complained further about the Stamp Act, the Alien and Sedition Acts, and the standing army. Marks asked Foulke, "What is this I hear of you, I am told you are going about this Business again. Did I not tell you if you could not do without it, you should come to my house and I would feed you for four of five days. You do this for the few Dollars you will get by it." Foulke denied this and asserted that he took the rates because it was the law, not because he needed the money. Conrad Marks knew this plainly, but saw an opportunity to rouse the people's class resentment and just could not resist.[46]

Just then Fries received word that Cephas Childs had stopped just outside of town at David Griffith's public house. Fries went out and brought him back to Roberts's tavern. John Jameson then interceded and advised Foulke to show the crowd his assessment papers, saying that if they could inspect them and see that they were legitimate, then he could be let go. Fries then agreed to inspect Foulke's papers, and he ordered Captain Kuyder to herd the men back out into the street in front of the tavern and to bring Foulke's horse to the back door. Fries took Foulke back into the kitchen and left Childs with the Hubers and the crowd. There he demanded Foulke's papers, looked them over, then walked him back out into the barroom and instructed him to wait while he repeated the process with Childs.[47]

While Childs waited for Fries and Foulke, Captain Kuyder indeed brought their mounts to the back door, but he ignored Fries order to clear the crowd from the bar and instead more and more agitated drunks poured inside. Many insulted Childs and mistook him for Roderock: "damn you Roderock, we have got you now, you shall go to the liberty pole and dance around it!" Childs later stated: "I told them my name was Cephas Childs. . . . I had no doubt many of them, though they did not know my face, knew my name." Then someone recognized him as coroner of the county, but said "if he is Childs, he is no better than the other." "During this time," Childs remembered, "I had several thumps, which seemed more with the knee than with the fist." Childs grew nervous, but one of the Hubers advised him to "keep a good heart, and you shall not be hurt." Conrad Marks then waved his sword at Childs. Someone said "he should not have gone about when they had forewarned him the day before, and they made him promise that he would not come again 'til farther orders —'til they knew how the law was." Exacting this type of forced apology or public affirmation from a victim was typical of eighteenth-century crowds. Further, the group said again how they wished to choose their own assessor. The crowd began damning the government, "taking their Maker's name in vain," Childs later complained, adding, "they damned the house tax and stamp act, and called me a stampler repeatedly, they damned the alien law and sedition law, and finally all the laws the present Congress had made. They damned the Constitution."[48]

In his testimony for the prosecution at Fries's first trial for treason, Childs emphasized that last charge by framing it in its own sentence. No other witness or deponent corroborated this claim, but there were several who reported similar remarks about the Fifth Congress and its laws. Further clouding that comment with suspicion was Child's admission that "I could not talk the German language."[49] But they were all pretty well drunk, so perhaps they were damning the Constitution too by this time. They had been relying on it for a month to protect them from the Direct Tax, and here were the assessors taking the rates anyway. Kuyder's, Marks's, and Mumbower's behavior revealed that many were tiring of restraint and wished to abandon the nonviolent constitutional route and resort to some good old-fashioned "rough music." In their drunken revelry, they boasted that between the Schuylkill and the Delaware Rivers they could raise 10,000 men, and they exaggerated the Upper Milford rumor that "General Washington had sent them account that they had 20,000 men all ready to assist them" should they call. During a round of toasts, Childs remembered some in the crowd saying: "they had fought for liberty, and would fight for it again. They said they would not have the government, or the President, and they would not live under such a damned government: 'we will have Washington'; others said 'No, we will have Jefferson, he is a better man than Adams: huzza for Jefferson!'" While the crowd challenged the constitutional authority of President Adams, they selected their former president and current vice-president as elites who could be trusted with the reins of federal power. So when they "damned the Constitution," they seemed to do so only in connection with the Adams administration which was deviating from *their* Constitution.[50]

Then Fries emerged with Foulke and traded him for Childs. Fries was furious that Kuyder had disobeyed him and ordered the bar cleared. He said to Childs, "I understand some of my men have abused and insulted you," and Childs added that Fries "really did appear to be really distressed for the usage I had received." At trial, Childs expressed indignation that Fries left him "amongst a parcel of intoxicated people," but added for the record that Fries "respected me, and did not wish me to be abused. . . . I told him I was not much injured, and therefore hoped he would not think about it." That last exchange is revealing. As was the case with Foulke, Fries knew Childs through his work. When this tax-resisting business ended, Fries knew he would likely have to go back to working with these men, at least until the Kirchenleute could begin to assume their positions. And as prosecution witnesses, Foulke and Childs testified that Fries worked diligently to protect them from injury, and they appreciated it. When Fries apologized to Childs for the "thumps" he had received, Childs in effect told him, "Don't worry about it, I'm OK, it's not your fault," and he was specifically telling the jury the same. To further impress upon the jury Fries's mediating influence, Childs, a prosecution witness, assured them that "while he was with me no person insulted me." So Childs seems to have lied about crowd's damning of the Constitution to contrast their radicalism with Fries's restraint, perhaps to affect the sentence or to help secure a pardon.[51]

When Fries demanded Childs's assessment papers, Childs only had papers relating to his work as coroner. Fries made a quick decision to fool the crowd and defuse the situation. He took the coroner's papers and went out into the street and cried to the crowd, "Hoho! My boys we have got what we wanted," eliciting "a considerable huzza." While Fries was trying to convince the crowd out front to disperse, Weidner and Marks pushed back into the kitchen. Weidner demanded the assessment papers that included his rate taken the day before, and Marks waved his sword. Childs remembered that Marks "shook me very hard . . . threatened me, and said I should be shot." William Thomas interceded on Childs's behalf, and then Fries came rushing back in to save Childs and Foulke. He returned their papers, led them out the back door, and held the bridle to help Foulke up onto his mount. He led them out of the crowd's sight and harms way, warning them "never to come back again to assess." According to Fries, when the men in the bar learned he had returned the papers to Foulke and Childs, "the people were much enraged, and sus-pected him of having turned from them and threatened to shoot him" as he headed from Quakertown to Jacob Fries's tavern. It would not have been at all surprising for the drunken mob to turn on its leader for denying them the pleasure of beating the assessors and for freeing them in exchange for no sat-isfaction whatsoever.[52]

That night, the people of Northampton County met to decide what to do about their friends, neighbors, and relatives who were about to be transported to Philadelphia for trial. Captain Jarret's light horse met without him because had gone to Philadelphia to post his own bail before Judge Peters. His men decided to muster the next morning, on March 7, to follow after a small delegation that would accompany Henry Shankweiler to Bethlehem, where he had promised to meet Marshal Nichols. At another meeting on March 6, Anton Stahler, captain of the volunteer infantry, had commanded his troops to meet early in the morning on March 7 at Jacob Ritter's tavern near Emmaus; from there they would march to Bethlehem and see about releasing the prisoners. One of Stahler's men, John Dillinger, Jr., had left that March 6 meeting and traveled to Bucks County that afternoon, where he saw the ruckus at Quakertown and informed the Bucks County people of the Northamptoners' intentions for March 7. Fries took action to reassert his authority and control over the Associators later that evening when he learned of Dillinger's report, and he called a meeting at his cousin's tavern. He saw an opportunity to restore the community's confidence in him, and he took it. At Jacob Fries's house that night, he called on his men to meet at Conrad Marks's tavern the next morning, to go to Bethlehem to assist their Northampton County neighbors. Fries drafted a paper affirming these intentions, and the men signed it and left each other for the night.[53]

Meanwhile, in Bethlehem, Marshal Nichols was just returning to the Sun Inn from making his arrests in Macungie, and he learned that some Northamptoners intended to rescue the prisoners. He called for twenty men that night; fifteen came in, including Eyerle and Balliet, and he deputized them all as a posse comitatus to guard the prisoners. He further called upon "General Brown," the new Republican congressional representative, "to remain at Bethlehem, as he had a very great influence in that county," but Brown refused, saying that he should go home, "as he had been so long from his family." Nichols then asked Representative Brown "to return in the morning, but he seemed to think there was no necessity for it, and did not." Brown was quick to intervene to stir partisan discontent but unwilling to get involved when his machinations threatened to disturb the peace. Nevertheless, the night passed quietly. The next day would be different.[54]

Early on the morning of Thursday, March 7, John Fries dressed in his "regimentals" and cocked his hat with a black feather, the black cockade that instantly identified him with the cause of Federalism. No one recorded how his men, who adorned their hats with tricolored French cockades, reacted to the sight of Fries's feather, but they all knew that he had been a Federalist prior to the fall elections. As supporters and admirers of General Washington, most of them had been as well. Moreover, the black feather was also a symbol of Washington's Society of Cincinnatus, and perhaps Fries was playing to their rumor that Washington would join them. Fries himself never suffered from such delusions, but he had proved his ability and willingness to manipulate the beliefs of his followers, however inaccurate. It is also possible that he cocked his hat knowing that he would lead any attempt to rescue the prisoners. Captain Jarret had just come through Milford Square a couple of days earlier on his way south to Philadelphia and had not been back through, so Fries would be the eldest and ranking Associator. Marshal Nichols did not know any of these people, so perhaps the black feather was meant to reassure Nichols that Fries meant him no harm and that despite their armed array, they really only sought to bail the prisoners.[55]

Fries and his youngest son, Daniel, rode to meet the others at Conrad Marks's tavern. They waited a while for Captain Kuyder, who had been extremely drunk the day before, but they learned he was too "ill" to attend. Apparently many others either suffered from the same affliction or resented Fries's apparent betrayal the day before because only twenty of them left the tavern, sometime between nine and ten o'clock. They followed Fries and Marks toward the Lehigh Hills, where they determined to go first to Millers Town to meet with the Northamptoners. As they progressed, Marks's son, returning from business in Northampton County, rode up and told the group that the Northampton County troops were already preparing to march to Bethlehem, so Fries and Marks redirected their course for that destination as well. At Emmaus they stopped at Jacob Ritter's tavern (Figure 5) to water their horses, where they learned that they were just behind the Northampton County men.[56]

In the meantime, Captain Stahler's men had just left Ritter's tavern and marched toward Bethlehem. Jarret's company of light horse was less organized. When they met at Gessey's tavern in Salisbury at eight o'clock that morning, Jarret himself was still absent, and the men quarreled over who should take the command. When the group nominated Samuel Toon, one of Jarret's lieutenants, he refused to lead the company because he had no horse. Daniel Schwartz charged in front of Toon, called him a coward, and said that "if not having a horse was his only excuse, [he] would give him a horse and a Dollar in money." They also argued for some time over whether they should wear their militia uniforms. When Samuel Toon and John Fogel refused to wear their "regimentals," the group abused them until they complied. Another man, Daniel Schwartz, Jr., "wanted to go along, but [his father] would not allow it, because he had no regimentals or uniform." When the boy persisted, his father allowed him to go, but only as a hostler to look after the horses. As in the case of other Revolutionary techniques such as liberty poles, liberty caps, and associations, the wearing of militia uniforms—in many cases by Revolutionary War veterans or their sons—further legitimized their actions. Moreover, they wanted to be sure that they were recognizable as a company of militia, not a common mob, because the militia was a constitutionally sanctioned body, preserved for the purpose of protecting the people's liberty not only against foreign invasion, but from the possible transgressions of their own government. Eventually, they decided to ride under the command of Andrew Shiffert, but before they could leave, Captain Stahler and his men arrived, and took charge of Jarret's men. The group of about one hundred then began the three-mile trip to Bethlehem. As Stahler's and Jarret's companies closed on Bethlehem, other Northampton County men had already arrived in town. [57]

In Bethlehem, Nichols and his deputies thankfully awoke to a quiet morning on March 7. By nine a.m., the only strangers arriving in town were a group of a dozen Lehigh Township men, who peacefully submitted themselves for arrest. An hour later, however, the peace began to deteriorate, as a report arrived that an armed force had gathered four miles southeast at Ritter's tavern. Then at ten a.m., Nichols learned that two armed men had wandered into the town, and he sent his deputies out to arrest them. The wanderers were

Figure 9. The Sun Inn, Bethlehem. Today the tavern is surrounded by city buildings, but in 1799 it sat almost alone at the top of the hill, surrounded by a spacious, gated yard. The Sun Inn is operated as a restaurant today. Photograph by Paul Douglas Newman.

Peter Keefer and Valentine Paulus, two confused troopers from Jarret's company who thought they were supposed to rendezvous in Bethlehem. The deputies led them into the tavern, where Nichols took their arms and jailed them with the other prisoners. Keefer and Paulus claimed at first to be out "on a shooting frolic" but when pressed by Nichols they admitted that they had come to town "to see what was best to be done for the country." If they came two at a time, Nichols believed he could handle them, but a larger force would be unstoppable and larger forces were coming.

Minutes later Henry Shankweiler rode into town with William Desh, David Shaeffer, and Jacob Klein, all of them armed, Klein in uniform. Two days earlier Shankweiler had promised to meet Nichols in Bethlehem on March 7, on the condition that Nichols would allow him to post bail and appear later in Philadelphia. He had claimed earlier that family necessities prevented him from traveling immediately to the city. Shankweiler said he had not come to submit but to "see his accuser" (another constitutional right) and post bail. Nichols explained that he was not authorized to accept bail and that his accuser was the United States government in Philadelphia. When Nichols asked the men why they were armed, they responded that "they were freemen and might go where they pleased with their arms." When pressed, they told the marshal that fifty more men were on their way, referring to their own company of light horse not far behind them. Dissatisfied with that news, Nichols disarmed the four men, placed them under arrest, and sent them upstairs under guard to join the sixteen prisoners plus Keefer and Paulus. So far so good, but just then Nichols received word that a large body of armed men had been spotted on the road headed for Bethlehem, confirming Shankweiler's warning.[58]

At about half past noon, Nichols made an important decision. He now possessed all his prisoners, including Shankweiler and the Upper Milford and the Lehigh men. He knew that a large armed force was within an hour of Bethlehem coming from the southeast. He knew that he could take his prisoners and march east one mile and then take the Easton-Philadelphia road south toward the capital. Instead, Nichols ordered dinner. He sat down to eat with Shankweiler, Klein, Desh, and Shaeffer. Tavernkeeper Joseph Levering fed the prisoners and the deputies as well. Besides his being hungry, there are several possible explanations for Nichols's decision. He was the law, why should he run? If he did run, encumbered with more than twenty prisoners, the armed forces in pursuit might quickly overtake them. At least the Sun Inn offered some defensive protection, and hundreds of townspeople as witnesses might deter the mob from employing violence. Perhaps he thought he could reason with the armed resistance and win them over to the cause of law and order. Or maybe confrontation was what he wanted, an opportunity to charge these insolent people, people who had insulted his person and his authority, with crimes greater than obstruction of process and rebuke them with stiff penalties to put them in their place. At trial, Nichols and the prosecution avoided discussion of his decision to dine at this critical hour, focusing instead on the "treason" committed by Fries and the others.[59]

After the meal, Nichols decided to send four of his deputies across the river to intercept the Northampton militia to persuade them against carrying out their plan. The marshal himself understood the political character of the resistance, and he picked for the job two Federalists—Judge John Mulhallon and Major William Barnet of the Northampton militia—and two Republicans—Isaac Hartzell and Christian Roth. The four left the tavern, crossed the Lehigh on the toll bridge south of town, and met the Northamptoners about a quarter mile down the road at about half-past-one. The combined force of Stahler's infantry, Adam Stahlneker's thirty riflemen, and Jarret's light horse now totaled nearly one hundred armed men, led by Samuel Toon and his trumpet, calling neighborhood Kirhenleute out to join the march. The light horse had their swords drawn, and one of the riflemen leveled his gun at Christian Roth then "some of his comrades pushed him back." When Mulhallon asked who led them, the soldiers democratically responded that "they were all commanders." Barnet ordered them to stop, but the troops followed Stahler, who shouted, "March on, march on!" The deputies rode beside them, continuing their appeals. When Roth asked them what they wanted, some replied that they had come for Shankweiler, "that they would give Bail for him and that he should have his Trial in his own County." Barnet reported that the people argued that none of the prisoners should "be taken to Philadelphia, but have been tried in Northampton County." Mulhollan later testified that "they wanted the prisoners, and that they wished to give security, and let them be tried in the county: that if they had done anything that was wrong, it was right they should suffer, but that it was not right to take them to Philadelphia." When they reached the toll bridge, Barnet again ordered the men "to desist and not to go to Bethlehem with their arms." John Mulhallon suggested that they stood a better chance of peacefully achieving their goal if they sent a delegation of three men across the river to meet with the marshal, instead of marching in force. The men agreed, elected a three-man delegation under Stahler, and gave "their Honor that none of their party should cross the bridge" if Nichols released at least Shankweiler, Keefer, and Paulus.[60]

The deputies and the three-man delegation crossed the bridge and proceeded to the Sun Inn. There Nichols conferred with them in German and agreed to release Keefer and Paulus, but he explained that he could not release Shankweiler because he had a warrant from a federal judge for his arrest and appearance. Meanwhile, shortly before two o'clock, John Fries and his Bucks County company reached the toll bridge and joined Stahler's Northampton County troops. The combined force now totaled 130 to 140 armed militia, as well as a crowd of unarmed but agitated participants numbering about twice that many who had joined the militia companies along the way. Fries asked where their commander had gone, and they told him about the delegation and that Captain Jarret had yet to join them. As the oldest and highest-ranking officer, Fries assumed command and suggested that they should all go into town to be sure that the marshal released the prisoners. Before crossing the bridge, they paused as Fries agreeably paid the toll for the entire group—this certainly was not the trademark of an unruly mob.[61]

The combined force entered the town of Bethlehem in military fashion, marching in step to the cadence of fife and drum, donning their liberty caps with "cockades of blue and white, blue and red," and wearing their regimentals. Just then the four deputies, the delegation, and the two freed prisoners were making their way down the hill, returning to the troops who they thought still waited on the other side of the bridge. Judge Mulhollan pleaded with the men to turn back, and when they refused he said he hoped they "would not hurt anybody." Fries said "No! if they would not hurt us," but then added, "This is the third day that I was out, I had a skirmish yesterday, and I mean to have another today if they do not let the prisoners clear." Fries led the force on. Deputy Christian Roth reported that the "horse preceded the foot . . . riding up two abreast . . . and then followed the foot, marching up in Indian file, when they came up the foot marched twice around the tavern, and placed themselves in front of the house, where they stood some time drawn up in single rank." Joseph Horsefield, another deputy, looked out the second story window and saw 130 armed men drawn up in close order and about 250 unarmed resisters crowded in front of the tavern. Fries's assurance two days before that he could muster 500–700 men was not far from the mark, as the total force was nearly 400. The disparity between the disciplined militia and the boisterousness of the crowd struck Horsefield. Occasionally some of the armed men pointed their weapons at the second-floor windows, especially when Judge Henry, Eyerle, or Balliet were visible, but they controlled themselves and stayed in rank. Some in the crowd shouted, "if Henry, and that damned Eyerle, and that damned pot-gutted Balliet were there, they would tear them to pieces." Meanwhile, incredibly, Joseph Levering kept his bar open, and liquor flowed out the door to the increasingly inebriated and obnoxious crowd. Private enterprise did not take a back seat to preserving the public peace that day. Taking thirty of his men, some armed, some not, Fries entered the tavern and found the marshal with his posse. Nichols anxiously requested that the riflemen wait outside; Fries agreed and disarmed himself.[62] He left Captain Stahler in command of the troops outside.[63]

Then the negotiations began. Over and over throughout the afternoon Fries offered to post bail for the Northamptoners and stated that he had "no objection" to the prisoners' trial, as long as "they were to be tried in their own courts, and by their own people." Time after time, Nichols refused, vowing to fulfill his duty. Nichols placed four armed guards on the stairs leading to the prisoners on the floor above, and conversed with Fries and others at the bar. About fifteen minutes into the negotiations, Nichols heard a thunderous series of huzzas from outside. Captain Henry Jarret had just arrived from Philadelphia and had whipped up the crowd, who gave him three cheers. When Jarret came inside, armed with a pair of pistols in his hands, he showed Nichols his receipt for bail he had posted in Philadelphia. Nichols begged him to use his influence to disperse the people, but Jarret replied "that he had no influence, that he could do nothing." At this point, Nichols finally ordered Levering "to close the bar, thinking there was madness enough without stimulating it."[64]

Two hours elapsed, and still they remained at an impasse. Had Fries and his men not been concerned with the constitutionality of the laws they defied or of the actions they took to defy them, they could easily have overrun the makeshift jail as other agrarian regulators had done over the previous three decades in America. They could have subdued the marshal, abused his posse, and forcibly taken the prisoners. Violence would have been the easy way to procure their release. Instead, the Kirchenleute under Fries were patient. Fries went so far as to assure Nichols "that he would vouch for his company that they would not hurt him," but he could offer no guarantees for the Northampton County men, especially as Captain Jarret had stirred the crowd into a fever. For his part, Nichols warned Fries that he would be hanged for his participation in this insurgency, but Fries refused to believe it, retorting that if the government sent an army to the region, the soldiers would join the people. Fries reasserted his belief that surely others in the American community perceived a breach of the unwritten social contract and could see the unconstitutionality of the laws.[65]

Still, according to John Barnet of Nichols's posse, the militia "kept regular order" for the entire two hours and "never separated." Meanwhile, the crowd became unruly.[66] Fries went out intermittently to calm them down. At about four o'clock, old Henry Huber grew frustrated at the militia's inaction. In middle age, he had captained the Lower Milford Associators during the Revolution as John Fries's superior.[67] Now elderly but still mindful of his Revolutionary service, Huber stood in the street in farmer's clothes and called out to eight or ten of his former company to follow him and storm the tavern. When Huber charged up the stairs to the front door, one of the deputies gave him a shove. The old man tumbled down, picked himself up, and launched into a tirade of cursing and obscenities. At this, Fries emerged at the door and shouted "Silence!" He later complained that the old man "was too much of a fool."[68]

Fries then consulted with the uniformed troops about the situation and vowed to try one more time to bail the prisoners. Fries disappeared back inside to see Marshal Nichols who had retreated to the second floor. The attempt by Huber to rush the jail prompted Nichols to instruct his posse to shoot anyone who tried to make it up to the second floor.[69] Fries made it about halfway up the stairs when he was stopped, and Nichols met him on the flight and once more refused the offer of bail. Fries warned Nichols that although it was not his intention to start a riot, he was unsure how much longer he could restrain his troops, who were beginning to shout for the prisoners' release. Nichols stood fast, telling him that only under armed duress would he release the prisoners. The militiamen's patience waned, and several called out to take the prisoners by force. Fries went back outside and once more consulted with the troops; this time he asked them what they wanted to do. It was well after four o'clock now, and twilight would soon set in. Frederick Heaney answered that "since they were come so far, it was a damned shame not to have them." Another shouted out that they "should go and do something pretty soon, for it was getting late."[70]

Caught between his own principles, the marshal's resolve, and a riot beyond his control, Fries decided to appease his men and the restless crowd by reentering the tavern with a second delegation, this time all of them armed except him. All the witnesses, including the marshal, agreed that Fries made it a point to disarm himself before each negotiation with the marshal. After handing his sword to a subordinate and announcing his plan to his troops, Fries begged them, "Please, for God's sake, don't fire *except* we are fired on first." They would demand the prisoners under force of arms but they hoped to avoid any bloodshed. Fries led them, and one by one they pushed their way into the tavern, with no violent altercations between them and the posse. His apprehension mounting, Nichols released the prisoners to defuse the crowd and to protect the lives of his deputies. He refused to accept Fries's offers for bail and chose instead to report the prisoners stolen rather than accept an unauthorized bond. Fries understood his position and left the tavern with the prisoners after double-checking to be certain that Reverend Eyermann was free. Within minutes, all parties dispersed, the streets emptied, and Fries's Rebellion peacefully concluded without gunfire, fisticuffs, or bloodshed.[71]

Following the "rebellion," the participants returned to their everyday activities, confident that their actions would not merit a government reprisal.

After all, they had tailored the rescue to conform to the Revolution's ideals and the written Constitution, using the Second Amendment's provision for a militia, offering bail, and refraining from violence—all in an effort to preserve their violated Sixth Amendment rights. Fries himself actually went back to work as a vendue crier and performed auctions out in public. This display of collective self-assurance further attests to the Kirchenleute perception of their actions as being constitutional as they defined the meaning and values represented by the document. The resisters believed that they had acted in accord with and in support of their Constitution, not against it, to preserve and not undermine its laws, in order to secure the liberty it promised. At most they were guilty of rioting, kidnapping federal prisoners, and obstruction of process, not treason as the Federalists would charge. As far as rebellions go, their action barely amounted to the "most unreasonable riot 'n rescue" that John Adams described fourteen years afterward, but it was precisely the kind of "little rebellion" that Jefferson called for "now and then" to maintain the public spirit of republicanism (even if he denied that it was). But Hamiltonian Federalists determined to treat it as if it was an act of civil war.[72]

Chapter 5
Repression

Federalist leaders—Hamiltonians especially—and even Republicans saw insurrection rather than riot or constitutional resistance in 1799. Both viewed the happenings in the Lehigh Valley that year through a set of republican lenses that overcorrected their vision concerning matters of domestic tranquility. But Federalists, especially those obsessed with social order, used Fries's Rebellion to justify their prior restrictions of individual liberties and military measures. The Hamiltonians' emphasis on an ordered public liberty blinded them to the popularity of democratic trends in post-Revolutionary America, and in 1799, it preconditioned them to view challenges to their policies as threats to order and to interpret questions to their elected authority as acts of sedition or treason. The deeply held beliefs of their conservative republican political culture, together with other circumstantial evidence, convinced Hamiltonians and other Federalists in March that a real rebellion was underway. Moreover, it at first appeared to be the French inspired insurrection that they had spent the entire Fifth Congress preparing to repel. As a result, neither President Adams nor his Hamiltonian advisers bothered to investigate the need for military force before applying it.

Four days after the rescue, on March 11, John Fenno, Jr.'s *Gazette of the United States* broke the story to Philadelphians, warning readers that this insurgence was more dangerous and more formidable than the western insurrection five years earlier. Fenno reported that "a most rebellious disposition pervades the whole county of Northampton, insomuch as no man dare avow his attachment to government; and that a sentiment of hostility to France jeopardizes his life. . . . These disturbances are related directly to the political posture between this country and France."[1] The next day William Cobbett's *Porcupine's Gazette* warned that "If the Provisional Army be not ratified without delay, a *civil war* or *surrender of Independence*, is not more than twelve month's distant."[2] The following week the *New York Daily Advertiser* charged that the cause of the "*mania* insurrection . . . is Jacobin Resolves, and the inflammatory and seditious movements of the French Party in the United States."[3]

A few days later the *Philadelphia Gazette* charged that the "Chiefs of the Northampton Insurrection already begin to imitate their revolutionary brethren in other parts of the world. . . . About the same time that a pair of emissaries arrived at Charleston from the French Directory, the sans culottes of Northampton raised the standard of rebellion. There is a singular coincidence in the schemes of these miscreants."[4] A week later Cobbett added that "merely to quell such an insurrection as this will answer but little purpose. It is a weed that has poisoned the soil, to crop off the stalk will only enable it to spring up again and to send out a hundred shoots instead of one. It must be torn up by the root."[5] A reporter in Trenton, New Jersey, worried "that the spirit of disaffection to the Federal Government . . . is spreading itself into the northern part of this state, bordering on Northampton County."[6] And on March 23, the *New York Daily Advertiser* alerted its subscribers that the rebels remained at large, and that "some of them [are] now on the way to this city!"[7] The Federalist press succeeded in fanning the sparks of resistance into the flames of rebellion for the imaginations of its partisan readers.

News of the rescue also shocked John Adams. Marshal William Nichols had made his way back to Philadelphia by Sunday, March 10, and had reported to Judge Peters that the prisoners had been stolen by "an armed force consisting of fifty horsemen, some in their military uniform, and as many foot." He mentioned nothing of Fries's reassurances that they intended no harm to himself or his deputies. Nichols merely shrugged his shoulders before the judge and explained that "the violence of the ARMED FORCE was not to be resisted."[8] Finally, he added, "I am well satisfied . . . that the laws of the United States cannot be executed by the officers of the Government, throughout the county of Northampton, without military aid; the people are determined to resist; they calculate largely on their strength in this State, and the aid they will have from the neighboring States, and particularly that of Virginia." Judge Peters relayed the information to President Adams on March 11. Peters reported to Secretary of State Timothy Pickering that "a daring combination, and treasonable opposition to the laws of the United States" had occurred in Northampton County and that the tax laws could not be enforced there "without a military force."[9] Pickering then alerted the president. Adams already knew of the rescue from Fenno's paper, and just before leaving Philadelphia for Quincy, he met hastily with his cabinet and issued a proclamation on March 12 demanding that the "insurgents of Northampton, Montgomery, and Bucks counties" cease their "treasonable proceedings . . . on or before Monday next, being the eighteenth day of the present month, to disperse and retire peaceably to their respective abodes."[10] This he did without any consultation with Governor Mifflin of Pennsylvania, whose government also resided in Philadelphia. Yet even before the proclamation, the people of the Lehigh Valley had done just what the president had ordered.

The proclamation ran in all of the papers, and by Friday, March 15, news of the president's warning reached the Lehigh region when that day's post brought the March 12 issue of the *Philadelphia Aurora* to George Mitchell's tavern. Mitchell took the paper to Conrad Marks's tavern and showed it to Marks, Fries, and Frederick Heaney, Fries's neighbor and his March 7 lieutenant. The four then decided to call a meeting on March 18—the day of the president's deadline—for all the people in the region to read the proclamation and to resolve their best course of action through consensus. On that Monday morning, over two hundred citizens of Bucks and Northampton Counties met at Marks's tavern to consider their response. Among them were Fries, Marks, Jarret, and other lesser leaders. To expedite a decision, each county appointed a committee of four members as representatives. The committeemen reached a consensus with little debate and ordered their neighbors "to desist from opposing any public officer in the execution of his office and enjoined upon the citizens to use their influence to prevent any opposition, and to give due submission to the laws of the United States." This they did in complete compliance with the presidential proclamation. And a week later Lower Milford held a township meeting at Mitchell's and unanimously voted to allow Samuel Clark to assess their homes. Fries was present but declined to vote, noting that it would be hypocritical of him to do so. He did remark at the meeting that he would willingly submit to federal authorities if presented with a warrant for his arrest.[11] No warrant came, however. And though the president's message labeled their actions as "treasonable," it did seem to offer the "insurgents" the opportunity to avoid trouble by retiring "peaceably to their respective abodes." That is precisely what they all decided to do.

Meanwhile, instead of Marshal Nichols with warrants, three Republican Pennsylvania politicians—Jonas Hartzell, Nicholas Kern, and Abraham Horn— traveled through the Lehigh region, making speeches to the people, urging them to cooperate with federal authorities. They were surprised when they learned that the people had already decided on such a course at their March 18 meeting, especially in light of the early accounts reported in the *Gazette of the United States* and Cobbett's paper. When they returned to Philadelphia on March 20, much earlier than they had expected, they began drafting a public letter to correct Fenno's and Cobbett's "audacious falsehoods." To one Republican newspaper they wrote: "We are warranted in saying that from the appearances in Northampton during our excursion, nothing like insurrection exists—that on the contrary, the most cordial disposition prevailed to submit to the laws."[12]

The resisters seem to have once more attempted to correct the mistakes made by the western insurgents in 1794. The Whiskey Rebels met several times at Brownsville and Parkinson's Ferry between August and October 1794 for votes on whether to submit to the laws. Majorities opted for peaceful submission each time, but a sizable minority led by David Bradford refused to submit and talked openly of secession. At the August 20, 1794 Brownsville vote, twenty-three representatives from the four disaffected western counties, or 40 percent, voted for secession against thirty-four favoring submission. Prior to this news, easterners had been slow to answer President Washington's call for volunteers, as only 1,000 militia had enlisted. Following the Brownsville vote, more than 10,000 joined the "Watermelon Army," including 28 men who were later Northampton and Bucks Counties resisters.[13] By contrast, the Lehigh Kirchenleute resistance displayed a remarkable unanimity in their profession to submit peacefully to the law and the assessments. They were as yet determined to keep a federal force from marching into their neighborhood, as their own actions and the reports from the Republican politicians attest.

Although Republican newspapers reported the general peacefulness of the region, the *Aurora* disapproved, "Yet we hear nothing but military movements."[14] Meanwhile, the Federalist press continued to issue unsubstantiated reports of "continued violence," blaming the French and the Francophile American Republicans.[15] But how the insurgents behaved or how they were reported to have acted did not matter to Adams or his party because even before the President spoke the administration had decided to send troops to the region. On March 11, the day before the proclamation, Adams and his Secretary of War James McHenry had already begun to build the "Eventual Army," still fearing French involvement and seeking a quick restoration of order.[16]

The proclamation is also important for understanding Adams's intentions concerning the charge of treason. In the March 12 proclamation, Adams—as yet without sufficient information—proclaimed the actions "amount to treason, being overt acts of levying war against the United States."[17] As a warning and a plea for peace, this proclamation did not necessitate such a specific indictment. A more qualified or tempered charge—sedition, conspiracy, obstruction of process, rescue, riot or disturbing the peace—would have allowed the prosecutors greater flexibility upon presentation of the evidence in the trial to come. But on March 12, Adams needed to make the charge in order justify his activation of the Eventual Army the day before. Just five days before Fries's rescue mission, on March 2, Congress had passed the Eventual Army Act, which gave "eventual authority to the President of the United States to augment the army" in case of invasion or domestic insurrection by calling forth and combining the militia of various states for up to three months of active duty without the consent of Congress.[18] Any lesser charge might necessitate only the response of Pennsylvania forces and open the door for Generals Hamilton and Washington to demand instead the use of the "New Army" still in creation. Adams had long distrusted the military ambitions of the former president and his treasurer and in 1798 had preferred naval defense and continued negotiations with France as the best method to secure the peace. Moreover, a quick suppression of the rebellion, whether in fact it was one or not, would necessitate a much smaller and cheaper force than the 1794 uprising had required.[19]

Adams's charge of treason, so early and so unsubstantiated, reveals his desire to flex the new muscle of a federalized militia instead of using regular troops. Hamiltonians would rather have used the "New Army," but they approved of the proclamation and the charge of treason to ensure executions, and thereby preclude other malcontents from considering armed resistance against federal authority. Adams, for his part, may have favored the charge of treason merely to obtain death sentences in order to provide himself with the opportunity to pardon the rebels, as Washington had done five years earlier. The treason charge in the proclamation covered the president's bets. If it was a French-directed insurrection, then the roar of public applause would drown out the groan of the gallows above the weight of hanging traitors. Conversely, if the affair amounted only to riot and rescue, the administration could vigorously pursue convictions to demonstrate the authority of the federal government and then show mercy with the use of the pardoning pen. Such a move would simultaneously display the power and the compassion of the federal government and the Federalist administration, earning them both the awe and the respect of the people. Adams's actions from the proclamation to the pardon, confirm these intentions.

With Congress in recess, President Adams activated the Eventual Army on March 11. That same day McHenry commissioned William MacPherson as a brigadier general in command of the expedition.[20] MacPherson, a Revolutionary War veteran who commanded a celebrated volunteer corps from Philadelphia known as "MacPherson's Blues," resigned his post as a brigadier general in the Pennsylvania Militia and became the only commissioned officer in the Eventual Army.[21] A week later, Hamilton advised Secretary of War James McHenry that "Whenever the government appears in arms, it ought to appear like a Hercules and inspire respect by display of strength."[22] At no time did the Hamiltonians expect that such a display should be offered by the Pennsylvania militia alone. While in reality the state could have easily handled the situation,

Federalists in Philadelphia demanded a federal force to uphold federal laws as a matter of jurisdiction, and besides, it still seemed to them that there was a very real possibility that the Northampton Insurrection was only the beginning of much more serious trouble.

When Pennsylvania governor Thomas Mifflin read President Adams's March 12 proclamation, it was the first he had heard from the president on the matter. Earlier in the decade, President Washington had corresponded regularly with the governor for more than a year about the resistance to the excise, several times after the resisters mustered at Braddock's Field; together the governor and the president had coordinated their response to the Whiskey Rebellion. Such federal cooperation would not come from the Adams administration. Adams's proclamation tied Mifflin's hands, and he waited for word from the executive office. By the fourteenth, he decided to address the General Assembly to suggest the passage of a resolution pledging full state support for any federal mission. The next day he addressed both houses and explained that "Though I have received no communication from the President . . . it is my duty as executive magistrate of Pennsylvania, to call your attention to the subject that if any measures ought to be taken on the part of the state, to cooperate with the federal government, they may be devised and authorized by the Legislature." The message was then referred to a committee to issue a joint response. On the twentieth, the Federalist-dominated Assembly announced that it found

cause of deep regret, that combinations to defeat the laws of the United States have for a second time made their appearance in the state of Pennsylvania, as such combinations are repugnant, not only to the pure principles of republicanism and the spirit of our constitution, but also highly dishonorable to the character of a portion of the citizens of our state. That laws tending to lay the burden on the most opulent part of the community should be opposed by those on whom they operated lightest, proves that the opposition has arisen from ignorance, or the most dark and malignant design.

The "spirit of our constitution" described by Federalists was far different than the Kirchenleute definition. Republicans in the Assembly then suggested an alternate resolution, that the state would "when required, cooperate with the general government . . . but as no such cooperation is now requested, this House considers their interference at present as wholly unnecessary," but Federalists defeated it by a two-to-one margin. Republicans learned that Fries was a Federalist, and they knew that many Germans in the disaffected region had in the past supported Federalist candidates. Under the leadership of Pennsylvanian Dr. George Logan, they attempted to pass another resolution calling for a state investigation into the causes of the insurrection.[23] In so doing, they believed they could distance themselves from the disorder while being assured that the Federalist majority who clamored to repress the rebellion would vote down the measure. This was a shrewd maneuver. By negating an investigation again by a two-to-one margin, the Pennsylvania Federalists drew suspicion away from the Republicans (who deserved it) and toward themselves.[24]

The Adams administration also knew that its partisan colleagues controlled the Pennsylvania Assembly and the administration cavalierly expected the Assembly's support. They were not disappointed. That same day Adams ordered Secretary of War McHenry to be sure to request the assistance of the Pennsylvania militia, and preparations were well underway to begin the expedition.[25] Volunteer cavalry from Philadelphia and militia cavalry from southeastern Pennsylvania would comprise the bulk of the Eventual Army, supported by thousands of militia from neighboring states. But they would not be alone. After he had issued his proclamation, Adams rushed off to his home in Quincy, Massachusetts and refused to return to Philadelphia to oversee the military operation, leaving it to McHenry. McHenry then heeded Hamilton's counsel and moved beyond the authority of the Eventual Army Act, mobilizing the regular army without the president's knowledge or Congress's approval. Hamiltonians attempted to exploit the "Northampton Insurrection" during the president's absence in order to further strengthen their argument for a powerful standing army.

The ink on the Eventual Army Act had barely dried when McHenry put it to action, but immediately the federal government displayed its ineptitude, and this troubled Hamiltonians, who required a good show to demonstrate their capacity to maintain order. McHenry hurried to assemble the force, but recruiting and coordinating troops from as far away as Windsor, Vermont, required weeks of preparation.[26] Through General Hamilton, McHenry ordered the Vermont artillerists, as well as two additional companies of artillery from West Point and new infantry recruits to the Provisional Army from Brunswick, New Jersey, to rendezvous at Newtown, Bucks County. To those units, Hamilton added two companies of infantry from Fort Jay, New York, on his own authority. In addition, McHenry ordered another company of artillery from Fort Mifflin, in Philadelphia, still another artillery company and engineers from Carlisle, and new Provisional Army infantry recruits from Frederick, Maryland, all to meet at Reading.[27] But the clock seemed to be ticking away, and McHenry was not moving as aggressively with regular troops as Hamilton and other High Federalists desired. Secretary of the Treasury Oliver Wolcott worried that an "affair which ought to have been settled at once will cost much time and perhaps be so managed to encourage other and formidable rebellions." He also complained that the president's absence from Philadelphia during the crisis left an air of weakness about the Federalists' authority. Wolcott cursed McHenry's sluggishness in a letter to Hamilton, asserting that "his operations are such as to confirm more and more a belief of utter unfitness for the situation."[28] Hamilton in turn advised George Washington that "everything continues to wear the character of feebleness, in respect to the measures for suppressing" the rebellion.[29]

General MacPherson, who preceded his army to the Lehigh region, also complained of McHenry's perpetual delays and exclaimed to Hamilton on his first day in the region that "the people . . . seem ripe for anything."[30] One of his lieutenants likewise confirmed "a general indisposition . . . to submit to the laws and that nothing but a display of force would reform them." General MacPherson wrote to Hamilton on March 25, complaining about McHenry's insistence upon coordinating militia for the Eventual Army: "I confess I could have wished a different mode of operation had been adopted and which I am convinced would have made a more serious and lasting impression, than my scampering through the Country with a Few Horse, But the Secretary thinks otherwise and I shall obey."[31] Hamilton, Pickering, Wolcott, and MacPherson all wanted to use the "New Army" in a grand display of martial power, not just for the insurgents, but for the American people at large and for European powers watching for any signs of weakness. But the very next day when MacPherson traveled through the countryside seeking guides and Federalist supporters, he saw nothing in the way of opposition, and over the next week he reported calm conditions back to his staff. He nevertheless warned them that the army should not consider the Kirchenleute's behavior as "indicative of any change for the better and I believe a reformation among them will not take place until the troops appear." The following day, April 3, he traveled through Reading on his way back to Philadelphia and reported to Major Ford that he "arrived at this place on Monday without anything happening to me of consequence, the people as I passed through the country appeared to view me with eyes of *suspicion*, but however I passed without anything like insult." Despite calm in the region as reported by the commander, the army marched from Philadelphia early the next morning.[32]

Exactly four weeks had elapsed since the rescue at the Sun Inn, and not a single act of violence had followed.[33] For two weeks before MacPherson's departure, the *Aurora* had published numerous reports of peacefulness in the region. On the very day that the citizens met and resolved to cease further resistance to the tax and to "retire peaceably to their respective abodes," the *Aurora* reported that the "insurrection of Northampton county is cooled down to an ordinary process at law, to which all the parties have voluntarily submitted."[34] Then, following the government announcement that troops would be raised to march on eastern Pennsylvania, the *Aurora* noted that even "FRIES has declared his readiness to submit, and to take his trial, whenever summoned thereto."[35] Although it was a Republican newspaper, the "friends of order" were not deaf to the *Aurora's* reports. And though Duane criticized the Federalists' military preparations, the Republican press joined its adversaries in condemning the rescue and the violation of the laws—removing themselves from the Federalist charges that Jeffersonians had had a hand in orchestrating the affair.

Republicans engaged in a quick revisionism to distance themselves from the radical popular constitutionalism of the Lehigh resisters.[36] William Duane's *Aurora* expressed "sincere regret" that "an opposition to the tax law of Congress has taken place in Northampton" and further remanded that no "Republican can justify the conduct of those people who resisted the marshal in the execution of his duty; it was highly reprehensible and ought to be punished."[37] Duane was quick to point out that Federalist assessor Jacob Eyerle had probably fomented the discontent to avenge his congressional loss in the autumn or that other Federalists had stirred the pot in order to improve the chances of their 1799 Pennsylvania gubernatorial candidate, James Ross. Duane was also the first to report that Fries himself was a Federalist, and by the summer he had transformed all the insurgents into Federalists. Finally, Duane denied that the insurgency had any connection with Republicans or with sophisticated popular attempts to nullify or repeal unconstitutional laws. Instead he asserted that the event was merely a riot by an ignorant mob and as such it did not amount to treason.[38] Jacob Schneider also quickly proclaimed that "none of the perpetrators of violence were subscribers to the *Readinger Adler.*"[39]

When Vice-President Jefferson, the author of the Kentucky Resolution for state nullification and the promoter of a "little rebellion now and then," learned of the tax resistance, he condemned it. "Insurrection," he warned, "would check the progress of public opinion" for nullification and "rally them around the government." "But keep away from all show of force," Jefferson continued, and the people "will bear down on the evil propensities of the government, by the constitutional means of election and petition."[40] Jefferson's quip about rebellions was never more than that, and by 1799 both he and the Republican press revealed the fundamental consensus that underlay the fledgling two-party system. "While the law exists," Duane chastised his readers, "it must be obeyed by every good citizen. There is no honest method to get rid of a bad tax or a bad law, but by prevailing on the legislature to repeal it."[41] In 1789, Thomas Jefferson cautioned against rigid constitutional adherence in a letter to James Madison, suggesting that the people should create wholly new constitutions for their states and the federal government every nineteen years because "the earth belongs in usufruct to the living." Opposition to Hamilton awakened a pragmatic strict constructionism in Jefferson as a tool to correct Federalist mishandling of the republican experiment.[42]

In 1798, Jefferson and Madison led the Republican Party in an attempt to strengthen their hand by augmenting the Constitution. Jefferson's "Kentucky Resolution" would grant state governments the right to interpret federal law and nullify unconstitutional statutes. Madison's "Virginia Resolution" called on state legislatures to collect petitions and influence their federal representatives to repeal national laws deemed unconstitutional. Both states sent their resolutions to other state governments in the winter of 1799 for consideration. Just four days after the rescue in Bethlehem, Pennsylvania, Federalists voted to disavow the Kentucky and Virginia Resolutions by a vote of 43–23, declaring, in an obvious reference to Fries's Rebellion, that "the principles contained in the resolutions . . . relative to certain measures of general government are calculated to excite unwarrantable discontents, and to destroy the very existence of our government, they ought to be, and are, hereby rejected." Republicans, in the minority, attempted but failed to excise the language referring to the resolutions' insurrectionary intentions.[43] While the two parties disagreed about the role of state governments in the federal legislative process, they agreed that the proper form of American governance, whether state or national, was a republican representative system. The Constitution provided the people with the roles of election and petition, and they would not be allowed to expand their power through popular precedent. Early in the 1790s, Jefferson and the Republicans welcomed and accepted the Democratic Societies, but their role in the Whiskey Rebellion made them a political liability. By 1799, Republicans and Federalists alike had rejected the more radical democratic innovations like the societies or the Kirchenleute direct action and had agreed that elected officials and appointed officers would legislate, execute, and interpret the laws with only the occasional consent of the people at times and places chosen by the government. Only after his presidency did Republican Thomas Jefferson begin to muse about using the principle of popular sovereignty to increase direct democracy on the local, state, and national levels, and then it was merely an intellectual exercise.[44] For all their rhetoric as the "friends of liberty," the Republicans of the late 1790s essentially enjoined the Federalists' counterrevolutionary contention that the age of democratic revolution ended with the construction of republican governments. The Kirchenleute resistance represented a rekindling of the Revolution's democratic flame, and thus an alternate idealistic definition of the Revolution's purpose and its future. Yet when they quickly realized that the Republicans rejected their conception of expanding democracy and that an army might march against them, they retreated to a realistic submission to the laws.

Notwithstanding the reports of calm, even from the Federalists' own General MacPherson, and although several rebels had surrendered themselves peacefully to authorities in Philadelphia, the army marched on April 4 to crush what they imagined to be a "mania insurrection" and "to inspire respect by display of strength."[45] Though the "rebels" never fired a shot, the Federalists, especially Hamiltonians, chose to see a rebellion in 1799 for a number of reasons. Federalist newspapers contributed greatly to the exaggerated notion of a rebellion, its supposed French and Republican direction, and the possibility that it might spread throughout the country if not checked with military measures. The hysteria generated by the pro-Federalist media certainly exacerbated the paranoia of Federalists like Timothy Pickering, but even the less extreme members of the party did not need to rely on newspaper accounts to form their perception of events up the Delaware. Personal experience and memories guided their thinking even more. The American tradition of riotous violence in response to taxation since the Stamp Act crisis three decades before also served to heighten the Federalist perception of rebellion.[46] And Shays's Rebellion and the Whiskey Rebellion obviously elevated their anxiety.

Further deepening the ethnocentric Federalists' suspicion of rebellion was the preponderance of German Americans in the rebel group. When South Carolina Federalist U.S. Representative Robert Goodloe Harper learned of the rescue, he advised James McHenry that the Germans were "ignorant, bigoted, numerous and united" and should be dealt with swiftly and sternly. He then put his money where his mouth was and volunteered to serve with the Eventual Army. Hamiltonian Federalist Uriah Tracy went even further in a racist diatribe to Oliver Wolcott. "The Germans" he wrote, "are both stupid, ignorant and ugly, and are to the Irish what the negroes of the south are to their drivers." The state's ethnic composition and its infamous legacy of rebellion prompted Wolcott to agree with President Adams that "Pennsylvania is the most villainous compound of heterogeneous matter conceivable."[47] In addition, the organization of resistance and its close proximity to the nation's capital in Philadelphia reinforced the Hamiltonian perception of insurrection. The rebels had appeared armed, in uniform, and under military command, and perhaps like the Paxton Boys only three decades before, they might march on Philadelphia. If they so decided, they could march to the capital city in less than two days.[48]

Still, the key to understanding how and why Hamiltonians made a rebellion out of a rather orderly kidnapping lay within their narrow, ordered conception of republicanism, much as the Kirchenleutes' actions stemmed from their broader, more democratic political culture. In particular, the Hamiltonian Federalists' understanding of liberty in an ordered republic and their conception of themselves as the protectors of the republic and sole guarantors of republican liberty preconditioned them to see rebellion in 1799. Inseparable from these beliefs was also the partisan desire to crush the Republican opposition that threatened Federalism. Although such a reaction is inexcusable in either a republican or democratic society, considering their frame of mind when the Quasi War erupted, it is little wonder that the Federalists sought to bind the Republicans with sedition bills and alien laws in addition to defending the nation from attack. Little wonder too that they saw rebellion rather than riot in Northampton, when the people took politics into their own hands and tested the constitutionality of Federalist legislation. Even if it was not really a rebellion, Federalists believed that it had to be crushed as if it were one in order to legitimize their rule, regain the respect and deference of the people, and sustain liberty with order.

In addition to all these reasons, the Hamiltonians' own national security program—itself an extension of that ordered conception of public liberty—still would have demanded that they send federal troops to the area, charge the rebels with treason, and push for executions. They reacted to Fries's rescue as if it were a rebellion because it was precisely what they had expected to see. The Hamiltonian fear of subversion became manifest in the March rescue, and the lens of national security transformed the "riot 'n rescue" into the "Northampton Insurrection." For ten months the Federalists had formed a national security framework to combat "internal invasion." Moreover, the Kirchenleute directly opposed the laws of that framework. They resisted the Direct Tax on houses, a tax that Hamilton himself had designed to fund the army and naval operations against the French. They denounced the "Alliance" and sedition laws. And Hamiltonians had suspected French and Republican agitation in the region since October when Timothy Pickering had learned from a friend in Northampton County about Republican campaigning there and had relayed that information to Washington and Hamilton.[49] Correspondence from the affected counties confirmed as well that the Fries Rebels "would join the French if they invaded the country."[50] At the outset, the Federalists—especially Hamiltonians—had little doubt that the rescue and tax resistance amounted to "treasonable proceedings" that demanded immediate repression.

In a short time, however, the Federalists began to realize that the situation was less serious than they had first thought, yet they continued to push for armed suppression. Hamilton himself conceded that the incident was less than the French-directed rebellion he had feared on March 18 when he warned McHenry "of magnifying a riot into an insurrection, by employing in the first instance, an inadequate force."[51] Wolcott, too, questioned even the "ignorant" Germans' capability "of being influenced."[52] On March 20, two days after the meeting at Conrad Marks's tavern, "some of the most violent opposers of the law" from Millers Town, Macungie Township in Northampton County—the center of the resistance—voluntarily surrendered themselves to authorities in Philadelphia. Herman Hartman, Adam Stephan, and Henry Shankweiler all delivered themselves peacefully to Judge Peters.[53] Nevertheless, President Adams feared that if they failed to crush the Northampton Insurrection, "it may . . . be nursed into something more formidable," or as Wolcott worried, "other and more formidable rebellions" would ensue.[54] In 1794 they had marched nearly 12,000 men west to put down the Whiskey Rebellion, had tried several insurgents for treason, and then had pardoned them. Clearly some of the people had not learned their lesson. Federalists, therefore, decided to use the military to repress the rebellion to make an example of the Kirchenleute for the rest of the nation as a further deterrent to insurrection during the Quasi War and beyond.

McHenry had hoped that MacPherson and the Eventual Army would be ready to deploy by March 28, but it was not until a week later, April 4, that the mission commenced.[55] Its objectives were to assist the marshal and his deputies to serve arrest warrants for more than one hundred men involved with both the tax resistance and the rescue, as well as to secure the region from further outbursts and to ensure that the assessors could finally take the rates. The latter objective was the condition for declaring pacification, and it was left for MacPherson to decide when to withdraw his forces. The force charged with these goals consisted of more than 600 regulars and 320 volunteer cavalry from Philadelphia City and militia cavalry from Philadelphia, Bucks, Montgomery, Chester, and Lancaster Counties. The volunteer and militia cavalry from the nearby counties were responsible for making the arrests, with the regular troops arrayed in support. Two thousand Pennsylvania and New Jersey militia would stand ready, surrounding the periphery to contain the rebellion and back up the main force.[56] McHenry here attempted to correct the mistakes of Washington's Watermelon Army by using mainly southeastern Pennsylvania troops to march directly into the disaffected area to make the arrests. Moreover, that direct force would be small in order to reduce the costs of the expedition, the reliance of the troops on the quarter of the insurgents, and the possibility of bloodshed. In 1794 the 12,000-man expedition to suppress the Whiskey Rebellion cost more than $1.2 million, denuded the fence rails and firewood from a swath of western Pennsylvania landscape, consumed local grain and livestock, and killed two innocent civilians and one suspected insurgent. McHenry was determined to secure order in a more orderly way, and he attempted to steer the military measures down a middle path between the president's desire to use only the militia-based Eventual Army and Hamilton's preference for the professional New Army.[57] This course earned him the contempt of both men. While Adams disapproved of McHenry's use of regulars, he later expressed pride that he had "suppressed an insurrection in Pennsylvania, and effectually humbled and punished the insurgents; not by assembling an army of militia from three or four States, and marching them in all the pride, pomp, and circumstance of war, at an expense of millions, but silently, without noise, and at a trifling expense."[58] Adams was right that the bills for the Eventual Army, tallying only $80,007, were a "trifling expense" by comparison to the cost of the 1794 action, but there was in fact a great deal of "pride, pomp, and circumstance" in 1799. And though there would be no pitched battles, the affair certainly was not suppressed "silently, without noise" from the perspective of local Kirchenleute.[59]

By April 3, the Philadelphia regulars stood ready, and the troops from New York and Vermont had reached Newtown. The next morning at eight o'clock MacPherson mustered his volunteer troops on Market Street and they paraded out of town, cheered on by the excited townspeople who huzzahed and threw their hats. One of the young soldiers called out "if some of the insurgents were not hanged or shot before their return they would never march a foot in public service again."[60] MacPherson took the Bethlehem road following the Wissahocken Creek north for about eighteen miles, and the next day the two bodies met at the Spring House Tavern, or "Dull's House," in Guinett Township, Montgomery County, and prepared to move together toward northern Bucks County the next day. Their first target was to capture the man who they thought was the ringleader of the conspiracy, John Fries. A disgusted William Duane chastised the mission in the *Aurora*, writing that it "appears perfectly well calculated to produce rather than to prevent discontent" because "there is no force to oppose them, no body in arms, nor even a riot to quell."[61]

That night MacPherson received intelligence that Fries would be calling a vendue on Saturday in Haycock Township, some thirty-five miles distant, and he determined to move quickly. On Friday, April 5, MacPherson's army reached David Sellers's tavern in Rockhill Township, Bucks County, and established headquarters there within riding distance of Fries's job in Haycock.[62] That morning he submitted two documents written in German to Sellers, which were to be distributed to the taverns and meeting places throughout the region. The first was a manifesto MacPherson had written in which he warned the people not to oppose the army or aid the fugitives it sought. He went on to explain the necessity and constitutionality of the Direct Tax to provide for national defense against France, and he lectured them on the meaning and function of republican representative government. Furthermore, he argued that the tax was fair because it was a progressive rate that burdened the rich more than the poor. Here MacPherson only referred to the House Tax, revealing his and the broader Federalist misunderstanding of the resisters' objection to the land tax, which was not progressive. Like other Philadelphia Federalists before him, MacPherson underestimated the Kirchenleute and thoroughly misdiagnosed the causes of discontent. Although the "necessity of employing arms against a number of our fellow citizens is painful," he apologized, "the consequences must be imputed to those whose traitorous conduct has produced these present disturbances, and not to government, who, according to their most sacred duties, are obliged to maintain order and enforce obedience to the laws." And lastly, he attempted to soothe the people's fears by promising that every "precaution shall be taken that the march of the troops shall not be troublesome to the citizens; all subsistence shall be punctually paid for, and the strictest discipline observed."[63]

The other paper MacPherson carried with him was an address to the Kirchenleute of Northampton County by the Reverend Justus Henry Christian Helmuth, the German-American Lutheran pastor from St. Michael's parish in Philadelphia. Helmuth was a devoted Federalist who had long used his pulpit for political sermons. On this occasion, he seems to have been sincerely concerned for the lives and the souls of some of his flock to the north. He believed they had been led astray by the Republican Party, a body enamored with the atheistic French, "a nation that aims at the overthrow and destruction of all religion." He urged the people to cease their treasonable opposition "during the sacred season of Lent!" and to remember Matthew 22: 21—"render unto Caesar."[64] A few days later "A Citizen of Northampton County" rebutted Helmuth's entreaty in the *Aurora*:

When I behold your *papal bull* with the military manifesto of General MacPherson in the same paper, I confess that for a moment I thought that the iron age of the world had again recurred. To see the man of God, and the man of war, proclaiming similar sentiments and acting in concert, was a phenomenon that no rational being could ever have anticipated. . . . That the general should have lugged France neck and heels into his manifesto is natural enough . . . but what had you to do with France? And how was the insurrection in Northampton County connected with that Republic?[65]

Apparently some Kirchenleute in Philadelphia had also taken exception to the minister's involvement when he preached a sermon on March 17 calling for the rebels to submit to the constituted authorities. Following the service a large crowd cornered Helmuth at the steps of St. Michael's. They denounced him for enterring so boldly into the political arena and hurled insults at him. One man called the minister an "Aristocratic English Bugger," to wild applause from the crowd.[66]

After MacPherson presented his manifesto and Helmuth's paper, he ordered four companies of calvary to set out to arrest John Fries. MacPherson had learned from David Penrose, one of Fries's neighbors, that Fries would be calling a vendue on Saturday at a place the locals called "Bunker Hill" in Haycock. Since MacPherson believed "that the people in that part of the Country, which is very disaffected, generally went armed," and since he had "an apprehension that the vendue might be no more than a cover for a seditious and armed meeting," he sent a powerful force to make the arrest, consisting of two squadrons of volunteer Philadelphia cavalry as well as militia cavalry from Germantown and Bucks County.[67] Earlier that morning Fries had received a warning that the troops would be out that day to arrest him. He professed that he was not afraid and reiterated his pledge to submit himself peacefully when the time came for his arrest. Fries was expecting the marshal to come back, perhaps with McPherson and a few armed reinforcements, but neither he nor his neighbors expected the three cavalry units that were quickly making their way toward them. After all, what violence had they done? Who had been hurt? Had they not tried to the best of their ability to conform to the Constitution? So he continued on toward Bunker Hill, followed by his son Daniel, and his constant companion, a tiny black dog called "Whiskey" that he had acquired on the expedition to suppress the Whiskey Rebellion.

By mid-morning, Fries was standing atop a cider barrel, calling an auction in German and in English, getting the best prices he could for a family in debt—a family he surely knew—when the crowd heard the clatter of hoofbeats and the rattle of sabers behind them. The people were aghast when some of the cavalry drew their swords and leveled their pistols. Fries at first stood his ground, prepared to submit peacefully, until he saw the troopers draw their weapons. Perhaps he remembered his own experiences with the Watermelon Army in 1794. It is possible that he had witnessed the bayoneting of Charles Boyd by a soldier in Myerstown, in nearby Dauphin County. Or perhaps he had seen the shooting death of a sick adolescent boy in Carlisle.[68] The young man was too ill to stand and an overzealous trooper accidentally shot him in the groin and he died a slow and miserable death. Fries at least knew of these tragedies and determined that he would not become another, so he jumped down from the barrel and ran into a nearby wood. The commander of the cavalry, Captain Porter, ordered all the people in the street to remain still until he could find and arrest Fries. But the terrified townsfolk ran pell mell, and the troopers chased them down. They took after one man whom they thought was Fries, pursuing him through fields and over fences, narrowly missing him with the blow of a sword, smashing it instead against a fence rail. One trooper fired his gun at another man supposed to be Fries, blowing a hole through his hat and grazing the skull of the terrified fleeing victim. The atrocities of Myerstown and Carlisle in 1794 were barely averted, and more by good luck than good management. McHenry had ordered MacPherson, "You will be particularly careful . . . to prevent, by the most pointed orders, any insults to the inhabitants, or unnecessary rigor towards the prisoners taken."[69] All this was indeed insulting and unnecessarily rigorous, perhaps criminally so. During the confusion, Captain Porter learned that Fries had escaped through the woods and was suspected to be hiding in the brier patch of a meadow not far away. Porter reassembled his men and redeployed them toward the meadow. Along the way they came across a lost little black dog, who, coincidentally, was looking for the same man. Within minutes Fries's own dog delivered him to his captors.

Having John Fries, Porter then ordered his men to find the prisoner's son. Daniel had taken cover in a bog where the ground was too soft and the cover too dense for the light horse to follow, and Porter called off the chase, preferring to deliver John Fries to the general. MacPherson had moved his forces to Quakertown while the cavalry was pursuing Fries, and just before sunset on only their third day out, Porter brought John Fries into custody. MacPherson was elated by the capture and complimented his lieutenants for their success. Following an examination at Quakertown by Judge Richard Peters, MacPherson sent Fries to Philadelphia under armed guard, where he was jailed to await his grand jury hearing.[70] To celebrate their victory and to observe the Sabbath, MacPherson rested the troops on Sunday, but Major Ford marched his men from Reading that day along the Reading-Allentown Road to rendezvous with MacPherson in Millers Town, Macungie Township, on April 8. The celebration would not last long. MacPherson considered Millers Town "the center of the insurrection," and he feared "an intention on the part of the Insurgents to make some stand there."[71]

As Ford's men approached Kutz Town, along the Berks-Bucks County border, a messenger rode up delivering MacPherson's good news concerning the capture of Fries. MacPherson warned him not to continue to Millers Town but to stop at Trexlertown about four miles to the west and to wait one day before marching into Macungie until MacPherson could come in from the southeast. "Our march astonishes the people," Ford scribbled in a quick note of congratulations to MacPherson, and he related that the people he encountered had offered no kind of resistance even though "some of them were so ignorant they thought the United States could not raise men enough."[72] The people surely did not expect such an army, but ignorance had little to do with their astonishment—they believed that they had tailored their actions to prevent such an extreme government reprisal. They understood the difference between their own resistance and that offered by the Whiskey Rebels five years before. Ford was right about the popular submission, however, as over the course of the following week, while the army first headquartered at Quakertown and Millers Town from April 8 to 14 and then at Allentown from April 15 to 19, most people rather calmly submitted themselves to arrest. By April 7, 13 of the 18 men charged with treason had surrendered themselves voluntarily, as had 7 of the 14 charged with obstruction of process and combining to defeat the laws.[73] Over the next twelve days the arrests and serving of warrants only became easier, as the troops served process on over 120 people.

On April 11, at Millers Town, MacPherson wrote to McHenry, "I ordered a general parade and review of the Troops for the purpose of Muster and to increase the impression which their arrival had made on the people." More than 1,000 troops, including more than six hundred regulars, paraded through the tiny town. All of Macungie Township comprised only 1,800 souls, and perhaps a quarter of them lived in Millers Town. MacPherson happily reported, "I had every reason to be satisfied with the state of their equipment, their martial appearance and their condition in general. There is reason to believe that good effect resulted from this measure."[74] Such "pride, pomp, and circumstance" scared the life out of some witnesses. The surgeon accompanying the expedition, Joseph Strong, reported that old John Kline "was delirious on account of his anxieties for his family, and great dread for the consequences of his arrest. I examined him and discovered that he was in a maniacal state."[75] On April 13, two days after the display, MacPherson wrote to Ford that there "is no disposition on the part of the inhabitants to oppose us." And Ford concurred that as "to any appearances of the people taking up arms I believe is entirely out of the question."[76]

The only resistance offered—which came simply in the form of evasion—surfaced in the face of military abuses, like the near disasters on April 6 when Porter's cavalry fired shots and swung their swords in pursuit of Fries. "Nearly all the male inhabitants, on the approach of the army, fled from their homes," one soldier noted in a letter, "and their wives and children exhibit a very unhappy scene of distress." Fries's neighbor and confidant, Frederick Heaney, was one of the men who fled. The soldiers arrived at his home late one night and woke his wife and infant daughter by banging on the door and threatening his life. Alone and scared, Heaney's wife took off, running out the back door to a neighbor's house for help. She was so terrified that she left her baby behind. When she and the neighbors returned, the soldiers had left, and she found her child safe and asleep.[77] Heaney eventually surrendered himself.

Another woman left alone by a fleeing husband, Catherine Mumbower, also feared for the lives of her husband, her children, and herself. Catherine's husband, John, had served as assessor Christian Heckenwelder's guide in Upper Milford when Heckenwelder's partner, Henry Kooken, was unavailable. Mumbower had led Heckenwelder around for much of the morning but had refused to continue in the afternoon when the townspeople threatened him. John fled before the troops when he learned they had a warrant for his arrest, and Catherine immediately went to Heckenwelder for help. Heckenwelder wrote and signed an affidavit clearing John of any wrongdoing and gave it to Catherine to present to the army. "I do hereby certify," the paper read, "that John Mumbower did not only suffer me to value his House, but that I also found a secure Night's Lodging in the same in that dark corner of the township (being the worst part) but also went along with me next morning to some neighbors as a guide, until he was prevented to proceed by his own neighbors." Nonetheless, within the week the army had arrested John Mumbower on the charge of conspiracy.[78]

Terrifying people like Mrs. Heaney or Catherine Mumbower in the middle of the night was not only a practical method of finding "rebels," it seemed to be a common tactic. Indeed, it was reminiscent of the "Terrible Night" or the "dreadful night" of November 13, 1794, when the Watermelon Army made more than 150 arrests in the middle of the night, bursting in upon terrified families, dragging half-naked men from their homes, forcing them to march shoeless for miles through mud and cold in rain and sleet to makeshift open-air prisons, sickening many and killing one man of exposure.[79] MacPherson's correspondence with Secretary McHenry reveals that most attempts to make arrests came after midnight.[80] One letter from the region provides particular detail: "The system of terror here I am sorry to say is carried far beyond what in my opinion what the public good requires. Detachments are out every day or night apprehending one or other individuals. . . . Conceive your home entered at the dead of night by a body of armed men, and yourself dragged from your wife and screaming children. These poor people . . . always consider that death awaits anyone who is seized, be he culpable or not."[81] Another letter complained that "the troops who derive their authority from the Federal Government, live at free quarter on the people," and still another lamented that "there are about seven detained in irons and I am grieved to see among them some old men, whose wrists are raw to the bone with the hand-cuffs."[82] And one more reported that "this expedition was not only unnecessary, but violently absurd. . . . I do verily believe that a sergeant and six men might have performed all the service for which we have been assembled . . . with such a loss of important time to us."[83] Doubtless many of the Eventual Army resented being called from their farms at planting time; they grumbled at their government and took out their frustrations on the hapless "insurgents" who had necessitated their muster. The Federalist *Gazette of the United States* countered these stories carried in the *Aurora* with this report: "We are informed by a gentleman who has been continually with the troops," Fenno wrote on April 19, "that their conduct has not only been irreproachable, but remarkable for discipline and good order."[84] In reality, their conduct probably lay somewhere in between the *Aurora's* and the *Gazette's* reports, but leaning distinctly toward the former.

By Monday, April 15, the troops moved on to the Allentown-Bethlehem area, making more arrests, serving warrants, and taking bail. There the mission saw its only fatality. Late that night a sentinel guarding the supplies heard some noises behind the wagons containing the cavalry provisions. Too frightened to investigate himself, he ran back to camp and alerted his company. Armed with their muskets, they accompanied him back to the wagons. When they got within several yards they stopped, and hearing the noises again they called out for whoever was in the shadows to show themselves, but the noise continued and grew louder and louder. One of the company declared that it must be the rebel army, marching up in the darkness. A platoon leader in front ordered his men to load and fire, and when they did a tremendous groan emanated from the back of the wagon, followed by a groundshaking thud. When one of the more courageous men volunteered to venture forth and police the area, he found the remains of the "rebel army"—a bull that had been snacking on the cavalry's hay hanging from the tail of a wagon.[85] This was the extent of both the popular resistance and deadly military force to date, but the mission was not over yet.

MacPherson had become so impressed with the popular submission that he wrote Jacob Eyerle and asked him to try to assess Upper Milford and Macungie "so as to gauge whether or not the people are generally disposed to submit peacefully to the execution of the laws." Within seventy-two hours, an elated Jacob Eyerle thanked MacPherson for his efforts in the region and informed him that "from every information I have been able to collect the law which for some time past has met with so much opposition is now peacefully submitted to."[86] In reality, MacPherson had little to do with this outcome because the people had agreed to submit to the valuations at their March 18 meeting, three weeks prior to the military occupation. Nevertheless, this test passed, MacPherson decided it was time to bring the regulars back home. By this time he had thirty-one prisoners and had accepted bail from another ninety-two. On April 18, MacPherson wrote to the secretary of war, "order is restored and the assessments going on in Hamilton and Penn Townships, I have thought that the further continuance of the Troops in this quarter will be unnecessary and have therefore resolved to march tomorrow."[87] On April 19, he led the troops out of Northampton County, through Bucks County, and into Reading in Berks County, where they would stay the night before leaving for Philadelphia on Saturday, April 20.

Since the first of the month, a Lancaster company of light horse had been making its way through Berks County, cutting down liberty poles. They reached Reading, meeting MacPherson's men, by Saturday morning April 20.[88] A week earlier, they had read a report in Jacob Schneider's April 9 *Readinger Adler* that blamed the federal troops for committing abuses among the Berks County people—not altogether unlike the *Aurora's* reports. "Captain Montgomery's Troops . . . according to their conduct here," Schneider wrote, "would be more apt to excite the people to insurrection and raise them against the government, than to enforce obedience . . . for they have effectively already taken measures . . . contrary to the laws of the land and directly against the Constitution."[89] On that morning Montgomery's troops paid a visit to Schneider's press. Federalist U.S. Representative Robert Goodloe Harper—MacPherson's volunteer aide-de-camp—led the troops to Schneider's door and demanded to know who had written the April 9 article. Schneider later reported that when he admitted that the work was his, they "tore the clothes from my body . . . like a banditti of robbers and assassins . . . and forcibly dragged me from my house before their captain." Montgomery then ordered his men to drag Schneider to the town square and, in front of the market house, to administer twenty-five lashes across his back with a knotted whip. A shocked crowd witnessed the first six blows before Captain Leiper's company of Philadelphia cavalry interrupted the beating and Leiper mercifully put a halt to Schneider's suffering.[90]

Three days later Schneider published a report of his beating. The *Aurora* followed directly with an article entitled "Order and Good Government," in which Duane chastised the Federalist army for Schneider's treatment "without any form of a trial." And when Duane learned that MacPherson had released all the regular troops on Monday, April 23, without any courts-martial proceedings despite complaints by German colonel and Republican U.S. Representative Joseph Heister, he asked, "Is there any substantial difference between FRIES and the actual conduct of the Lancaster Troop? None—they both put the laws at defiance, and they are both criminal—but what is the difference in the eyes of the Federalists?"[91] Of course Duane was wrong, there was a difference between Harper, Montgomery, and Fries. Fries exercised restraint whereas Harper and Montgomery gladly employed the use of violence. But Duane, like other Republicans, was happy to heap condescension upon Fries and his neighbors to de-legitimize such direct democracy that subverted the authority of elected leaders and yet criticize the Federalists as undemocratic militarists. Robert Goodloe Harper quickly answered the charges against him in an open letter to the *Aurora* and the Federalist press. He denied the charges that the troops "lived at free quarter on the people" and that old men were chained with wrists "raw to the bone," but he freely admitted and justified his involvement in the whipping of Jacob Schneider. Harper saw nothing wrong with beating a man for publishing reports that he considered unnecessarily critical, especially since they offended his own honor and that of the entire mission.[92] Harper went on to explain that MacPherson had decided to leave the matter for the civil courts to decide in order to release the troops as soon as possible. The *Aurora* printed six affidavits confirming Schneider's version of events later that month, but no convictions were ever secured for the beating.[93] Then in early May an armed mob visited William Duane's printing office and demanded to know the identity of an anonymous correspondent whom Duane had quoted regarding Schneider's beating. One thug held a gun to his head and threatened to kill him and others then beat him severely, but Duane never revealed his source.[94]

In the end, it seems Schneider's and Duane's fears about the effect of the federal force were not unfounded. In three weeks they had spent $80,000 from the federal treasury, beat up one newspaper editor and inspired the thrashing of another, terrified women and children, killed a bull, nearly shot one man through the head and almost splayed another in two. While this was certainly an improvement over the performance of the Watermelon Army in 1794, it was still an unnecessary use of military force against a civilian population. Not once did the "rebels" offer anything resembling armed resistance as had the Massachusetts Regulators, and unlike the Whiskey Rebels, they had unanimously voted to submit to the laws two weeks before the army marched. MacPherson complained that the "Terror which they [the insurgents] have inspired among the peaceable part of the Inhabitants has rendered even the well affected averse from giving intelligence, and they appear to conceal their plans with great ease."[95] Yet the ease of their concealment came not from the "Terror" but in reality from the fact that the "rebels" had nothing to conceal. There was no planned resistance. Their plan was to nonviolently obstruct the collection of the Direct Tax until the Sixth Congress responded to their petitions and until they were sure that other counties and other states were complying with the tax. Some expected to be prosecuted for their refusal to pay the rate, and perhaps for disturbing the peace, but none even remotely expected to be charged with treason and sedition and to be hunted down by a federal army. They had intended to oppose the tax and the Sedition Act in such a way as to prevent a repeat of the Watermelon Army's abuses or the open battle of Shays's Rebellion. They did not intend to be insurgents. The irony of the situation must have been particularly bitter, yet still they submitted and wisely did not allow the military presence to inspire retaliation.

General MacPherson released most of the regulars on the Monday following Schneider's whipping, and by Wednesday he and his volunteers triumphantly rode back to Philadelphia, "met near the city by the Infantry and Artillery Blues, together with the Volunteer Grenadiers who escorted him" into cheering crowds along the streets of town.[96] A week later, with John Fries's trial for treason well underway, MacPherson in a public ceremony "thanked all those troops, regular and militia, for sacrificing their time and effort," and he especially thanked his aide-de-camp, Robert Goodloe Harper, and Captain Montgomery's Lancaster light horse.[97]

Despite the easy success and the Kirchenleutes' complete compliance with the occupying force, Hamilton and McHenry still feared the explosiveness of the region. They demanded that the militia stay on guard. Throughout the summer, letters between them and their field commanders traveled back and forth with orders for the positioning of regular troops still stationed in the area and arguments over the size of the around-the-clock military guard necessary to prevent the rescue of Fries.[98] In July, correspondence from the discontented counties still warned Hamilton and McHenry that the people "would join the French if they invaded the country."[99] Yet even more than for preemptive reasons, Hamiltonians calculated their overreaction to assert their authority and to protect their conception of ordered liberty. As the trials approached in late April, President Adams and the Hamiltonians began to see the truth. The French had nothing to do with the tax resistance or the rescue, and the Kirchenleute had no subversive or insurrectionary designs. Nevertheless, the Hamiltonians persisted in their pursuit of treason convictions and executions for the leaders of the resistance. The image of John Fries swinging from a gallows would serve as another component of their national security framework by upholding public order and warning the people against any future challenges to the wisdom or authority of Federalist government. While their original misconception of the tax resistance and rescue as an insurrection may be understandable, the Hamiltonian demand for the execution of undeserving men certainly was not. It revealed to the Republicans, other more moderate Federalists, President Adams, the American people, and especially the Kirchenleute, the possible dangers in republican government when the governors not only lose faith in the governed, but also hold them in contempt.

Chapter 6
Injustice

As John Adams found in 1800, it was (and still is) difficult to describe the Kirchenleute tax resistance and the rescue of federal prisoners as an insurrection. While they certainly broke the law, the question is, which laws did they break? It is a far stretch to contend that they committed treason and "levied war" against the government of the United States, as those terms and the Federalist prosecution team implied. At the same time, the events of 1798 and 1799 were too organized, nonviolent, and politically sophisticated to be dismissed as a riot. In fact, the Sedition Act best describes the crimes committed by the Kirchenleute. Its first section outlawed conspiracies and combinations with the intent to oppose any measure of government and prescribed fines not to exceed $5,000 and prison terms not longer than five years. In April the prosecution sought twenty-seven indictments against ninety-one persons for conspiracy, rescue, and obstruction of process.[1] But in March, the Federalist press had warned the people that the "Northampton Insurrection" was only the beginning of a French-directed system of terror that ultimately would embroil the infant nation in a bloody civil war between Federalist supporters of republican government and the Francophile democrats of the opposition party. As a result, Federalist District Attorney William Rawle, the same prosecutor of the Whiskey Rebels in 1795, sought eleven indictments for treason and secured ten true bills.

Treason, sedition, insurrection, rebellion, obstruction, and rescue were the words used by Hamiltonians, Federalist prosecutors, and the Federalist bench to describe the winter's events. Of those terms, only the last two seem to accurately reflect the experience. This was a nonviolent obstruction of one law and a vocal constitutional opposition to the package of Federalist legislation in the Fifth Congress. It represented a logical, if radical, extension of the Revolutionary theory of popular sovereignty that, while not immediately threatening federal authority, could in time diminish its ability to rule. Federalists, and perhaps even Republicans, must have wondered what if other people in other states began making the same democratic demands? How long would it be until the central government died a death of a thousand cuts? Of course, creative revolutionaries could have imagined a safer, more direct popular role to be appended to the Constitution to augment the right of petition, perhaps some sort of national system of initiative and referendum, but neither infant political party intended to be so boldly democratic. Republicans advocated petitioning and state government nullification while Federalists spurned all questioning of elected national authority. Both parties believed that people must be made to know that representative republicanism, not direct democracy, was the legitimate source of lawmaking in America: elected representatives made and executed laws and the people's role in legislation began and ended on Election Day. They could petition, but they had no right to disobey established laws whether under reconsideration or not. Hamiltonians, other Federalists, and even Republicans created the "Northampton Insurrection" out of the resistance movement and rescue in order to make these points crystal clear to other would-be democratic popular constitutionalists.

The legal proceedings against John Fries and his Lehigh Valley neighbors began even before MacPherson and his men returned from the field. On April 12, a federal grand jury heard the case against Fries on the charge of treason, fulfilling the goals of the president's proclamation a month before. In the days that followed, the grand jury remained extremely busy, indicting ninety-one other "rebels" on felony and misdemeanor charges varying from treason and conspiracy to rescue, prison breach, obstruction of process, and "uttering seditious statements."[2] With the exception of the treason counts, the Sedition Act proved an effective Federalist tool for indictment. While Fries sat in jail, guarded around the clock and denied visitation (even by his wife), some anonymous Philadelphia Republicans worked to provide him with legal counsel.[3] Their first choice was an obvious one, celebrated Republican lawyer and former Pennsylvania secretary of state Alexander James Dallas. To balance the defense team in the eyes of the jury, they approached a local Federalist attorney (and Quaker) William Lewis, without telling either of the two about the other—Dallas and Lewis were bitter rivals. When the two learned of their unexpected partnership, sparks quickly flew. The older and more experienced Lewis insulted Dallas's courtroom abilities, and Dallas brashly challenged him to a duel. Only the lead prosecutor, U.S. District Attorney William Rawle, could mediate the squabble and cool off the heated tempers. Dallas and Lewis mutually apologized and agreed to work together on what all three of the lawyers agreed would be an extremely important case for the legal future of the young nation.[4]

The defense planned to undo the precedent of bringing treason charges for the action of combining to defeat a single federal law that William Rawle had established in the cases of *U.S. v. Vigol* and *U.S. v. Mitchell* in the 1795 Whiskey Rebellion trials. Rawle argued then, and he planned to do so again in

1799, that such a combination in arms was indeed "levying war against the United States." Not coincidentally, Lewis had served on the defense team opposite Rawle in 1795, so he was a natural choice for Fries's defense.[5] In his charge to the grand jury, Associate U.S. Supreme Court Justice James Iredell accepted the 1795 definition of treason when he instructed the jurors that "if . . . the intention was to prevent by force of arms the execution of any act of the Congress . . . altogether . . . any forcible opposition . . . was a levying of war . . . and of course an act of treason." "But," he continued, "if the intention was merely to defeat its operation in a particular instance . . . it did not amount to the crime of treason." Iredell's charge played right into the prosecution's hands, and he had to know that was true since the other judge presiding over the case with him, Judge Richard Peters, had presided over the *Vigol* and *Mitchell* cases in 1795. But Iredell went further. In order to justify the treason count, he spent several minutes explaining the danger of the international crisis with France to the jury. He then finished with this charge: "If you suffer this government to be destroyed, what chance have you for any other? . . . Anarchy will ride triumphant, and all lovers of order, decency, truth and justice be trampled under foot. May that God, whose peculiar providence seems often to have interposed to save these United States from destruction, preserve us from this worst of all evils!"[6] Judge Iredell made it clear to the members of the grand jury that it was their duty to help the Almighty preserve the union. They did not disappoint him, returning a true bill of indictment against John Fries.

Jury selection for Fries's trial began in the last days of April, and the sensational trial opened to his plea of "Not Guilty" before an overflowing gallery on April 30 in front of Peters and Iredell.[7] Peters had accompanied the Eventual Army the month before and and headed the investigations into the tax resistance in the Lehigh region. It is thus questionable whether he should have remained on the bench for Fries's trial because of his preformed opinions. Prior to the trial, Judge Iredell already had decided that the defendants were guilty of treason. A week after the rescue he had recorded that he hoped to see "some of the insurgents punished."[8] And just days before the trial was scheduled to begin, Timothy Pickering wrote to both judges explaining to them why he believed that Fries was guilty of treason. Pickering later told Adams that he "knew that the two judges were perfectly agreed as to the treasonable matter" before the trial began, and that they agreed upon "the guilt of the prisoner."[9] Lewis understood the prejudice and presented a pretrial motion to remove the trial from Philadelphia to the region of the alleged criminal conduct. Making matters worse, the jury was stacked against his client. Seven were from Philadelphia, two were from Northampton County, and only three were from Fries's home county of Bucks. Only two of the jurors spoke German. Lewis cited the Judiciary Act of 1789, "That in cases punishable with death, the trial shall be had in the county where the offense was committed" and argued that a Philadelphia trial violated his client's Sixth Amendment constitutional rights as well. Peters and Iredell would not tolerate any delays, however, and they informed Lewis that justice was blind regardless of the venue.[10] Fries never had much of a chance for a fair trial.

In spite of their prejudices, Peters and Iredell were on the bench when Rawle's assistant, none other than Northampton Federalist and former U.S. Representative Samuel Sitgreaves, opened the prosecution's case. Sitgreaves was still bitter that these same Kirchenleute rebels had defeated his handpicked Federalist successor, Jacob Eyerle, in the October elections. The case he presented was not solely of his own making, however; William Rawle deserves most of the credit since his prosecution of Vigol and Mitchell had created the notion that armed opposition to defeat a federal law constituted treason. But even without those precedents, the prosecution would have had little choice but to pursue a treason conviction in light of the president's March 12 proclamation and the pressure from other Federalist politicians and the Federalist media. The prosecution's case was thus no surprise to anyone.

When Sitgreaves opened with the charge of treason, he had to thoroughly explain the law, "which shall consist only in levying war" against the United States "or in adhering to their enemies or giving them aid and comfort." He planned to apply the first part of that definition against Fries, but he knew from the first this would be a difficult task, given the nonviolent posture of the tax resistance and rescue. No matter, Sitgreaves argued, because "war may be sufficiently levied against the United States, although no violence may be used, and although no battle may be fought." "If the arrangements are made," he explained, "and the numbers of men actually appear so as to procure the object they have in view by intimidation as well as by actual force, that will constitute the offense." In other words, the intent to levy war was the same as actually levying war if the perpetrators achieved their goals. Furthermore, treason was to "defeat the operation of the laws of the government; any insurrection, I will be bold to say, to defeat the execution of public laws amounts to treason," and the motives for such actions were immaterial.[11] Sitgreaves's definition was indeed bold. He intended to show that the Kirchenleute's use of the militia and their carrying of arms—actions they believed they were constitutionally entitled to take in defense of perceived violations of their constitutional rights— signified their intention to levy war, and that only the marshal's prudence, not Fries's, had forestalled actual warfare. He claimed that "Fries ordered his men to fire" at Everhard Foulke in front of Enoch Roberts's tavern on March 6 (though he produced no witness to testify to this), that Fries sometimes carried "a large horse pistol" and a sword, and that Fries talked of "skirmishing" with federal officials.[12] He and Rawle charged that Fries had intended to obstruct the federal law and had led the armed force into Bethlehem on March 7 and that the combination of those acts constituted treason.

Sitgreaves continued speaking for most of the day until the court adjourned, waiting for the next morning, Wednesday, May 1, to bring forth witnesses. Over the following five days, Sitgreaves and Rawle called the first of their eighteen witnesses, consisting of rebuffed assessors, the marshal, his deputies, and even Judge Peters himself. The charge of treason only required two witnesses of the "overt act of levying war," but even eighteen did not seem to be enough. Most of them provided the jury with hearsay testimony from other sources not present, and Peters and Iredell admitted it all. Jacob Eyerle's testimony was full of hearsay, such as: "Mr. Dixon told us," and "a person who was along with me, I do not recollect who, told me that they were," and most incredible, "I had received information . . . from the commissioner in Bucks, that he had received information from a gentleman in Philadelphia that . . ." By the twentieth century, hearsay testimony had become inadmissible in American courts, but in 1799 it was fair game even for capital cases like Fries's.[13]

Rawle and Sitgreaves began with the Northampton County common pleas judge William Henry, who had been with Marshal Nichols in Bethlehem at the rescue and had taken depositions in Millers Town in January. They opened with Henry in order to impress the jury right out of the gate with an authoritative and credible witness. Henry testified to the general dissatisfaction with the tax law in Northampton County and then about the particulars of the March 7 rescue. Rawle and Sitgreaves followed Henry with members of the posse: William and John Barnett, Christian Winters, Christian Roths, Philip Schlaugh, Joseph Horsefield, John Mulhollan, and U.S. Mashal William Nichols. Then they turned to assessors Jacob Eyerle, James Chapman, Cephas Childs, and John Roderock, and finally to witnesses from Lower Milford, including some of the smaller fish such as Samuel Toon, Andrew Shiffert, John Dillinger, William Thomas, and George Mitchell. Rawle and Sitgreaves finished with their most credible witness, none other than Judge Peters himself, on Monday morning, May 6. One can only imagine the impression this made on the jury, to see the impartial judge presiding over that very case give testimony for the prosecution. Here is just one gem from his testimony wherein he speculates on what might have happened without a military suppression, arrests, or trials: "I did believe that unless the army had gone through the whole country, there would have been the most atrocious instances of violence."[14] Peters testified mostly about events he had heard about through his deposition work in the region while MacPherson's army was capturing the rebels. He also spoke of

John Fries's signed admission of guilt concerning the rescue, evidence he had taken on April 6 in Quakertown. By the end of the prosecution's case, Fries did not have a chance, and events both inside and out of the courtroom ensured it.

Before, during, and after the prosecution's presentation, Federalist newspapers and Hamiltonian politicians all clamored for Fries's and others' convictions. A treason conviction would carry a death sentence, and a dead John Fries would serve as a significant deterrent to popular outbursts criticizing government and challenging its authority, stemming future insurrections that might threaten the government and subject the United States to foreign invasion. The call for executions had begun even before their capture. On March 30, before the trial, the Federalist *Porcupine's Gazette* had demanded that "the principals of the insurrection must be eradicated, or anarchy must ensue."[15] Hamiltonians such as Timothy Pickering believed that Washington's leniency with the Whiskey Rebels had allowed such a spirit of insurrection to survive in 1799.[16] Another Hamiltonian, Senator Uriah Tracy of Connecticut insisted that "if some executions are not had of the most notorious offenders—I shall regret the events of leniency in '94 & '99—as giving a fatal stroke to government."[17] In 1794 none of the principal leaders of the insurrection had been apprehended, much to the government's embarrassment. David Bradford, the most influential and most radical of the leaders, fled the country and never faced a jury. This time they had a "leader," and they were determined not to let him slip away.

On the day that the prosecution rested, Senator Tracy noted the popular sympathy for Fries exhibited in the streets before the courthouse. Fearful of the political effects of the trial, Tracy begged of McHenry, "Why in God's name is not the Alien law enforced?"[18] Tracy was referring to the Irish and Germans demonstrating in the streets as well as the accused, and he asked a very astute question, one that no other Federalist had yet bothered to consider. Not until a week after Fries's conviction for treason did John Adams wonder, "Is Fries a native or a foreigner?"[19] Adams, Pickering, Wolcott, McHenry, and Hamilton all knew from the beginning that most of the resisters were German speakers. Yet not once in the two months since the rescue had even one of them inquired of Fries's citizenship. All of them had a hand in the Alien Act, and Adams had signed it into law, but when an opportunity arose to consider it they balked. They chose to ignore the Alien Act, designed to defuse such situations peacefully with deportations and instead demanded that Rawle charge Fries with treason in order to secure his execution. Even though the Alien Act would not have applied to Fries, an American-born citizen, Adams and the Hamiltonians did not know this and their failure even to consider it further attests to their intention to make an example of Fries through the charge of treason. Also indicted for sedition was the Reverend Jacob Eyermann, and as a recent immigrant, he did fit the bill for the Alien Act, but the Federalist prosecution ignored it in his case as well. In Fries's and Eyermann's cases, multiple laws had been broken, so the Alien Act, while it might have more expediently removed the problem if it had applied, seemed insufficient to procure justice for the injured party, the United States. What would have been an even better fit for Fries's crime would have been the Sedition Act. And that is precisely what Dallas and Lewis were prepared to argue.

Dallas opened the defense case on Monday afternoon, and his address to the jury lasted well into the next day. Thomas Carpenter, the court reporter, recorded over twenty-three pages of a speech spanning more than seven hours in which Dallas traced the crime of treason from its English common law origins, through colonial law, and into the present. He argued that Fries and his neighbors did not intend to "levy war against the United States." They had only opposed one specific law, not the laws of the United States in general, and the absence of violence should have mitigated the accusation of the action or even intention of levying war. Moreover, the moment that they "effected the rescue," Dallas pleaded, "did they not disperse?"[20] They were guilty only of kidnapping federal prisoners and obstructing taxes. They certainly did not intend to overthrow the government of the United States or break from the Union. Fries was guilty of a crime, Dallas conceded, but that crime was sedition, not treason. "Is it not the very phrase of that act," Dallas asked the jury, "that if any person shall combine to intimidate an officer from the performance of his duty, he shall be deemed guilty of a high misdemeanor, and be punished with fine and imprisonment?"[21] The defense, then, would argue not the facts of the case but the law itself and seek to undermine the prosecution's attempt to use English common law and its own precedents from 1795 that broadened the definition of treason to any intentions of impeding any federal law.

During the prosecution's case, the defense had only cross-examined witnesses with questions about whether Fries was armed, about local doubts that the Direct Tax was really a law, and questions leading to motive in order to show the jury the prosecution's political bias. Now, during the defense's case, Dallas called four witnesses in rapid succession. Three neighbors, John Jameson, Jacob Huber, and Israel Roberts, testified to Fries's nonviolent demeanor during the rescue and his willingness to submit to the authorities afterward. Assessor Everhard Foulke likewise testified that Fries offered them no violence and that there appeared to be no French connection to the resistance. Dallas wanted the case to go to the jury straight away. They had been sequestered for more than a week already, and they appeared agitated at the redundancy of the prosecution's many witnesses. Indeed, one observer complained that it "has been a fatiguing, tedious trial," and he bragged that he had "made a royal escape from being a juryman since they have been confined in one room ever since they were impaneled, excepting when at court."[22] The defense rested late in the day on May 7, in less than two days' time, and the next morning the lawyers began their closing remarks to the jury. Dallas opened on the eighth and concluded about sundown, and the judges allowed Sitgreaves to proceed until about midnight. The trial was reaching its ninth day, an unusually long trial for the eighteenth century, and everyone wanted it to end. William Rawle had the last word on May 9, and Judge Iredell delivered his charge to the jury late that evening: "If you are satisfied that the prisoner at the bar was engaged in the affair at Bethlehem, and that affair was connected with the previous arrangements, you must convict him." He agreed with Sitgreaves's definition of treason, that the use of armed men to intimidate officers and defeat the execution of a federal law constituted "levying war against the United States," repudiating the defense counsels' argument that sedition, not treason, had been committed. Rawle also spent a great deal of time comparing the events of 1799 to those of 1794 to cement his precedent for the broad construction of treason.[23] Judge Iredell then advised the jury to convict if they found evidence to convince them beyond a reasonable doubt that Fries was the leader of the armed rescue. He left them almost no choice but to convict.

It took the jury less than three hours to return to the court, sometime before midnight, finding John Fries guilty of treason.[24] "Though Judge Peters and myself were clear that such ought to be the verdict," Iredell confided to his wife, "we both felt a great deal when it was actually pronounced. I could not bear to look upon the poor man, but, I am told, he fainted away. I dread the task I have before me in pronouncing sentence on him."[25] The bloodthirsty Federalist press was not so moved. "This is *liberty* reader," Cobbett exclaimed, "This is the very *soul of liberty*. You shall never hear me inveigh against *republicanism* if I find *all the Courts of Justice* like this—I do not care what you call the government, provided you will ensure me such judges and juries."[26] The same day, Pickering concurred in a letter to the president that exemplified the Hamiltonian position:

This conviction is of the highest importance to vindicate the violated laws and support the Government . . . an example or examples of conviction and punishment of such high handed offenders are essential to ensure future obedience to the laws . . . and to suppress future insurrections. The examples appear singularly important in Pennsylvania, where treason and rebellion have so repeatedly reared their heads. And painful as is the idea of taking the life of a man, I feel a calm and solid satisfaction that an opportunity is now presented in executing the just sentence of the law, to crush that spirit, which if not overthrown and destroyed, may proceed in its career and overthrow the Government.[27]

The job was now only half complete; the judges would not proclaim sentence until Monday, May 13. And on that day, Hamiltonians indeed felt vindicated when Judges Peters and Iredell sentenced Fries to death. Finally, the Federalists could breathe easy. A traitor would hang, unlike the outcome of Pennsylvania's Whiskey Rebellion. Neither were any of the leaders hanged in Massachusetts in 1787, as most escaped to Vermont. Only two lesser men, John Bly and Charles Rose, had swung beneath the gallows.[28] Perhaps that had been enough, Hamiltonians believed, since Massachusetts had not seen a repeat of Shays's Rebellion in more than a decade. In 1799, however, John Fries, a leader, would make a capital example for Pennsylvania and the rest of the nation as well.

But on May 15, William Lewis pulled the rug out from under the Hamiltonian designs. He presented evidence to Judge Iredell that one of the jurors, a Northampton County German named John Rhoads, "declared a prejudice against the prisoner after he was summoned," by vowing that Fries ought to hang.[29] Lewis presented three witnesses who contended that they had seen Rhoads at a Philadelphia tavern around the beginning of April. When Nicholas Mayer remarked that it "was hard that they [the accused] should be so long in prison and so far from home," Rhoads contested that it "was very right" and that the government "should hang every one of them." Concerning Fries in particular, he added that "a man like him ought to be hung who brings on such a disturbance."[30] Cornered and intent on securing a legitimate conviction beyond Republican reproach, Iredell reluctantly declared a mistrial that spared Fries for the time being. He scheduled a second trial for the later that summer, but another yellow fever epidemic closed the courts and clogged the fall docket so that Fries would wait until the following April for his second trial for treason. Timothy Pickering was shocked; "that juror only thought and spoke as every other person did who was equally informed of the facts, without any symptom of malice."[31] But Pickering and his Hamiltonian associates were confident that the next trial would deliver Fries to his just demise.

In the meantime, there were other trials. On May 10, Judges Iredell and Peters heard the cases against Henry Shiffert, Christian Ruth, Henry Stahler, Daniel Schwartz, Sr., Daniel Schwartz, Jr., and George Shaeffer. The April grand jury had indicted them all on counts of conspiracy, obstruction, and rescue under the Sedition Act. They all plead not guilty, but William Rawle procured testimony that the men had written and signed a paper, the 600-man association from Upper Milford, Williams, and Upper and Lower Saucon Townships that bound them together to oppose and obstruct the tax assessors. On May 15 the jury came back and convicted Ruth and Stahler of rescue, Shaeffer and Schwartz, Sr., of conspiracy, and acquitted the younger Schwartz. Iredell meted out sentences of fines between $40 and $400 and jail terms of eight months. The court held over still more cases until the fall session, including Fries's.[32]

The "rebellion" did not pass from the public mind or the Federalists' concerns while the court recessed for the summer. Just days after Fries received his temporary reprieve, the German-language *Unpartyische Harrisburg Zeitung* published an editorial condemning Fries's conviction as a traitor. The Federalists' pursuit of the treason charge could not have been based upon the definition of that crime, but "it is grounded on the word expedient, a ground that has produced the sedition and Alien bills, a standing army in time of peace of which the Constitution knows nothing. And if Congress and the Judges pass the bounds prescribed to them by the Constitution . . . by reason and justice how far may they go? When will they stop? Who will not be declared guilty by a Marshal's jury?" The essay appeared in other German presses across the state and caught the attention of William Rawle, who charged the *Zeitung* editors Benjamin Meyer and Conrad Fahnstock with sedition.[33]

On the same day that Judge Iredell declared the mistrial in Fries's case, President Adams wrote to Oliver Wolcott and requested that he obtain from Fries's defense attorney, William Lewis, a full written account of the insurrection.[34] It at first seems odd that the president sought the opinion of the defense lawyer over that of the presiding judges, but Adams had good reason. He had heard a rumor that after the trial Fries had admitted to a clerk of the prison "that *great men* were at the bottom of this business."[35] Fries was likely referring to the Republican politicians who had stirred up the region in the October elections. But both the Republican and the Federalist press were proposing suspects. Adams thus made this unorthodox request in an effort to determine if the Fries Rebellion really did have its roots in France or among the pro-French Republican opposition, or even among begrudged local Federalists, and to learn more about the facts of the case to evaluate the merit of the treason charge. Because of the January depositions taken by Judge Henry and the April depositions collected by Judge Peters, Adams must have known about the influence of U.S. Representatives McClenachan and Brown, Pennsylvania State Representatives Isaac Hartzell and Abraham Horn, and State Senator Nicholas Kern in persuading the people to resist the assessment. Indeed, when Oliver Wolcott wrote to the president on May 11 informing him of Fries's allusion to "*great men*," the treasurer remarked that "B. McClenachan, of the House of Representatives, was certainly an agitator among the insurgents."[36]

Why Adams, the Hamiltonians in his cabinet, and the Federalist prosecution team failed to pursue their Republican adversaries is a mystery. The accusations in the depositions were clear, and they were substantiated by several witnesses, yet the prosecution summoned none of the Republican politicians as witnesses, nor filed sedition charges against them. Only the vituperative Federalist press dared to single them out for chastisement. Perhaps this is evidence of an early consensus within the party leadership that convicting and executing simple men would suffice. Perhaps the Federalists were happy to hunt "Jacobins" so long as they were newspaper editors or common farmers but still understood the utility of Jeffersonian leaders to manage the more democratic impulses of their constituents. But following only a year after the famed incident on the floor of the U.S. House of Representatives when Vermont Republican Matthew Lyon spat in the face of Connecticut Federalist Roger Griswold (for which Griswold later beat Lyon with a hickory stick,) such Federalist deference to Republican politicians is perplexing.[37]

Adams wanted to get to the bottom of the business and requested a full account from the defense team. If Dallas had been Fries's only counsel, Adams would never have made the request. But Adams trusted Lewis's opinion as a good Federalist, and as early as December the president had tempered his opinion of the affair in his annual address to Congress, when he simply referred to the tax resistance as an "ungrateful return" in which some people "openly resisted the law." Nowhere in his speech did he use the words treason, insurrection, or rebellion.[38]

Meanwhile, the government removed the prisoners from Philadelphia for the summer to Norristown in Montgomery County to escape the yellow fever epidemic that gripped the city. A guard of infantry kept Fries under close supervision, but the jailors treated most of the others rather fairly. Many left the jail to work as laborers for local farmers during the day to send money home to their families and returned to the jail only at night. In spite of this liberal treatment, yellow fever did make its way through the close quarters of the jail that summer, incapacitating many and claiming the life of two men, David Shaeffer and Michael Schmoyer of Macungie Township.[39]

The fever cut short the work of the fall session of the U.S. Circuit Court, but the system succeeded in indicting editors Meyer and Fahnstock for sedition although they did not submit themselves, nor were they apprehended for trial. Judges Richard Peters and Bushrod Washington, the former president's nephew, also presided over the trials of Morris Schwelein, George Britson, Isaac Young, and James Jackson. These men were indicted then tried and convicted of sedition for erecting the liberty pole at the Hembolts' Christmas party nearly a year before. Ironically, the prosecution principally charged them with treason for the sign they hung about the pole proclaiming "No Gagg Law" in opposition to the Sedition Act. The court indicted and tried the minister Jacob Eyermann for prison breach, conspiracy to oppose the Direct Tax law, and counseling and advising an unlawful combination and conspiracy, the latter two charges of course being brought under the auspices of the Sedition Act. Eyermann had fled Pennsylvania after his rescue on March 7, making his way into New York, where he was apprehended and brought back to Pennsylvania for trial. On October 16, William Rawle prosecuted the case, but Eyermann could afford no attorney, and none was offered to him save for advice from the bench. Rawle called six witnesses, including Judge Peters, William Nichols, and Jacob Eyerle, who again regaled the jury with an earful of hearsay testimony. Judge Washington delivered the charge to the jury: "From all the testimony, it appears that the prisoner, in his previous conduct, took pains to stir up the discontents, and that the armed force came to Bethlehem to rescue him. . . . Farther, his subsequent conduct proves his offence . . . he fled from his country, and secreted himself." The judge gave the jury no choice, and in fifteen minutes they returned with a verdict of "Guilty of all three counts." Judge Washington sentenced Eyermann to one year in prison and fined him $50.[40] The fall court completed a few more misdemeanor cases, but it held over twenty other misdemeanor cases and the lengthy treason trials, including Fries's and those of his neighbors Gettman and Heaney, for the spring session.

On April 16, 1800, a Philadelphia grand jury again considered the case of John Fries and once more returned a true bill of indictment against him for treason. The second trial was set for April 24. This time, Samuel Chase, the Federalist Supreme Court justice, sat on the federal district court bench in Philadelphia alongside Judge Peters. Judge Chase had followed the "insurrection" closely the year before, once writing to Judge Iredell that he was "concerned to hear of the Insurrection in Northampton." "I hope a body of horse and foot are ordered to seize the insurgents," he added, and a year later he still considered the event an insurrection.[41] He had also monitored Fries's first treason trial, and he desperately wanted to prevent the second from matching its length because there were 107 cases on the spring docket. So in the week after the indictment, Chase wrote a legal brief stating his opinion concerning the crime of treason in which he extended the concept of "levying war" to match the broad interpretation put forward by the prosecution team the year before. The defense would only be permitted to argue the facts of the case in this trial, not the law. Moreover, they would not be permitted to make arguments stemming from English common law, as they had also done a year earlier, to draw the comparison between the Federalist application of treason to outrageous monarchical usage of the charges in the years before the "Glorious Revolution of 1688" and the adoption of the "English Bill of Rights." On April 23, he presented the paper to the defense, the prosecution, and the jury and stated that his opinion would serve as the court's definition of treason.

Lewis and Dallas were dumbfounded by this unprecedented move. Their entire defense depended upon the argument that Fries's actions—while illegal—did not conform to the constitutional standard of treason, but rather to sedition. One observer reported that Lewis slowly rose from his seat, lifted the papers, and threw them down on the table in disgust.[42] The two attorneys walked out, leaving the prisoner at the bar stunned and visibly shaken. That night Lewis and Dallas conferred with their client in the city jail. The three considered the situation and concluded that only two options were available. They could continue as his counsel and most assuredly lose the case, or they could withdraw and he could refuse counsel and lose anyway but stand a better chance for a pardon because the public would undoubtedly sympathize with a simple man fighting alone for his life against the federal government. The latter course, they decided, would be the only chance to save Fries's life because Chase's decision to interpret the law all but ensured his conviction. Also that night Judges Peters and Chase paid a visit to William Rawle at his home. According to Rawle, "Peters began by expressing an apprehension that the counsel for Fries would decline acting for him. Judge Chase observed that he could not suppose that that would be the case." Rawle agreed with Peters that "the counsel for Fries would not proceed, unless the papers were withdrawn, and they were permitted to go on in their usual way." Chase disagreed but Peters and Rawle insisted, fearing that trying Fries without counsel would raise public sympathy for the accused and cast a pall over the trial and his conviction and execution. So they designed to retrieve and destroy all the copies of Chase's written opinion, including the copy thrown down by Lewis.

The next morning Lewis and Dallas entered the courtroom, and Lewis angrily charged that the "Court has prejudged the law of the case—the opinion of the court has been declared—after such a declaration the counsel can have no hope of changing it—the impression of it must remain with the jury—the counsel, therefore, will not act in behalf of the prisoner." "You are at liberty to proceed as you think proper," Chase hastily blurted, "address the jury and lay down the law as you think proper." Rawle remembered that "Mr. Lewis answered with considerable warmth [and not a little sarcasm], 'I will never address myself to the court upon a question of law in a criminal case.'" At this point, according to Dallas, Peters leaned over to Chase and said, "I told you so; I knew they would take the stud."[43] Now it was Chase's turn to be stunned. Having no other option, he asked the prisoner to choose other representation. Fries refused counsel, and "a profound silence" fell over the courtroom.[44] Chase then appointed himself to represent the interests of the accused—Fries could not have been in worse hands, and his fate appeared to be sealed.[45] But Chase had painted himself into the only corner that Lewis and Dallas believed might save their client's life. Perhaps a defenseless man could generate enough public sympathy to soften the heart of the president with the authority to pardon him. And Lewis, of course, knew that Adams had been contemplating that course of action for almost a year.

William Rawle opened the prosecution's case with a ten-minute address to the jury. Like Chase, he also wanted a much quicker trial, and with the absence of a defense counsel there was no need for longwinded speeches. Besides, with Chase's definition of treason guiding the court, all he needed to prove was that Fries had led the armed forces into Bethlehem and released the prisoners. After his brief introduction, Chase advised Fries, "you will attend to all the evidence that will be brought against you; will attend to their examination, and ask any questions you please of the several witnesses."[46] With that opening, Rawle began calling and questioning witnesses in rapid succession. Before the day had ended, no less than twenty prosecution witnesses had testified that they had seen John Fries lead the rescue party on March 7, 1799.

Fries remained quiet most of the day, allowing the testimony to go uncontested until the marshal, William Nichols, took the stand late in the afternoon. Still concerned about his own reputation, Nichols testified again that Fries and his men presented him with an irresistible force and that the rebels' threats of violence compelled him to release the prisoners. Once more Nichols failed to recount the offer to bail the prisoners. Fries could take no more. "When the conversation passed between you and I," the prisoner blurted from the bar, "did I not ask you if these prisoners could not be admitted to bail?—I said I would come forward and risk my life, that you would not be hurt—Was it so or was it not?" Chase immediately admonished Fries for his outburst and warned him against asking questions that could incriminate him. But Fries persisted, rightfully so, and Chase allowed the question. "Very possibly," Nichols shrugged. "Had I any arms when I came up to you?" Fries snapped back. In the light of previous testimony, Nichols could only answer "No." Later in the day Fries questioned prosecution witness William Thomas on the same incident, and Thomas also testified that Fries was unarmed. When assessor Everhard Foulke took the stand, Fries also questioned him about the events of March 6 in Quakertown, when Foulke, Roderock, and Childs had been accosted by a Lower Milford mob. "When I took you from the people to the back kitchen," Fries asked, "and away out of the house backward, and helped you onto your horse, did I or not desire you to go out of the way, so that the people should not see you?" "Yes," Foulke confirmed, "you did take me out the back way, and said, Captain Kuyder was then commanding the people in the front of the house; you did desire me to keep out of their way."[47] Fries did very well for himself, but he was no match for William Rawle and the Federalist judge, Samuel Chase.

After court adjourned that evening, two disturbing episodes transpired, casting a darker shadow of opprobrium over the already controversial trial. Right after the jury left the courtroom, one of the jurors, John Taggert, asked to see Judge Chase in his chambers. He told the judge that he felt uneasy deciding this case, admitting that while he had never expressed a wish to see the defendant hang, like the boisterous John Rhoads the year before, he nonetheless had publicly expressed his opinion on several occasions that he thought Fries a "very culpable man." Chase dismissed the juror's concerns out of hand and told him that it was too late to replace him, even though alternates were available.[48] Minutes later the bailiffs escorted the jury from the court and out into the crowded street, where people eagerly awaited news from inside the courtroom. In the crush between the court and the tavern where the jury would be sequestered, one of the jury members, Charles Deshler, lost hold of the bailiff's coat and became separated from the group. He called out to the bailiff several times, but he could not be heard over the din. Having no idea where he was supposed to go (or no desire to go there), he lodged in the first inn he found with a vacancy. The next morning the court officials reported the incident to Chase, and since Deshler had been seen in public out of sequestration that night, Chase quickly dismissed him from the panel and assigned an alternate—the very action he said he could not take only the day before to the juror who had declared a prejudice against the defendant.[49] It was actions like these, combined with his interpretation of the law of treason prior to the trial, that led to Chase's impeachment in 1804 by the House of Representatives. In the Senate he narrowly escaped conviction and removal from the U.S. Supreme Court. His conduct in *U.S. v. John Fries* comprised the first of several charges against him.

The next day, April 25, Rawle speedily finished with his last two witnesses and rested the case for the people of the United States. Fries did not call any witnesses, and Chase asked Rawle to make his case to the jury. Rawle was very uneasy about addressing the jury against a man with no counsel and pleaded with the bench that "under the circumstances, I feel very great reluctance to fulfill, what would in other circumstances be my bounden duty. . . . I therefore shall rest the evidence and the law here." Chase shot back that though there "is great justice due to a prisoner arraigned on a charge so important as the present: there is great justice also due to the government." "It is a painful talk," Peters agreed, "but we must do our duty."[50] With that, Rawle lamented and applied the law to the facts for the jury, which he did for about ten minutes. When he finished, Chase advised Fries, "you are at liberty to say any thing you please to the jury," and Fries responded, "It was mentioned that I collected a parcel of people to follow up the assessors, but I did not collect them; they came and fetched me out from my house to go with them."[51] Chase then delivered his charge to the jury:

The court are of the opinion that a combination, or conspiracy to levy war against the United States is not treason, unless combined with an attempt to carry such combination, or conspiracy, into execution; some actual force, or violence, must be used, in pursuance of such design to levy war; but that it is altogether immaterial, whether the force used is sufficient to effectuate the object; any force connected with the intention, will constitute the crime of levying war.[52]

Once again the jury was left with little choice but to convict. In less than two hours, they returned with a guilty verdict. A week later Chase reconvened the court for sentencing, and he ordered Fries to be hanged on May 23. Unlike the trials, the executions would take place in the region where the crimes were committed. Chase ordered the gallows to be constructed at the intersection of the Bethlehem and Norristown Roads in Quakertown in front of Enoch Roberts's tavern.[53] Fries did not receive his trial in his neighborhood, but he was scheduled to meet the hangman there.

In the course of the three sessions from April 1799 through May 1800, the court convicted thirty-two others of lesser crimes under the Sedition Act—conspiracy, rescue, obstruction of process, and seditious expressions—and it meted out prison sentences ranging from two months to two years and fines from $40 to $1000. Of eleven men charged with treason, ten stood trial and juries acquitted seven. Juries acquitted or refused to indict nearly two-thirds of all the accused, but in contrast to what had happened in 1795, they convicted the leaders. John Gettman and Frederick Heaney were Fries's friends and neighbors and had served as his lieutenants on March 7, 1799. They were slated to hang on either side of him on May 23, 1800. Northampton Captain Henry Jarret received the stiffest fine, $1,000, and the longest jail time, two years, along with Bucks County captain Valentine Kuyder and Lower Milford tavern-keeper Conrad Marks. Millers Town tavernkeeper Henry Shankweiler and the Reverend Jacob Eyermann each got one year and fines, and Northampton County miller Herman Hartman received a sentence of six months and a day in jail and fined $150.[54] Now Hamiltonians were smugly confident that at long last the government would defend its shores, uphold its honor, and preserve the public order necessary for liberty to survive in their republican society by executing John Fries and his two neighbors and making an example of them and the rest of the convicts. Events over the next three weeks would not only spoil these designs but would also bode ill for the future of the Federalist Party and, Hamiltonians believed, for the future of the infant republic.

The loudest calls for John Fries's execution resonated from Hamiltonians who believed that President Adams was veering from the path of Federalism. A series of confrontations transpiring over the two previous years had created a Hamiltonian conception of a disloyal John Adams. The intraparty confrontation began over the establishment of the "New Army" in the summer of 1798. Adams had nominated his son-in-law, Col. William Smith, to the office of adjutant general. Crying nepotism, Secretary of State Timothy Pickering had vehemently opposed the nomination of the "bankrupt" Colonel Smith and tirelessly lobbied the Senate against him. His efforts paid off, as Congress decisively rejected Smith. Upon learning of Pickering's role in the matter, Adams was outraged and so the estrangement began. Pickering remarked years later that Adams "has never forgiven me, his hatred is implacable." Ironically, Pickering's first complaints against the Adams administration surfaced in the same week as the passage of the Direct Tax.[55]

Later that summer Adams passed over General Hamilton as second in command of the New Army under the semiretired George Washington. Adams appointed George Washington commander-in-chief, and Washington reluctantly accepted under the conditions that he decide upon his principal officers and that he would not enter into active duty except in an emergency.[56] Washington named Hamilton, Henry Knox, and Charles Pinckney, in this order of authority, as his choices for his major-generals. Thus, with Washington serving inactive duty, Hamilton, as second in command, would run the army. The Senate quickly approved these nominations, but final determination of their rank in the chain of command rested with the president. While Washington had made it clear that Hamilton was to be his second, Adams had other plans. Without consulting Washington or his cabinet, Adams placed General Knox second to Washington and suggested Hamilton's position be fifth or sixth down the line from the commander.[57] This drew fierce criticism from Hamilton's friends, especially Timothy Pickering. An angered Pickering remarked that "the President has an extreme aversion to Hamilton—a personal resentment—and if he followed his own wishes and feelings alone, would scarcely have given him the rank of brigadier."[58] In a September 13 letter to General Washington, Pickering requested that he appeal to the president. Washington readily obliged and chastised Adams, charging that he "had departed from . . . a solemn compact." "After this," Pickering remarked, "the President found himself under the mortifying necessity of treading back his own unadvised steps, and altering the three commissions of the major-generals, to make them conformable to General Washington's arrangements." Irate over the challenge to his authority, Adams wrote a seething letter to McHenry, charging that he and Pickering had "crammed Hamilton down my throat."[59]

With Hamilton controlling the army, Adams became convinced that peace with France was imperative. While war was actually the last thing that Hamilton wanted, Adams knew that many of his followers had been eager to declare war that spring. The president decided that peace must be negotiated with the French in spite of the humiliating XYZ Affair and his own vow to "never send another minister to France without assurances that he will be received, respected and honored."[60] So in his address to Congress in December 1798, Adams announced his decision to send the Ellsworth mission to France. Hamiltonians were enraged. Not only was Adams's concession "at the expense of [national] honor," as Hamilton lamented, but as Pickering also bemoaned, "not one officer about him had any knowledge of his design" and "Mr. Stoddert [Secretary of the Navy] and Mr. Lee [Attorney General] reprobated the mission to France, as well as Wolcott, McHenry and myself."[61] Nonetheless, Adams persisted with his conviction and, to the dismay of the Hamiltonians, dispatched the mission to France in the autumn of 1799 despite intervening troubles and persisting cabinet pleas to delay it.

Then, in the early days of May 1800, came the most serious of the president's moves against the Hamiltonians to date. On the fifth he called James McHenry into his office and asked for his resignation as secretary of war. Adams charged that McHenry had biased Washington to place Hamilton atop his list of major-generals and on Hamilton's suggestion had advised a suspension of the mission to France.[62] McHenry resigned the following day. Five days later Pickering received a letter in which Adams announced that he "perceive[d] a necessity of introducing a change in the administration of the office of the State." Pickering was not as accommodating as McHenry. "After deliberately reflecting on the overture you have pleased to make me," Pickering facetiously replied, "I do not feel it to be my duty to resign." Adams immediately issued Pickering a terse, one-sentence reply stating that "You are hereby discharged from any further service as Secretary of State."[63]

The Hamiltonians were stunned. Even Charles Cotesworth Pinckney, Adams's ally and running mate in the upcoming election, expressed astonishment in a letter of condolence to Pickering.[64] But slowly the president's action in this case and in that of the mission to France began to make sense to his intraparty opponents. Both actions appeared to them as attempts to appease the Republican Party and smelled of a conspiracy between the Federalist president and Jefferson, his Republican opponent and vice-president. Hamilton wrote to Pickering on May 15, "I perceive that you as well as Mr. McHenry are quitting the Administration. . . . Allow me to suggest, that you ought to take with you copies and extracts of all such documents as will enable you to *explain* both *Jefferson* and *Adams*. . . . The time is coming when men of real integrity must unite against all conspiracies.[65] After almost two years of discord and despite suspicions of conspiracy, the Hamiltonians were ready to relinquish their support for Adams's reelection. The President's behavior in the case of John Fries would be the final straw.

When the time came for Fries to stand trial once again, President Adams was entertaining second thoughts about the sentence. He had read the opinion and description of the rebellion offered by Fries's defense attorney a year earlier and had decided that Fries and his men were guilty only of inciting a riot and kidnapping federal prisoners. They were not French-directed traitors deserving of the rope. They were merely "miserable Germans," he concluded, "as ignorant of our language as they were of our laws."[66] In the meantime, Adams had received four separate pleas for clemency from sixteen of the convicts with the stiffest sentences, including Fries, Gettman, and Heaney.[67] Adams was already determined to issue a general pardon to all the convicted "insurgents," but he recalled the fury he had incited when he decided to send the Ellsworth delegation to France without consulting his advisers. Therefore, on this occasion he sought to conciliate his party by first conferring with his cabinet, or what remained of it after the dismissal of Pickering and McHenry. Upon his request, Wolcott, Lee, and Stoddert presented their opinions to the president on May 20. Adams already knew his cabinet's opinion. The preceding September he had asked for the opinion of Attorney General Charles Lee concerning pardons if the court ordered executions. Lee responded that "Pennsylvania, possessing very many good, is not without a considerable number of bad citizens, some of whom are ignorant, refractory, headstrong, and wicked. . . . I think an exemplary punishment of rebellious conduct is more necessary and will be more salutary in that state than in any other, and therefore that considerations of public policy require that the most criminal of the insurgents should be left to the due and impartial course of the law."[68] Pickering reported, to no surprise, that Lee and Stoddert were "convinced in the opinion that Fries ought to be executed and Mr. W[olcott] gave his opinion that all three of the traitors should suffer death agreeably to the sentence of the court." Nevertheless, it was on May 21, as "Preparations were making for the execution . . . When Lo!" Pickering angrily exclaimed, "the pardon was issued." It came in a presidential proclamation, the *Aurora* wrote, granting "ABSOLUTE PARDON to all and every person or persons concerned in the said insurrection."[69] William Duane exclaimed:

This measure called for by the public voice, and by the more solemn dictates of justice and humanity, entitles Mr. Adams to praise . . . it was dictated by . . . the most laudable and praiseworthy motives. . . . This case, however, we trust will operate with salutary effect on those who are entrusted with every branch of government. It will, we trust, point out to the executive of the present and future day, the delicacy with which the people should be treated.[70]

Adams ordered Charles Lee to issue pardons for Heaney, Gettman, and Fries on May 21, less than forty-eight hours before their execution. Adams had had all his information and could have issued the pardon weeks before, but he had waited for several reasons. He had stalled to give the appearance of lengthy, thoughtful deliberation. If he had moved too quickly, he might have undermined the authority of the court in the eyes of the people and members of his own party. Few people knew that Adams had been in contact with William Lewis and that he had been deliberating for almost a year. Adams also wanted to take the time to consult his cabinet, even though he had already made up his mind and was prepared to issue the pardon against their unanimous disapproval. Perhaps the president wanted a clean start with his new cabinet members after the restructuring and at least wanted to create the appearance that he valued their advice. There was also the drama of drawing the thing out for effect. Although Adams had convinced himself that the convicts were guilty only of "riot 'n rescue," he wanted to impress fully upon the American people that obstructing federal laws was not a legitimate option in a representative republic. Waiting until the last moment would leave the convicted, their families, and neighbors, and other Americans holding their breath. In the case of the Massachusetts Regulation, authorities had publicly carted several Shays Rebels to the gallows. The authorities had hooded and noosed the condemned and had told them they had just seconds to live, before revealing the pardons at the last second. Adams did not play for this level of drama, but a forty-eight-hour span allowed Philadelphia newspapers to print the news and to disseminate it throughout most of eastern Pennsylvania by the date of execution. Many people likely learned of the reprieve on the day they had thought Fries would hang.[71]

From this point onward, Hamiltonians got to work against Adams's bid for reelection. Even after the cabinet dismissals, none of the Hamiltonians had even suggested abandoning the president. But after the pardon, they followed Pickering's lead, and one by one withdrew their support from John Adams. Fracturing the party and risking the loss of the executive office to the Republicans seemed worth the gamble.

News of the pardon first shocked and then outraged Timothy Pickering. Suddenly, the president's behavior of the last two years made sense. As Hamilton had suspected just a week prior to the pardon, there seemed to him to be a conspiracy, or as Pickering wrote to Benjamin Goodhue, "*there was a coalition*," in which Adams was attempting "to secure the office of the Vice-President under Jefferson." "You well know Mr. Adams anxiety to be in office," he continued, "and that he in your last conversation with him, complained that after forty years of public service, he must return to Quincy and follow the plough," as he believed Jefferson's election inevitable. Indeed, after "the pardons of Fries, Gettman and Hainey," Pickering exclaimed, "I can believe Mr. Adams capable of anything to promote his personal views." And it was this "*new system of politics-the coalition*," the ex-secretary charged, which "can alone account for the astonishing act . . . of *grace* to the Jacobins."[72] While there is no evidence to substantiate Pickering's and Hamilton's charges that Adams colluded with Jefferson, it is certainly likely that Adams viewed the pardon as a helpful tool toward his own reelection in the fall, especially in Pennsylvania, a state he had lost to Jefferson in 1796.

More than astonishment and outrage, the Hamiltonians felt betrayed by the president's latest deviation from the road of Federalism. Hamiltonians now feared that this man they had formerly considered one of their own, a most virtuous republican citizen, would betray the nation as a Republican partisan. Timothy Pickering best illustrated this sentiment when he wrote to his son that it was "distressing to find an early patriot and one who thro' thirty or forty years of public life had sustained the reputation of integrity, and who now, capable in his old age, of being influenced by such unworthy motives. It tends to destroy the public confidence; the people knowing not whom to trust, will suspect *all*: and yet without the confidence of a nation in its government, its affairs cannot be well administered."[73]

The Hamiltonians strictly adhered to the Federalist brand of republicanism that could not conceive of liberty without order. Adams, it seemed, threatened to destroy that order by defecting to the Republican cause. The pardons of the Fries Rebels sounded the call to abandon the Adams ship. Pickering jumped overboard as early as May 28, when he wrote that "the cause of federalism (which we consider to be the cause of our country) will be as little or as less in jeopardy under Mr. Jefferson than under Mr. Adams. But we shall all strive to place General Pinckney in the chair."[74] Next went McHenry, on June 16, when he informed Federalist George Cabot of Massachusetts that he certainly would not support Adams on a ticket with Pinckney because "it is clear to my mind that we shall never find ourselves in the straight road of Federalism while Mr. Adams is President."[75]

The schism became a chasm on July 1, when Hamilton began the composition of his pamphlet entitled "A Letter from Alexander Hamilton, Concerning the Public Conduct and Character of John Adams, Esq. President of the United States."[76] Hamilton designed the letter to vindicate his character as a patriot and to destroy the president's campaign for reelection. Intended for circulation among a few influential Federalists in the twilight of the campaign, the letter sought to persuade these influential people to support Pinckney for president. Hamilton wanted Adams out of office. Like Pickering, he realized that Pinckney's chances were slim and that Jefferson would likely be elected. "Under Adams as under Jefferson the government will sink," Hamilton theorized, and "The party in the hands of whose chief it shall sink will sink with it and the advantage will be on the side of his adversaries."[77] When it came time to rebuild the Federalist ship of state, Hamilton clearly wanted High Federalists to be in charge of the yard.

Oliver Wolcott remained unconvinced that deserting the president was the proper political maneuver. In September, advising Hamilton against the writing and distribution of the Letter, Wolcott assured him that Adams "is sufficiently successful in undermining his own credit and influence." Days earlier, George Cabot had similarly responded to Hamilton, admitting that while "it is true there is an apparent absurdity in supporting a man whom we know to be unworthy of trust . . . Adams and Pinckney are to be voted for together."[78] Both men were still hopeful that General Pinckney could muster enough electoral votes to edge out both Jefferson and Adams. Within a month, however, Wolcott finally conceded that dream with a reluctant approval of Hamilton's letter.[79] Thus he joined Pickering, McHenry, and Hamilton and disembarked from the Adams candidacy, leaving Cabot behind.

While Hamilton's letter was still at press, Aaron Burr obtained a copy and released it to the *Aurora*, which published extracts on October 25.[80] In order to avoid misrepresentation by newspaper editors quoting him out of context, Hamilton decided to release the entire letter as a pamphlet for public distribution. As Hamilton hoped, the letter damaged Adams's bid for reelection, but it simultaneously ruined his own career and divided the party. Appropriately, the *Aurora* advertised the sale of Hamilton's pamphlet as, "The Last Speech and Dying Words of Alexander Hamilton," as it effectively alienated him from much of the Federalist Party, which still supported the president.[81] Unfortunately for Hamilton, his career was not all he would lose at the hands of Aaron Burr. This was one incident among several that eventually led to the infamous duel on the cliffs at Weehauken.

Hamilton's letter is also significant in that it clarifies the Hamiltonian reasons that motivated many Federalists to withdraw their support from John Adams. Hamilton emphasized Adams's decision to send a peace envoy to France without consultation with his cabinet, the dispatch of that mission in the "dangerous" autumn of 1799 "without a ratification of assurance by the New Directory," and "the dismission of the two Secretaries, PICKERING and M'HENRY," without "any new or recent cause for their dismission."[82] But this was not all; there remained one final and even more perplexing presidential action that drew Hamilton's contempt.

"The last material occurrence in the administration of Mr. Adams of which I shall take notice, is the pardon of *Fries*," Hamilton charged. This, he wrote, was "the most inexplicable part of Mr. Adams' conduct."[83] The pardoning of the Fries Rebels, who—by resisting Hamilton's own Direct Tax—had threatened the Republic by raising the possibility of civil war, proved to Hamiltonians that John Adams was a danger to the nation. He refused to uphold the High Federalist conception of ordered public liberty with executions and therefore could not be trusted. Hamilton concluded his criticism of Adams with this remark concerning the pardon:

It shows him so much at variance with himself, as well as with sound policy, that we are driven to seek a solution for it in some system of concession to his political enemies; a system the most fatal for himself, and for the cause of *public order*, of any that he could possibly devise. It is by temporizing like these, that men at the head of affairs, *lose the respect* of both friends and foes—it is by temporizings like these, that in times of fermentation and commotion, Governments are prostrated, which might easily have been upheld by an *erect and imposing attitude*.[84]

For Hamilton and Pickering, the pardon of Fries and his insurgents was indeed the last straw. Wolcott and McHenry could hardly disagree; they followed their Federalist allies and deserted Adams. Thus, with the defection of four of the men who had constituted the heart of the Federalist Party in the executive branch just a few years earlier, and with Washington's death earlier that year, the party's outlook in future elections indeed looked grim. This is not to say that the pardon of Fries was solely responsible for the Federalist defeat in 1800. That election was extremely complex, and even when it was clear that the Republicans had won, the issue was still undecided as Jefferson and Burr held an equal number of electors, although Pennsylvania played a crucial role in throwing those electors to the Republicans. Nor was the pardon the only or even the most important issue that divided Hamiltonians from the president. However, as Hamilton wrote, it was the last in a litany of "offenses" and was "the most inexplicable."

Although the execution of John Fries might not have salvaged the election for the divided Federalists, it might have been just enough to quiet Hamiltonian criticisms about the presidents' overtures to France, prevent Hamilton's letter, and perhaps allow the Federalists to survive the election and reorganize under a conservative consensus. But that is all conjecture. Instead, Adams issued the pardons, and the Hamiltonians broke from the party in the summer of 1800. Hamilton wrote his letter, the Republicans took office, and the Federalists began their disintegration. In their hunger for order and thirst for power, the paranoia and hypersensitivity to matters of honor endemic to the Hamiltonians' political culture began to eat away at the Federalist Party. Republicans would feast upon Federalist misfortunes for years to come, championing themselves as "democrats" saving the people from Federalist "aristocracy," while offering Americans a steady fare of wars with Corsairs, Indians, and ultimately

Great Britain, in addition to gradually increased federal spending, a Second Bank of the United States, new protective tariffs, and eventually more indirect taxes. Meanwhile, the Kirchenleute continued to choose their own plate, balancing their diet between Republicans and Federalists, between national, state, and local concerns, still obsessed with one primary and democratic goal: pursuing their own happiness.

Epilogue: Die Zeiten von '99

Three and a half decades after President Adams issued the pardons, a decade after his death, and nearly two decades after the death of John Fries, Fries's Rebellion had still not been forgotten. In the autumn of 1836, the nation was caught in the grips of a bitterly contested presidential election between two rival political parties. In the Lehigh Valley, Andrew Jackson's Democrats resurrected the Hamiltonian ghost to frighten the Kirchenleute away from the Whig Party.

Both the Federalists and the Republicans of the first party system had faded away after the War of 1812, and a second party system reappeared after a market crash and depression a decade later. Federalists had opposed President Jefferson's purchase of Louisiana, the mission to explore it, and the embargo on U.S. trade during Napoleon's wars, among other expensive policies. When President Madison favored trade with France and war with England, it was too much. In 1814, New England Federalists contemplated secession from the Union and displayed the unfortunate timing of publicizing their thoughts at the Hartford Convention the moment that Great Britain called for peace. This was a death knell for the Federalist Party, but it was not the fatal blow. That came from Republicans who had usurped the Federalists' agenda. Republicans, not Federalists, had gone to war with a European power, built the first U.S. Military Academy, and sponsored domestic fiscal programs that looked peculiarly Federalist. Republican Congresses authorized federal internal improvements such as the national road, rechartered the Bank of the United States, and passed protective tariffs for manufactures.

The "Era of Good Feelings" witnessed the destruction of the first party system and the rise of the National Republicans, but nonpartisanship did not last long. A panic in 1819 led to a devastating economic depression at the same time that the question of slavery's expansion into Missouri divided Congress on sectional lines, portending civil war. In the ensuing presidential election of 1824, the issues were slavery, the economy, foreclosures, and the Bank of the United States, which held the liens and seemed to grow and grow. The National Republicans divided between the personalities of Andrew Jackson, a western

Figure 10. "Die Zeiten von '99." Image on a political handbill printed by Edwin Huetter, Allentown, October 29, 1836. The image reportedly appeared during presidential elections between 1828 and 1840. Image courtesy of Lehigh County Historical Society, Snyder Manuscripts.

Revolutionary War veteran and War of 1812 hero who opposed the Bank of the United States as the enemy of the common man, and John Quincy Adams, the former president's son, who supported the bank as an engine of national commercial expansion. When no candidate secured a majority of electors and the decision was thrown into the House of Representatives, Jackson believed that Speaker Henry Clay used his influence to steal the election from him and give it to Adams. After several votes, Adams finally emerged with the majority and assumed the presidency, naming Henry Clay as his secretary of state and, so it seemed to some, his heir apparent to the executive office because Jefferson, Madison, Monroe, and Adams had all held that post as well. After this election, a Democratic Party opposing the Bank of the United States and favoring the expansion of slavery coalesced around Jackson, while Bank supporters, road builders, manufacturers and laborers gradually assumed the Whig moniker, extolling their role as keepers of the Revolution. Jackson and the Democrats got their revenge in 1828 and 1832, capturing the White House and the Congress. Jackson dismantled the Bank of the United States, and Congress passed "Gag Laws" outlawing the distribution of abolitionist literature through the federal mail and automatically tabling any antislavery petitions.[1]

In 1836, Jackson vowed to step down and the Whigs ran their own war hero, William Henry Harrison, "Ole Tippecanoe" of Indian War fame, against the Democrats' Martin Van Buren, the "little magician" whose behind-the-scenes work in the 1820s had created the Democratic Party. Whigs hoped Harrison's record would win them the west as well as patriots in the east. Democrats were quick to expose this "spin" for their constituents with spin of their own, especially in the Lehigh Valley. On October 29, 1836, Edwin Huetter, the Democratic editor of Allentown's *Der Unabhaeugniger Republikaner*, ran a pamphlet entitled "Die Zeiten von '99," ("The Times of '99") in which three figures labeled "Heaney—Fries—Gettman" were shown hanging dead from a gallows. The cartoon tried to link the aristocratic, militaristic, and taxing Federalist Party of 1799 with the contemporary Whigs. "This is the fate which the Federalists intended for the Free Republicans in 1799," the handbill charged, warning that Whigs like General Harrison would treat the people the same as had the Federalists, who had abused the Kirchenleute a generation before. Jackson, though a warrior himself, had won most of their votes as the "Man of the People" who fought against the influence and corruption of the Bank of the United States, in spite of his own corrupt behavior and that of the state banks and other private "pet banks" into which he illegally shifted government funds. The greater irony is that Fries, Gettman, and Heaney almost went to the gallows in part for their demands for free speech and their opposition to the Sedition Act, and it was the Democrats who violated the First Amendment in 1836 by gagging the abolitionists. But the Democrats claimed that Harrison "admitted that he was in favor of having the three patriots Fries, Gettman, and Heaney hanged from the gallows, because they dared as free Americans, to criticize the then government." In 1836 most Kirchenleute, indeed most of Pennsylvania, went for Van Buren as the Democrats exploited the memory of Fries's Rebellion.[2] Time and partisan intrigue worked together to blur the real meaning of Fries's Rebellion for subsequent generations of Kirchenleute. While Fries's Rebellion revived the spirit of the Revolution and played a pivotal role in local, state, and national politics, they ultimately resulted in very little in the way of lasting democratic change in either party politics or the agrarian economy. However, the "Times of '99," had had a significant impact upon the Kirchenleute in their development as American and Pennsylvania citizens.

In the short run, there was sincere hope that a reenergized democratic consciousness could affect real political reform. First after the rebellion came the state elections for governor and the Assembly in the fall of 1799, which occurred as Michael Schmoyer and David Shaeffer were dying of yellow fever in the Norristown jail, and scores of others, including John Fries, were beginning their fifth month of imprisonment while awaiting their trials. Thomas Mifflin, the affable governor who attempted to stay above partisanship but who increasingly leaned Republican late in the decade, was stepping down. The Federalists ran James Ross from Pittsburgh to court the western voters where the Republicans held a decided majority. While the Federalists had held firm in their vote to augment the Eventual Army in March, they had given in to Republican demands to expand the state militia and to increase fines for delinquency with a new militia bill on April 9. Republicans exploited the insurrection and the delinquent militia returns of sectarian pacifists both to demonstrate their own attachment to "order" and to continue to use the militia as a political organizing tool (as well as a club to thump their opposition). Federalists, who were responsible for the force of nearly 3,000 men in the state that was suppressing the insurrection at that very moment, were outmaneuvered.[3] But Pennsylvania Federalists did some maneuvering of their own with Ross's candidacy. Ross had opposed Hamilton's standing army while a senator in 1794 and had not voted on any of the legislation from the Fifth Congress's second session, and unlike his Republican opponent, he spoke German. According to Cobbett, Ross would "talk Federalism out of doors, while he opposed it within the Senate."[4]

Against Ross, the Republicans nominated Chief Justice Thomas McKean of the Pennsylvania State Supreme Court. McKean was probably the most widely known Republican, and his name certainly attracted an ethnic vote.

Like Ross for the Federalists, McKean seems to have been the Republicans' choice to move toward the political center; as historian Harry M. Tinkcom has noted, "he had nothing in common with the 'liberty pole' school of democracy." McKean opposed the democratic state constitution of 1776, supported the conservative republican Constitution of 1790, and advocated property qualifications for voting and office-holding. Perhaps his most aristocratic moment came as a delegate to Pennsylvania's ratifying convention for the U.S. Constitution, when he said on the record, "despotism, if wisely administered, is the best form of government invented by the ingenuity of man." And yet the Republicans sold him to the people as one of the "boys of '76."[5] Federalists and Republicans did not offer Pennsylvanians much of a choice in 1799, but the parties tried to convince them that they did.

From the first, McKean and his camp sought to associate Ross's name with two things: the Federalist Fifth Congress and the Federalists' military excursion into the Lehigh region. The *Aurora* ignored Ross's actual record and invented one for him: "Do not the friends of James Ross, and James Ross himself vote for standing armies, Loans at Eight per centum . . . High public salaries, Increase of Public Debt, Heavy taxes, Excises, Imposts, House tax, poll tax, window tax, hearth tax, Cattle and horse tax, land tax, Alien Bills and Sedition or Gag Bills to cram everything down your throats?"[6] While it is clear that Duane was appealing to the sentiments that gave rise to Fries's Rebellion by falsifying Ross's record, he was careful nonetheless not to sanction the uprising. Ross's Federalist supporters were more direct and countered that a vote for Ross would be a vote "to preserve the happiness and independence of their country; to suppress the spirit of anarchy and insurrection; to retain the true republican characteristics—equality of rights and subjection to the Constitution and laws established by the will of the whole society."[7] Federalists also circulated German handbills entitled "An Ernest Reputation for the Germans of Pennsylvania," praising Ross, who "almost had the appearance of a brave, strong German." The rebellion, the handbills stated, had stained Germans' honor and they could clear it only by voting for Ross, and if they did not, they would be "as cursed as the Irish."[8] Here the Federalists aimed directly at breaking up the new Republican coalition in Philadelphia, playing the politics of ethnic division. Perhaps it would work in the backcountry, because Germans and Irish had come to blows in a Dauphin County riot just a few years earlier. Schneider's *Readinger Adler* warned the Kirchenleute that a vote for Ross and the rest of the Federalist ticket would be a vote for their own enslavement, and he printed a letter by German Revolutionary War hero Peter Muhlenberg endorsing McKean. The *Aurora* printed Muhlenberg's statement as well, and added, "He is the Moses of the German Israelites . . . who will lead the people out of the house of bondage. He calls on you in the name of McKean. Unite! Unite!"⁹

But more than the recent civil disorder or national and international events colored the elections of 1799. There were important state concerns as well. McKean's platform included several issues that mattered to the Kirchenleute: tax relief, direct election of justices of the peace and militia captains, and continued expansion of the jurisdiction of justices of the peace and sheriffs. The first plank had obvious appeal, and the third was already underway. In March 1799, Germans from both parties in the Assembly passed a temporary statute extending the powers of justices of the peace and sheriffs concerning recovery of debt, collection of rents, and actions of trespass. Previously, these had been the domain of the courts, whose proceedings and records were transacted in English only. Now their local magistrates could adjudicate local economic matters in the local tongue. McKean and the Republicans seized on the popularity of this measure, promised to extend it should they win the executive's chair and the Assembly, and vowed to make the local magistrates elected officials.¹⁰

As a result, the German-American vote accounted for over half of McKean's support, carrying 35 of 39 election districts in the heavily German counties of Northampton, Berks, Dauphin, Northumberland, Montgomery, Fayette, Chester, Cumberland, Lancaster, and Philadelphia. In Millers Town, Macungie Township, the Northampton County home of Henry Shankweiler, the people favored McKean by a vote of 574 to 76. Northampton County defeated Ross by almost 4 to 1. Federalists like Alexander Graydon, a Dauphin County prothonotary removed by McKean in favor of a German, later blamed the Federalists' defeat on the German vote and the influence of Fries's Rebellion.¹¹ Graydon was right. Statewide the election was tight. Ross actually won one more county than McKean, but the judge took the popular vote by just over 5,000 ballots. According to one state historian, "it seems fairly obvious that McKean's margin of victory came from the 'window tax' counties" of Berks, Bucks, Northampton, and Montgomery, where the Republicans polled a six thousand vote majority.¹² Voter turnout was extraordinary. In Northampton County, the rate was 83 percent, and in Bucks County it was 85 percent, and the Republicans made the most of it, taking not only the governor's chair but winning forty-one of seventy-six House seats as well, seizing the majority for the first time. In the Senate, the Federalists held their edge, but the Republicans gained ground in Northampton County, sending Kirchenleute Thomas Mewhorter to the new capitol in Lancaster.¹³ As Pennsylvania historian Sanford Higginbotham wrote: "the high handed methods of Federalism in 1798 and 1799, the Alien and Sedition Acts, the direct taxes, and the suppression of Fries's Rebellion were exploited by an alert Republican Party to create a tradition of terrorism."[14] This was an ominous turn for the national hopes of the Federalist Party, who had lost Pennsylvania to Jefferson once in 1796 and who would face even stiffer odds of carrying the Keystone State in 1800.

Pennsylvania Federalists could see the handwriting on the wall, and as early as December 1799 they took action to try to salvage the upcoming presidential election and their own authority in the state. In previous contests, Pennsylvania had chosen its presidential electors by a general election, but when Senate Republicans introduced a bill on December 19 to do so again, Federalists blocked them by a party-line vote of fourteen to nine. Instead, the Senate wanted to apportion the electors by district polling, in particular, they wanted to gerrymander districts that strengthened the Federalists' chances. The Republican-dominated House followed eleven days later by passing a bill supporting the general election method. When the Republicans were in the minority in 1796, however, they had opposed this scheme.[15] By the end of the session there was no agreement, as John Fries's second trial for treason produced a second conviction, and John Adams followed the lead of his predecessor and offered complete pardons to all the "insurgents." He even extended a pardon to Whiskey Rebel David Bradford just two days after the Bethlehem jailbreak. Bradford was the western insurgent from 1794 who had fled to Spanish territory and was the lone rebel excluded by Washington's pardons. Adams had good reason to believe that his own pardons would have an ameliorating effect on the electorate, after all, the people had elected him after Washington's pardons in 1795.[16]

Summer came and went without an agreement by Pennsylvania's House and Senate, and by October 1800 the state faced its annual elections. Republicans, using the county committee organizations they had begun establishing in 1797, trounced the Federalists. Federalists by then had also begun organizing at the county level, but they were unable to overcome the national party's repressive program, graphically illustrated during Fries's Rebellion, and their rival's adoption of a localist agenda. Republicans won six of seven available Senate positions, though Federalists retained a slim majority of two seats there, and the party of Jefferson took the State House by a margin of fifty-five to twenty-three, increasing its margin of majority from six to thirty-two. After the elections, Governor McKean called the Assembly to a special session in order to decide on a system for apportioning electors in the rapidly approaching presidential election, which featured President Adams and Charles Cotesworth Pinckney on the Federalist ticket and Thomas Jefferson and Aaron Burr representing the Republicans. Too late to coordinate a general election, the Republican House favored a joint vote by both houses to determine the lot of the electors, while the insecure Federalist Senate held out for a concurrent vote of the separate bodies. Needless to say, the House spurned the Senate bill, and the Senate turned up its nose at the House measure. At issue were fifteen electoral votes, and the Senate, bowing to the majority in the House, compromised on November 13, allowing the House to decide eight electors while retaining seven for itself.

In the final national tally of electors Jefferson and Burr each polled 73 votes, to 65 for Adams, 64 for Pinckney, and 1 for John Jay. Republicans captured a majority of the House of Representatives as well. Burr embarrassed Jefferson by refusing to capitulate, and the affair was settled in a bitter round of congressional voting that extended dangerously close to Inauguration Day in March, when Jefferson finally prevailed. It was not at all clear whether the Federalists would give up the House or the presidency in March 1801. Governor McKean promised Jefferson that he would use the state militia to arrest Pennsylvania Federalists should they fail to abdicate their positions, and Governor James Monroe promised to use the Virginia militia to seize a federal arsenal. Plans to use military force by the Republican governors of the nation's largest two states had been in the works for more than a year.[17] Many expected violence, but none came. Instead, the ousted Federalist representatives, and their president, left the capital after the Sixth Congress, and power transferred peacefully to the Republicans in an event that has since come to be known as the "Revolution of 1800." Thomas Jefferson, in one of the most famous inaugural speeches, pronounced that a national republican consensus had triumphed over partisanship when he expressed, "We are all republicans—we are all federalists."

In the "Revolution of 1800," the Pennsylvania House pledged eight votes to the Republicans while the Senate checked seven for the Federalists. Had the Senate refused to compromise and Pennsylvania failed to vote, Jefferson and Burr would still have won, although the victory would have been one vote narrower. Had Pennsylvania apportioned its electors through a general ticket, the Jeffersonian margin of victory would have been much wider. In the congressional races that fall, Pennsylvanians cast 24,108 votes for Republican candidates against only 8,964 for Federalists. The Kirchenleute returned Robert Brown to Congress with a resounding vote of confidence. Northamptoners marked 2,344 out of 2,482 ballots for Brown.[18] Had they been able to participate directly, the Kirchenleute would have played a significant role in Jefferson's revolution. Yet in reality, they had played their part a year earlier when they had helped to elect a Republican governor and a month earlier when they had sent a massive Republican majority to the Pennsylvania House. After the elections in 1800, Republicans must have thought that they could regularly count on the Kirchenleute, especially those from the region of Fries's Rebellion. They would be wrong.

After 1800 the Kirchenleute added their experiences in Fries's Rebellion to their world-view and became even more distrustful of extralocal, non-German-speaking governments, whether controlled by Republicans or Federalists. When the Republicans came into national power, they repealed all federal internal taxation in 1802 (such as excises and "Stamp" duties), but they still attempted to collect the Direct Tax to meet the Fifth Congress's expenditures. By 1803, thirteen states were still in arrears and two states had made no payments to the Treasury at all; and by 1812, 6 percent of assessments still remained uncollected. But the third and fifth districts of Pennsylvania paid theirs. Republicans also repealed the Sedition Act, drastically cut the New Army, relying instead on the Navy and state militia, and allowed the charter of the Bank of the United States to expire in 1811. Jefferson's administration exerted its vigor in western Indian policy, the Louisiana Purchase, naval warfare in the Mediterranean, and schemes of internal improvements. These national policies seemed benign to Kirchenleute liberties, and allowed them to turn their attention back to state and local concerns, particularly to support candidates who spoke their language, who demonstrated republican virtue, or who would be most effective as voices for local control in Lancaster, the new state capital.[19]

But the Fries Rebels would not neatly join the Republican Party. Between 1801 and 1809, the people of Millers Town, the center of Fries's Rebellion, many times voted overwhelmingly for German-speaking Federalist candidates, as for example they favored Federalists Abraham Rinker and George Acker for the state assembly in 1806. Moreover, earlier in 1802 they and other German townships had elected Rinker as their sheriff, ousting Republican Nicholas Kern. Across the Lehigh River, the people in "Ohl's district" also supported Federalists as often as Republicans, as Northampton County continued to send a mix of Republicans and Federalists to the State House throughout the decade. William Barnet, John Ross, William Lattimore, George Acker, and James Wilson were regular Federalist favorites, and Isaac Hartzell, Thomas Mewhorter, and John Coolbaugh represented the Republicans. At no time in the decade that followed Fries's Rebellion did the Republicans hold more than two of Northampton County's four seats, and from 1801 to 1805 the Federalists held three of the four seats.[20]

At the same time, the Republicans at the state level were increasing their majority in the House, and in 1802, they captured the entire Senate. Yet those were years during which the party was rent with schism between German Simon Snyder's supporters, who advocated judicial and constitutional reform and local control, and McKean's supporters who preferred the status quo. One Republican faction was headed by William Duane and his *Aurora*, Michael Lieb and his city Germans, and Simon Snyder and his Pennsylvania House of

Representatives, for which he was the new Speaker. They stood in opposition to the governor and his faction, and Pennsylvania Federalists played a middle role but tended to support the latter. As Speaker of the House, Simon Snyder, the Northumberland County son of a Palatinate immigrant, initiated a bill in December 1802 to give permanent power and still greater authority to the 1799 law expanding the reach of justices of the peace. Governor McKean vetoed the bill, citing that untrained men without juries would be responsible for deciding cases of up to $100. McKean was fresh from his second victory over Federalist James Ross, in which he had widened his margin of victory considerably, polling 47,879 to Ross's 17,037, and he apparently felt comfortable enough to oppose exactly the kind of legislation that he and the Republicans had promised when beginning their "Revolution" in 1799.[21]

In the 1805 gubernatorial race, McKean squared off against Snyder, and only with the help of Germans Joseph Heister and Peter Muhlenberg did the governor win his third term. In that election, Millers Town voters followed Muhlenberg's advice and took McKean over Snyder. Heister and Muhlenberg pitted their German-ness and reputations against the lesser known Snyder, and urged the Kirchenleute to reelect the Republican champion of 1799. But one-quarter of Northampton County's votes went to Snyder anyway. Northamptoners replaced Republican Isaac Hartzell in the State Senate with Federalist William Lattimore, but in that same election they chose Captain Henry Jarret to be their sheriff.[22] The Kirchenleute had not become lockstep Republicans. But if the 1808 election, featuring Simon Snyder, can be read as a popular endorsement for Snyder's proposals in 1802 and the more radical Republicans' attempts at constitutional reform in 1805, then the Kirchenleute's 1798–99 attempts to broaden popular sovereignty were still visible. In 1805 radicals pushed for a constitutional convention to amend the constitution of 1790 in a democratic direction: to elect senators every year instead of every four, to reduce executive patronage, particularly among justices of the peace, to elect judges and limit their terms, and to reform other judicial procedures. McKean's men styled themselves as Constitutional Republicans and narrowly defeated Snyder and the reformers. In his third term, McKean proposed to limit the radical Republican oppositionist press by calling for a bill to force newspapers to print proof of their allegations, to require editors to provide security for their good behavior, and to give the courts the power to suppress the papers when grand juries were presented with cases of libel. Radicals, of course, conjured up the specter of the Sedition Act. They brought impeachment charges against the governor, mostly over cases of inappropriate appointments and dismissals. With McKean reaching his three-term limit, Snyder became the Republican favorite in 1808, and he easily defeated Federalist James Ross. Snyder made good on his pledge to expand local control, but like his predecessors and followers he did not expand the franchise. Northampton County favored Snyder by a two-to-one margin. While Ohl's district also went for Snyder, Millers Town narrowly favored Federalist James Ross in a tight race, once again proving that the Kirchenleute would not be beholden to one political party. Captain Anthony Stahler, a veteran and leader of Fries's Rebellion, also ran for State Assembly that year. He ran as a Federalist and he lost. Frederick Heaney, once convicted of treason and sentenced to death with John Fries, moved to Northampton County sometime after his pardon and beat Captain Henry Jarret for the sheriff's office in 1808.[23] Jarret did all right for himself. Five years later he captained a troop of light horse from Lower Nazareth Township in the War of 1812, reprising his role in the American Revolution and Fries's Rebellion.[24]

In 1815, John Adams reflected on his pardon of the Fries Rebels, and asked, "What good, what example would have been exhibited to the nation by the execution of three or four obscure, miserable Germans . . . Pitiful puppets danced upon the wires of jugglers behind the scene or underground."[25] How wrong the president was in some ways. These people certainly were not miserable, and though misinformed by disingenuous Republican politicians, they danced on their own. But he was right in issuing the pardon. The pardons had an enormous impact upon the pardoned, their families, and their neighbors. First, of course, was John Fries. The pardon added eighteen years to his life, which he spent traversing Bucks County crying auctions and watching his children provide grandchildren until his death in February 1818, at the age of 68. He was laid to rest in an unmarked grave beside Christ Reformed United Church in Charles Town (see Figure 2).

The rebellion and its aftermath had even more significant consequences for Fries's Kirchenleute neighbors and their children, not only in the Lehigh Valley but across the state as well. The Federalists' aristocratic attitude, the antidemocratic national security framework, and the military and judicial repression of the resistance led the Kirchenleute to the Republicans in 1799 and 1800, but their own desire for republican government and local democratic control led them to support candidates for local, state, and national offices who seemed best suited to meet those needs, regardless of their party. This in turn opened doors to local, state, and national political office.[26] In 1814 the predominantly Kirchenleute townships of the southwestern corner of Northampton County successfully split and formed Lehigh County, providing the residents of Upper Milford, Macungie, Heidelberg, and Lehigh Townships and the Saucon Valley with even greater local control, as they divorced themselves from Easton and congregating instead at a new, closer, and German county seat in Allentown. They had started that campaign in the winter of 1799, as they opposed the Direct Tax and the Sektenleute assessors appointed by Easton Federalist Samuel Sitgreaves.[27]

In the first half of the nineteenth century, political parties and the Kirchenleute used and reused the memory of Fries's Rebellion at election time and placed more and more German Americans into local, state, and national offices under the Republican, Federalist and, later, the National Republican and Democratic Parties. In 1808, Pennsylvania-German politicians invoked the memory of the 1799 opposition movement to place the first German American in the governor's chair, even though some of the resisters themselves supported James Ross. Simon Snyder was only the first of many German Americans who controlled that office thereafter. In the 1828 and 1836 presidential campaigns, the Democrats used the still vivid memory of the rebellion to capture Pennsylvania German votes for Andrew Jackson and Martin Van Buren. The real memories of "Die Zeiten von '99" had faded away, but the importance of local control against large, centralizing governmental powers remained with them. By then, Jackson's hypocrisy did not matter. Compared to John Quincy Adams, he seemed to be a "Man of the People" in many Kirchenleute minds. But neither the Republicans nor the Democrats democratized Pennsylvania or the United States as much or as rapidly as the Kirchenleute's behavior in 1799 suggest they desired. Judicial reforms came slowly in Pennsylvania, and even with a new state constitution in 1838 that made more local offices elective and curtailed the power of the governor and the Supreme Court, voting was still limited to taxpayers. Meanwhile, the Kirchenleute gradually relinquished their status as freeholders.[28]

The Kirchenleute continued to protect themselves from the economic contraction of the early nineteenth century, but time and economic expansion gradually took their toll. In 1800, the five townships of heaviest Direct Tax opposition were home to 1,151 families; 868 (75 percent) owned land averaging more than 100 acres in size, and 783 owned homes. In 1810, Heidelberg, Upper Milford and Macungie were home to 5,500 people residing in 889 households. Although tax returns for 1813 show only 752 (85 percent) still owning land, many households had become homes to several adults, revealing that the number of taxable men (937) increasingly outpaced the number of dwellings. And the size of farms began to dwindle. Two hundred eighty-seven (38 percent) owned less than fifty acres of land (a dramatic change from 1800), barely enough to sustain a family. Another 134 owned less than one hundred acres, meaning that 56 percent of landowners possessed too little to divide among their children or to compete effectively in the national market economy that roads and canals were already creating and railroads would expand in the near future. The region's youthfulness in the last quarter of the eighteenth century strained its land supply in the first quarter of the nineteenth and, combined with the nation's economic transition to a market economy, changed and challenged the lives, identities, and the world-views of Kirchenleute in eastern Pennsylvania.

The numbers were similar in Lower Milford. There in 1820, 1,195 people lived in 281 households. Three hundred and ten owned some taxable property, while 231 owned land (82 percent). Again, as in the Northampton County townships, the number of landholders had risen, but the size of the holdings had diminished. One hundred and five (45 percent) owned less than fifty acres, and another 74 owned less than one hundred. Seventy-seven percent possessed inadequate amounts of land for their families.[29] These figures help to explain why the Kirchenleute refused to pledge themselves solely to one party or another, whether for state or national politics, preferring to choose candidates who best met their needs of local economic protection and political control. In this respect they were drawing upon their past as much as their present, following the examples set by their ancestors in Pennsylvania's provincial politics over the preceding century. Multiple experiences, past and present, continued to provide the structural contexts that informed the Kirchenleute's political options and the decisions they would make. These choices, in turn, continuously altered those contexts creating new ones for agents to add to their history and use to determine new courses of action.

Therefore, in spite of the Kirchenleute's economic worries and their failure to effect real democratic change, the "rebellion's" political effects did carry important political and cultural ramifications. In a tangible, political sense, the federal government did not attempt to lay another direct tax until the Civil War, well after most resisters from the 1798–99 period had passed away. As a result, in an abstract sense the resisters did successfully defend their ideas of the Constitution and republicanism and at least asserted their perceived right of democratic direct action. In so doing, the Lehigh region Kirchenleute built for themselves another span in their bridge to an American identity, adding to the other sections they had constructed throughout the century before. Fries's Rebellion was their second American Revolution, and it not only confirmed their political citizenship earned by the first, but it also paved the way for a new social and cultural status as Americans. Their German heritage and identity would be remembered for generations, and indeed is still not forgotten, but with the dawning of the nineteenth century, German Americans in Pennsylvania were rapidly becoming much more American than German. In the nineteenth century, democratic politics came to be defined by interest groups: ethnocultural, class, occupational, agricultural, mercantile, industrial, religious, reform-oriented, and others. It would become as "American" to tout the interests of one group over those of the whole in the nineteenth century as it had been to sacrifice the interests of the few to those of common good in the eighteenth. The Kirchenleute had readied for that transition. Throughout the nineteenth century in Pennsylvania, they zealously protected their language and culture from the common school movement and demanded their American right to participate in Pennsylvania politics as Germans.[30] Being American meant the right to remain German while adhering to political principles that translated liberty as freheit. There seemed to be no contradiction to the Kirchenleute, who in the Revolution had attempted to exclude sectarian "Tories" from local and state government in the name of democracy. That too was American.

Even more generally, Fries's Rebellion reveals the attitudes of its participants about their role in republican politics in the decades immediately following the War for Independence. They are instructive of the democratic and localist idealism and the popular application of ideological principles unleashed by the American Revolution. They also testify to the localists' interest and participation in state and federal politics. The Kirchenleute resisters, ordinary citizens whom historians commonly label "the inarticulate," were in fact politically literate and vocal. While some may have been "ignorant of our language" in John Adams's estimation, they were not ignorant "of our laws." Language and ethnicity were immaterial in a republic based on principles, not bloodlines or factions, and the laws sanctioned by popular sovereignty belonged to Germans as much as to Anglo Americans, to the governed as well as the governors. The resisters understood the republican system and applied the logic of natural law to expand it democratically with the tactics of direct action. The land and the laws belonged to them. They belonged to people, not parties, placemen, opportunists, or governments. The Kirchenleute tax resisters perceived of themselves as American citizens, constitutionally entitled to protect the liberty secured by the Revolution. The republican ideology that forged the Revolution and that the governing elite used to create the Constitution stressed the virtue of the average citizen and the necessity of political engagement on the part of common men, teaching the electorate that regardless of class or culture they were political equals. Fries's Rebellion reveals how well the Kirchenleute learned these lessons and, to the Federalists' surprise and chagrin, how well they had taught their pupils. Subsequent Americans have alternately forgotten and relearned these democratic lessons, but the central idea of the Revolution—popular sovereignty—has remained in word and spirit to be revived, re-interpreted, and re-engaged by the people, sometimes with and sometimes without the consent of their governors. As long as the people retain that notion of popular sovereignty, the Revolution will endure and the story of Fries's Rebellion will remain relevant.

Notes

Prologue

1. Richard D. Peters, ed., *The Public Statutes at Large of the United States of America*, 106 vols. (Boston: Little and Brown, 1845), "An Act Authorizing the President of the United States to raise a Provisional Army," May 28, 1798, 1: 558–61; "An Act to Provide for the Valuation of Lands and Dwelling Houses and the enumeration of Slaves within the United States," July 9, 1798, 1: 580–91; "An Act to Lay and Collect a Direct Tax within the United States," July 14, 1798, 1: 597–604; "An Act Respecting Alien Enemies;" July 6, 1798, 1: 577; "An Act for the Punishment of Certain Crimes Against the United States," July 14, 1798, 1: 596–97.

2. On the evolution, symbolism, and importance of liberty poles and their use in the American Revolution, see Peter Shaw, *American Patriots and the Rituals of the Revolution* (Cambridge, Mass.: Harvard University Press, 1981), 182–84. See also Simon Newman, *Parades and the Politics of the Street: Festive Culture in the Early American Republic* (Philadelphia: University of Pennsylvania Press, 1997), 172–76; and David Waldestreicher, *In the Midst of Perpetual Fetes: The Making of American Nationalism, 1776–1820* (Chapel Hill: University of North Carolina Press, 1997).

3. Deposition of John Romig, January 29, 1799, William Rawle Papers, "Insurrections in Western Pennsylvania," 2 vols., 2: 10, Historical Society of Pennsylvania. All Fries's Rebellion material is in volume 2. Page numbers will be provided when available, but many documents were inserted after Rawle compiled the original collection and were not paginated. When no pagination exists, I have attempted to record the date of the deposition when possible.

4. Military Abstracts Card File for Revolutionary War, 1775–1783, Active Duty Militia, microfilm 3903, roll 93, Pennsylvania State Archives.

5. German Lutherans and Reformed in Pennsylvania often stood on opposite sides of local, state, and national political issues in the 18th century, partly as a result of their competition for Protestant, German-speaking pastors, who were in short supply, and for the resources of land, buildings, and money that made a parish. Of course there was also a theological divide between Lutheranism and Calvinism. But in the Lehigh Valley, the Protestants were threatened religiously and politically by the sectarians in their midst, especially the Moravians, who sought to take advantage of the Protestants' ministerial shortage and bickering divisions through their own proselytizing. Moravians in Northampton County and English-speaking Quakers in Bucks County also held the most prized county and municipal offices throughout the region. It was in the face of this dual threat that Lehigh Valley Reformed and Lutherans put aside their differences in the 1770s, 1780s, and 1790s to form Union churches and homogenized themselves as Kirchenleute. On these issues, see Kenneth W. Keller, "Diversity and Democracy: Ethnic

Politics in Southeastern Pennsylvania, 1788–1799" (Ph.D. dissertation, Yale University, 1971); Keller, *Rural Politics and the Collapse of Pennsylvania Federalism* (Philadelphia: American Philosophical Society, 1982); Laura Becker, "Diversity and Its Significance in an Eighteenth-Century Pennsylvania Town," in Michael Zuckerman, ed., *Friends and Neighbors: Group Life in America's First Plural Society* (Philadelphia: Temple University Press, 1982), 196–221; Charles H. Glatfelter, "The Colonial Pennsylvania German Lutheran and Reformed Clergymen" (Ph.D. dissertation, Johns Hopkins University, 1952); Benjamin Rush, *An Account of the Manners of the German Inhabitants of Pennsylvania* (Philadelphia: Samuel Town, printer, 1875), 45–46; and especially Patricia Bonomi, "'Watchful Against the Sects': Religious Renewal in Pennsylvania German Congregations, 1720–1750," *Pennsylvania History* 50 (October 1983); 273–83; Owen S. Ireland, *Religion, Ethnicity, and Politics: Ratifying the Constitution in Pennsylvania* (University Park: Pennsylvania State University Press, 1995).

6. On the eighteenth-century German migration to Pennsylvania and North America, see Aaron Fogleman, *Hopeful Journeys: German Immigration, Settlement, and Political Culture in Colonial America, 1717–1775* (Philadelphia: University of Pennsylvania Press, 1996); and Marianne S. Wokeck, *Trade in Strangers: The Beginnings of Mass Migration to North America* (University Park: Pennsylvania State University Press, 1999).

7. These statistics were gleaned from *United States Direct Tax of 1798: Tax Lists for the State of Pennsylvania* (Washington, D.C.: National Archives Microfilms Publications, 1962), reels 8, 9, 10, 12; Bucks County, Pennsylvania, Tax Assessments 1798, Bucks County Historical Society, Doylestown, Pennsylvania; and Pennsylvania Septennial Census 1786, Records of the General Assembly, House of Representatives, Septennial Census Returns, 1779–1863, microfilm, roll 1, Pennsylvania State Archives.

8. Terry Bouton, "A Road Closed: Rural Insurgency in Post-Independence Pennsylvania," *Journal of American History* 87 (December 2000): 855–87. See also Leland Baldwin, *Whiskey Rebels: Story of a Frontier Uprising* (Pittsburgh: University of Pittsburgh Press, 1939), 56–59.

9. "Petition of Sundry Inhabitants of the Township of Lower Milford in the County of Bucks to President of the Supreme Executive Council," April 15, 1785, Records of Pennsylvania's Revolutionary Government (frame 39, reel 22), Pennsylvania State Archives. Terry Bouton's "A Road Closed" pointed me toward this petition.

10. John Armstrong and John Boyd to John Dickinson, August 7, 1784, Records of Pennsylvania's Revolutionary Government, Executive Correspondence and Petitions, 1777–1790, Pennsylvania State Archives (frame 409, reel 21).

11. Bouton, "A Road Closed," 855–56.

12. Bouton overlooks this distinction in his essay, preferring to see the similarities of what he calls the "Pennsylvania Regulation" as a class struggle. Clearly, the agrarian Kirchenleute who marched to quell the western insurrection in 1794 did not possess a very strong agrarian class consciousness then, but perhaps after their contact with western non-German farmers they began to develop notions of their broader agrarian interests and identity. Stephen Nolt argues that during the era of the Early Republic, Pennsylvania Germans were in the process of forming a political consciousness that was both parochial and national; Stephen M. Nolt, *Foreigners in Their Own Land: Pennsylvania Germans in the Early Republic* (University Park: Pennsylvania State University Press, 2002).

13. See Ireland, *Religion, Ethnicity, and Politics.*

14. Keller, *Rural Politics.*

15. Bouton, "A Road Closed," covers this extensively. See also his dissertation, "Tying Up the Revolution: Money, Power, and the Regulation in Pennsylvania, 1765–1800" (Ph.D. dissertation, Duke University, 1996), and Bouton, "'No wonder the times were troublesome': The Origins of Fries Rebellion," *Pennsylvania History* 67 (Winter 2000): 21–42. I agree that this populist tradition played an important role in the tax resistance of 1798 and 1799, but I do not believe that it was the only factor nor necessarily the most important one. A complex combination of ideological, ethnic, religious, local, state, and national political issues as well as economic factors and class influenced the Kirchenleute's decision to regulate the federal government's extension of its authority.

16. Mifflin Administration, Appointments File, Bureau of Commissioners and Elections, Records of the Department of State, Bucks File, especially August 12, 1791, August 24, 1791, January 2, 1795, December 26, 1797. Pennsylvania State Archives. See also Keller, *Rural Politics,* 5.

17. Kammerer was the president of the German Republican Society of Pennsylvania.

18. On the "counterrevolution" in Pennsylvania and the Constitutions of 1776 and 1790, see Robert L. Brunhouse, *The Counter-Revolution in Pennsylvania, 1776–1790* (Harrisburg: Pennsylvania Historical and Museum Commission, 1942).

19. Keller, *Rural Politics,* 17–18. *Pennsylvania House Journal,* 1798–99, 96, 117, 152, 181, 202–23, 228, 248, 269; Mifflin Administration, Appointments File.

20. Simon Newman, "The World Turned Upside Down: Revolutionary Politics, Fries' and Gabriel's Rebellions, and the Fears of the Federalists," *Pennsylvania History* 67 (Winter 2000): 5–20, makes a fascinating argument that the Kirchenleute in 1798 and the slaves and free blacks in Richmond in 1800 were cognizant of and acting upon principles of the French Revolution, Wolf Tone's failed Irish Rebellion, and the successful revolt in San Domingue. Fries himself was reported by several deponents and witnesses to have denounced the French, not surprising because until 1798 he was a Federalist, but that is not to say that his neighbors were not infected by transatlantic Jacobin democracy.

21. Nolt, *Foreigners in Their Own Land,* 43.

22. I am grateful to Robert Churchill for our many discussions and conference correspondence about the idea of popular nullification. For his perspective, see Robert Churchill, "Popular Nullification, Fries' Rebellion, and the Waning of Radical Republicanism, 1798–1801," *Pennsylvania History* 67 (Winter 2000): 105–40. Churchill refers to the Northampton Insurrection as a "revolutionary libertarian resistance movement," and he sees the resisters primarily as ideological reactionaries. (This latter characterization is my assessment of his general argument, not his stated opinion.) While a strain of "revolutionary libertarianism" or localism certainly pervaded the Kirchenleute ideology, it was equally informed by ethnoreligious and economic factors in addition to local, state, national, and international politics. For a similar argument about the convergence of local, state, national and international political issues, see Alan Taylor, *William Cooper's Town: Power and Persuasion on the Frontier of the Early American Republic* (New York: Knopf, 1995).

23. On the Democratic-Republican Societies, see Eugene Perry Link, *Democratic-Republican Societies, 1790–1800* (New York: Columbia University Press, 1942); Philip S. Foner, *The Democratic-Republican Societies, 1790–1800: A Documentary Sourcebook of Constitutions, Declarations, Addresses, Resolutions, and Toasts* (Westport, Conn.: Greenwood

Press, 1976); Matthew Schoenbachler, "Republicanism in the Age of Democratic Revolution: The Democratic-Republican Societies of the 1790s," *Journal of the Early Republic* 18 (Summer 1998): 237–61. For an excellent regional study specific to Pennsylvania see Jeffrey A. Davis, "The Democratic-Republican Societies of Pennsylvania, 1793–1796" (Ph.D. dissertation, Washington State University, 1996).

24. On the Shays and Whiskey Rebellions, see Leonard Richards, *Shays's Rebellion: The American Revolution's Final Battle* (Philadelphia: University of Pennsylvania Press, 2002); David Szatmary, *Shays Rebellion: The Making of an Agrarian Insurrection* (Amherst: University of Massachusetts Press, 1980); Baldwin, *Whiskey Rebels*; Davis, "Democratic-Republican Societies of Pennsylvania"; Dorothy Fennel, "From Rebelliousness to Insurrection: A Social History of the Whiskey Rebellion" (Ph.D. dissertation, University of Pittsburgh, 1991); Thomas P. Slaughter, *The Whiskey Rebellion: Frontier Epilogue to the American Revolution* (New York: Oxford University Press, 1986).

Chapter 1. Liberty

1. *Philadelphia Aurora and General Daily Advertiser*, March 12, 1799, and Washington *Herald of Liberty*, April 15, 1799. For other accounts of women warning off assessors, see the testimony of John Romig and Isaac Schmyer in Thomas Carpenter, *The Two Trials of John Fries, on an Indictment for Treason* (Philadelphia: William W. Woodward, printer, 1800), 185–86.

2. Pictured originally in O. P. Knauss, "History of Macungie," in Charles Rhoads Roberts et al., *History of Lehigh County*, vol. 1 (Allentown: Lehigh County Historical Society, 1914).

3. Useful for the concept of multivalent constructions of liberty is Michael Kammen, *Spheres of Liberty: Changing Perceptions of Liberty in American Culture* (Ithaca, N.Y.: Cornell University Press, 1986). For a discussion of the economic definitions of liberty and a "moral economy" in the post-Revolutionary era, see Ruth Bogin, "Petitioning and the New Moral Economy of Post-Revolutionary America," *William and Mary Quarterly* 3rd ser. 45 (July 1988): 391–425.

4. For a superb discussion not only of the volatility of the 1790s but also of the Federalist and Republican Party's views on popular participation, see James Roger Sharp, *American Politics in the Early Republic: The New Nation in Crisis* (New Haven, Conn.: Yale University Press, 1993).

5. On the construction of the "myth" of popular sovereignty at the founding of the nation, see Edmund S. Morgan, *Inventing the People: The Rise of Popular Sovereignty in England and America* (New York: W.W. Norton, 1988), 263–87, and especially 303–6.

6. Deposition of Phillip Schlough before Judge Richard Peters, April 15, 1799, Rawle Papers; deposition of Israel Robert, no date, Rawle Papers. The word "snakes" may be "shakers,"—smudged eighteenth-century ink muddies the translation.

7. Deposition of Andrew Schlichter, given before Judge Richard Peters, April 6, 1799, Rawle Papers, 2: 41. Emphasis in original.

8. Deposition of John Jarret, April 10, 1799 given before Judge William Henry, Rawle Papers, 2: 2.

9. Deposition of Henry Ohl, given before Judge William Henry, April 27, 1799, Rawle Papers, 2: 91.

10. *Oracle of Dauphin and Harrisburg Daily Advertiser*, January 23, 1799.

11. Deposition of John Lersass, given before Judge William Henry, February 1, 1799, Rawle Papers, 2: 2.

12. "Lehigh Association," draft in Rawle Papers, 2: 6.

13. Carpenter, *Two Trials*, 68.

14. Deposition of John Fogel, Jr., before Judge William Henry, January 29, 1799, Rawle Papers, 2: 2.

15. Examination of Henry Shiffert before Judge Richard Peters, April 14, 1799, Rawle Papers.

16. Deposition of Philip Wescoe, recorder and date unknown, Rawle Papers.

17. For Adams quote, see John Adams to James Lloyd, March 31, 1815, Adams Family Papers, Massachusetts Historical Society. For earlier antiquarian accounts of "Fries's Rebellion" that portray it as an example of German ignorance or misunderstanding, see W. W. H. Davis, "The Fries Rebellion in Bucks and Northampton Counties, Pennsylvania, in 1799," unpublished essay read before the Historical Society of Pennsylvania March 9, 1891, W.W.H. Davis Collection, Spruance Library, fol. 163, Bucks County Historical Society; Davis, *The Fries Rebellion of 1799* (Doylestown, Pa.: Doylestown Publishing, 1899); Frank M. Eastman, *The Fries Rebellion* (New York, 1923); Donald A. Gallager, "Revolting Taxes and Tax Revolts," *Old York Road Historical Society Bulletin* 38 (1978): 43–48; Alexander Boyd Hamilton, "Fries Insurrection," unpublished essay, Society Collection—John Fries, Historical Society of Pennsylvania; Lewis R. Harley, "Fries Rebellion," *Historical Sketches, Historical Society of Montgomery County* 1 (1895): 313–26; Frederic Hartz, "The Fries Rebellion of 1799," *Bucks County Panorama* 18 (January 1976): 9–13, 43; William J. Heller, *History of Northampton County and the Grand Valley of the Lehigh*, 3 vols. (New York: American Historical Society, 1920), 1: 143–48; Joseph Mortimer Levering, *A History of Bethlehem, Pennsylvania, 1741–1892* (Bethlehem, Pa.: Times Publishing, 1903), 565; Judith Ann Meier, "The Federal Direct Tax of 1798: The Window Pane Tax," *Bulletin of the Historical Society of Montgomery County* 22 (Spring 1981): 358–79; Henry L. Snyder, "Muskets in the Milfords," unpublished essay, A. Weaver Collection, Lehigh County Historical Society, and Snyder, "Unique Aspects of the Trials of John Fries," *Proceedings of the Lehigh County Historical Society* 23 (September 1960): 48–59; Ellen Swartzlander, "John Fries, Pie Plate Patriot," unpublished essay, Spruance Library, MSC 164, fol. 180, Bucks County Historical Society; Theodore G. Tappert, "Helmuth and the Fries Rebellion in 1799," *Lutheran Quarterly* 17 (1965): 265–69; Nancy Wylie, "The Red Lion: Site of the 1799 Tax Rebellion," *Bucks County Panorama* 17 (April 1975): 40–41; "Some Brief Account of the Excise Insurrection Which Took Place in 1798–1799 in Pennsylvania," author unknown, unpublished essay, c. 1820, Society Miscellaneous Collection—John Fries, Historical Society of Pennsylvania. For earlier, more scholarly accounts that also characterize the event as one of a parochial nature or involving cultural misunderstanding, see Norman Victor Blantz, "Editors and Issues: The Party Press in Philadelphia, 1789–1801" (Ph.D. dissertation, Pennsylvania State University, 1974), 209; Gerard Clarfield, *Timothy Pickering and American Diplomacy, 1795–1800* (Columbia: University of Missouri Press, 1969), 210; Robert W. Coakley, *The Role of Federal Military Forces in Domestic Disorders, 1789–1878*, Army Historical Series (Washington, D.C.: Center of Military History, U.S. Army, 1988), 69–77; Noble Cunningham, Jr., *The Jeffersonian Republicans in Power: Party Operations 1801–1809* (Chapel Hill: University of North Carolina Press, 1963), 80; Alexander DeConde, *The Quasi-War: The Politics and Diplomacy of the Undeclared War with France, 1797–1801*

(New York: Scribner's, 1966), 196–99; David Hackett Fischer, *The Revolution of American Conservatism: The Federalist Party in the Era of Jeffersonian Democracy* (New York: Harper and Row, 1965), 223; Sanford W. Higginbotham, *The Keystone in the Democratic Arch: Pennsylvania Politics, 1800–1816* (Harrisburg: Pennsylvania Historical and Museum Commission, 1952), 17, 25–27; Peter P. Hill, *William Vans Murray, Federalist Diplomat: The Shaping of Peace with France, 1797–1801* (Syracuse, N.Y.: Syracuse University Press, 1971), 141; John R. Howe, *The Changing Political Thought of John Adams* (Princeton, N.J.: Princeton University Press, 1966), 206; Richard H. Kohn, *Eagle and Sword: The Federalists and the Creation of the Military Establishment in America, 1783–1802* (New York: Free Press, 1975), 193, 251, 266; James Owen Knauss, "Social Conditions Among the Pennsylvania Germans in the Eighteenth Century, as Revealed in German Newspapers Published in America" (Ph.D. dissertation, Cornell University, 1917), 160–65; Stephen G. Kurtz, *The Presidency of John Adams: The Collapse of Federalism, 1795–1800* (Philadelphia: University of Pennsylvania Press, 1957), 358; Gilbert Lycan, *Alexander Hamilton and American Foreign Policy: A Design for Greatness* (Norman: University of Oklahoma Press, 1970), 350; John C. Miller, *The Federalist Era: 1789–1801* (New York: Harper and Brothers, 1960), 247–49; Page Smith, *John Adams*, 2 vols. (New York: Doubleday, 1962), 2: 1004–5, 1010, 1033; Harry M. Tinkcom, *The Republicans and Federalists in Pennsylvania, 1790–1801* (Harrisburg: Pennsylvania Historical and Museum Commission, 1950), 215–19; Leonard D. White, *The Federalists: A Study in Administrative History* (New York: Macmillan, 1956), 237–52; Richard Charles Wolf, "The Americanization of the German Lutherans, 1683–1829" (Ph.D. dissertation, Yale University, 1947), 369–71.

18. Louis Weinstein, "The Fries Rebellion" (Master's thesis, Temple University, 1939), 3–13. Weinstein's thesis differed little from Davis's narrative of events in *The Fries Rebellion of 1799*, except for Weinstein's limited use of depositions taken by U.S. District Attorney William Rawle. See also Peter Levine, "The Fries Rebellion: Social Violence and the Politics of the New Nation," *Pennsylvania History* 40 (July 1973): 241–58; Sue Taishoff, "Parties, Political Culture, and Latent Values: The Fries Rebellion and Partisan Behavior in Southeastern Pennsylvania" (Master's thesis, University of Virginia, 1973); Derek C. Smith, "The Fries Rebellion: Ideology and Insurrection in the Early American Republic" (Master's thesis, Claremont Graduate School, 1995). Dwight Henderson and Jane Shaffer Elsmere have studied John Fries's two trials, focusing on their significance for the evolution of the American definition of treason as well as Samuel Chase's role in Fries's second trial. Dwight F. Henderson, "Treason, Sedition, and Fries Rebellion," *American Journal of Legal History* 14 (1970): 308–17; Jane Shaffer Elsmere, "The Trials of John Fries," *Pennsylvania Magazine of History and Biography* 103 (October 1979): 432–45. For other mono-causal interpretations, see Stanley Elkins and Eric McKitrick, *The Age of Federalism, 1788–1800* (New York: Oxford University Press, 1993), 696–700; Robert Churchill, "Popular Nullification, Fries' Rebellion, and the Waning of Radical Republicanism, 1798–1801," *Pennsylvania History* 67 (Winter 2000): 105–40; Simon Newman, "The World Turned Upside Down: Revolutionary Politics, Fries' and Gabriel's Rebellions, and the Fears of the Federalists," *Pennsylvania History* 67 (Winter 2000): 5–20; Whitman D. Ridgway, "Fries in the Federalist Imagination: A Crisis of Republican Society," *Pennsylvania History* 67 (Winter 2000): 141–60. Terry Bouton's economic interpretation in "'No wonder the times were troublesome': The Origins of Fries Rebellion" works only by overlooking a considerable body of evidence that suggests that constitutional, political, and ethnoreligious concerns remained as important as economic ones.

Even my own "The Fries Rebellion and American Political Culture, 1798–1800," *Pennsylvania Magazine of History and Biography* 119 (January/April 1995): 37–74; "The Federalists' Cold War: The Fries Rebellion, National Security, and the State, 1790–1800," *Pennsylvania History* 67 (Winter 2000): 63–104; and "'Slavery and Taking the Liberty Away': Fries Rebellion and the Language of Popular Opposition," forthcoming in Jean Soderlund et al., eds., *Backcountry Crucibles: The Lehigh Valley from European Settlement to Steel* (Lehigh, Pa.: Lehigh University Press) attribute too few factors to the Kirchenleute language and ideology of resistance. In the former two articles, I had not yet incorporated the resisters' real economic concerns and I had only conceived of their ideology as a backward-looking, conservative defense of republican rights won during the Revolution. In the latter, written and submitted in 1999, I was beginning to broaden my conception of the Lehigh resistance, thanks to conferences and conversations with Marcus Rediker, Whit Ridgeway, Simon Newman, Owen S. Ireland, and Robert Churchill. The works published in *Pennsylvania History* in 2000 by Terry Bouton, Robert Churchill, Owen S. Ireland, Simon Newman, and Whit Ridgeway have been integral in my reassessment and reevaluation of Fries's Rebellion.

19. An exception is Keller, "Diversity and Democracy," chapter 7, passim; and Keller, *Rural Politics*, 25–28. Keller attributes the resistance to both local ethnoreligious conflict and state Republican Party machinations in 1798.

20. On the construction of popular ideologies, especially for the purpose of political protest, see George Rude, *Ideology and Popular Protest* (London: Lawrence and Wishart, 1980), and Rude, *The Crowd in History: A Study of Popular Disturbances in France and England, 1730–1848* (New York: Wiley, 1964). I am indebted to Katherine Reist for help in developing the language metaphor. Also on premodern popular ideology in the Atlantic world and America, see E. P. Thompson, "The Moral Economy of the English Crowd in the Eighteenth Century," *Past & Present* 50 (1971): 76–136; and Bogin, "Petitioning and the New Moral Economy."

21. It is important to note here that I have drawn these examples of language and actions from reports by rebuffed tax assessors and local constabulary, as well as by resisters themselves.

22. Philip Abrams, *Historical Sociology* (Ithaca, N.Y.: Cornell University Press, 1982). Abrams refers to this process as the "problematic of structuring," and he traces the development of this way of theorizing about sociology and history in "a single unified programme of analysis" from Emil Durkheim, Karl Marx and Freidrich Engels, and Max Weber to more recent "historical sociologists" who believe that the past should be used to understand the present and guide action in the future. Anthony Giddens, *New Rules of Sociological Method: A Positive Critique of Interpretative Sociologies,* (New York: Basic Books, 1976) called this process "structuration."

23. Carl Becker, *The History of Political Parties in the Province of New York, 1760–1776* Bulletin of the University of Wisconsin Series, vol. 2, no. 286 (1909; reprint Madison: University of Wisconsin Press, 1960).

24. On the Radicals and the Revolutionary movement in Pennsylvania, see Carl Bridenbaugh and Jessica Bridenbaugh, *Rebels and Gentlemen: Philadelphia and the Age of Franklin*, 2nd ed. (1942; reprint London: Oxford University Press, 1968); Brunhouse, *The Counter-Revolution in Pennsylvania*; John Frantz and William Pencak, eds., *Beyond Philadelphia: The American Revolution in the Pennsylvania Hinterland* (University Park: Pennsylvania State University Press, 1998); Eugene R. Harper, *The Transformation of*

Western Pennsylvania, 1770–1800 (Pittsburgh: University of Pittsburgh Press, 1991); Richard A. Ryerson, *The Revolution Is Now Begun: The Radical Committees of Philadelphia, 1775–1776* (Philadelphia: University of Pennsylvania Press, 1978).

The literature on republicanism as a historical construct to understand the ideology behind the decision making in the Revolutionary era is vast. Principal studies include Bernard Bailyn, *The Ideological Origins of the American Revolution* (Cambridge, Mass.: Harvard University Press, 1967); Gordon S. Wood, *The Creation of the American Republic, 1776–1787* (Chapel Hill: University of North Carolina Press, 1969); Wood, *The Radicalism of the American Revolution* (New York: Knopf, 1991); and Lance Banning, *The Jeffersonian Persuasion: The Evolution of a Party Ideology* (Ithaca, N.Y.: Cornell University Press, 1978), among others. For historiographic essays, see Robert E. Shalhope, "Toward a Republican Synthesis: The Emergence of an Understanding of Republicanism in American Historiography," *William and Mary Quarterly* 3rd ser. 29 (January 1972): 49–80; Shalhope, "Republicanism and Early American Historiography," *William and Mary Quarterly* 3rd ser. 39 (April 1982): 334–56; Daniel T. Rodgers, "Republicanism: The Career of a Concept," *Journal of American History* 79 (June 1992): 11–38.

25. Davis, *Fries Rebellion*, 9–10, details John Fries's military record. Through the depositions in the Rawle Papers and the trial testimony in Carpenter, *Two Trials*, and the *Criminal Case Files of the U.S. Circuit Court for the Eastern District of Pennsylvania, 1791–1840*, Records of the District Courts of the United States, National Archives and Records Administration (Washington D.C.: National Archives Microfilm Publications, 1976, 7 reels), reels 1 and 2, I compiled a sample of 211 people from Northampton, Bucks, Montgomery, and Berks Counties who participated in either the tax resistance, the writing and signing of petitions or associations, or the rescue. The 70 direct relatives were matched when possible by census and probate records, otherwise by surname and township matches; and adding these to those 83 veterans, raises the percentage of those directly connected to the Revolution to at least 72.5 percent. That number is undoubtedly low because it does not account for cousins or nephews with different surnames. Military records were compiled from Military Abstracts Card File for Revolutionary War, 1775–1783, Pennsylvania State Archives; and Active Duty Militia, Miscellaneous Payments and Continental Units, Pennsylvania State Archives, microfilm, reels 3891–3909. In previous publications, my sample number has differed. When I wrote "The Fries Rebellion and American Political Culture," I had only gathered 187 names. In my dissertation I identified 215. Recently, I have determined that four people I originally believed were resisters probably were not, so I have omitted them from the sample, yielding the present 211. Also, in the intervening years I was able to make a more exhaustive search of military records, which increased the numbers of veterans and relatives of veterans from 60 and 61 to 83 and 70 respectively.

26. Eugene R. Slaski, "The Lehigh Valley," in Frantz and Pencak, eds., *Beyond Philadelphia*, 46–66. See also Francis S. Fox, *Sweet Land of Liberty: The Ordeal of the Revolution in Northampton County Pennsylvania* (University Park: Pennsylvania State University Press, 2000).

27. Nolt, *Foreigners in Their Own Land*, 20.

28. Deposition of Israel Roberts, recorder and date unknown, Rawle Papers, 2: 2.

29. Deposition of Michael Bobst, given before Judge William Henry, January 28, 1799, Rawle Papers. For other examples of associations, see deposition of John Moritz, given before Judge Richard Peters, April 8, 1799, deposition of Daniel Reisch, given

before Judge William Henry, January 29, 1799, deposition of Daniel Weidner, given before Judge Richard Peters, April 6, 1799, deposition of Philip Stettler, given before Judge William Henry, January 28, 1799, Lehigh Association draft, 2: 16, deposition of Valentine Kehmlig, given before Judge Richard Peters, April 10, 1799, deposition of George Mitchell, given before Judge Richard Peters, date unknown, deposition of Peter Zeiner, given before Judge Richard Peters, April 16, 1799.

30. Deposition of Michael Bobst, given before Judge Richard Peters, April 10, 1799, Rawle Papers.

31. Deposition of George Ringer, given before Judge William Henry, January 28, 1799, Rawle Papers.

32. U.S. Congress, *Annals of Congress*, 5th Cong., 3rd sess., 2795. For more on the wave of petitions from over 18,000 Pennsylvanians and from all over the United States, see, 2985–3002.

33. I say at least 187, but there are several "Millers" and "Smiths" who of course very well may have been German. Actually, there are no names that I can say are definitely not German.

34. A. G. Roeber, *Palatines, Liberty, and Property: German Lutherans in Colonial British America* (Baltimore: Johns Hopkins University Press, 1993), especially chapters 1–4, passim. Stephen Nolt defines their political culture upon emigration as "peasant republicanism," in which "they related to governing powers as subjects who requested privileges and performed traditional duties," but that would begin to change in Pennsylvania, Nolt, *Foreigners in Their Own Land*, 30–31.

35. Fogleman, *Hopeful Journeys*, 147–48, 150, 140. For German immigrants concern for the attainment and security of private property and their engagement in Pennsylvania's colonial politics to achieve that security, see chapter 5. See also Nolt, *Foreigners in Their Own Land*, 12–13.

36. *Annals*, 5th Cong., 1st sess., June 17, 1797, 331, July 3, 1797, 393–407.

37. Fogleman, *Hopeful Journeys*, chapter 6, passim.

38. Fogleman, *Hopeful Journeys*, 150.

39. U.S. Bureau of the Census, 1790, 1800, Northampton County.

40. Slaski, "Lehigh Valley," 65.

41. Roeber in, *Palatines, Liberty, and Property* expertly details the Kirchenleute creation of a revolutionary ideology in eighteenth-century America.

42. Jean Stauffer Hudson, "Emmaus, Pennsylvania: Conflict and Stability in an Eighteenth Century Moravian Community" (Ph.D. dissertation, Lehigh University, 1977), 157–64.

43. These figures were compiled from "Upper Milford Evangelical Lutheran Church and Cemetery, Dillingersville Cemetery," Lehigh County Historical Society; "Church Record of the Upper Milford Reformed Congregation, New Zion's Reformed Church, 1757–1885," "Old Zionsville Reformed Church," "Solomon's United Church of Christ Cemetery," "Burials at Heidelberg Church," "Heidelburg Union Church Cemetery," "Chestnuthill Church, Upper Milford, 1773–1787"; *Collections of the Genealogical Society of Pennsylvania* V, 251 "Zion Lutheran Church, Old Zionsville, 1758–1903" (Philadelphia, 1910); Charles F. Seng, "Tombstone Inscriptions, Chestnuthill Cemetery" (Allentown, Pa.: Lehigh County Historical Society, 1967); "Christ Union Church Cemetery, Trumbauersville, Lower Milford" Bucks County Historical Society; "St. John's Evangelical Lutheran Cemetery, Spinnerstown, Lower Milford"; "Records of Trumbauersville Reformed

Church, 1769–1842" Bucks County Historical Society; Charles F. Seng, "Tombstone Inscriptions, Old Cemetery Great Swamp Church" (Newtown, Pa.: Bucks County Historical Society,1969).

44. No copy is extant, but Ethan Allen Weaver describes Pomp's letter to the editor in "'The American Eagle': The First English Newpaper Printed in Northampton County, Pennsylvania," *Pennsylvania Magazine of History and Biography* 23 (January 1899): 70.

45. Charles H. Glatfelter, *Pastors and People: German Lutheran and Reformed Churches in the Pennsylvania Field, 1717–1793* (Breinigsville, Pa.: Pennsylvania German Society, 1981).

46. On the process of "ethnicization" for Kirchenleute and Pennsylvania Germans, see Nolt, *Foreigners in Their Own Land*. On the concept of ethnicization in immigration studies, see John Higham, "Integrating America: The Problem of Assimilation in the Nineteenth Century," *Journal of American Ethnic History* (Fall 1981); Philip Gleason, "American Identity and Americanization," in William Patterson et al., eds., *Concepts of Ethnicity* (Cambridge, Mass.: Belknap Press of Harvard University Press, 1982), 57–68. The term "ethnicization" entered immigration studies with Victor Greene, *For God and Country: The Rise of Polish and Lithuanian Ethnic Consciousness in America* (Madison: University of Wisconsin Press, 1975).

47. While the resistance to the laws of the 5th Congress was spread broadly across the state—in Berks, Dauphin, Northumberland, Westmoreland, York, Chester, and Philadelphia Counties—the most concerted opposition to the Direct Tax took place in the Lehigh Valley region of Northampton, Bucks, and Montgomery counties (Map 2). Given the virulence of the Republican Party in Berks County, it seems surprising that the assessors were permitted to value and collect the tax there. But Berks was virtually an ethnically homogeneous county, nearly all its citizens were of German ancestry, and most of them were Kirchenleute. So the Federalists who received commissions to tax the rural areas outside of Reading were likely to be Kirchenleute as well, and those who were not knew better than to push the assessments. Berks County residents, therefore, did not suffer the indignity of being taxed by "Tories," and the charges of a Federalist monarchical conspiracy seemed somewhat less plausible.

48. Sharp, *American Politics in the Early Republic.*

49. See especially Davis, "The Democratic-Republican Societies of Pennsylvania, 1793–1796."

50. On the development of the national party struggle in the 1790s, see Lance Banning, *Jeffersonian Persuasion*; Elkins and McKitrick, *Age of Federalism*; Sharp, *American Politics in the Early Republic.*

51. For the party struggle in Pennsylvania, see Kenneth Keller, *Rural Politics*; and Keller, "Diversity and Democracy." For the elections of 1796 see chapter 6, passim.

52. Nazareth, Pennsylvania, Bicentennial, Inc., *Two Centuries of Nazareth, 1740–1940* (Nazareth, Pa.: Item Publishing Company., 1940), 75; Keller, "Diversity and Democracy," 196.

53. *Readinger Adler*, November 29, 1796.

54. For the standard interpretation of the influence of "country" ideology on Jeffersonian opposition in the 1790s, see Banning, *Jeffersonian Persuasion.*

55. Wokeck, *Trade in Strangers*, 9.

56. Abbot Emerson Smith, *Colonists in Bondage: White Servitude and Convict*

Labor in America, 1607–1776 (Chapel Hill: University of North Carolina Press, 1947), 320–23. Smith estimates that perhaps one-half to two-thirds of Germans came to Philadelphia as either indentures (pre-contracted in Europe) or redemptioners (shipped with a contract to be purchased in the colony), most as the latter.

57. Bouton, "A Road Closed," 859.

58. On these topics see Alfred F. Young, ed., *The American Revolution: Essays in the History of American Radicalism* (Dekalb: Northern Illinois University Press, 1976); Brendan McConville, *These Daring Disturbers of the Public Peace: The Struggle for Property and Power in Early New Jersey* (Ithaca, N.Y.: Cornell University Press, 1999); Richards, *Shays's Rebellion*; Szatmary, *Shays' Rebellion*; Alan Taylor, *Liberty Men and Great Proprietors: The Revolutionary Settlement on the Maine Frontier, 1760–1820*; Michael Bellesiles, *Revolutionary Outlaws: Ethan Allen and the Struggle for Independence on the Early American Frontier* (Charlottesville: University Press of Virginia, 1993).

59. Jacob Arndt to John Nicholson, April 21, 1787, Records of the Comptroller General, General Correspondence, 1776–1809, Pennsylvania State Archives, microfilm 4865, roll 3.

60. Bouton, "'No wonder the times were troublesome,'" 28–30; Bouton, "A Road Closed," 858–64.

61. Pennsylvania Septennial Census 1800, rolls 1, 4, numbers 242, 245.

62. Lucy Simler, "The Landless Worker: An Index of Economic Social Change in Chester County, Pennsylvania, 1750–1820," *Pennsylvania Magazine of History and Biography* 114 (April 1990): 163–99.

63. "Petition of the Citizens and Inhabitants of Lower Milford and part of Richland Township," Records of the Department of State, Bureau of Commissions, Elections and Legislation, Appointment and Commission Books for Civil Officers, 1790–1973, Bucks File, 1795, Pennsylvania State Archives.

64. These figures were tabulated using *United States Direct Tax*, reels 8, 9, 10, 12; Bucks County, Pennsylvania, Tax Assessments, 1798; Northampton County, Pennsylvania, County Rate 1798, 1799.

65. *Gazette of the United States*, March 20, 1799.

66. James T. Lemon, "Household Consumption in Eighteenth-Century America and its Relationship to Production and Trade: The Situation Among Farmers in Southeastern Pennsylvania," *Agricultural History* 41 (1967): 59–70.

67. Kenneth Keller compiled these county averages from the Direct Tax lists, Keller, *Rural Politics*, 9. Northampton County resisters were ahead of the county average because in 1798 Northampton County spread over a vast northern distance of undeveloped or underdeveloped land controlled mainly by speculators, dragging down the average values.

68. The statistics in this paragraph were culled from U.S. Bureau of the Census, 1790, Bucks County, Northampton County; Pennsylvania Septennial Census, 1786, 1800; *Direct Tax of 1798*, Bucks County, Northampton County, reels 8, 9, 10, and 12.

69. Bouton, "No wonder the times were troublesome," 30–33.

70. *Philadelphia Aurora*, January 12, 1799.

71. Bouton, "No wonder the times were troublesome," 33–34.

72. E. Gordon Alderfer, *Northampton Heritage: The Story of an American County* (Easton, Pa.: Northampton County Historical and Genealogical Society, 1953), 69–91, 174.

73. *Direct Tax of 1798*, Bucks County, reel 8.

74. Examination of John Fries, given before Judge Richard Peters, April 6, 1799, in Carpenter, *Two Trials*, 81–82.

75. For Northampton officeholders, see County Election Returns for Federal, State, and Local, 1790–1850, Department of State, Pennsylvania State Archives, microfilm, reels 679–88; and Appointments File for Civil Officers, 1790–1968, Bureau of Commissions, Elections, and Legislation, Department of State, microfilm, reels 675–78. On the controversy over the prothonotary appointment in 1798, see Keller, *Rural Politics*, 20.

76. "The Memorial of divers freemen Inhabitants of the County of Bucks," January 1, 1795, Appointments File for Civil Officers, roll 1, frame 110; "Petition of the Inhabitants of Lower Milford and Richland Townships," 1794, frames 291–92.

77. Deposition of Judge John Mulhallon, given before Judge Richard Peters, March 23, 1799, Rawle Papers, 2: 2.

78. Wood, *Radicalism of the American Revolution*, especially chapters in part 2, "Republicanism," passim. On the Revolution's democratizing effect on women, see Mary Beth Norton, *Liberty's Daughters: The Revolutionary Experience of American Women, 1750–1800* (Boston: Little, Brown, 1980); Linda Kerber, *Women of the Republic: Intellect and Ideology in Revolutionary America* (Chapel Hill: University of North Carolina Press, 1980); Ronald Hoffman and Peter J. Albert, *Women in the Age of the American Revolution* (Charlottesville: University of Virginia Press, 1989). On democratization within the family, see Jay Fliegelman, *Prodigals and Pilgrims: The American Revolution Against Patriarchal Authority, 1750–1800* (New York: Cambridge University Press, 1982). On religion, see Nathan O. Hatch, *The Democratization of American Christianity* (New Haven, Conn.: Yale University Press, 1989). On the Revolution's effect on slave owners, slaves, and free blacks, see William Freehling, "The Founding Fathers and Slavery," *American Historical Review* 77 (February 1972): 81–93; Winthrop Jordan, *The White Man's Burden: Historical Origins of Racism in the United States* (New York: Oxford University Press, 1974); Ira Berlin, *Many Thousands Gone: The First Two Centuries of Slavery in North America* (Cambridge, Mass.: Belknap Press of Harvard University Press, 1998); Arthur Zilversmit, *The First Emancipation: The Abolition of Slavery in the North* (Chicago: University of Chicago Press, 1967). See also a variety of essays in Ira Berlin and Ronald Hoffman, eds., *Slavery and Freedom in the Age of the American Revolution* (Charlottesville: University of Virginia Press, 1983), particularly Richard S. Dunn, "Black Society in the Chesapeake, 1776–1810"; Philip D. Morgan, "Black Society in the Low Country, 1760–1810"; Gary Nash, "Forging Freedom: The Emancipation Experience in Northern Seaport Cities, 1775–1820"; Mary Beth Norton, Herbert Gutman, and Ira Berlin, "The Afro-American Family in the Age of Revolution"; A.J. Raboteau, "The Slave Church in the Era of the American Revolution"; Benjamin Quarles, "The Revolutionary War as a Black Declaration of Independence."

79. Deposition of Jeremiah Trexler, given before Judge Richard Peters, April 14, 1799, Rawle Papers, 2: 77.

80. *Annals*, 5th Cong., 3rd sess., 2795. For more on the wave of petitions from over 18,000 Pennsylvanians and from all over the United States, see 2985–3002.

81. Deposition of James Jackson, given before Justice of the Peace John Curwan, October 23, 1799, Rawle Papers; *Oracle of Dauphin and Harrisburg Daily Advertiser*, February 6, 1799, January 23, 1799, March 20, 1799. For other examples of liberty poles

throughout the Lehigh Valley region, see deposition of Philip Arndt, given before Peter Rhoads, September 17, 1798, Rawle Papers; *Kline's Carlisle Weekly Gazette*, January 23, 1799, and *Oracle of Dauphin*, January 16, 1799.

82. Deposition of Jon Fogel, Jr., given before Judge William Henry, January 29, 1799, Rawle Papers, 2: 2; deposition of James Jackson, given before Justice of the Peace John Curwan, October 23, 1799; *Oracle of Dauphin*, January 9, 1799.

83. For the last two decades, scholars have debated the usefulness of republicanism to understanding post-Revolutionary American society. Many contend that classical republican values continued to influence American thought and action through the eighteenth century and into the first two decades of the nineteenth. See particularly Banning, *Jeffersonian Persuasion*, and Banning, "Quid Transit? Paradigms and Process in the Transformation of Republican Ideas," *Reviews in American History* 17 (June 1989): 199–204; Drew McCoy, *The Elusive Republic: Political Economy in Jeffersonian America* (Chapel Hill: University of North Carolina Press, 1980); and John Murrin, "Self Interest Conquers Patriotism," in Jack P. Greene, ed., *The American Revolution: Its Character and Limits* (New York: New York University Press, 1987).

Others contend that the Revolution either unleashed liberalism, democracy, and individualism in America or simply confirmed those qualities, which preexisted. Liberalism, for them, was the dominant ideological construct throughout this era and forward into the nineteenth century. See especially, Joyce O. Appleby, *Capitalism and a New Social Order: The Republican Vision of the 1790s* (New York: New York University Press, 1984); Appleby, "Republicanism in Old and New Contexts," *William and Mary Quarterly* 3rd ser. 43 (January 1986): 20–34; Isaac Kramnick, "'The 'Great National Discussion': The Discourse of Politics in 1787," *William and Mary Quarterly* 3rd ser. 45 (January 1988): 3–32; and Wood, *Radicalism of the American Revolution*, part 3, "Democracy," passim.

Contemporaries would have been confused by the twentieth-century academic debate on this issue. They would have recognized elements of both classical republicanism and liberalism in their own thoughts and actions. Even before the Revolution, in the world of American politics framed by classical republican thought, kernels of liberalism were widespread. Throughout the colonies, citizens came to expect their governments to be responsive to their individual needs. In places of ethnic and religious diversity, such as Pennsylvania and New York, party politics liberalized the political world further by providing voters with a choice of candidates. And in Pennsylvania, requirements for naturalization and voting declined steadily through the colonial era. The Revolution demonstrably excited the elements of liberalism, democracy, and individualism inherent within republicanism. Yet this does not mean that liberalism supplanted republicanism as the dominant mode of thought in the 1790s. Indeed, I would argue that neither was dominant, nor were they separate, but rather two sides to the same coin. For similar arguments, see Lance Banning, "Jeffersonian Ideology Revisited: Liberal and Classical Ideas in the New American Republic," *William and Mary Quarterly* 3rd ser. 43 (January 1986): 3–19; and Pauline Maier, "The Transforming Impact of Independence, Reaffirmed: 1776 and the Definition of American Social Structure," in James E. Henretta et al., eds., *The Transformation of Early American History: Society, Authority, and Ideology* (New York: Knopf, 1991). Liberalism, democracy, and the politics of self-interest would eventually come to dominance, but not for another generation—when the mostly rural, agrarian veterans of the Revolution and their children passed on control of the country to men who inherited a nation on the brink of a national market economy financed by banks, interconnected by bridges, roads, canals, steamboats, and railroads, and steered by the consumer.

84. "Petition of Remonstrance of Sundry Inhabitants of the Township of Lower Milford," 1785, Executive Correspondence and Petitions, Records of Pennsylvania's Revolutionary Governments, Pennsylvania State Archives, microfilm roll 22, frame 39.

85. Deposition of John Lersass, given before Judge William Henry, February 1, 1799, Rawle Papers, 2: 2.

86. Testimony of Christian Heckewelder, Carpenter, *Two Trials*, 185; deposition of John Lersass, given before Judge William Henry, February 1, 1799, Rawle Papers, 2: 2.

87. Thompson, "Moral Economy of the English Crowd in the Eighteenth Century"; Rude, *Ideology and Popular Protest*, chapter 2, passim, and Rude, *The Crowd in History*.

88. For accounts of the conservatism of eighteenth-century political protests in America, see Paul Gilje, *Rioting in America* (Bloomington: Indiana University Press, 1996), chapters 1–4, passim; and *The Road to Mobocracy: Popular Disorder in New York City, 1763–1834* (Chapel Hill: University of North Carolina Press, 1987); Pauline Maier, "Popular Uprisings and Civil Authority in Eighteenth-Century America," *William and Mary Quarterly* 3rd ser. 27 (January 1970): 3–35, and Maier, *From Resistance to Revolution: Colonial Radicals and the Development of American Opposition to Britain, 1765–1776* (New York: Knopf, 1972); Gordon S. Wood, "A Note on Mobs in the American Revolution," *William and Mary Quarterly* 3rd ser. 23 (October 1966): 634–42.

For accounts of the radicalism of eighteenth-century social protest, see Alfred F. Young, ed., *The American Revolution: Explorations in the History of American Radicalism* (Dekalb: Northern Illinois University Press, 1976).

89. For an excellent example of middle-colony pluralism and its attendant cultural, religious, and economic competition that often resulted in crowd action, see Brendan McConville, *These Daring Disturbers of the Public Peace: The Struggle for Property and Power in Early New Jersey* (Ithaca, N.Y.: Cornell University Press, 1999).

90. Gilje, *Rioting in America*, 25; see also Brook Hindle, "The March of the Paxton Boys," *William and Mary Quarterly* 3rd ser. 3 (October 1946), 461–86.

91. On the radicalism and violence of eighteenth-century public protest, with particular attention to Pennsylvania examples, see Thomas P. Slaughter, "Crowds in Eighteenth Century America: Reflections and New Directions," *Pennsylvania Magazine of History and Biography* 115 (January 1991): 3–34.

92. Keller, "Diversity and Democracy," 50.

93. Northampton County Quarter Sessions Papers, Northampton County Archives, see especially December 1785, June 1791, September 1791, December 1791 for cases of riot and armed road closings. Every docket from both decades contains dozens of cases of assault and battery, armed robbery, rape, mischief, riot, and other violent crimes. In spite of the sectarian presence, violence was no stranger to the Lehigh Valley.

94. Gilje, *Rioting in America*, 63.

95. Davis, *Fries Rebellion*, 10, discusses Fries's military record, and Jarret's Whiskey Rebellion service can be found in Records of the Office of Comptroller General, Western Expedition Accounts, Pennsylvania State Archives, microfilm, reels 4262 and 4265. Of the sample of 211 resisters, 28 had marched west in 1794 to put down the insurrection. This direct experience witnessing the federal government dealing with popular, violent dissent is another contributing factor that explains the purposeful attempts to refrain from violence in the Lehigh Valley in 1798–199.

96. Deposition of George Lintz, given before Judge William Henry, January 29, 1799, Rawle Papers, 2: 2.

97. Deposition of John Wetzel, given before Judge William Henry, January 29, Rawle Papers. For other examples of similar threats, see deposition of Henry Strauss, given before Judge William Henry, February 16, 1799, deposition of Alexander Benjamin, given before Justice of the Peace Abraham Bachman, March 28, 1799, deposition of Simon Seller, given before Judge William Henry, May 21, 1799, examination of Henry Kooken, given before Judge William Henry, no date given, deposition of Christian Heckewelder, given before Judge Richard Peters, April 13, 1799.

98. Deposition of James Williamson, given before Judge Richard Peters, April 15, 1799, Rawle Papers.

99. Slaughter, "Crowds in Eighteenth-Century America," rebukes the "consensus school"—particularly Jack P. Greene, *Pursuits of Happiness: The Social Development of Early Modern British Colonies and the Formation of American Culture* (Chapel Hill: University of North Carolina Press, 1988), 140, 199; Maier, *From Resistance to Revolution*; Maier, "Popular Uprisings and Civil Authority," and Gilje, *Road to Mobocracy*—for their portrayal of eighteenth-century extralegal mob action as conservative, acceptive of authority, and diminishing in its violent character. To challenge the consensus model, Slaughter points to example after example of mob violence in Pennsylvania, stressing its continuity from the colonial era, thorough the Revolution and the founding of the nation, and into the nineteenth century. He then offers his own model to explain the peculiarly violent nature of American mob action: the concept of liminality. Liminal theory "is a threshold state betwixt and between existing orders and Aliminars . . . are between identities" or "in politics they are between allegiances." Slaughter continues to explain that "liminal status can be the consequence of comparative economic and/or educational deprivation; it can be ethnically, racially, and/or gender based; and it can be the consequence of living on a territorial frontier." Living on various forms of frontiers, "living at the fringes of power—cultural, political, and economic—people on the frontier are typically, perhaps definitionally contemptuous of authority . . . forced to rely on a justice less influenced by law . . . and lived in a more interpersonally violent world" (12–14). Yet there are exceptions to Slaughter's model just as he found exceptions to the consensus model. In almost every way, the Fries Rebels were liminars—ethnically, politically, territorially, and linguistically. However, when the time came to mobilize for extralegal action they were conspicuously non-violent in an age when political violence was indeed the norm. And their actions represented attempts to reaffirm their place within their concept of the existing political order rather than an endeavor to overthrow it. Indeed, they opposed their Federalist leaders not in contempt for national political authority, but to hold them accountable to the federal Constitution that granted that power and to defend their conception of the Constitution. For another account of the extent and typicality of interpersonal and political violence in the eighteenth century, see Thomas P. Slaughter, "Interpersonal Violence in a Rural Setting: Lancaster County in the Eighteenth Century," *Pennsylvania History* 58 (April 1991): 98–123.

100. On "Hillsborough Painting," see Shaw, *American Patriots and the Rituals of the Revolution*, 185–86, and on other violent rituals, 26–47.

101. Deposition of Philip Wescoe, date and recorder unknown, Rawle Papers, 2: 95.

102. On partisan politics in the 1790s, and particularly on the varying strains of "Federalism" in the party of Washington, see Elkins and McKitrick, *Age of Federalism*,

and Sharp, *American Politics in the Early Republic.* Hamiltonian Federalism will be explored further in the succeeding chapters.

Chapter 2. Order

1. Kammen, *Spheres of Liberty.*
2. Bailyn, *Ideological Origins*; Wood, *Radicalism of the American Revolution.* For a clear and concise explanation of the dual meaning of liberty between 1765 and 1800, see Banning, *Jeffersonian Persuasion,* 126–27.
3. Wood, *Creation of the American Republic, 1776–1787.*
4. Max Farrand, ed., *The Records of the Federal Constitution of 1787,* 4 vols. (New Haven, Conn.: Yale University Press, 1911), 1: 282–311.
5. Farrand, *Records of the Federal Constitution.*
6. On Antifederalism, see especially Celia Kenyon, "Men of Little Faith: The Anti-Federalists on the Nature of Representative Government," *William and Mary Quarterly* 3rd ser. 12 (January 1955): 3–43; and Gordon S. Wood, "Interests and Disinterestedness in the Making of the Constitution," in Richard Beeman et al., *Beyond Confederation: Origins of the Constitution and American National Identity* (Chapel Hill: University of North Carolina Press, 1987), 69–109.
7. For the development of this concept within republicanism, its use in Britain, and its export to America see J. G. A. Pocock, *The Machiavellian Moment: Florentine Political Thought and the Atlantic Republican Tradition* (Princeton, N.J.: Princeton University Press, 1975).
8. It is not the purpose of this book to unfurl the many contours of 1780s and 90s Federalism; that subject alone comprised a considerable, insightful, and provocative synthesis by historians Elkins and McKitrick, *The Age of Federalism.* Instead, the following portrayal of the Federalists and the discussions of them in the subsequent chapters will focus mainly upon Alexander Hamilton and his followers, referred to above as Hamiltonians, because they were at the center of this story. They devised the defensive measures and the Direct Tax and spearheaded them through Congress. They labeled the resistance a "rebellion," pushed for the military suppression of the rebellion, most loudly demanded the execution of its leaders, and withdrew themselves from the majority of the Federalist Party in the summer and fall of 1800 after President Adams sent a peace mission to France and issued pardons to the rebels. They created the context for the Kirchenleute's popular constitutional dissent.
9. This sentiment is clearly described in David F. Epstein, "The Case for Ratification: Federalist Constitutionalist Thought," in Leonard W. Levy and Dennis J. Mahoney, eds., *The Framing and Ratification of the Constitution* (New York: Macmillan, 1987), 301. For other key Federalists' fears of democratic politics and beliefs that the political role of the people in a republic ended at the polls, see Winfred E. A. Bernhard, *Fisher Ames: Federalist and Statesman, 1758–1808* (Chapel Hill: University of North Carolina Press, 1965); John Malsberger, "The Political Thought of Fisher Ames," *Journal of the Early Republic* 2 (Spring 1982): 1–20; Stephen E. Patterson, "The Roots of Massachusetts Federalism: Conservative Politics and Political Culture Before 1787," in Ronald Hoffman and Peter J. Albert, eds., *Sovereign States in an Age of Uncertainty* (Charlottesville: University

of Virginia Press, 1981); Glenn A. Phelps, *George Washington and American Constitutionalism* (Lawrence: University of Kansas Press, 1993); Richard E. Welch, Jr., *Theodore Sedgwick, Federalist: A Political Portrait* (Middletown, Conn.: Wesleyan University Press, 1965); and Melvin R. Zahniser, *Charles Cotesworth Pinckney, Founding Father* (Chapel Hill: University of North Carolina Press, 1967).

10. I have drawn on a number of sources to form my view of conservative Federalist ideology. Some of the more complete treatments can be found in Appleby, *Capitalism and a New Social Order*, Appleby, "The New Republican Synthesis and the Changing Political Ideas of John Adams," *American Quarterly* 25 (December 1973): 578–95; James M. Banner, *To the Hartford Convention: The Federalists and the Origins of Party Politics in Massachusetts* (New York: Knopf, 1970); Banning, *Jeffersonian Persuasion*; Richard Buel, *Securing the Revolution: Ideology in American Politics, 1789–1815* (Ithaca, N.Y.: Cornell University Press, 1972); Manning J. Dauer, *The Adams Federalists* (Baltimore: Johns Hopkins University Press, 1968); Elkins and McKitrick, *The Age of Federalism*; Fischer, *The Revolution of American Conservatism*; John R. Howe, Jr., "Republican Thought and the Political Violence of the 1790s," *American Quarterly* 19 (Summer 1967): 147–65; Kammen, *Spheres of Liberty*; Linda Kerber, *Federalists in Dissent: Imagery and Ideology in Jeffersonian America* (Ithaca, N.Y.: Cornell University Press, 1970); McCoy, *The Elusive Republic*; Miller, *Federalist Era*; Sharp, *American Politics in the Early Republic*; Marshall Smelser, "The Federalist Period as an Age of Passion," *American Quarterly* 10 (Winter 1958): 391–419; Slaughter, *Whiskey Rebellion*; Gerald Stourzh, *Alexander Hamilton and the Idea of Republican Government* (Stanford, Calif.: Stanford University Press, 1970); Wood, *The Creation of the American Republic*; and Wood, *Radicalism of the American Revolution*.

11. For another treatment of the Federalists as the "friends of order" against rebellious disorder, see Todd Estes, "Liberty and Order: Revolutionary Democracy and the Problem of Governance in the Early American Republic" (Ph.D. dissertation, University of Kentucky, 1995), 51–114.

12. Hamilton to Edward Carrington, May 26, 1792, in *The Papers of Alexander Hamilton*, 27 vols., ed. Harold C. Syrett (New York: Columbia University Press, 1961–1987), 11: 444.

13. On Alexander Hamilton, see Jacob Cooke, *Alexander Hamilton* (New York: Scribner's, 1982); Forrest McDonald, *Alexander Hamilton: A Biography* (New York: W.W. Norton, 1979); John C. Miller, *Alexander Hamilton: Portrait in Paradox* (New York: Harper, 1959); Stourzh, *Alexander Hamilton*.

14. For Hamilton's understanding of Britain and the balance of power, and the course of action the U.S. should pursue between France and Britain, see Hamilton to George Washington, July 15, 1790, *Papers of Alexander Hamilton*, 6: 493–96; and Hamilton to Washington, September 15, 1790, 6: 36–57.

15. For a clear definition of Hamiltonian foreign policy, see Stourzh, *Alexander Hamilton*, 126–70; and Reginald Horsman, *The Diplomacy of the New Republic, 1776–1815* (Arlington Heights, Ill.: Harlan Davidson, 1985), chapter 2, "The British Connection," passim.

16. For the Federalist ideology behind Hamiltonian schemes of finance and the connection between domestic and foreign policy, see Banning, *Jeffersonian Persuasion*, 126–47; Elkins and McKitrick, *Age of Federalism*, chapter 2, "Finance and Ideology," 77–131; McCoy, *Elusive Republic*, 132–35, 146–65.

17. Wood, *Radicalism of the American Revolution*, 243.

18. On the "Shays'" and "Whiskey" rebellions, see sources in Prologue note 24 above, and Robert A. Gross, *In Debt to Shays: The Bicentennial of an Agrarian Rebellion* (Charlottesville: University Press of Virginia, 1993). On Democratic Societies, see Davis, "Democratic-Republican Societies of Pennsylvania"; and Eugene P. Link, *The Democratic-Republican Societies, 1790–1800* (New York: Columbia University Press, 1942). On the various secession attempts and conspiracies, see Sharp, *American Politics in the Early Republic*; on Vermont, see Bellesiles, *Revolutionary Outlaws*.

19. Thomas Jefferson to William Stephens Smith, November 13, 1787, in *The Papers of Thomas Jefferson*, 25 vols., ed. Julian P. Boyd et al. (Princeton, N.J.: Princeton University Press, 1950–1992), 12: 582; James Madison, "Government of the United States," published originally in the *National Gazette*, February 4, 1792, reprinted in *The Papers of James Madison*, 17 vols., ed. William T. Hutchinson et al. (Chicago: University of Chicago Press, 1962–1991), 9: 248.

20. Hamilton to George Washington, September 9, 1792, *Papers of Alexander Hamilton*, 12: 344–47; Tench Coxe to Hamilton, October 19, 1792, 12: 592–602; Hamilton to Washington, August 2, 1794, 17: 15–19.

21. Bailyn, *Ideological Origins of the American Revolution*, 36, 48, 61–63, 65, 73, 84, 112–19.

22. "Americanus, No. 1," *Dunlap and Claypoole's American Daily Advertiser*, January 31, 1794; "Pacificus," Nos. 1–10, *Gazette of the United States*, June 29, July 3, 6, 10, 13–17, 27, 1793; "The Cause of France," 1794, *Papers of Alexander Hamilton*, 17: 585–86.

23. Hamilton feared British military might. In addition, his domestic programs, court style politics, and commercial republican ideology depended on stable economic and political relations with the British. The agrarian republicanism of Jefferson and Madison, on the other hand, demanded freer trade and wide access to foreign markets, and they feared the opportunities for corruption that Hamilton's economic programs could create. While they did not advocate literal adherence to the 1778 Franco-American Treaty of Alliance to assist the French in their own war with England in 1793, they scorned attachments to Great Britain as corrosive to liberty and republican virtue, and Jefferson worked diligently as secretary of state to prevent a Proclamation of Neutrality that would discriminate against the French in favor of the British. As of the 1790s, Jefferson and Madison still held to the radical republican or "Whig oppositionist thought" that had formed their perception of a British conspiracy against liberty in 1776. Through the decade of the nineties, they viewed the Hamiltonian economic program and subsequent Federalist "pro-British" policies together as a monarchical conspiracy against liberty, designed to undermine republican government in America. Hamilton to Carrington, May 26, 1792, *Papers of Alexander Hamilton*, 11: 439. McCoy, *Elusive Republic*, 136–65. In *The Elusive Republic* and in "Republicanism and American Foreign Policy: James Madison and the Political Economy of Commercial Discrimination, 1789–1794," *William and Mary Quarterly* 31 (October 1974): 633–46, Drew McCoy discusses the foreign policy of Jeffersonian republicanism. For the evolution of Jeffersonian-republican opposition ideology, see Banning, *Jeffersonian Persuasion*.

24. Hamilton to Carrington, May 26, 1792, *Papers of Alexander Hamilton*, 11: 444; Wolcott to Hamilton, March 31, 1797, 20: 572; Wolcott to Hamilton, December 8, 1796, 20: 435–36; Pickering to Hamilton, April 9, 1798, 21: 409.

25. Gilje, *The Road to Mobocracy*, 71–119; Fisher Ames's memorable remark is on p. 3.

26. The literature on the first party system is vast, see particularly: Banning, *Jeffersonian Persuasion*; Buel, *Securing the Revolution*; Elkins and McKitrick, *Age of Federalism*; Sharp, *American Politics in the Early Republic* An excellent recent interpretation is Stuart Leibiger, *Founding Friendship: George Washington, James Madison, and the Creation of the American Republic* (Charlottesville: University Press of Virginia, 1999).

27. Link, *Democratic-Republican Societies*, 16. Aside from Link, the most modern and sophisticated interpretations of the Democratic-Republican societies, which treat them within the scope of the history of voluntary associations in America, are Elkins and McKitrick, *Age of Federalism*, 451–61, and Davis, "Democratic-Republican Societies Pennsylvania." Much of my analysis flows from their arguments. See also Philip S. Foner, *The Democratic-Republican Societies, 1790–1800: A Documentary Sourcebook of Constitutions, Declarations, Addresses, Resolutions, and Toasts* (Westport, Conn.: Greenwood Press, 1976), on French Jacobin clubs 10, 67, 153; quoted material on 180, 255, 359.

28. For further sources on the "Whiskey Rebellion," see Boyd, ed., *The Whiskey Rebellion: Past and Present Perspectives*; Jerry A. Clouse, *The Whiskey Rebellion: Southwestern Pennsylvania's Frontier People Test the American Constitution* (Harrisburg: Pennsylvania Historical and Museum Commission, 1994); and Mary K. Bonsteel Tachau, "The Whiskey Rebellion in Kentucky," *Journal of the Early Republic* 2 (Fall 1982): 239–59.

29. Elkins and McKitrick, *Age of Federalism*, 226; Hamilton to George Washington, August 2, 1794, *Papers of Alexander Hamilton*, 17: 15–19; Hamilton to Washington, September 9, 1792, 12: 344–47; Hamilton to Washington, September 2, 1792, 12: 311–12.

30. Marco M. Sidi, "The Democratic-Republican Societies at the End of the Eighteenth Century: The Western Pennsylvania Experience," *Pennsylvania History* 60 (November 1993): 288–304.

31. Quoted in Stephen E. Ambrose, *Undaunted Courage: Meriwether Lewis, Thomas Jefferson, and the Opening of the American West* (New York: Simon and Schuster, 1996), 39.

32. "President's Address to Congress," *Annals*, 3rd Cong., 2nd sess., November 19, 1794, 787–92.

33. Madison to James Monroe, December 4, 1794, *Papers of James Madison*, 15: 406. On the Federalists' manipulation of the symbols and images of George Washington for political advantage, see Simon P. Newman, "American Popular Political Culture in the Age of the French Revolution" (Ph.D. dissertation, Princeton University, 1991), chapters 2 and 3, passim.

34. Newman, "American Popular Political Culture," 281–87; Miller, *Federalist Era*, 168.

35. Quoted in Newman, "American Popular Political Culture," 286–87.

36. See chapter 1. Nazareth, Pennsylvania, Bicentennial, Inc., *Two Centuries of Nazareth, 1740–1940* (Nazareth, Pa.: Item Publishing Company., 1940), 75; Keller, "Diversity and Democracy," 196.

37. On these points, see Gilje, *Road to Mobocracy*; Newman, "American Popular Political Culture," 338–53; and Estes, "Liberty and Order," 244–45.

38. See especially Alexander DeConde, *Entangling Alliance: Politics and Diplomacy Under George Washington* (Durham, N.C.: Duke University Press, 1958), on Genet, 200, 235–36, 250, 252–53, 260, 278–79, 283–84, 305, on Fauchet, 409–15, on Adet, 425–28, 456, 472, 476; and Albert Hall Bowman, *Struggle for Neutrality: Franco-American Diplomacy During the Federalist Era* (Knoxville: University of Tennessee Press, 1974), on Genet, 81–83, on Fauchet, 199–203, and on Adet, 204, 233, 263–67.

39. "No Jacobin," Nos. 1–8, *American Daily Advertiser,* July 31, August 5, 8, 10, 14, 23, 26, 28, 1793.

40. George Washington, "Proclamation," in *Writings of George Washington* 14 vols., ed. Worthington Chauncey Ford (New York: G.P. Putnam's Sons, 1889–1893), 3: 430–31.

41. *Writings of George Washington,* 3: 4.

42. For accounts of Genet's mission, see Harry Ammon, *The Genet Mission* (New York: W.W. Norton, 1973); Maude H. Woodfin, "Citizen Genet and his Mission" (Ph.D. dissertation, University of Chicago, 1928); William F. Keller, "American Politics and the Genet Mission" (Ph.D. dissertation, University of Pittsburgh, 1951).

43. Hamilton, "Relations with France, 1795–1796," *Papers of Alexander Hamilton,* 19: 526–27; Wolcott to Hamilton, March 31, 1797, 20: 569–574; Hamilton, "Relations with France," 19: 527; *Philadelphia Aurora,* October 27, November 15, 1796.

44. *Minerva & Mercantile Evening Advertiser,* December 8, 1796; Hamilton to Rufus King, December 16, 1796, *Papers of Alexander Hamilton,* 20: 444; Hamilton to Jeremiah Wadsworth, November 8, 1796, 20: 376.

45. Hamilton, "Relations with France," *Papers of Alexander Hamilton,* 19: 526; Timothy Pickering to Noah Webster, November, 1, 1797, in *The Timothy Pickering Papers,* ed. Frederick S. Allis (Boston: Massachusetts Historical Society, 1966, microfilm, 69 reels), 7: 412; Hamilton, "Relations with France," *Papers of Alexander Hamilton,* 19: 326–27. See Genet's instructions in Frederick Jackson Turner, ed., "Correspondence of the French Ministers to the United States, 1791–1797," *Annual Report of the American Historical Association for the Year 1903* (Washington, D.C.: Government Printing Office, 1904), 2: 201–11. He was instructed also to rouse the citizens of Louisiana, Florida, and Canada to rise up against their Spanish and British governors. On the Kentucky mission, see Thomas Jefferson, "Anas," in *The Writings of Thomas Jefferson,* 20 vols., ed. Andrew A. Lipscomb (Washington, D.C.: Thomas Jefferson Memorial Association, 1904), 1: 235–37. Other accounts of Genet's activity in the southwest can be found in Harold D. Peters, "Citizen Genet and the American West, 1793–1794" (Ph.D. dissertation, University of West Virginia, 1972); Frederick Jackson Turner, "The Origins of Genet's Projected Attack on Louisiana and the Floridas," *American Historical Review* 3 (July 1898): 650–71; Turner, "The Policy of France Toward the Mississippi Valley in the Period of Washington and Adams," *American Historical Review* 10 (January 1905): 249–79; Archibald Henderson, "Isaac Shelby and the Genet Mission," *Mississippi Valley Historical Review* 6 (March 1920): 445–69.

46. H. Marshall to Pickering, December 15, 1796, *Pickering Papers,* 20: 423; Hamilton to McHenry, May 15, 1797, in *The Life and Correspondence of James McHenry: Secretary of War Under Washington and Adams,* ed. Bernard C. Steiner (Cleveland: Burrow Bros., 1907), 212; McHenry to George Washington, July 9, 1797, 256–57; Captain William H. Harrison to McHenry, August 13, 1797, 263–64. See also Pickering to McHenry, January 17, 1810, 272–73.

47. Pickering to Rufus King, June 20, 1797, *Pickering Papers,* 37: 190; Pickering to Andrew Ellicott, July 28, 1797, 222; McHenry to George Washington, July 9, 1797, *Life and Correspondence of James McHenry,* 256–57; Pickering to Rufus King, June 20, 1797, *Pickering Papers,* 37: 190, emphasis in the original; Hamilton to McHenry, May 15, 1797, *Life and Correspondence of James McHenry,* 212.

48. Elkins and McKitrick, *Age of Federalism,* 643–53. On French depredations on

American commercial shipping, see Bowman, *Struggle for Neutrality*, 179–182, 193, 200, 203–4, 248; Clarfield, *Timothy Pickering*, 76; DeConde, *Entangling Alliance*, 141–63; DeConde, *The Quasi War*, 8–12; Hill, *William Vans Murray*, 108, 166, 176–93; Lawrence S. Kaplan, *Colonies Into Nation: American Diplomacy, 1763–1801* (New York: Macmillan, 1972), 216–58; Lycan, *Alexander Hamilton and American Foreign Policy*, 144.

49. On Pinckney's rejection, see Bowman, *Struggle for Neutrality*, 263, 274, 280; DeConde, *Entangling Alliance*, 390–91.

50. Hamilton to Timothy Pickering, March 29, 1797, *Papers of Alexander Hamilton*, 20: 556–58.

51. Hamilton to Pickering, March 22, 1797, *Papers of Alexander Hamilton*, 20: 545–47; *Annals*, 5th Cong., 1st sess., March 25, 1797, 49. Wolcott also agreed with Hamilton's ideas for defense, agreeing on the need to raise revenue, arm merchant vessels, defend the coast, fortify ports, enroll an army, and empower the executive to arrest vessels and persons intending to raid American commercial ships; Wolcott to Hamilton, March 31, 1797, *Papers of Alexander Hamilton*, 20: 569–74.

52. Hamilton to Smith, April 5, 1797, *Papers of Alexander Hamilton*, 21: 20–21; Hamilton to Smith, April 10, 1797, 29–41, quotes 30–33, 40.

53. Hamilton to Pickering, May 11, 1797, 81–84, emphasis in original. For Hamilton's defensive plans, see 38–41; quoted material on pp. 39–40.

54. *Papers of Alexander Hamilton*, 41.

55. C. Vann Woodward, "The Age of Reinterpretation," *American Historical Review* 66 (October 1960): 1–19; this essay with the "age of free security" argument still appears as the first selection in a significant reader on American foreign policy, Thomas G. Paterson and Dennis Merrill, eds., *Major Problems in American Foreign Relations*, vol. 1, *To 1920*, Major Problems in American History Series (Lexington, Mass.: D.C. Heath, 1995). Melvyn Leffler correctly points out that a "national security" model can and should serve as a framework for studying the history of American foreign policy in the eighteenth and nineteenth centuries, in "National Security," *Journal of American History* 77 (June 1990): 143–52, quote 151. For one such treatment, see James Chace and Caleb Carr, *America Invulnerable: The Quest for Absolute Security from 1812 to Star Wars* (New York: Summit Books, 1988). For other accounts that use the national security state model for Cold War studies, see Michel Crozier, Samuel P. Huntington, and Jose Watanuki, *The Crisis of Democracy: Report on the Governability of Democracies to the Trilateral Commission* (New York: New York University Press, 1975); Robert Gilpin, *War and Change in World Politics* (New York: Cambridge University Press, 1981); Samuel P. Huntington, *American Politics: The Promise of Disharmony* (Cambridge, Mass.: Harvard University Press, 1981); Paul M. Kennedy, *The Rise and Fall of the Great Powers: Economic Change and Military Conflict from 1500 to 2000* (New York: Random House, 1987); Klaus Knorr, *Power and Wealth: The Political Economy of International Power* (New York: Basic Books, 1973); Melvyn Leffler, *A Preponderance of Power: National Security, the Truman Administration, and the Cold War* (Stanford, Calif.: Stanford University Press, 1992); Leffler, "The American Conception of National Security and the Beginnings of the Cold War, 1945–1948," *American Historical Review* 89 (April 1984): 346–90; Kenneth N. Waltz, *Theory of International Politics* (Reading, Mass.: Addison-Wesley, 1979).

56. McHenry to Hamilton, April 19, 1797, Steiner, *Life and Correspondence of James McHenry*, 51–52; Hamilton to McHenry, April 29, 1797, 61–68.

57. "President's Speech to Congress," *Annals*, 5th Cong., 1st sess., May 16, 1797, 54–59.

58. *Annals*, 5th Cong., 1st sess., June 5, 1797, 239–348.

59. Peters, ed., *Statutes*, "An Act prohibiting, for a limited time, the Exportation of Arms and Ammunition; and for encouraging the importation thereof," July 14, 1797, 1: 520; "An Act to provide for the further Defense of the Ports and Harbors of the United States," June 23, 1797, 1: 521–22; "An Act making additional appropriations for the support of Government, for the year 1797," July 10, 1797, 1: 534–35; "An Act providing a Naval Armament," July 1, 1797, 1: 523–25; "An Act laying Duties on stamped Vellum, Parchment, and Paper," July 6, 1797, 1: 527–32; "An Act authorizing a loan of Money," July 8, 1797, 1: 534.

60. Peters, *Statutes*, "An Act authorizing a detachment from the Militia of the United States," June 24, 1797, 1: 522.

61. DeConde, *Quasi War*, 25–30.

62. For accounts of the XYZ Affair, see Bowman, *Struggle for Neutrality*; Hill, *William Vans Murray*; William Stinchcombe, *The XYZ Affair* (Westport, Conn.: Greenwood Press, 1980). For the increased French attacks on American shipping following the incident, see Elkins and McKitrick, *Age of Federalism*, 645.

63. Pickering to Hamilton, April 9, 1798, *Papers of Alexander Hamilton*, 21: 409.

64. Thomas M. Ray, "'Not One Cent for Tribute': The Public Addresses and American Popular Reaction to the XYZ Affair, 1798–1799," *Journal of the Early Republic* 3 (Winter 1983): 389–412; DeConde, *Quasi War*, 80–84.

65. Hamilton to Washington, May 19, 1798, *Papers of Alexander Hamilton*, 21: 466–67, emphasis in original.

66. Pickering to Harper, March 21, 1798, cited in DeConde, *Quasi War*, 84; *Annals*, 5th Cong., 2nd sess., April 28, 1798, 1531; Knox to Adams, June 26, 1798, cited in Elkins and McKitrick, *Age of Federalism*, 647; *Annals*, 5th Cong., 2nd sess., May 8, 1798, 1640–41.

67. John Robison, *Proofs of a Conspiracy Against All the Religions and Governments of Europe, Carried on in the Secret Meetings of Free Masons, Illuminati, and Reading Societies* (Edinburgh, 1797, reprint New York, 1798); Vernon Stauffer, *New England and the Bavarian Illuminati* (New York: Columbia University Press, 1918), 10–11.

68. David Tappan, *A Discourse Delivered in the Chapel of Harvard College, June 19, 1798* (Boston, 1798), 13–20.

69. Jedediah Morse, *A Sermon, Exhibiting the Present Dangers, and Consequent Duties of the Citizens of the United States of America. Delivered at Charlestown, April 25, 1799* (Charlestown, Mass., 1799), 10–11, 15–17, emphasis in original. On the extent of conspiracy theories throughout American history, and especially in response to the French Revolution in the 1790s, see David Brion Davis, ed., *The Fear of Conspiracy: Images of Un-American Subversion from the Revolution to the Present* (Ithaca, N.Y.: Cornell University Press, 1971), 35–65.

70. Fisher Ames, "Laocoon," in *The Works of Fisher Ames* 2 vols., ed. Seth Ames (Boston: Little, Brown, 1854), 2: 114–15.

71. DeConde, *Quasi War*, 103–8.

72. Bowman, *Struggle for Neutrality*, 306–85; DeConde, *Quasi War*; Hill, *William Vans Murray*; Horsman, *Diplomacy of the New Republic*, 42–78; Kaplan, *Colonies into Nation*, 259–96; Kohn, *Eagle and Sword*, 193–276; Lycan, *Alexander Hamilton and American Foreign Policy*, 318–409; Stinchcombe, *The XYZ Affair*.

73. Ames to Pickering, July 10, 1798, *Works of Fisher Ames*, 1: 233–34.

74. Peters, *Statutes*, "An Act for an additional appropriation to provide and support a Naval Armament," March 27, 1798, 1: 547; "An Act to provide an additional Armament for the further protection of the trade of the United States," April 27, 1798, 1: 552; "An Act to establish an Executive Department, to be denominated the Department of the Navy," April 30, 1798, 1: 553–54; "An Act supplementary to the act providing for the further defense of the ports and harbors of the United States," May 3, 1798, 1: 554–55; "An Act to enable the President of the United States to procure Cannon, Arms, and Ammunition, and for other purposes," May 4, 1798, 1: 555–56; "An Act to authorize the President of the United States to cause to be purchased, or built, a number of small vessels to be equipped as galleys or otherwise," May 4, 1798, 1: 556; "An Act to amend the act," entitled, "An act providing a Naval Establishment," June 22, 1798, 1: 569; "An Act in addition to the act more effectually to protect the Commerce and Coasts of the United States," June 28, 1798, 1: 574–75; "An Act supplementary to the act," entitled "An act to provide additional Armament for the further protection of the trade of the United States, and for other purposes," June 30, 1798, 1: 575–76; "An Act for the establishing and organizing a Marine Corps," July 11, 1798, 1: 594–96; "An act to make a further appropriation for the additional Naval Armament," July 16, 1798, 1: 608–9; "An Act making certain additional appropriations for the year one thousand seven hundred and ninety eight," July 16, 1798, 1: 611; "An Act more effectually to protect the Commerce and Coasts of the United States," May 28, 1798, 1: 561; "An Act further to protect the Commerce of the United States," July 9, 1798, 1: 578–80; "An Act to suspend the commercial intercourse between the United States and France," June 13, 1798 1: 565–66; "An Act to declare the treaties heretofore concluded with France, no longer obligatory on the United States," July 7, 1798, 1: 578.

75. Banning, *Jeffersonian Persuasion*, 44–45, 49–50, 54, 56, 59, 64, 69, 75, 180, 222–24, 259–64, 277–78, 293–99; Lois G. Schwoerer, *"No Standing Armies!" The Antiarmy Ideology in Seventeenth-Century England* (Baltimore: Johns Hopkins University Press, 1974).

76. Peters, *Statutes*, "An Act authorizing the President of the United States to raise a Provisional Army," May 28, 1798, 1: 558–61. On the Senate bill, see *Annals*, 5th Cong., 2nd sess., April 17, 1798, 542–44, April 23, 1798, 546, May 22, 1798, 559–61. On the congressional history of the Provisional Army, see Elkins and McKitrick, *Age of Federalism*, 595–98; and Kohn, *Eagle and Sword*, 224–26.

77. Kohn, *Eagle and Sword*, 73–88, 91–127, 139–57, 174–89.

78. *Annals*, 5th Cong., 2nd sess., July 9, 1798, 605; July 12, 1798, 609; July 14, 1798, 611, 613–14; July 3, 1798, 2084; July 5, 1798, 2088–93; July 6, 1798, 2114; July 7, 1798, 2128–32; July 16, 1798, 3785–87. See also Kohn, *Eagle and Sword*, 227–28.

79. Kohn, *Eagle and Sword*, 47–48.

80. Peters, *Statutes*, "An Act giving eventual authority to the President of the United States to augment the Army," March 2, 1799, 1: 725–27. Another national security act, still in force today, was prompted by the actions of Dr. George Logan, a wealthy Philadelphia Quaker and prominent Republican supporter. In the summer of 1798, after meeting with Thomas Jefferson and Edmond Genet, Logan traveled to Paris and conducted meetings with French officials of the Directory without any official authorization. When he returned in the autumn of 1798, he reported to President Adams and informed him that the French were ready to receive a new American minister and open peace talks. Adams, perturbed at Logan's impetuous behavior but nonetheless polite,

heard what Logan had to say and then consulted his cabinet. He asked Pickering, "Is this constitutional, for a party of opposition to send embassies to foreign nations?" Pickering and others were outraged, and Congress prepared the "Logan Act" to prohibit any private United States citizen from conferring with any foreign government "with an intent to influence the measures or conduct of any foreign government . . . in relation to any disputes or controversies with the United States." Frederick B. Tolles, *George Logan of Philadelphia* (New York: Oxford University Press, 1953), 153–204; Adams to Pickering, November 2, 1798, in *The Life and Works of John Adams, Second President of the United States*, 10 vols., ed. Charles Francis Adams (Boston: Little, Brown, 1851), 6: 615; Peters, *Statutes*, "An Act for the punishment of certain Crimes therein specified," January 30, 1799, 1: 613.

81. *Annals*, 5th Cong., 2nd sess., May 3, 1798, 1578.

82. Peters, *Statutes*, "An Act Concerning Aliens," June 25, 1798, 1: 570–72; "An Act respecting Alien Enemies," July 6, 1798, 1: 577–78. Elkins and McKitrick, *Age of Federalism*, 590–91; Peters, *Statutes*, "An Act in addition to the act," entitled, "An Act for the punishment of certain crimes against the United States," July 14, 1798, 1: 596–97. Keller, *Rural Politics*, 21–23; Catherine Herbert, "The French Element in Pennsylvania in the 1790s," *Pennsylvania Magazine of History and Biography* 108 (October 1984): 451–69; Herbert, "The Pennsylvania French in the 1790s: The Story of Their Survival" (Ph.D. dissertation, University of Texas, Austin, 1981); Catherine Christians Spaeth, "Purgatory or Promised Land? French Emigres in Philadelphia and Their Perceptions of America During the 1790s" (Ph.D. dissertation, University of Minnesota, 1992).

83. Hamilton to Wolcott, June 29, 1798, *Papers of Alexander Hamilton*, 21: 522; *Annals*, 5th Cong., 2nd sess., July 2, 1798, 596; James Morton Smith *Freedom's Fetters: The Alien and Sedition Laws and American Civil Liberties* (Ithaca, N.Y.: Cornell University Press, 1956), 94–130. The original Senate bill, as proposed by James Lloyd of Maryland, had been more extreme. It contained a section dealing with treason as well as sedition, in which Lloyd maintained that the crime of treason could be committed during peacetime. He suggested that although the United States was not officially at war with France, the French were in reality the enemies of America and that Americans who gave aid and comfort to the French should be considered traitors and summarily executed. Lloyd's presumption that it was possible to have enemies during peacetime shocked most, but many Federalists in the Senate agreed with him. It would not be until the twentieth century when an idea this radical could win a majority in Congress or at large. See also John C. Miller, *Crisis in Freedom: The Alien and Sedition Acts* (Boston: Little, Brown, 1951).

84. Hamilton to Pickering, June 7, 1798, *Papers of Alexander Hamilton*, 21: 495.

85. I calculated these figures from the acts listed in Peters, *Statutes*; see especially, 5th Congress, 1: *Stat. 1*, chapters 3, 17; 1: *Stat. 2*, chapters 23, 37, 38, 39, 52, 53, 65, 82, 84, 86; 1: *Stat.3*, chapters 13, 15, 16, 42, 44.

86. *Universal Gazette*, May 17, 1798.

87. On the Federalist obsession with the central government's need for effective methods of taxation in the days prior to the Philadelphia Convention, see Roger H. Brown, *Redeeming the Republic: Federalists, Taxation, and the Origins of the Constitution* (Baltimore: Johns Hopkins University Press, 1993).

88. New York Assembly, *An Act For Raising Certain Yearly Taxes Within This State*, February 9, 1787, in *Papers of Alexander Hamilton*, 21: 500–501.

89. Oliver Wolcott to George Washington, April 23, 1790, in *Memoirs of the Administrations of Washington and Adams*, 2 vols., ed. George Gibbs (New York: William Van Nordon, 1846), 2: 345.

90. Hamilton to Theodore Sedgwick, January 20, 1797, *Papers of Alexander Hamilton*, 20: 473–75.

91. *Annals*, 4th Cong., 1st sess., April 1, 1796, 841–55; April 4, 1796, 855–56.

92. *Annals*, 4th Cong., 2nd sess., December 14, 1796, 2635–2713. Wolcott announced that after much deliberation, three possible courses existed. The first option would be a federal requisition from the states, but this he declared was out of the question since such a system "utterly failed under the late Confederation, and to remedy which, was one great object of establishing the present Government." Second, the government could levy and collect a direct tax using the laws already in existence for each state. While this option had the advantage of using pre-existing systems of taxation formulated by representatives close to the people who understood their constituents' ability to pay, a direct national tax needed to be uniform, Wolcott insisted, and the fact that not all state laws used the same indicators or levied the same rates could lead to sectional antagonisms. The last and only legitimate option to Wolcott's mind was a direct tax on property.

93. *Annals*, 4th Cong., 2nd sess., January 12, 1797, 1843–1942, quote 1865.

94. Hamilton to Smith, January 19, 1797, *Papers of Alexander Hamilton*, 20: 468; Hamilton to Sedgwick, January 20, 1797, 473–75; Hamilton to Sedgwick, January, 1797, 499–504; Hamilton to Wolcott, June 6, 1797, 21: 98–101; Hamilton to Wolcott, June 8, 1797, 103–4; Hamilton to Smith, June 10, 1797, 106–7.

95. Hamilton to Sedgwick, January 20, 1797, *Papers of Alexander Hamilton*, 20: 474.

96. Hamilton to Sedgwick, January, 1797, *Papers of Alexander Hamilton*, 20: 501–4.

97. Hamilton to Smith, June 10, 1797, *Papers of Alexander Hamilton*, 21: 106–7.

98. Hamilton to Wolcott, June 6, 1797, *Papers of Alexander Hamilton*, 21: 98–101; Hamilton to Wolcott, June 8, 1797, *Papers of Alexander Hamilton*, 103–4.

99. *Annals*, 5th Cong., 1st sess., June 17, 331, July 3, 393–407; Peters, *Statutes*, "An Act laying duties on stamped vellum, parchment and paper," July 6, 1797, 1: 523–25; "An Act to postpone for a limited time, the commencement of the duties imposed by the act" entitled "An act laying duties on stamped vellum, parchment and paper," December 15, 1797, 1: 536.

100. Hamilton to Sedgwick, March 15, 1798, *Papers of Alexander Hamilton*, 21: 361–63.

101. Gibbs, *Memoirs of the Administrations of Washington and Adams*, 2: 65–66.

102. *Annals*, 5th Cong., 2nd sess., July 9, 1798, 3758–70; Peters, *Statutes*, "An Act to provide for the calculation of Lands and Dwelling Houses, and the enumeration of Slaves within the United States," July 9, 1798, 1: 580–91; "An Act to lay and collect a direct tax within the United States," July 14, 1798, 1: 597–605.

103. Lee Soltow, "America's First Progressive Tax," *National Tax Journal* 30 (March 1977): 53–58.

104. For the history of African-Americans in Pennsylvania in the eighteenth and early nineteenth centuries, see Gary Nash, *Forging Freedom: The Formation of Philadelphia's Black Community, 1720–1840* (Cambridge, Mass.: Harvard University Press, 1988).

105. Gibbs, *Memoirs of the Administrations of Washington and Adams*, 2: 66.

106. Peters, *Statutes*, "An Act to enable the President of the United States to borrow money for the public service," July 16, 1798, 1: 607–8; "An Act making certain appropriations; and to authorize the President to obtain a Loan on the credit of the direct tax," July 16, 1798, 1: 609–10.

107. Davis, *The Fries Rebellion*, 1–13; Weinstein, "The Fries Rebellion," 14–33.

Chapter 3. Resistance

1. *Philadelphia Aurora*, October 19, 1797. See also Keller, "Diversity and Democracy," 214–15. My account of the Berks and the Northampton, Bucks, Montgomery elections which follows is from Keller, "Diversity and Democracy," 224–34.

2. *Readinger Adler*, July 3, 10, 17, 1798. Tinkcom, *Republicans and Federalists in Pennsylvania*, 215–16.

3. *Reading Weekly Advertiser*, June 2, 9, 16; July 3, 7, 14, 17, 1798.

4. *Reading Weekly Advertiser*, September 27, 1798.

5. *Readinger Adler*, September 18, October 2, 9, 1798.

6. Federalist lawyer Mark John Biddle reported this rumor in the *Reading Weekly Advertiser*, September 29, 1798.

7. Keller, "Diversity and Democracy," 229.

8. In favor of Everhard Foulke was "Petition of the Inhabitants of Richland Township" December 8, 1794.

9. "Petition of the Inhabitants of Richland Township" December 8, 1794; in favor of George Weikert in the 1794 contest with Everhard Foulke was "Petition from the Inhabitants of Lower Milford and Richland Townships," December 5, 1794, "Petition from the Inhabitants of Lower Milford and Richland Townships," January 1, 1795, "Petition from the Inhabitants of Lower Milford and Richland Townships," January 2, 1795, in Appointments File for Civil Officers, Records of the Department of State, Bureau of Commissions, Election, and Legislation, Pennsylvania State Archives.

10. "Petition of the Inhabitants of Richland Township," January 22, 1795, in Appointments File for Civil Officers, Records of the Department of State, Bureau of Commissions, Election, and Legislation, Pennsylvania State Archives.

11. For the best account of the ethnic, economic, and religious divisions that drove eastern Pennsylvania politics in the 1790s, see Keller, *Rural Politics*.

12. *Philadelphia Gazette*, October 4, 1798.

13. On the influence of the Philadelphia press in the region during the election and in the winter of 1799, see *Philadelphia Gazette*, April 15, 1799.

14. See especially *Readinger Adler*, September 18, October 2, 9, 1798.

15. Tinkcom, *Republicans and Federalists in Pennsylvania*, 215–16.

16. Deposition of John Jarret, given before Judge William Henry, April 10, 1799, Rawle Papers, 2: 62.

17. See Chapter 2, note 80, above.

18. Deposition of Andrew Schlichter, given before Judge Richard Peters, April 6, 1799, Rawle Papers, 2: 41, emphasis in original; deposition of John Wetzel, Sr., given before Judge William Henry, January 29, 1799, 2: 8. For another account of Hartzell's activities, see deposition of Michael Bobst, given before Judge Richard Peters, April 10, 1799, 2: 4.

19. Deposition of Henry Ohl, given before Judge William Henry, April 27, 1799, Rawle Papers, 2: 91.

20. The parody was reported to Timothy Pickering in a letter from George Ball. Pickering then related it to Washington in a letter on October 27, 1798, in *Pickering Papers*, 9: 522, emphasis in original.

21. Deposition of Henry Ohl, given before Judge William Henry, April 27, 1799, Rawle Papers, 2: 91.

22. Deposition of James Williamson, given before Judge Richard Peters, April 15, 1799, Rawle Papers, 2: 78.

23. Deposition of Michael Bobst, given before Judge Richard Peters, April 10, 1799, Rawle Papers, 2: 58.

24. Testimony of Joseph Horsefield, Carpenter, *Two Trials*, 41.

25. Deposition of John Romig, given before Judge William Henry, January 29, 1799, Rawle Papers, 2: 10.

26. *Philadelphia Aurora*, April 11, 13, 1799.

27. *Philadelphia Universal Gazette*, November 1, 1798.

28. Clark swore his deposition, however, which suggests he did not attend Quaker meeting.

29. Testimony of Jacob Eyerle, Carpenter, *Two Trials*, 45.

30. On political opposition in Berks County, see *Oracle of Dauphin*, January 9, 16, 23; February 6, March 6, 13, 20, 1799.

31. Testimony of Jacob Eyerle, Carpenter, *Two Trials*, 45; deposition of Philip Arndt, given before Sheriff Peter Rhoads, September 17, 1798, Rawle Papers, 2: 1.

32. Edmund S. Morgan and Helen M. Morgan, *The Stamp Act Crisis: Prologue to Revolution* (Chapel Hill: University of North Carolina Press, 1953), 161–63, 173, 180–81; Gilje, *Rioting in America*, 46–47. See also Arthur M. Schlesinger, "Liberty Tree: A Genealogy," *New England Quarterly* 25 (1952): 435–58; On revolutionary rituals, see Shaw, *American Patriots and the Rituals of the Revolution*, 26–47, on Hillsborough paintings see 185–86.

33. Gilje, *Rioting in America*, 55; Baldwin, *Whiskey Rebels*, 103, 169, 179, 187, 193, 206, 208; on Jay's effigies see Miller, *Federalist Era*, 168.

34. On the integrative role of political rituals as agents in political action—more than simply mirrors of contemporary public opinion—see Catherine M. Bell and David I. Kertzer, *Ritual Theory, Ritual Practice* (New York: Oxford University Press, 1992); Susan G. Davis, *Parades and Power: Street Theatre in Nineteenth-Century Philadelphia* (Berkeley: University of California Press, 1988); David I. Kertzer, *Ritual, Politics, and Power* (New Haven, Conn.: Yale University Press, 1988); Albrecht Koschnik, "Political Conflict and Public Contest: Rituals of National Celebration in Philadelphia, 1788–1815," *Pennsylvania Magazine of History and Biography* 118 (July 1994): 209–48; Sally Falk Moore and Barbara G. Myerhoff, eds., *Secular Ritual* (Assen, Netherlands: Van Gorcum, 1977); Sean Wilentz, ed., *Rites of Power: Symbolism, Ritual, and Politics Since the Middle Ages* (Philadelphia: University of Pennsylvania Press, 1985).

35. Testimony of William Nichols Carpenter, *Two Trials*, 39. For the desire among the post-Revolutionary generation to live up to their predecessors' republican ideals and actions, and eventually their willingness and desire to prove it on the battlefield against the same enemy their parents had faced, see Steven Watts, *The Republic Reborn: War and the Making of Liberal America, 1790–1820* (Baltimore: Johns Hopkins University Press, 1987).

36. Deposition of James Jackson, given before Justice of the Peace John Curwan, October 23, 1799, Rawle Papers, 2: 131.

37. *Oracle of Dauphin*, January 9, 16, 23, February, 6, March 6, 13, 20, 1799.

38. *Kline's Carlisle Weekly Gazette*, January 23, 1799.

39. Jeffrey A. Davis, "Guarding the Republican Interest"; see also Eugene P. Link, *The Democratic-Republican Societies, 1790–1800* (New York: Columbia University Press, 1942).

40. On the eighteenth-century republican conception of militias, see Maier, "Popular Uprisings and Civil Authority in Eighteenth-Century America," 3–35; on the role of the militia in the Revolution, see John Shy, "The American Revolution: The Military Conflict Considered as a Revolutionary War," in Stephen G. Kurtz and James H. Hutson, eds., *Essays on the American Revolution* (Chapel Hill: University of North Carolina Press, 1973), 121–56; on the Pennsylvania politics surrounding the militia, see Keller, *Rural Politics*.

41. Davis, *Fries Rebellion*, 38–39; testimony of Jacob Eyerle, Carpenter, *Two Trials*, 47.

42. Testimony of Jacob Eyerle, *Two Trials*, 47.

43. Testimony of Jacob Eyerle, *Two Trials*, 47.

44. Deposition of James Williamson, given before Judge Richard Peters, April 15, 1799, Rawle Papers.

45. Deposition of George Ringer, given before Judge William Henry, January 28, 1799, Rawle Papers, 2: 7; deposition of Daniel Reisch, January 29, 1799, 2: 8; deposition of John Wetzel, Jr., 2: 9; deposition of John Butz, 2: 9; deposition of John Shymer, given before Judge Richard Peters, March 8, 1799, 2: 19; deposition of John Moritz, April 8, 1799, 2: 56; deposition of Christian Heckenwelder, April 13, 1799, 2: 68; examination of Henry Kooken, given before Judge William Henry, 2: 94; testimony of Jacob Eyerle, Carpenter, *Two Trials*, 50.

46. An excellent source for investigating the ritualization of interpersonal violence during the Revolutionary struggle is Shaw, *American Patriots*. On violence in the North Carolina Regulation see A. Roger Ekirch, *"Poor Carolina": Politics and Society in Colonial North Carolina, 1729–1776* (Chapel Hill: University of North Carolina Press, 1981), and M. L. M. Kay, "The North Regulation, 1766–1776: A Class Conflict," in Young, ed., *The American Revolution*. On Stamp Act violence see Morgan, *The Stamp Act Crisis: Prologue to Revolution*, and on Boston specifically see Gary Nash, *The Urban Crucible: Social Change, Political Consciousness, and the Origins of the American Revolution* (Cambridge, Mass.: Harvard University Press, 1979).

47. Testimony of Jacob Eyerle, Carpenter, *Two Trials*, 49.

48. W. J. Rorabaugh, *The Alcoholic Republic: An American Tradition* (Oxford: Oxford University Press, 1979), 27–28; David W. Conroy, *In Public Houses: Drink and the Revolution of Authority in Colonial Massachusetts* (Chapel Hill: University of North Carolina Press, 1995); Peter Thompson, *Rum Punch and Revolution: Taverngoing and Public Life in Eighteenth-Century Philadelphia* (Philadelphia: University of Pennsylvania Press, 1999).

49. See the many letters between state tax collectors, especially Robert Levers and Jacob Arndt from Northampton County, to State Comptroller General John Nicholson in 1786 and 1787 in Records of the Comptroller General, General Correspondence, 1776–1809, Pennsylvania State Archives, microfilm reels 4865, 4868.

50. Testimony of Jacob Eyerle, Carpenter, *Two Trials*, 48–50.

51. Deposition of James Williamson, given before Judge Richard Peters, April 15, 1799, Rawle Papers, 2: 78.

52. Deposition of Valentine Bobst, given before Justice of the Peace, Michael Bobst, April 18, 1799, Rawle Papers, 2: 84.

53. Alan Tully, "Literacy Levels and Educational Development in Rural Pennsylvania, 1729–1775," *Pennsylvania History* 39 (July 1972), 301–12; for signatures on petitions, see Records of the Department of State, Bureau of Commissions, Elections, and Legislation, Appointment and Commission Books for Civil Officers, 1790–1793, Appointment File for Civil Officers, 1790–1868, Pennsylvania State Archives, microfilm reels 675–78, 875–94.

54. Deposition of John Rein, given before Judge William Henry, January 28, 1799, Rawle Papers, 2: 5; deposition of George Lintz, January 29, 1799, 2: 7; deposition of Michael Bobst, given before Judge Richard Peters, April 10, 1799, 2: 58; deposition of Captain Henry Hunsecker, April 14, 1799, 2: 72; deposition of Samuel Kisler, given before Judge William Henry, January 28, 1799, 2: 6.

55. Deposition of Captain Henry Hunsecker, given before Judge Richard Peters, April 14, 1799, Rawle Papers, 2: 72.

56. Deposition of Henry Strauss, given before Judge William Henry, February 16, 1799, Rawle Papers, 2: 15–16.

57. *Oracle of Dauphin*, January 23, 1799.

58. *Philadelphia Aurora*, January 12, 1799.

59. *True American*, March 28, 1799.

60. *Farmers' Register*, January 9, 1799.

61. *Oracle of Dauphin*, November 21, 1798, for quote. The series, signed anonymously by "A Farmer," "A Quiet Citizen," and "Parvo Contentus," ran on December 12 and 26, 1798; January 23, 30, and February 6, 13, 1799.

62. Carpenter, *Two Trials*, 114.

63. Testimony of John Sneider, John Serfass, Carpenter, *Two Trials*, 222–23; deposition of Conrad Kroesy given before Judge William Henry, February 1, 1799, Rawle Papers, 2: 11; deposition of John Serfass, given before Judge William Henry, February 1, 1799, 2: 11. An amusing anecdote here is that Thomas Carpenter, the secretary of the court who recorded the two trials of John Fries, spelled Kroesy's name as it sounded phonetically to him: Crazy. Thus the testimony contains wonderful exchanges between the defense and the witnesses like: "Did I not tell you when at Crazy's house?" or "What did you hear at the Crazy house?"

64. Deposition of Jacob Eyermann, given before Judge Richard Peters, June 14, 1799, Rawle Papers, 2: 119; testimony of William Nichols, Carpenter, *Two Trials*, 41, 221; testimony of William Thomas, 63.

65. Deposition of George Graeff, given before Judge William Henry, January 28, 1799, Rawle Papers, 2: 5; deposition of Gottfried Roth; deposition of Peter Evy, 2: 6.

66. Deposition of John Fogel, Jr., given before Judge William Henry, January 29, 1799, Rawle Papers, 2: 10; examination of Henry Shiffert, given before Judge Richard Peters, April 14, 1799, 2: 71; Deposition of Adam Wetzel, April 11, 1799, 2: 64a; deposition of John Fogel, Sr., October 4, 1799, 2: 123.

67. Deposition of John Butz, given before Judge William Henry, January 29, 1799, Rawle Papers, 2: 9; deposition of Jacob Sterner, given before Judge William Henry, January 29, 1799.

68. Deposition of George Ringer, given before Judge William Henry, January 28, 1799, Rawle Papers., 2: 7; Deposition of Daniel Reisch, January 29, 1799, 2: 8; Deposition of John Wetzel Jr., 2: 9; Deposition of John Butz, 2: 9.

69. For the chain of events surrounding the Upper Milford assessment, see Testimony of Jacob Eyerle, Carpenter, *Two Trials*, 45–52; testimony of Christian Heckenwelter, 185; deposition of John Shymer, given before Judge Richard Peters, March 8, 1799, Rawle Papers, 2: 19.

70. Deposition of John Shymer, given before Judge Richard Peters, March 8, 1799, Rawle Papers, 2: 19; deposition of John Moritz, April 8, 1799, 2: 56; deposition of Christian Heckenwelder, April 13, 1799, 2: 68; examination of Henry Kooken, given before Judge William Henry, date unknown, 2: 94; Carpenter, *Two Trials*, testimony of Jacob Eyerle, 50. The testimonies and depositions detailing the chain of events disagree with one another, and I have endeavored to recreate the narrative of events in as logical a manner as possible.

71. Deposition of Philip Kremer, given before Jacob Bush, February 13, 1799, Rawle Papers, 2: 13; deposition of Jacob Brown, February 14, 1799, 2: 14; deposition of Michael Bobst, given before Judge William Henry, January 28, 1799, 2: 4; deposition of George Miller, 2: 4; deposition of Isaac Shimer, given before Judge Richard Peters, April 8, 1799, 2: 52; deposition of David Okly, 2: 53; deposition of Peter Zeiner, April 16, 1799, 2: 82; deposition of Matthias Lieby, given before Judge Michael Bobst, April 18, 1799, 2: 89; testimony of Judge William Henry, Carpenter, *Two Trials*, 82–83.

72. Deposition of Jacob Sterner, given to Judge Henry, January 29, 1799, Rawle Papers, 2: 10; Davis, *Fries Rebellion*, 44–45; testimony of Judge Richard Peters, Carpenter, *Two Trials*, 79–80.

73. Deposition of Henry Strauss, given before Judge William Henry, February 16, 1799, Rawle Papers, 2: 15–16, spelling in original.

74. Deposition of Michael Bobst, given before Judge Richard Peters, April 10, 1799, Rawle Papers, 2: 58; deposition of Adam Wetzel, given before Judge Richard Peters, April 11, 1799, 2: 64; deposition of John Fogel, Jr., given before Judge Richard Peters, April 10, 1799, 2: 123.

75. *Philadelphia Aurora*, March 12, 1799.

76. Testimony of John Romig, Carpenter, *Two Trials*, 185; testimony of Isaac Schmyer, 186. For the democratic impact of the American Revolution on women, see Norton, *Liberty's Daughters*.

77. Deposition of John Shymer, given before Judge Richard Peters, March 8, 1799, Rawle Papers, 2: 19; deposition of Valentine Kehmlig, April 10, 1799, 2: 63; deposition of Duvall Albrecht, 2:63; deposition of John Fogel, Jr., April 13, 1799, 2: 69; deposition of Henry Strauss, given before Judge William Henry, February 16, 1799, 2: 15–16; deposition of John Jarret, April 10, 1799, 2: 62; examination of John Moor, 2: 63a.

78. Deposition of John Fogel, Jr., given before Judge Richard Peters, April 13, 1799, Rawle Papers, 2: 69; deposition of Michael Bobst, given before Judge Richard Peters, 2: 58.

Chapter 4. Rebellion

1. Testimony of Jacob Eyerle, Carpenter, *Two Trials*, 45–46.
2. Testimony of James Chapman, Carpenter, *Two Trials*, 67–68.

3. Military Abstracts Card File; *Direct Tax of 1798*, Lower Milford Township, Bucks County.

4. For the petitions, see Records of the Department of State, Bureau of Commissions, Elections, and Legislation, Appointment Files for Civil Officers, 1790–1968, Bucks File, January 1, 1795, August 12, 1791, December 5, 1794, January 2, 1795, January 22, 1795, May 7, 1796, October 3, 1798. On the Foulkes, see *Direct Tax of 1798*, Richland Township, Bucks County. A quick reference for the Direct Tax records for the first district of Bucks County, comprising its twelve northernmost townships is Harry C. Adams, ed., *The Direct Tax of 1798: In the Second District, Third Division of Pennsylvania, Twelve Townships in the Upper Part of Bucks County* (Bedminster, Pa.: Adams Apple Press, 1994).

5. "Petition of the Inhabitants of Lower Milford," August 12, 1791, Records of the Department of State, Bureau of Commissions, Elections, and Legislation, Appointment Files for Civil Officers, 1790–1968, Bucks File.

6. Bouton, "A Road Closed," discusses the concept of "rings of protection" that Pennsylvania agrarians used to protect their property in the late eighteenth century.

7. Testimony of James Chapman, Carpenter, *Two Trials*, 68.

8. Biographical information on Fries was gleaned from a number of sources, including: Carpenter, *Two Trials*; Davis, *Fries Rebellion*, 1–14, 137–43, appendices; Hamilton, "Fries Insurrection," *Direct Tax of 1798*, Lower Milford Township, Bucks County; Military Abstracts Card File.

9. Davis, *Fries Rebellion*, 11.

10. On Joseph Galloway, see Julian P. Boyd, *Anglo-American Union: Joseph Galloway's Plans to Preserve the American Empire, 1774–1788* (New York: Octagon Books, 1970).

11. Davis, *Fries Rebellion*, 8. For an example of the mixed motives of average Patriots, see John Shy, "Hearts and Minds in the American Revolution: The Case of "Long Bill" Scott and Peterborough, New Hampshire," in Shy, ed., *A People Numerous and Armed: Reflections on the Military Struggle for American Independence* (New York: Oxford University Press, 1976).

12. Shy, "Hearts and Minds," 8–9, Military Abstracts Card File; on the Revolutionary War in Bucks County, see Owen S. Ireland, "Bucks County," in Frantz and Pencak, eds., *Beyond Philadelphia*, 23–45.

13. Davis, *Fries Rebellion*, 141.

14. Wayne Bodle, "This Tory Labyrinth: Community, Conflict, and Military Strategy During the Valley Forge Winter," in Michael Zuckerman, ed, *Friends and Neighbors: Group Life in America's First Plural Society* (Philadelphia: Temple University Press, 1982), 231–34; Ireland, "Bucks County," 38–39. Fries's participation in this battle was related by his son Daniel to Davis in *Fries Rebellion*, 8–9.

15. Ireland, "Bucks County."

16. *Direct Tax of 1798*, Lower Milford Township, Bucks County; Military Abstracts Card File.

17. Records of the Department of State, Bureau of Commissions, Elections, and Legislation, Appointment Files for Civil Officers, 1790–1968, Bucks File, January 1, 1795, August 12, 1791, December 5, 1794, January 2, 1795, January 22, 1795, May 7, 1796, October 3, 1798.

18. Hamilton, "Fries Insurrection"; testimony of Cephas Childs, Carpenter, *Two Trials*, 77.

19. Davis, *Fries Rebellion*, 8–9; *Direct Tax of 1798*, Lower Milford Township, Bucks County.

20. Hamilton, "Fries Insurrection"; Davis, *Fries Rebellion*, 8–11; examination of John Fries, given before Judge Richard Peters, April 6, 1799, William Rawle Papers, 2: 43.

21. U.S. Constitution, art. 1, sec. 9.

22. Examination of Samuel Clark, recorder and date unknown, Rawle Papers, 2: 93; Davis, *Fries Rebellion*, 14.

23. Deposition of John Jameson, recorder and date unknown, Rawle Papers, 2: 92; deposition of George Mitchell, given before Judge Richard Peters, date unknown, 2: 95; deposition of Isreal Roberts, recorder and date unknown, 2: 100; testimony of Israel Roberts, Carpenter, *Two Trials*, 114; testimony of James Chapman, 67–701; Davis, *Fries Rebellion*, 15–17.

24. Testimony of Everhard Foulke, Carpenter, *Two Trials*, 188–89; testimony of James Chapman, 67–70; testimony of Israel Roberts, 113–15, 189–90.

25. Testimony of Everhard Foulke, Carpenter, *Two Trials*, 188–89, testimony of James Chapman, 67–70.

26. Examination of Samuel Clark, recorder and date unknown, Rawle Papers, 2: 93; deposition of George Mitchell, given before Judge Richard Peters, date unknown, 2: 95; testimony of James Chapman, Carpenter, *Two Trials*, 68, testimony of Isreal Roberts, 114; Davis, *Fries Rebellion*, 17–19.

27. *Annals* 5th Cong., 3rd sess., January 28, 1799, 2795; February 21, 1799, 2955; *Oracle of Dauphin*, January 6, 1799.

28. *Annals*, 5th Cong., 3rd sess., January 31, 1799, 2807; February 13, 1799, 2906; February 21, 1799, 2955; February 25, 1799, 2985.

29. *Annals*, 5th Cong., 3rd sess., February 25, 1799, 2990–92.

30. *Annals*, 5th Cong., 3rd sess., February 25, 1799, 2990–92.

31. Testimony of Richard Peters, Carpenter, *Two Trials*, 79; testimony of William Nichols, 37.

32. Testimony of William Nichols, Carpenter, *Two Trials*, 37; Davis, *Fries Rebellion*, 48; Deposition of Jeremiah Trexler, given before Judge Richard Peters, April 14, 1799, Rawle Papers, 2: 77.

33. Testimony of William Nichols, Carpenter, *Two Trials*, 37.

34. Testimony of William Nichols, Carpenter, *Two Trials*, 37–38; testimony of Jacob Eyerle, 50; Davis, *Fries Rebellion*, 49–53.

35. Examination of Samuel Clark, Rawle Papers, 2: 93; testimony of James Chapman, Carpenter, *Two Trials*, 67–70.

36. Testimony of John Roderock, Carpenter, *Two Trials*, 71; testimony of William Thomas, 58–63, 187; Davis, *Fries Rebellion*, 26–27; deposition of George Mitchell, given before Judge Richard Peters, date unknown, Rawle Papers, 2: 95.

37. Affirmation of John Roderock, given before Judge Richard Peters, March 22, 1799, Rawle Papers, 2: 25; affirmation of James Chapman, testimony of John Roderock, Carpenter, *Two Trials*, 71; testimony of Israel Roberts, 114–15; Davis, *Fries Rebellion*, 27–29.

38. Deposition of Daniel Weidener, given before Judge Richard Peters, April 6, 1799, Rawle Papers, 2: 39; deposition of George Mitchell, date unknown, 2: 95.

39. Testimony of John Roderock, Carpenter, *Two Trials*, 71; Davis, *Fries Rebellion*, 23, 28–29; affirmation of Everhard Foulke, given before Judge Richard Peters, March 22, 1799, Rawle Papers, 2: 25; examination of Samuel Clark, recorder and date unknown, 2: 93.

40. Testimony of William Thomas, Carpenter, *Two Trials*, 59, 187.

41. Testimony of William Thomas, Carpenter, *Two Trials*, 60.

42. Testimony of John Roderock, Carpenter, *Two Trials*, 72; testimony of Everhard Foulke, 115, 188–89; prosecutor Samuel Sitgreaves claimed in his opening statement at Fries's first treason trial in 1799 that Fries gave the command to fire, but even Roderock, his best witness, would not testify to it. See chapter 6 below.

43. Testimony of William Thomas, Carpenter, *Two Trials*, 58–60, 187–88.

44. Testimony of William Thomas, Carpenter, *Two Trials*, 59–60; testimony of Jacob Huber, 113; testimony of Everhard Foulke, 188–89.

45. Testimony of William Thomas, Carpenter, *Two Trials*, 60; *Direct Tax of 1798*, Lower Milford Township, Bucks County; Military Abstracts Card File.

46. Testimony of Everhard Foulke, Carpenter, *Two Trials*, 115–16, 188–89.

47. Testimony of John Jameson, Carpenter, *Two Trials*, 110–13; testimony of Everhard Foulke, 115–16; testimony of Cephas Childs, 73–79.

48. Testimony of Cephas Childs, Carpenter, *Two Trials*, 73–79.

49. Testimony of Cephas Childs, Carpenter, *Two Trials*, 73.

50. Testimony of Cephas Childs, Carpenter, *Two Trials*, 73–74.

51. Testimony of Cephas Childs, Carpenter, *Two Trials*, 73–79.

52. Testimony of William Thomas, Carpenter, *Two Trials*, 60; testimony of John Roderock, 72; testimony of John Jameson, 111; testimony of Everhard Foulke, 115–16, 188–89; testimony of Cephas Childs, 73–79; examination of John Fries, given before Judge Richard Peters, 81–82; Davis, *Fries Rebellion*, 30–37; affirmation of Everhard Foulke, given before Richard Peters, March 22, 1799, Rawle Papers, 2: 25; affirmation of John Roderock, 2: 26–27; affirmation of Henry Johnston, March 27, 1799, 2: 35; deposition of John Dillinger, Jr., April 11, 1799, 2: 65a; deposition of John Jameson, recorder and date unknown, 2: 92; deposition of Frederick Atoss, given before Judge William Henry, April 6, 1799, 2: 41.

53. Deposition of John Dillinger, Jr., given before Joseph Horsefield, March 17, 1799, Rawle Papers, 2: 22; examination of Samuel Schwartz, recorder and date unknown, 2: 60; deposition of Daniel Weidener, given before Judge Richard Peters, April 6, 1799, 2: 39; deposition of David Penrose, given before William Rodman, April 5, 1799, 2: 39.

54. Testimony of William Nichols, Carpenter, *Two Trials*, 38; Davis, *Fries Rebellion*, 49.

55. Testimony of Christian Roths, Carpenter, *Two Trials*, 36; testimony of Samuel Toon, 56.

56. Deposition of Daniel Weidener, given before Judge Richard Peters, April 6, 1799, Rawle Papers, 2: 39; deposition of George Mitchell, date unknown, 2: 95; testimony of William Thomas, Carpenter, *Two Trials*, 61.

57. Deposition of Samuel Toon, given before Joseph Horsefield, March 15, 1799, Rawle Papers, 2: 21; deposition of John Fogel, Jr., given before Judge Richard Peters, April 13, 1799, 2: 69; testimony of Samuel Toon, Carpenter, *Two Trials*, 53–54; testimony of Andrew Shiffert, 56–57. On the contemporary, popular perception of the Second Amendment's meaning, see Pauline Maier, "Popular Uprisings and Civil Authority," 32–33.

58. Testimony of Joseph Horsefield, Carpenter, *Two Trials*, 41, testimony of William Nichols, 39; deposition of Christian Winters, given before Judge Richard Peters, March 23, 1799, Rawle Papers, 2: 31; examination of Peter Keefer, April 10, 1799, 2: 59; deposition of Joseph Horsefield, given before Judge William Henry, March 8, 1799, 2: 18.

59. Testimony of Joseph Horsefield, Carpenter, *Two Trials*, 43.

60. Deposition of Samuel Toon, given before Joseph Horsefield, March 15, 1799, Rawle Papers, 2: 21; deposition of Andrew Shiffert, 2: 24; deposition of John Mulhallon, given before Judge Richard Peters, March 23, 1799, 2: 28; deposition of Christian Roth, 2: 29; testimony of John Mulhollan, Carpenter, *Two Trials*, 45, testimony of John Barnet, 31.

61. Testimony of William Thomas, Carpenter, *Two Trials*, 61; testimony of Judge William Henry, 27.

62. Deposition of John Mulhallon, given before Judge Richard Peters, March 23, 1799, Rawle Papers, 2: 28; deposition of Christian Roth, 2: 29; deposition of William Barnet, 2: 30; deposition of William Thomas, April 6, 1799, 2: 40; examination of John Klein, 2: 44; deposition of John Kemmerer, April 10, 1799, 2: 66; testimony of William Henry, Carpenter, *Two Trials*, 25.

63. Testimony of Christian Winters, Carpenter, *Two Trials*, 34–35; testimony of Joseph Horsefield, 43.

64. Testimony of Joseph Horsefield, Carpenter, *Two Trials*, 43.

65. Testimony of William Nichols, Carpenter, *Two Trials*, 39–41; testimony of John Barnet, 33.

66. Testimony of John Barnet, Carpenter, *Two Trials*, 31–34.

67. Military Abstract Card File.

68. Testimony of William Thomas, Carpenter, *Two Trials*, 66; testimony of George Mitchell, 66.

69. Testimony of Jacob Eyerle, Carpenter, *Two Trials*, 46.

70. Testimony of William Thomas, Carpenter, *Two Trials*, 62.

71. Testimony of John Barnet, Carpenter, *Two Trials*, 30; testimony of William Nichols, 40, testimony of William Thomas, 187; testimony of Cephas Childs, 73–79; testimony of William Barnet, 30; testimony of George Mitchell, 66; testimony of John Roderock, 70–73.

72. Davis, *Fries Rebellion*, 9; Lester J. Cappon, ed., *The Adams-Jefferson Letters* (New York: Simon and Schuster, 1959), 346.

Chapter 5. Repression

1. *Gazette of the United States*, March 11, 1799.

2. *Porcupine's Gazette*, March 12, 1799.

3. *New York Daily Advertiser*, March 23, 1799, emphasis in original.

4. *Philadelphia Gazette and Universal Daily Advertiser*, March 16, 1799.

5. *Porcupine's Gazette*, March 30, 1799, emphasis in original.

6. *Oracle of Dauphin*, April 10, 1799, article dated Trenton, New Jersey, March 26.

7. *New York Daily Advertiser*, March 23, 1799.

8. *Philadelphia Gazette and Universal Daily Advertiser*, March 11, 1799, emphasis in original.

9. *American State Papers, Miscellaneous*, vol. 1, *1789–1809* (Washington, D.C.: Gales and Seaton, 1834), 1: 185–86.

10. The proclamation appears in full in Francis Wharton, S*tate Trials of the United*

States During the Administrations of Washington and Adams (Philadelphia: Carey & Hart, 1851), 458–59.

11. Testimony of George Mitchell, Carpenter, *Two Trials*, 66–67, testimony of John Jameson, 112, testimony of Jacob Huber, 113, testimony of Isreal Roberts, 113; examination of Samuel Clark, recorder and date unknown, Rawle Papers, 2: 93; *Philadelphia Gazette and Universal Daily Advertiser*, March 20, 1799; Davis, *Fries Rebellion*, 67–72.

12. *Kline's Carlisle Weekly Gazette*, March 27, April 10, 1799.

13. Slaughter, *Whiskey Rebellion*, 192–204; Clouse, *Whiskey Rebellion*, 33; Baldwin, *Whiskey Rebels*, chapters 9–11, passim; for records relating to the Pennsylvania militia and the Western Expedition, see Western Expedition Accounts, 4262, 4265.

14. See especially *Philadelphia Aurora*, March 15, 16, 22, 23, 25, April 3, 1799; *Oracle of Dauphin*, March 27, April 10, 1799; *Herald of Liberty* (Washington, Pa.), April 1, 1799; *Philadelphia Aurora*, March 15, 22, 28, and April 1, 1799.

15. *Porcupine's Gazette*, April 5, 1799; *Oracle of Dauphin*, April 10, 1799.

16. Adams advised McHenry to begin assembling the force, and McHenry commissioned William MacPherson Brigadier General of the expeditionary force that same day, *Papers of Alexander Hamilton*, 22: 378–88.

17. Wharton, *State Trials*, 459.

18. Peters, *Statutes*, 1: 726, March 2, 1799, "An Act giving eventual authority to the President of the United States to augment the Army."

19. On the split between Adams and the High Federalists over the New Army, see Kohn, *Eagle and Sword*; Elkins and McKitrick, *Age of Federalism*, 714–19.

20. Syrett, *Papers of Alexander Hamilton*, 22: 378–88.

21. Gertrude MacKinney and Charles F. Hobson, eds., *Pennsylvania Archives*, 138 vols. (Harrisburg: Commonwealth of Pennsylvania, 1931), 9th ser., 2: 1507, March 22, 1799.

22. Hamilton to McHenry, March 18, 1799, Steiner, *Life and Correspondence of James McHenry*, 433.

23. *Journal of the First Session of the 9th House of Representatives of the Commonwealth of Pennsylvania* (Philadelphia: Hall and Sellers, 1799), March 14, 15, 20, 1799, 311; *Pennsylvania Archives* 9th ser., 2: 1503, March 15, 1799; *Philadelphia Aurora*, March 25, 1799; *Kline's Carlisle Weekly Gazette*, March 27, 1799.

24. Tinkcom, *Republicans and Federalists in Pennsylvania*, 217.

25. Davis, *Fries Rebellion*, 75; *Philadelphia Aurora*, March 22, 1799; *Kline's Carlisle Weekly Gazette*, March 27, 1799.

26. McHenry to Hamilton, March 15, 1799, *Papers of Alexander Hamilton*, 22: 540; McHenry to Hamilton, March 22, 1799, 22: 577–78; Wolcott to Hamilton, April 1, 1799, 23:1–3. *Porcupine's Gazette*, March 28, 1799 reported troops mobilizing in Trenton, New Jersey, Baltimore, and Winchester, Virginia and preparing to march to Philadelphia.

27. See McHenry's orders to McPherson in *American State Papers, Miscellaneous*, 1: 188–89; and the correspondence between McHenry and Hamilton in Steiner, *Life and Correspondence of James McHenry*, 432–33; McHenry to Hamilton, March 15, 1799, *Papers of Alexander Hamilton*, 22: 539–54; Hamilton to MacPherson, March 22, 1799, 579; McHenry to Hamilton, 577–78; MacPherson to Hamilton, 581; Wolcott to Hamilton, 23: 1–3; Davis, *Fries Rebellion*, 78; Robert W. Coakley, *The Role of Federal Military Forces in Domestic Disorders, 1789–1878* (Washington, D.C.: Center of Military History, U.S. Army, 1988), 72–73.

28. Wolcott to Hamilton, April 1, 1799, *Papers of Alexander Hamilton*, 23: 1–3.

29. Hamilton to Washington, April 3, 1799, *Papers of Alexander Hamilton*, 23: 7–8.

30. MacPherson to Hamilton, March 22, 1799, *Papers of Alexander Hamilton*, 22: 579.

31. MacPherson to Hamilton, March 25, 1799, *Papers of Alexander Hamilton*, 22: 584–85.

32. Report of Mr. Eddy to General MacPherson, March 24, 1799, Memorandum from General MacPherson, March 25, 1799, General MacPherson to Major Ford, April 2, 1799, General MacPherson to Major Ford, April 3, 1799 in MacPherson Manuscripts, Military Papers, Correspondence, March-April, 1799, Historical Society of Pennsylvania.

33. Davis, *Fries Rebellion*, 72, claims that Balliet was severely beaten by a Northampton mob sometime after the President's Proclamation, but no evidence of this exists in the depositions or trial testimony, and it is very unlikely that William Rawle would not have used such an incident in his prosecutions. Moreover, Balliet did not swear a warrant and no record of this incident exists in the Northampton County Archives.

34. *Philadelphia Aurora*, March 15, 1799.

35. *Philadelphia Aurora*, March 22, 1799, emphasis in the original. For other accounts of tranquility in Northampton, Bucks and Montgomery counties prior to April 4, see March 28, 1799, April 1, 1799.

36. Churchill, "Popular Nullification," 130; Churchill makes a persuasive case that Republicans as a party sought to silence the idea of popular nullification.

37. *Philadelphia Aurora*, March 16, 22, 1799.

38. *Philadelphia Aurora*, March 25, April 5, April 30, July 15, 1799; *New London Bee*, January 8, 1800; *Newark Sentinel of Freedom*, September 23, 1800. I am indebted to Robert Churchill for the latter two references.

39. *Readinger Adler*, March 20, 1799.

40. Jefferson to Edmund Pendleton, February 14, 1799, in *Writings of Thomas Jefferson*, 7: 356. I am indebted to Robert Churchill for this reference.

41. *Philadelphia Aurora*, March 16, 1799.

42. On Jefferson's conception of popular constitutionalism, see Lance Banning, *Jefferson and Madison: Three Conversations from the Founding* (Madison: Madison House, 1995), 27–55, for the letter from Thomas Jefferson to James Madison, September 6, 1789, see 166–71.

43. On the Kentucky and Virginia Resolutions, see Elkins and McKitrick, *Age of Federalism*, 719–26; Sharp, *American Politics in the Early Republic*, chapter 9, passim; Banning, *Jeffersonian Persuasion*, chapter 9, passim; *Journal of the First Session of the 9th House of Representatives of the Commonwealth of Pennsylvania*, March 11, 1799, 289–92.

44. Ellis, *American Sphinx*, 222–23; Banning, *Jefferson and Madison*, 57–91, see particularly Jefferson to Madison, September 6, 1789, reprinted, 166–71, and Jefferson's musings on "ward republics" in his July 12, 1816 letter to Samuel Kercheval, reprinted, 218–25.

45. *Philadelphia Aurora.*, March 21, 1799 reported that Henry Shankweiler, Herman Hartman, and Adam Stephan came to Philadelphia and surrendered themselves to the Marshall.

46. See references in Chapter 1 above.

47. Thomas J. Archdeacon, *Becoming American: An Ethnic History* (New York: Free Press, 1983), 20; John Higham, *Send These to Me: Jews and Other Immigrants in Urban America* (Baltimore: Johns Hopkins University Press, 1975), 19; Robert Goodloe Harper to James McHenry, March 26, 1799, Steiner, *Life and Correspondence of James McHenry*,

433–34; Uriah Tracy to Oliver Wolcott, August 7, 1800, in Gibbs, *Memoirs of the Administrations of Washington and Adams*, 2: 230; Adams to Wolcott, April 2, 1799, 2: 230.

48. Brook Hindle, "The March of the Paxton Boys," recounts the Philadelphians fears of backcountry discontent only three decades earlier.

49. George Ball to Timothy Pickering, October 27, 1798, *Pickering Papers*, 9: 522.

50. Report from Capt. John Adlum to McHenry, July 22, 1799, Steiner, *Life and Correspondence of James McHenry*, 437.

51. Hamilton to McHenry, March 18, 1799, Steiner, *Life and Correspondence of James McHenry*, 433.

52. Wolcott to John Adams, May 11, 1799, Adams, *Life and Works of John Adams*, 8: 644–45.

53. *Philadelphia Aurora*, March 22, 1799.

54. Adams to Wolcott, April 2, 1799, Gibbs, *Memoirs of the Administrations of Washington and Adams*, 2: 230; Wolcott to Hamilton, April 1, 1799, *Papers of Alexander Hamilton*, 23: 1–3.

55. *Philadelphia Aurora*, March 22, 1799; *Porcupine's Gazette*, April 4, 1799.

56. *Papers of Alexander Hamilton*, 22: 378–88; Davis, *Fries Rebellion*, 80; *New York Daily Advertiser*, March 30, 1799.

57. For the problems associated with the Watermelon Army, see Slaughter, *Whiskey Rebellion*, chapter 13, passim, Clouse, *Whiskey Rebels*, chapters 12 and 13, passim.

58. Adams, *Life and Works of John Adams*, 10: 153.

59. *American State Papers, Finance* (Washington, D.C.: Gales and Seaton, 1832), 1: 661.

60. *Porcupine's Gazette*, April 4, 1799; *Philadelphia Aurora*, April 6, 1799; *Oracle of Dauphin*, April 10, 1799; Davis, *Fries Rebellion*, 80.

61. *Philadelphia Aurora*, April 6, 1799.

62. MacPherson to James McHenry, April 6, 1799, Adams Family Papers, Library of Congress. I am indebted to Whit Ridgeway for references to the MacPherson correspondence in the Adams Family Papers.

63. MacPherson's Manifesto appears in Wharton, *State Trials*, 461–63.

64. Theodore G. Tappert, "Helmuth and the Fries Rebellion in 1799," *Lutheran Quarterly* 17 (1965): 265–69.

65. *Philadelphia Aurora*, April 11, 1799.

66. *Kline's Carlisle Weekly Gazette*, March 20, 1799.

67. MacPherson to McHenry, April 6, 1799, Adams Family Papers.

68. Baldwin, *Whiskey Rebels*, 225–28; Slaughter, *Whiskey Rebellion*, 204–05.

69. Instructions to General MacPherson, March 21, 1799, *American State Papers, Miscellaneous*, 1: 188–89.

70. *Kline's Carlisle Weekly Gazette*, April 17, 1799; *Porcupine's Gazette*, April 8, 1799; Davis, *Fries Rebellion*, 91–95, 97; MacPherson to Major Ford, April 6, 1799, MacPherson Manuscripts.

71. MacPherson to McHenry, April 8, 1799, Adams Family Papers.

72. Ford to MacPherson, April 7, 1799, MacPherson Manuscripts.

73. Samuel Sitgreaves to MacPherson, April 7, 1799, MacPherson Manuscripts.

74. MacPherson to McHenry, April 18, 1799, Adams Family Papers.

75. *Oracle of Dauphin*, May 22, 1799.

76. MacPherson to Ford, April 13, 1799, Ford to MacPherson, April 14, 1799, MacPherson Manuscripts.

77. Davis, *Fries Rebellion*, 109–10, 13.

78. Christian Heckenwelder to MacPherson, April 9, 1799, MacPherson Miscellaneous Collection, Historical Society of Pennsylvania; William Nichols to MacPherson, April 16, 1799, W. M. Hornor Collection, Historical Society of Pennsylvania.

79. Slaughter, *Whiskey Rebellion*, 217–18.

80. MacPherson to McHenry, April 8, 18, 1799, Adams Family Papers. I am indebted to Whit Ridgeway for these references.

81. *Philadelphia Aurora*, April 11, 1799.

82. Davis, *Fries Rebellion*, 108–10.

83. Davis, *Fries Rebellion*, 139.

84. *Gazette of the United States*, April 19, 1799.

85. Davis, *Fries Rebellion*, 111.

86. MacPherson to Eyerle, April 16, 1799, MacPherson Manuscripts; Eyerle to MacPherson, April 19, 1799, Hornor Collection.

87. MacPherson to McHenry, April 18, 1799.

88. *Reading Weekly Advertiser*, April 17, 1799.

89. *Readinger Adler*, April 9, 1799.

90. *Readinger Adler*, April 23, 1799; *Oracle of Dauphin*, May 8, 1799.

91. *Readinger Adler*, April 23, 1799; *Philadelphia Aurora*, April 24, 27, 30, 1799.

92. Harper was a South Carolinian, and as Bertram Wyatt Brown makes clear in *Southern Honor: Ethics and Behavior in the Old South* (New York: Oxford University Press, 1982), a southern man's honor was his most important possession in the antebellum age, and it was worth preserving at all costs.

93. *Philadelphia Aurora*, May 10, 24, 1799; *Porcupine's Gazette*, May 15, 1799; *Oracle of Dauphin*, May 22, 1799.

94. *Philadelphia Aurora*, May 16, 1799.

95. MacPherson to McHenry, April 18, 1799, Adams Family Papers.

96. *Kline's Carlisle Weekly Gazette*, May 1, 1799.

97. *Porcupine's Gazette*, May 8, 1799.

98. The following correspondence is in *Papers of Alexander Hamilton*: Hamilton to McHenry, May 25, 1799, 23: 148; McHenry to Hamilton, May 28, 23: 152–53; McHenry to Hamilton, June 4, 23: 164; Hamilton to McHenry, June 6, 23: 171; McHenry to Hamilton, June 6, 23: 172; Hamilton to David A. Ogden, June 7, 23: 175; Ogden to Hamilton, June 7, 23: 176; Hamilton to Capt. John Adlum, June 8, 23: 178; McHenry to Hamilton, July 2, 23: 236; Adlum to Hamilton, July 22, 23: 280; Hamilton to Adlum, August 23, 23: 343; Richard Peters to Timothy Pickering September 12, 23: 411; McHenry to Hamilton, September 13, 23: 411; Hamilton to Lloyd Moore, September 16, 23: 412; McHenry to Hamilton, September 20, 23: 445–46.

99. Report from Capt. John Adlum to McHenry and Hamilton, July 22, 1799, Steiner, *Life and Correspondence of James McHenry*, 437.

Chapter 6. Injustice

1. For details of all the court proceedings in April, May, and October 1799, and the second round of trials in April and May, 1800, see *Criminal Case Files of the U.S. Circuit Court for the Eastern District of Pennsylvania, 1791–1840* (Washington,

D.C.: National Archives and Records Administration, 1976, microfilm, 7 reels: from RG-21, Records of the District Courts of the United States, National Archives), reels 1, 2.

2. Forty-four were indicted for conspiracy, thirty-two for conspiracy, rescue and obstruction, eleven for treason, and one for uttering seditious statements, *Criminal Case Files*, reels 1, 2.

3. *Philadelphia Aurora*, April 27, 1799.

4. Raymond Walters, Jr., *Alexander James Dallas: Lawyer, Politician, Financier, 1759–1817* (Philadelphia: University of Pennsylvania Press, 1943), 80.

5. Walters, *Alexander James Dallas*, 79–85; Jane Shaffer Elsmere, "The Trials of John Fries," *Pennsylvania Magazine of History and Biography* 103 (October 1979): 432–45.

6. Wharton, *State Trials*, 480–81.

7. For accounts of the trial's sensational appeal, see Wolcott to Adams, May 11, 1799, Adams, *Life and Works of John Adams*, 8: 644–45; and Adams to Pickering, May 17, 1799, 8: 649.

8. James Iredell to Hannah Iredell, March 14, 1799, in Griffith McRee, ed., *The Life and Correspondence of James Iredell*, 2 vols. (New York: Peter Smith, 1949), 2: 546–48.

9. Pickering to Adams, May 10, 1799, Adams, *Life and Works of John Adams*, 8: 643–44.

10. Carpenter, *Two Trials*, app. No. 1, 1–9.

11. Carpenter, *Two Trials*, 19–24.

12. Wharton, *State Trials*, 494–95.

13. Testimony of Jacob Eyerle, Carpenter, *Two Trials*, 45–52.

14. Wharton, *State Trials*, 535.

15. *Porcupine's Gazette*, March 30, 1799.

16. Timothy Pickering to James Pickering, June 7, 1800, *Pickering Papers*, 13: 542.

17. Uriah Tracy to McHenry, May 6, 1799, Steiner, *Life and Correspondence of James McHenry*, 436.

18. Uriah Tracy to McHenry, May 6, 1799, Steiner, *Life and Correspondence of James McHenry*, 436.

19. Adams to Wolcott, Adams, *Life and Works of John Adams*, 8: 650.

20. Wharton, *State Trials*, 542.

21. Wharton, *State Trials*, 545.

22. A. Reeder to John Arndt, May 9, 1799, Rawle Papers, 2: 103.

23. Wharton, *State Trials*, 583–84.

24. The most complete account of the trial is in Carpenter, *Two Trials*, 1–175. For newspaper accounts, see *Kline's Carlisle Weekly Gazette*, May 15, 1799; *Philadelphia Aurora*, May 15, 1799; *Porcupine's Gazette*, May 9, 10, 11, 13, 1799, emphasis in original; *Oracle of Dauphin*, May 15, 1799.

25. Elsmere, "Trials of John Fries," 438

26. *Porcupine's Gazette*, May 10, 1799, emphasis in original.

27. Pickering to Adams, May 10, 1799, *Pickering Papers*, 37: 417.

28. Richards, *Shays's Rebellion*, 41.

29. *Philadelphia Aurora*, May 15, 1799; Wharton, *State Trials*, 608–9.

30. *U.S. v. John Fries*, April 1799, deposition of Herman Hartmann, deposition of Nicholas Mayer, deposition of Daniel Heverly, deposition of John Rhoad, May 14, 1799, *Criminal Case Files*, reel 1.

31. Pickering to Rufus King, May 22, 1799, *Pickering Papers*, 11: 140.

32. *Criminal Case Files*, reel 2.

33. *Unpartyische Harrisburg Zeitung*, May 21, 1799; see *U.S. v. Mayer and Fahnestock*, October 1799, *Criminal Case Files*, reel 1.

34. Adams to Wolcott, May 17, 1799, Gibbs, *Memoirs of the Administrations of Washington and John Adams*, 2: 240.

35. Wolcott to Adams, May 25, 1799, Gibbs, *Memoirs of the Administrations of Washington and John Adams*, emphasis in original.

36. Wolcott to Adams, May 11, 1799, Adams, *Life and Works of John Adams*, 8: 644–45.

37. Aleine Austin, *Matthew Lyon: "New Man" of the Democratic Revolution, 1749–1822* (University Park: Pennsylvania State University Press, 1981).

38. "Speech of the President to Both Houses of Congress, December 3, 1799," in *State Papers and Public Documents of the United States from the Accession of George Washington to the Presidency, Exhibiting a Complete View of Our Foreign Relations Since That Time* 10 vols. (Boston: T.B. Wait, 1817), 4: 285–89.

39. Timothy Pickering to Richard Peters, September 14, 1799, Peters Papers, vol. 10, p. 58, Historical Society of Pennsylvania; Davis, *Fries Rebellion*, 123.

40. Carpenter, *Two Trials*, 220–25.

41. Chase to Iredell, March 17, 1799, McRee *Life and Correspondence of James Iredell*, 2: 548–49.

42. Horace Binney, "The Leaders of the Old Bar of Philadelphia," *Pennsylvania Magazine of History and Biography* 14 (1890): 18.

43. Testimony from Chase's 1805 impeachment trial before the U.S. Senate can be found in Wharton, *State Trials*, 613–27.

44. Binney, "Leaders of the Old Bar," 19–20.

45. Walters, *Alexander James Dallas*, 82–83.

46. Carpenter, *Two Trials*, 181.

47. Carpenter, *Two Trials*, 184, 189.

48. Davis, *Fries Rebellion*, 125; *United States v. John Fries*, April 1800, *Criminal Case Files*, reel 2, contains records of the jury challenges, with the names of the jurors and alternates.

49. *U.S. v. John Fries*, April 1800, *Criminal Case Files*, reel 2.

50. Carpenter, *Two Trials*, 191–92.

51. Carpenter, *Two Trials*, 195.

52. Carpenter, *Two Trials*, 197.

53. *U.S. v. John Fries, U.S. v. John Gettman and Frederick Heaney*, April 1800, *Criminal Case Files*, reel 2.

54. Carpenter, *Two Trials*, 226.

55. Pickering to Charles Pinckney, May 25, 1800, Pickering to Hamilton, July 10, 1798, *Pickering Papers*, 13: 520, 37: 316.

56. Forrest McDonald, *Alexander Hamilton: A Biography* (New York: W.W. Norton, 1979), 340.

57. McDonald, *Alexander Hamilton*, 341.

58. Pickering to Washington, September 13, 1798, *Papers of Alexander Hamilton*, 9: 309–10.

59. Pickering to Charles Pinckney, May 25, 1800, *Pickering Papers*, 13: 520.

60. McDonald, *Alexander Hamilton*, 342.

61. Letter from Alexander Hamilton," *Papers of Alexander Hamilton*, 25: 169–234; Pickering to George Cabot, February 21, 1799, Pickering to Charles Pinckney, May 25, 1800, *Pickering Papers*, 10: 528, 13: 520.

62. James McHenry to John McHenry, May 20, 1800, Gibbs, *Memoirs of the Administrations of Washington and John Adams*, 2: 346–48.

63. Adams to Pickering, May 10, 1800, Pickering to Adams, May 12, 1800, Adams to Pickering, May 12, 1800, *Pickering Papers*, 13: 498, 500, 500a.

64. Pinckney to Pickering, May 25, 1800, *Pickering Papers*, 520.

65. Hamilton to Pickering, May 15, 1800, *Pickering Papers*, 26: 118, emphasis in original.

66. Jane Shaffer Elsmere, "Trials of John Fries," *Pennsylvania Magazine of History and Biography* 103 (October 1979): 442.

67. Adams, *Life and Works of John Adams*, 9: 15; Davis, *Fries Rebellion*, 130.

68. John Adams to the Heads of the Departments, May 20, 1800, and The Heads of the Departments to John Adams, May 20, 1800, Adams, *Life and Works of John Adams* 9: 57–59, 59–60; Charles Lee to Adams, September 2, 1799, 9: 21–23.

69. Timothy Pickering to James Pickering, June 7, 1800, *Pickering Papers*, 13: 542; *Philadelphia Aurora*, May 22, 24, 1800, emphasis in original.

70. *Philadelphia Aurora*, May 22, 1800.

71. Richards, *Shays's Rebellion*, 39–40.

72. Pickering to Benjamin Goodhue, May 26, 1800, Pickering to Samuel Gardener, June 21, 1800, Timothy Pickering to James Pickering, June 7, 1800, *Pickering Papers*, 13: 526, 551, 542, emphasis in the original.

73. Pickering to James Pickering, June 7, 1800, *Pickering Papers*, 542.

74. Pickering to David Humphreys, May 28, 1800, *Pickering Papers*, 11: 166.

75. McHenry to Cabot, June 16, 1800, Gibbs, *Memoirs of the Administrations of Washington and Adams*, 2: 371.

76. Hamilton to McHenry, July 1, 1800, Gibbs, *Memoirs of the Administrations of Washington and Adams*, 376.

77. Hamilton to Theodore Sedgwick, May 10, 1800, *Papers of Alexander Hamilton*, 25: 173.

78. Wolcott to Hamilton, September 3, 1800, Cabot to Hamilton, August 23, 1800, *Papers of Alexander Hamilton*, 397, 77.

79. Wolcott to Hamilton, October 1, 1800, Gibbs, *Memoirs of the Administrations of Washington and Adams*, 2: 430.

80. Syrett provides a history of the "Letter" in *Papers of Alexander Hamilton*, 25: 173–174.

81. *Philadelphia Aurora*, October 31, 1800.

82. "A Letter from Alexander Hamilton," October 24, 1800, *Papers of Alexander Hamilton*, 25: 211, 214, 216, 221–22, emphasis in original.

83. *Papers of Alexander Hamilton*, 225–27, emphasis in original.

84. *Papers of Alexander Hamilton*, 225–27, emphasis mine, spelling in original.

Epilogue: Die Zeiten von '99

1. A few works on these political subjects are Cunningham, *Jeffersonian Republicans in Power*; Ronald P. Formisano, *The Transformation of Political Culture: Massachusetts*

Parties, 1790s-1840s (New York: Oxford University Press, 1983); Michael F. Holt, *The Rise and Fall of the American Whig Party: Jacksonian Politics and the Onset of the Civil War* (New York: Oxford University Press, 1999); Holt, *Political Parties and American Political Development: From the Age of Jackson to the age of Lincoln* (Baton Rouge: Louisiana State University Press, 1992); Robert Remini, *Henry Clay: Statesman for the Union* (New York: W.W. Norton, 1991); Charles Sellers, *The Market Revolution: Jacksonian America, 1815–1846* (New York: Oxford University Press, 1991).

2. Keller, *Rural Politics*, 52–53; *Der Unabhaeugniger Republikaner*, October 29, 1836; Rudolf Hommel, "The Fries Rebellion," newspaper article in unknown journal, in Ray A. Weaver Collection, Henry L. Snyder Manuscripts, fol. 3, PF 516 SNY, Lehigh County Historical Society.

3. Keller, *Rural Politics*, 13.

4. Quoted in Keller, *Rural Politics*, 29.

5. Tinkcom, *Republicans and Federalists in Pennsylvania*, 224, 225.

6. *Philadelphia Aurora*, October 8, 1799.

7. Ross circular, May 27, 1799, quoted in Tinkcom, *Republicans and Federalists in Pennsylvania*, 229–30.

8. *Ein Ernstlicher Ruf an die Deutschen in Pennsylvanien* (Lancaster, Pa., 1799).

9. *Readinger Adler*, June 25, July 2, 9, 16, October 1, 1799; *Philadelphia Aurora*, July 30, 1799.

10. Keller, *Rural Politics*, 2, 36–48.

11. Tinkcom, *Republicans and Federalists in Pennsylvania*, 215–41; Keller, *Rural Politics*, 48–55; *Easton American Eagle*, October 17, 1799; Higginbotham, *Keystone in the Demo-cratic Arch*, 25–27; Alexander Graydon, *Memoirs of a Life, Chiefly Passed in Pennsylvania* (Harrisburg, Pa., 1811), 358–59, 361.

12. Tinkcom, *Republicans and Federalists in Pennsylvania*, 238–39.

13. Keller, *Rural Politics*, 41, Tinkcom, *Republicans and Federalists in Pennsylvania*, 241.

14. Higginbotham, *Keystone in the Democratic Arch*, 326.

15. For the elections of 1799 and 1800 in Pennsylvania, including the House and Senate struggle over apportioning the electoral vote for the presidential election, see Tinkcom, *Republicans and Federalists in Pennsylvania*, chapters 12, 13, passim.

16. A valuable discussion of Adams's pardons can be found in Ridgway, "Fries in the Federalist Imagination," 149–53.

17. Sharp, *American Politics in the Early Republic*, 268–71.

18. Dauer, *Adams Federalists*, 257–58.

19. Soltow, "America's First Progressive Tax," 57.

20. *Northampton Farmer and Easton Weekly Advertiser*, October 18, 1806. For other elections with returns by district, see Easton *American Eagle* October 16, 1800, October 17, 1801, October 12, 1802, October 11, 1803, October 20, 1804, October 12, 1805; *Northampton Farmer and Easton Weekly Messenger*, October 17, 1807, October 15, 1808; *Pennsylvania Herald and Easton Intelligencer*, October 19, 1808, October 18, 1809. For election results for state and local offices for Northampton County, see Records of the Department of State, Bureau of Commissions, Elections, and Legislation, Appointments File for Civil Officers, microfilm rolls 1–3, Pennsylvania State Archives.

21. Tinkcom, *Republicans and Federalists in Pennsylvania*, 215–41.

22. Easton *American Eagle*, October 12, 1805.

23. *Northampton Farmer and Easton Weekly Advertiser*, October 15, 1808.

24. Weaver, "'The American Eagle'," 72.

25. Adams to James Lloyd, March 31, 1815, Adams, *Life and Works of John Adams*, 10: 153.

26. Keller, *Rural Politics*, 52–53.

27. Keller, *Rural Politics*, 19.

28. Randall M. Miller and William Pencak, eds., *Pennsylvania: A History of the Commonwealth* (University Park: Pennsylvania State University Press, 2002), 166–69. Moreover, the new state constitution specifically excluded free blacks from the poll. So while Pennsylvania bucked the national trend toward "Universal White Manhood Suffrage," it played right along with the decidedly undemocratic national treatment of African Americans.

29. United States Census, Northampton County, 1810, Bucks County, 1820; Charles F. Seng, ed., "Tax Assessment, Lehigh County, 1813," Lehigh County Historical Society; Bucks County, Pennsylvania, Tax Assessments, 1820.

30. Nolt, *Strangers in Their Own Land*, chapters 2, 3, passim.

Index

Acknowledgments

Over a decade of developing, researching, and writing this book, I taxed the time, energy, and abilities of many people. To them, I owe a considerable debt of gratitude and the acknowledgement that the remaining faults in this book rest with the author alone.

Many burdened themselves by reading various versions of the full-length manuscript. Lance Banning was a most encouraging dissertation director, and he served with Thomas Cogswell, Lee Elioseff, Philip Harling, George Herring, and Daniel Blake Smith on a Ph.D. committee that provided valuable guidance. Others who read and commented on the entire manuscript in its various stages include Paul Gilje, Owen S. Ireland, William Pencak, Peter Potter, and Thomas Slaughter. Thomas J. Kiffmeyer paid the price several times, reading or listening to most of every draft, continually encouraging me to write and rewrite, and extending such a friendship that will pay dividends for years to come.

Many other colleagues, friends, students, and editors shouldered a load as well, critiquing various selections of the work or providing valuable support: James Alexander, George Boudreau, Robert Brigham, Robert Churchill, Jeffrey A. Davis, Paul Doutrich, Richard S. Dunn, Todd Estes, Craig Thompson Friend, John Craig Hammond, Robert Jackman, Albrecht Koschnik, Francois LeRoy, Kyle Longley, Cathy Matson, Robert Matson, Holly Mayer, Simon Newman, David Nichols, James Powell, Ian M. G. Quimby, Marcus Rediker, Katherine Reist, Whitman Ridgway, Richard Alan Ryerson, Daniel J. Santoro, Nick Sarantakes, Matthew Schoenbachler, William Shade, Jean Soderlund, Ray Wrabley, Michael Zuckerman, Drew Funka, Michael Bradley McCoy, and Jim Stutzman. The last three are brave students from the University of Pittsburgh at Johnstown who read portions of the manuscript and provided me with the undergraduate's perspective. Bob Lockhart offered encouragement and expert editing decisions, and most important, he challenged me to demonstrate the significance of an event many have heretofore considered insignificant, allowing me the freedom and proffering me the necessary advice to write the book I should have written in the first place. Alison Anderson, Ellie Goldberg, and the copyeditors at the University of Pennsylvania Press saved me from many errors, so many that they cannot be expected to have caught them all.

Librarians at the University of Pittsburgh at Johnstown, University of

Pittsburgh, University of Kentucky, University of Pennsylvania, Bucks County Historical Society's Spruance Library, Northampton County Historical and Genealogical Society, Lehigh County Historical Society, Lancaster County Historical Society, Northampton County Archives, the National Archives and Records Administration in Washington, D.C. and Philadelphia, the Library of Congress, Pennsylvania State Archives, the David Library of the American Revolution, and the Historical Society of Pennsylvania also provided valuable assistance. The funds and support from several institutions must also be noted. A Hallam Dissertation Fellowship from the University of Kentucky and a University of Pittsburgh at Johnstown summer research grant provided monetary assistance while the award of a dissertation fellowship in 1995 from the McNeil Center for Early American Studies afforded collegiality and accessibility to resources. An invitation to guest lecture on the bicentennial of Fries's Rebellion for the Lawrence Henry Gipson Institute at Lehigh University granted similar benefits in 1999.

Additionally, I exacted a levy from a number of friends, relatives, and coworkers. Tom and Kathy Kiffmeyer, Leon and Annette Magruder, Mark, Maryann, Eric, Paul and Rusty Magruder, Mike and Jo Hopwood, John Castrege, Mike and Sharon Sandt, and my parents, Doug and Peggy Newman (whose financial and supportive roles also cannot be understated) all opened their homes and cupboards to me, issuing an immeasurable subsidy in lodging and support. Peggy Adams, Steve Biddle, Dick Helm, David Long, and James R. Mann also forfeited their time and energy to this, and other, Fries's Rebellion projects. Mary Lavine, Christine Herchelroath, and Monica Kovacic created the maps, and Sharon Wilson and Andrea Leibfried offered technical help. Bonnie Hunt, Wilson Savitz, Allan Stafford, Dale Eck, and Paul Reimel led me through "the Milfords," showing me from house to tavern to mill as local guides had done for hapless House Tax assessors two centuries before. "Smokin'" Joe Heffley assisted in the final editing and indexing, rearranging his schedule to help me meet a deadline. And Bethany Winters deserves great credit for her brilliant service as a research assistant: tabulating figures, cleaning up the quirks created by a shift in word processing programs, and reading, critiquing, copyediting, and indexing the book. Her service and friendship in the final stages of this project were invaluable to its completion.

Other friends and students lent support that, while not directly connected to this project, certainly made it possible. Although they are too many to name they should know that they too belong here and that I am most grateful for their support. Among them are my students at the University of Pittsburgh at Johnstown who have been among my best allies and teachers, and to them I offer this work.

But those whom I taxed most heavily live in my own home, and the absence of a rebellion there can only be the result of unconditional love and boundless patience, so it is to my family I dedicate this work. Forrest and the dissertation project were born together, and both competed for my time. As a child, Forrest has developed and shared a natural sense of justice and an unquenchable curiosity that have been an inspiration. Leo has had to contest for my attention with both Forrest and this dissertation-turned-book project. Watching and helping Leo struggle to overcome the hurdles of autism gave me the courage to see this endeavor through to publication when I was ready to abandon it. With this project behind them, my children will surely subject me to an audit and claim their arrears in time and companionship deferred. I hope the book is worth it, and I look forward to repaying them with interest.